INTRODUCTION TO GLOBAL MILITARY HISTORY

'Excellent. It integrates the land, air and maritime aspects of conflict and strikes a reasonable balance between the context and the events of the history of war and conflict.'

Stanley Carpenter, *Professor of Strategy and Policy,*
US Naval War College, Newport, Rhode Island

'An excellent stimulus to thought and to further study . . . very good on the theoretical underpinning of military history, the distinction between wars and battles and the necessity of examining strategy in the political context.'

Dan Todman, *Lecturer in Modern History,*
Queen Mary, University of London

This lucid account of military developments around the modern world begins with the American War of Independence and the French Revolutionary Wars and continues chronologically to the latest conflicts in the 2000s. It combines global coverage with thought-provoking analysis, dealing not only with the military aspects of conflict but also with the social, cultural, political and economic aspects and consequences of such conflict. By placing the familiar or known alongside the largely unknown, it forces the reader to reassess the standard grand narrative of military history that rests on assumptions of Western cultural and technological superiority. It will be essential reading for students in universities worldwide, whether studying modern military history, modern world history, history and international relations or war and society.

Specially designed to be user-friendly, *Introduction to Global Military History* offers:

- Chapter introductions and conclusions to assist study and revision
- 'Voices of war' sourced extracts from the field of war
- Case studies in each chapter to support the narrative and provoke discussion
- Vivid engravings, plans, paintings and photos to bring the conflicts alive
- A 12-page colour map section plus 21 other integrated maps
- Annotated references from the latest publications in the field

Jeremy Black is Professor of History at the University of Exeter. He is a leading military historian whose books include *Rethinking Military History* (Routledge, 2004), *World War Two: A Military History* (Routledge, 2003), *European Warfare, 1494–1660* (Routledge, 2002), *European Warfare, 1660–1815* (Routledge, 1994) and *Why Wars Happen* (1998). He is editor of the Routledge Warfare and History series and has lectured extensively in North America, Europe and Australasia.

INTRODUCTION TO GLOBAL MILITARY HISTORY

1775 to the present day

Jeremy Black

Routledge
Taylor & Francis Group

LONDON AND NEW YORK

First published 2005 by Routledge
2 Park Square, Milton Park, Abingdon, Oxon OX14 4RN

Simultaneously published in the USA and Canada
by Routledge
270 Madison Ave, New York, NY 10016

Routledge is an imprint of the Taylor & Francis Group

© 2005 Jeremy Black

Typeset in Adobe Garamond by
Florence Production Ltd, Stoodleigh, Devon
Printed and bound in Great Britain by
TJ International Ltd, Padstow, Cornwall

British Library Cataloguing in Publication Data
A catalogue record for this book is available from the British Library

Library of Congress Cataloging in Publication Data
Black, Jeremy.
Introduction to global military history: 1775 to the present day/Jeremy Black.
    p. cm.
  Includes bibliographical references and index.
1. Military history, Modern. I. Title.
D295.B53 2005
909.8–dc22   2005008577

ISBN 0–415–35394–7 (hbk)
ISBN 0–415–35395–5 (pbk)

FOR OLIVER COLVILLE

CONTENTS

ILLUSTRATIONS

PLATES

MAPS

BOXES

ACKNOWLEDGEMENTS

I have benefited greatly from the advice of seven anonymous readers, from the comments of Paul Mackenzie and Rick Schneid on individual chapters, and from the advice of Armstrong Starkey on the battle of Tippecanoe. I would like to thank Moira Taylor for being a most helpful editor and Alan Fidler for his valuable assistance at the copy-editing stage. The opportunity to develop some of these ideas presented by the invitations to speak at the 2004 History Institute for Teachers held in Philadelphia by the Foreign Policy Research Institute, the Australian Defence Force Academy, the Australian Land Warfare Centre, the universities of New South Wales, Ohio and Tasmania, Adelphi, High Point, William Paterson, Rutgers and Roger Williams universities, the 2004 program on the American War of Independence of the University of Virginia's Division of Continuing Education, the 2004 Summer School of the University of Oxford's Department for Continuing Education, a conference on the History of War in Global Perspective held at the Mershon Center of Ohio State University in 2004, and at the Centre de Cultura Contemporània de Barcelona was most welcome. I would like to thank Roger Burt for giving me the opportunity to practice black-powder shooting. It is a great pleasure to dedicate this book to Oliver Colville, a good friend.

LIST OF ABBREVIATIONS

AWM   Canberra, Australian War Memorial
NATO   North Atlantic Treaty Organization
RAF   Royal Air Force (British)
RMA   Revolution in Military Affairs
UN   United Nations
USA   United States of America

INTRODUCTION

The guiding principles of this book are that it be global and a textbook. The first demands a range of comprehension, the second a degree of explication. These, in combination, pose a considerable challenge. At the same time, the book is a major opportunity as no such work has yet been produced in the twenty-first century; there is therefore the opportunity to introduce readers to new developments. The latter include not only the extent to which confrontation and conflict after 1990 no longer revolved around the Cold War between the USA and the Soviet Union that had dominated international relations from 1945 until 1990, but also the extent to which the asymmetrical warfare seen in the 1990s and 2000s, for example in Somalia, Afghanistan and Iraq, creates a need to re-examine earlier struggles in order to probe the precursors of this type of warfare.

This is the major intellectual thrust of the book. It moves away from the idea that there is a clear hierarchy of importance in military history and an obvious pattern of development, focused on conflict between the great powers, and instead looks at the importance of conflict between these powers and others, and also amongst the latter. Arguments are drawn out across national and chronological boundaries.

As a result, there will be more discussion of Asian developments than might have been expected in a book of this type written twenty years ago. This is also appropriate because, throughout the entire period covered in this book, the bulk of the world's population lived in East and South Asia, with China and, secondly, India being particularly populous. As a consequence, it is necessary to devote attention to their military history, not least by moving aside from the notion that they were somehow passive victims of the inexorable rise of Western military dominance. Instead, the nature of the latter looks more tentative, contingent and short term than might have seemed the case in the past. If Anglo-French forces occupied China's capital, Beijing, in 1860, they still lacked the capability to control large sections of China. In India, British rule depended in large part on the co-operation of important sections of native society, and also rested on the use of Indian troops.

Asian military history is not therefore treated as a mere adjunct of that of the West, or indeed as it is often done for the period down to the 1920s as an aspect of the impact of the West on the non-West. Instead, there is an attempt to treat Asian developments as integral to those of the period. In part, this entails noting parallels. In Chapter 3, where nineteenth-century state-building and the opposition to it are considered, this involves the Taiping rebellion in China as well as developments in Europe and the USA.

The relationship between Western and 'Third World' powers and peoples is an important theme in this book, with particular attention devoted to the often overlapping processes of colonialism and decolonization. In addressing this relationship, there is a determined effort to move beyond Eurocentricity, as there also is in devoting due attention to military developments among non-Western powers and, in addition, conflict between them. This entails abandoning the notion of a hierarchy of military capability and effectiveness. Instead the very differing nature of fitness for purpose in very varied political environments and with reference to contrasting goals emerges clearly. As a result, however, it is difficult to compare performance in difference contexts between militaries both within a given period and over time.

Readers will appreciate that these themes do not make it clear how best to organize the book, because there are questions of weighting between and within the sections, as well as the serious issues of how best to divide the book into sections and how to allocate topics to sections. It is foolish to pretend that these issues do not arise. Instead, an awareness of them can serve a valuable educational function, as it is important, in discussing a subject, to consider how best to organize it. To give some examples from this book, and these are far from a full list: the unconventional periodization of the nineteenth century, with Chapters 2 and 3 separated at 1830, as explained on p. 50, is ripe for discussion. So also is the thematic divide between Chapters 8 and 9: in fact, the wars of decolonization discussed in the former are closely connected with the Cold War. Moreover, the second Vietnam war, the conflict in which the USA intervened directly from 1962, was, in its origins at least, a war of decolonization: unfinished business from the Geneva conference of 1954 following France's defeat. The classification of conflicts is a particularly appropriate topic for debate.

In light of the older 'war and society' approach to military history and the current 'cultural turn' in the subject (see pp. 276–8), there is a determined engagement within the book with the nature of the social, cultural, political and economic context, not least in order to discuss the degree of bellicosity in societies and cultures, and the causes and consequences of conflict. How each nation maintained itself in the realm of force, specifically how expectations of security were met, is an important factor in understanding military developments. Clearly, a balance has to be set between context (which tends to be the approach taken in universities), and conflict and the military dimension (the approach taken in the military academies), and this is not easy. If who serves and why, and who pays, how much, and why, are important to military history, how conflict was waged must not be forgotten. The 'cultural turn' in military history, in the sense of the emphasis on strategic and organizational cultures, and on different attitudes to suffering, requires attention, but, at every stage, it is necessary to remember that fighting is a central aspect of military capability and that the 'war and society' approach, while valuable, should not drive out concern with conflict.

Fighting is far from a constant, but while the tools of war, especially the weapons and the means of getting to the conflict zone, vary greatly, it is important to note the shared element of the need to handle people successfully. A sense of continuity can be seen in an extract from the draft report by 30 Corps, part of the British Eighth Army, dated 21 November 1942, after its victory over a German–Italian army at El Alamein in Egypt:

> The operations proved the general soundness of our principles of training for war, some of which had been neglected during previous fighting in the [North African] desert. In all forms of warfare, new methods should never disregard basic principles. The operations involved a reversion, with the difference due to the development in weapons, to the static warfare of the war of 1914–18. This reversion should not be regarded as an isolated exception unlikely to recur . . . our organisations and weapons must remain suitable both for mobile and periodical static operations.
>
> (AWM. 3 DRL/6643 3/9, p. 1)

Alongside an awareness of continuity, there is in this study an attempt to integrate land, naval and, eventually, air aspects of conflict. Too often these were dealt with as separate books, or in separate chapters within books. This underrates the extent to which common issues, objectives and problems affected developments in different spheres, and also the role of combined operations.

The extent to which war and preparation for war have moulded the modern world directs attention to the causes of military success. This is even more the case because the hopes expressed, first in the shadow of nuclear weaponry and then in the aftermath of the Cold War, that war had become obsolescent now increasingly look questionable.

CHAPTER 1

The World of War in the Late Eighteenth Century

INTRODUCTION

Variety was the keystone of conflict in this period. The last quarter of the century is frequently presented in terms of the origins of modern war, with the American War of Independence (1775–83) and the French Revolutionary Wars (1792–99) seen as bringing in a new age of warfare. Problematic as that idea is for the Western world, it makes little sense on the world scale. Indeed, on land, the major power was China, and there were no significant changes in Chinese war-making in the last quarter of the century. Yet, as frequent and large-scale British campaigning in India in these years clearly indicated, the worlds of Western and Asian war-making were not separate, and part of the importance of this period was that it saw significant advances for European powers, not only the British conquest of Mysore in southern India but also major defeats of the Ottoman Turks by the Russians in the Balkans. Elsewhere, the struggles between Western and non-Western peoples also led to success for the former in the Ohio country in the 1790s, as the newly independent American state expanded. Meanwhile, having established a colony at Botany Bay in Australia in 1788, the British extended their control at the expense of the native Aborigines.

The theme of variety thus extends not only to the range of combatants but also to the different types of conflict. It is not always easy to categorize the wars. For example, the American War of Independence can be seen as both civil war and a war of imperial control. The entry into the war of France (1778), Spain (1779), and the Dutch (1780), all against Britain, ensured also that the conflict became a genuinely worldwide struggle: it included an ultimately unsuccessful American attempt to invade Canada in 1775 and 1776, and a similarly unsuccessful Franco-Spanish attempt to invade Britain in 1779, as well as conflict in the Mediterranean, where the British lost the island of Minorca but held Gibraltar, and also in the West Indies. There was also conflict between Britain and France in the Indian Ocean, and a struggle for control over the supply of slaves from West Africa to the New World. There was an important related war in India between the French-backed Sultan of Mysore, first Haidar Ali and, after his death, his son Tipu Sultan, and the British.

Although its significance as a new type of war is often exaggerated, the American War of Independence was an important conflict because it led to the creation of a state that was to be the successful superpower of the twentieth century and whose values were to play a key role in moulding the modern world. France came to the aid of both the Americans and Mysore, but their politics and goals were very different. It is therefore appropriate to begin this book with the successful revolution that overthrew British control of the thirteen colonies.

Plate 1.1 *The Siege of Gibraltar, 1782* by George Carter, 1784. Captured by Britain in 1704, Gibraltar was besieged by Spain from 1779 to 1783 during the American War of Independence. The ability of the British navy to relieve the fortress on three occasions enabled it to survive the long siege. National Army Museum, neg 83763.

THE AMERICAN WAR OF INDEPENDENCE, 1775–83

The image is clear, the message obvious. Across a sun-kissed meadow, dappled with shade, lines of British soldiers, resplendent in red, move slowly forward, while brave American Patriots crouch behind trees and stone walls ready to blast these idiots to pieces. Frequently repeated on page and screen, the image has one central message: one side, the American, represented the future in warfare, and one side, the American, was bound to prevail. Thus, the war is readily located in both political and military terms. In both, it apparently represents the triumph of modernity and the start of a new age: of democracy and popular warfare. The linkage of military service and political rights therefore proved a potent contribution. Before these popular, national forces, the *ancien régime*, the old order, with its mercenaries, professionals, and unmotivated conscripts, was bound to crumble and its troops were doomed to lose. Thus, the political location of the struggle, in terms of the defining struggle for freedom, helps locate the conflict as the start of modern warfare, while considering the war in the latter light helps fix our understanding of the political dimension. Definition in terms of modernity also explains success, as most people assume that the future is bound to prevail over the past.

In making the war an apparently foregone conclusion, this approach has several misleading consequences. First, it allows historians of the period to devote insufficient attention to the fighting and, instead, to focus on traditional (constitution-framing) and modish (gender *et al.*) topics, neglecting the central point: no victory, no independence, no constitution, no newish society. Secondly, making British defeat inevitable gravely underrates the Patriot (not all Americans fought the British) achievement. Thirdly, it removes the sense of uncertainty in which contemporaries made choices.

The war needs rethinking. It has to be understood as a formidable challenge for the Patriots. Britain in 1775 was the strongest empire in the world. Other states, especially (but not only) China and Russia, had larger armies, but no other state had Britain's capacity for force projection. Britain not only had the largest navy in the world, but also a navy that had soundly beaten the second largest navy, that of France, as recently as 1759. With this navy, Britain had a network of bases, especially around the North Atlantic. The navy also rested on the best system of public finances in the world. The National Debt, guaranteed by Parliament, enjoyed international confidence to an extent unmatched among Britain's rivals, and the British could therefore borrow, and in large amounts. Indeed the War of Independence was to be waged by the British without a serious financial crisis. In part, this reflected the buoyancy of government customs revenues, based as they were on Britain's central role in Europe's global trading system.

Rich, Britain was also politically stable. The government of Frederick, Lord North had just won the general election of 1774. Under the Septennial Act, it did not have to fight another election until 1781. In fact, perfectly legally, it was to hold the next election in 1780, and to win that. The opposition criticized the war in America, but the government was in control of Parliament and this was not lost until early 1782: there was a collapse in parliamentary confidence after defeat at Yorktown the previous October.

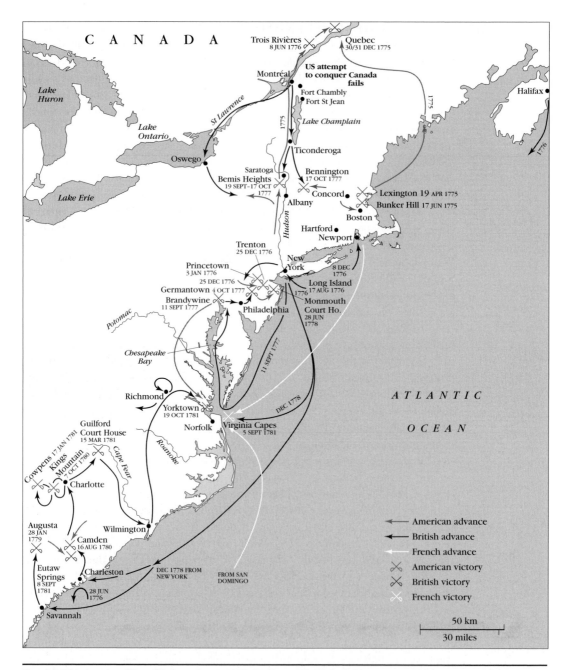

Map 1.1 The American War of Independence, 1775–83. From *The Oxford Companion to Military History* (2003), p. 41, edited by Richard Holmes, by permission of Oxford University Press.

As far as North America was concerned, the British army had plenty of experience in fighting there, and successfully so, as a result of conquering Canada from the French from 1758 to 1760 during the Seven Years War (otherwise known as the French and Indian War). Compared to Havana and Manila, which the British had captured from Spain in 1762 (prefiguring the American achievement in taking both from Spain in 1898), the eastern seaboard of North America was a relatively benign area for British operations. The killer diseases of the Tropics, such as yellow fever, were absent. It was also an area particularly vulnerable to amphibious operations, in which the British were especially skilled. In 1775, 75 per cent of the American population of European and African descent lived within 75 miles of the coast, and this included most people who counted politically. Their vulnerability to seapower was accentuated by the poorly-developed state of the roads and bridges, which led to an emphasis on coastal traffic, and also because inland towns such as Philadelphia were also ports reachable up rivers. All the major towns could be reached by water, while the eastern seaboard of North America is bisected by waterways that help maritime penetration: round Charleston, further north, the Chesapeake, the Delaware and Long Island Sound, and, countering any American

Plate 1.2 *Destruction of the American Fleet at Penobscot Bay, 14 August 1779*, by Dominic Serres. A victory for a smaller British squadron that indicated that the Americans were not as successful in amphibious operations as the more experienced British could be. The Massachusetts militia on land fled into the woods: on offensive operations they were not necessarily an impressive force. National Maritime Museum, BNC 0425.

invasion of Canada, the St Lawrence. The last, for example, enabled a British naval squadron to relieve Quebec in 1776 as soon as the ice melted.

Once ashore in North America, the British did not have to face a new type of foe, nor a revolution on the battlefield. Pressed by George Washington, the commander of the American national army – the Continental Army – to adopt the form of a conventional European army, the Americans relied on the volley fire and linear formations with which the British were familiar. The major difference to conflict in Europe was that the general absence of cavalry from the battlefield ensured that troops fought in a more open order. Also, compared to war in Europe, both sides employed relatively few cannon. The Americans did not inherit a significant artillery park, but there was also, for both sides, a question of fitness for purpose (the use of appropriate methods) which is so often a rule in military history. In this case, the great distances within America and the poor nature of inland communications discouraged a reliance on cannon, which were relatively slow to move. As a result, although cannon played a role in battles, such as the indecisive one at Monmouth Court House (28 June 1778), these clashes were not characterized by the efficient exchanges of concentrated and sustained artillery fire seen in Western and Central Europe, nor did the Americans match the development of artillery standardization and organization then being pursued by the French.

Nor were there new weapons that might make a difference. One was tried and, had it worked, it would have changed the war, but, as yet, the submarine could not fulfil its potential: the dependence on human energy for propulsion and on staying partially above the surface for oxygen made it only an intimation of the future. On land, the Americans found the rifle very useful in sniping, but its slow rate of fire and inability to carry a bayonet gravely reduced its value as a battlefield weapon. Anyway, the British also had riflemen.

Organizationally, however, the British were challenged by the Patriots. The major role of the American militia created a particular problem for the British. This was true both in operational terms, for example by restricting the range of the British supply gatherers, and in the political context of the conflict, especially in harrying Loyalists. At the outset of the Revolution, militia overcame royal governors, and defeated supporting Loyalists. On 9 December 1775, the Earl of Dunmore, the last royal governor of Virginia, was defeated by Virginia militia at Great Bridge; Josiah Martin, his North Carolina counterpart, following on 27 February 1776 at Moore's Creek Bridge. These successes helped give the Americans strategic depth. Furthermore, the militia could provide at least temporary reinforcements for the Continental Army. It helped to ensure that the British were outnumbered, and thus limited their effectiveness as an occupation force.

Lastly, the political context was crucial. Had all the colonies in the western hemisphere rebelled, then the British would not have stood a chance, but the economically most crucial ones (the West Indies sugar islands, such as Jamaica and Barbados), and the strategically vital ones (those with naval bases, such as Nova Scotia, Jamaica, Antigua), did not rebel. As a result, the British had safe bases – to both the north and the south of the thirteen colonies, from which to mount operations. When, in March 1776, General Sir William Howe withdrew from Boston, leaving the Patriots victoriously in control of the thirteen colonies, he did not have to retreat to Britain. Instead, he sailed to Halifax, Nova Scotia, a key naval base, and rebuilt his force, so that that summer the Empire could strike back, with British forces landing on Staten Island at the start of the New York campaign. The eventually successful British defence of Canada in 1776 ensured that, as with East Florida (modern Florida minus the panhandle), there were also land frontiers across which the Patriots could be attacked.

More serious were the Loyalists, for this was a civil conflict, the first major American civil war. Loyalists fought and died for their vision of America, just as Patriots did, and in some areas, especially Georgia, North Carolina, the eastern shore of the Chesapeake, and parts of New Jersey and New York, Loyalists were numerous. Furthermore, the boundaries between Patriots and noncommitted, and noncommitted and Loyalists, were porous, not fixed. Politically, the British had to move as many Americans as possible across these boundaries; and American strategy provided them with their opportunity. The American emphasis on position warfare in order to protect their major cities – New York in 1776, Philadelphia in 1777, and Charleston in 1780 – gave the British opportunities to defeat their opponents and thus to affect opinion within America.

Beginning, on both sides, as what was seen as likely to be a short conflict, the war became a lengthy struggle that pitted the world's leading maritime power against a portion of its subjects. It proved relatively simple for the Patriots to drive the poorly prepared British from the rebellious thirteen colonies, especially outside Massachusetts, as the British concentrated their forces there. When, under threat from American artillery positions, they withdrew from Boston in March 1776 there were no British bases left in these colonies; but the British then made a formidable attempt to regain the colonies. Helped by the fact that in 1776 they were at war with no other power, they sent the largest army they had hitherto deployed abroad. Its arrival on Staten Island in the summer of 1776 signalled a major attempt to regain both the initiative and control, inaugurating the second stage in the war which, unlike the first, was to end with neither side in complete territorial control. Indeed, at the close of the conflict, the British were to evacuate Charleston and New York: the Americans were not strong enough to drive them away.

For the Americans to sustain this effort it was necessary that the war was a political as much as a military struggle, one in which the revolutionaries had to convince themselves and the British that there was no alternative to independence. The resulting politicization of much of the American public, and the motivation of many of their troops, was an important aspect of what was to be seen as modern warfare: in the West, a notion of popular commitment was important to this definition. There was little, however, of the emphasis on large armed forces and the mass production of munitions that were to be such obvious aspects of the industrial, or total, warfare waged by Western states in the late nineteenth, and early and mid-twentieth centuries.

A popular fight for independence was not unprecedented. Within the Western world, it was possible, for example, to point to the Swiss in the thirteenth century and the Dutch in the sixteenth century, both of whom had overthrown Habsburg forces and created republics. In the eighteenth century itself, the American revolution was only one of a number of popular uprisings within the British Empire, but those by the Jacobites in Scotland in 1715 and 1745, and by nationalists in Ireland in 1798, were all suppressed. The uniquely successful character of the American revolution focuses attention on the political and military factors that were specific to this struggle. Among them, it is important to emphasize the distance between the colonies and Britain. Indeed, America was the first of the European transoceanic colonies to rebel, and it led the way to the successful rebellion of Haiti against France in the 1790s, and of the Spanish and Portuguese colonies in the New World in the 1810s and 1820s.

Campaigning in North America posed serious problems for the British, particularly with logistics (supplies), and with defining an appropriate strategy that could translate triumph in battle into victory in the war. War, then, as at the present day, is a matter of forcing one's will on an opponent, and although victory in battle can help achieve this end it is not generally enough. The political problem for the British was that they needed to persuade the Americans to surrender: they had insufficient forces to conquer and occupy more than a portion of the thirteen colonies, and, partly as a result, the war, as John Adams, a prominent Patriot, claimed, had been lost by the British before the fighting had begun. This was certainly true in New England, Adams's base, where there were few Loyalists, but was less the case elsewhere.

Furthermore, persuading the Americans was a matter, as the British saw it, of getting them to return to their loyalty: to inflict so punitive a defeat that this return would be grudging, and only enforced by an expensive occupation force, seemed pointless. Instead, the goal was that of the defeat of the main American field force, with the hope that this would lead the rebels to negotiate. Based on wishful thinking, this goal was confused by the further emphasis on seizing key American positions; while both policies were to be supported by a naval blockade that so weakened the American economy that negotiations seemed sensible. Defeats were inflicted by the British, and major cities captured and held – New York from 1776, Newport from 1776 to 1780, Philadelphia in 1777–1778, Savannah from 1778 and Charleston from 1780 – but neither was sufficient. Instead, the defeat of a British force near Saratoga on 19 September and 7 October 1777 (and its surrender on 17 October) by an American army that was not the main American field force indicated the limitations of the British perception of the Americans, as did the American ability to continue fighting after cities had been captured. For example, despite the surrender of a large American force when Charleston surrendered on 12 May 1780, it proved impossible for the British to enforce control over the Carolinas. Despite a further victory at Camden on 16 August 1780, the British could not craft an acceptable political strategy and also could not crush dispersed forces of defeated Patriots.

They were helped, nevertheless, by the problems facing the Americans. To create and sustain an effective army was no easy task, and the Americans faced many difficulties in doing both. Money and supplies were serious issues, and much of George Washington's correspondence is an account of organization and improvization under pressure. The anti-authoritarian character of the Revolution and the absence of national institutions made it difficult to create a viable national military system for land and, even more, seapower. Initial enlistments for one year did not amount to a standing army. In early 1777, for example, Washington's army was badly affected by desertion, expiring enlistments, and supply problems. There were difficult negotiations over the militia, as seen in Washington's letter to the Pennsylvania Council of Safety on 29 January: 'If some mode is not adopted for obliging the officers of the militia to return the arms and accoutrements that are lent to them, we shall be in the greatest want of them when the regular regiments are raised.' On 3 February, he wrote to Jeremiah Wadsworth: 'The present unsettled state of the Commissary's department in this quarter, makes me fearful, that unless some measures are fallen upon to reconcile the jarring interests of these who act, or pretend to act, under the appointments of Colonel Trumbull, that the army will in a little while want supplies of every kind.'

These problems, did not disappear. In 1780, Nathanael Greene resigned as quartermaster-general because of his anger with civilian politicians and what he saw as their responsibility for his failure to meet the logistical demands of the Continental Army. Such a clash looked ahead to later disputes between the American military and their civilian overseers.

The Americans also faced a central strategic dilemma. They could not defeat the British other than in the limited (but important) sense of denying them victory in North America and hoping that this would lead them to abandon the struggle. As John Paul Jones showed in 1778 and 1779, the Americans had ships able to operate in British waters, but they lacked a fleet, let alone the amphibious capacity and strike force to take the war to the British Isles: at the battle off Flamborough Head on 23 September 1779, Jones's fleet was two American and two French ships, none of them large warships. Indeed the Americans did not have such a fleet when conflict with Britain resumed in the war of 1812–15. France and Spain possessed such a capability, but their joint invasion attempt on southern England in 1779 was, partly due to disease amongst the invasion fleet, as unsuccessful as others separately mounted during the century, and, without that, Britain could stay in the struggle.

This was a real problem for the Americans, as only a brief conflict had been envisaged in 1775. Instead of a willingness to fight overawing King George III, and forcing him to negotiate, the British, in 1776, sent a major army to defeat the Revolution. The struggle then became more sustained and bitter than had at first seemed likely. Even worse, in 1778, the British displayed a determination to continue the struggle in North America on land even after French intervention. This was against the advice of the British opposition, and despite the fact that the British now faced challenges in home waters, the Mediterranean, the West Indies, West Africa and India, challenges that expanded when the war widened to include Spain in 1779 and the Dutch in 1780.

Did any of this matter? After all, the British at one stage or another held all the major towns in North America, and they won a series of major battles, including Long Island (27 August 1776), Brandywine (11 September 1777), and Camden (16 August 1780). Yet, the Patriots were willing to continue fighting. In short, there was a basic strategic problem for both sides: that neither could knock out their opponent, however many battles they won. In short, the war would have to end, as indeed it did, with a compromise peace. Even after the surrender of a British army at Yorktown on 19 October, the British held on to New York City and Charleston, and the close of the war partitioned British North America, with Canada remaining with George III.

Whether this could have been changed by repeated victory depended on how far Patriot resilience would have survived defeat. The willingness of Charleston to accept the consequences of British victory in South Carolina in 1780, and to return to its allegiance to George III, was instructive, and poses a question mark against bombastic claims of liberty or death. The voluntaristic character of American military service was a problem, and in 1776 the British nearly succeeded in turning it against the rebels. As the British scored one victory after another in the New York campaign between August and December 1776, Washington's army all but disintegrated. Men laid down their arms and returned home. At the same time, covered by the British advance, Loyalists came forward in numbers in New Jersey.

As a result, Washington's Trenton campaign, especially his successful surprise attack on Trenton on 25 December 1776, was a make-or-break operation. It was important for its results for both sides. Richard Henry Lee wrote to George Washington on 27 February 1777:

> I really think that when the history of this winter's campaign comes to be understood, the world will wonder at its success on our part. With a force rather inferior to the enemy in point of numbers, and chiefly militia too, opposed to the best disciplined troops of Europe; to keep these latter pent up, harassed, and distressed. But more surprising still, to lessen their numbers some thousands by the sword and captivity!

By stemming the tide of British success, Washington led them to abandon much of New Jersey. This had disastrous political and military consequences. The local Loyalists were hit hard, which compromised future chances of winning Loyalist support in the middle colonies. Militarily, the British advance on Philadelphia, the location of the American Continental Congress, in 1777 was mounted not rapidly by land from Trenton but instead, slowly, by sea via the Chesapeake. Philadelphia did not fall until 26 September 1777. By then, General John Burgoyne's force was very exposed near Saratoga. It was to surrender on 17 October. A speedier victory near Philadelphia in 1777 would have put General William Howe, the British commander in North America, in a better position to mount operations that would have made it harder for the Americans to concentrate against Burgoyne. This would also have given substance to the plan of cutting the thirteen colonies in half along the Hudson Valley, a move that would have dramatically reduced the articulation of American power and made it more a series of local forces, which the British could try to fight and/or negotiate with separately.

Washington's victory at Trenton also revitalized resistance and permitted Congress to raise a new army, including many who agreed to serve for three years, a luxury Washington had never enjoyed before. Yet it had been a gamble, a dangerous operation that was dependent on surprise and, anyway, partly miscarried. It is worth asking what if Washington had failed to achieve surprise, if the

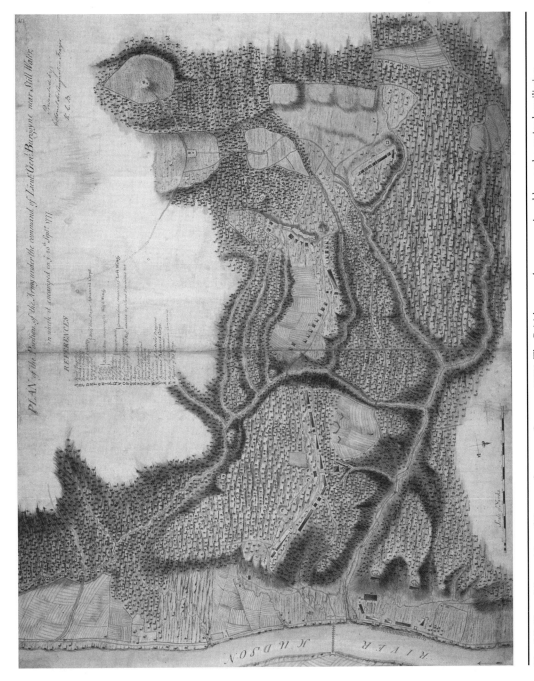

Map 1.2 Plan of the position of Burgoyne's army at Saratoga, 1777. The British surrender was a serious blow and a major humiliation. BL. Add. 57715 no 5. © British Library.

Hessian garrison at Trenton had driven him back to Pennsylvania, or if the British had continued to garrison New Jersey. Not only is it unclear that Congress would have been able to raise a new army for 1777, but also uncertain that the Americans, who were anyway to be defeated that year at Brandywine (11 September), could have put up a better effort earlier in the year had it been in the aftermath of a defeat at Trenton.

Late 1776 was not the only low ebb. By 1780, the Americans faced growing exhaustion and war-weariness. The absence of major engagements in the middle colonies in 1779 and 1780 did not indicate a disinclination to fight. However, the manpower situation in both armies was a testimony to the strains they were suffering from. The British had lost one army at Saratoga, and now had other pressing commitments, while the Americans were finding it increasingly difficult to sustain a major army. As a result, both sought new support: the British looked to the Loyalists, especially in the South, the Americans to French intervention in America, rather than the West Indies. The war therefore became a curious interplay of cautious moves and bold aspirations, as increasingly exhausted participants played for stakes that had been made higher as a consequence of the new factor of the intervention of French naval power, and in an atmosphere that the changing arithmetic of naval strength helped to make volatile for both sides.

Hyper-inflation had wrecked the American economy, and the war indeed reduced median household wealth by more than 45 per cent. The resources that existed were mismanaged. The limited credit-worthiness of Congress, and the reluctance of the states to subordinate their priorities and resources to Congress, meant that the army had to live from hand to mouth. Much of the supplying of the Continental Army relied on the issue of largely worthless certificates. In January 1781, short of pay, food and clothes, and seeking discharge, both the Pennsylvania line and three New Jersey regiments were to mutiny. The Pennsylvania mutiny was to be ended only by concession, including the discharge of five-sixths of the men.

This episode is a reminder of the precarious nature of the Revolution militarily, and the extent to which the situation did not improve as the Revolution continued. This provides a different perspective on the war. Both sides faced serious difficulties and had major drawbacks. Militarily, this meant both that there was everything to play for and that managing limitations was as important as grasping opportunities. Politically, these drawbacks also ensured not only that there was everything to play for but also that whichever side was better able to accept its weaknesses and persist was likely to win the struggle of will.

In 1780 this was still unclear. It was a year of disappointment for Britain's opponents. The French expeditionary force that arrived in Newport achieved nothing, while Washington was unable to shake British control of New York. His troops were increasingly demoralized. The British still controlled the sea, and, if their impact in the interior was limited, they revealed at Charleston, and around the Chesapeake, an ability to use their amphibious forces to considerable effect, taking the initiative, harrying their opponents and disrupting the American economy.

That year, the southern British strategy was successful – at least until Patrick Ferguson's defeat at King's Mountain on 7 October. In the middle colonies,

General Sir Henry Clinton, who had succeeded Howe as commander-in-chief in 1778, had a plan for crushing Washington by advancing on his position in New Jersey, and forcing battle on the outnumbered Americans. Had Clinton achieved that objective he would have moved against the French when they landed that year in Rhode Island. The French would not have been able to withdraw into the interior. With Washington's army gone, Clinton would probably also have captured West Point, thanks to the treachery of Benedict Arnold, and thus gained naval access to the entire Hudson Valley.

But he told nobody in New York about this plan, and before he returned from Charleston, the Loyalists, who were convinced that Clinton was incapable of decisive action, had persuaded General Wilhelm von Knyphausen, the commander of the Hessian auxiliary forces, to land in New Jersey with a smaller force than Clinton had envisaged. By the time Clinton returned there was no chance for surprise, and he pulled back to New York after the indecisive Springfield raid (7–23 June 1780). This was the last major campaign north of Virginia, and it was an important morale-boosting encounter for the Revolutionaries: a fighting withdrawal by the Americans in the face of large British forces was followed by the establishment of a stronger defensive position, and a British retreat that led to the abandonment of New Jersey.

Despite the anxieties expressed in Britain in 1778, French entry into the war had not obliged the British to abandon New York, nor had it led to another attack on Canada, nor to the permanent postponing of operations in the South. Similarly, the British position had not collapsed outside America, and, by the beginning of 1781, Britain had lost few possessions outside North America.

The close of 1780 saw the central themes of the 1781 campaign in America already clear: the need for Franco-American co-operation if a major blow was to be struck against the British; British problems in the South; the rising importance of the Chesapeake in military operations; and the crucial role of naval power. The contrasting results of the campaigns of 1780 and 1781 indicate, however, that these circumstances and problems made nothing inevitable.

Although Springfield, King's Mountain, and Banastre Tarleton's defeat at Cowpens on 17 January 1781 did not involve the main field armies, they ended the impression of Britain successfully gaining the initiative, tarnished the Southern strategy, and indicated that it had not had any significant consequences for the British in the middle colonies.

After then, it was unclear that the British could have won. The combination of Washington's strategy of attrition in the middle colonies and Greene's strategy of partisan warfare in the South denied the British effective control of the areas in which they operated. A different balance of naval power and advantage would have led to a successful British withdrawal from Yorktown in September or October 1781, but this would not have led to victory. Instead, having fought their way to impasse in the middle colonies and the South, the British would have had to evacuate Virginia.

French intervention in the war was also important in turning one type of American success (avoiding being defeated) into another type of success (defeating Britain). French intervention also transformed the conflict into a worldwide struggle that seriously tested the British Empire. Having earlier supplied weapons, France entered the war on the American side in 1778, Spain following a year later. Thanks to much shipbuilding by these powers in the late 1760s and 1770s, the British were now outnumbered at sea, and were unable to gain control of either European or American waters. French naval success in blockading a British army at Yorktown in the *Chesapeake* in 1781 was crucial to the triumph of the American and French besiegers on land, and the resulting surrender by Earl Cornwallis of

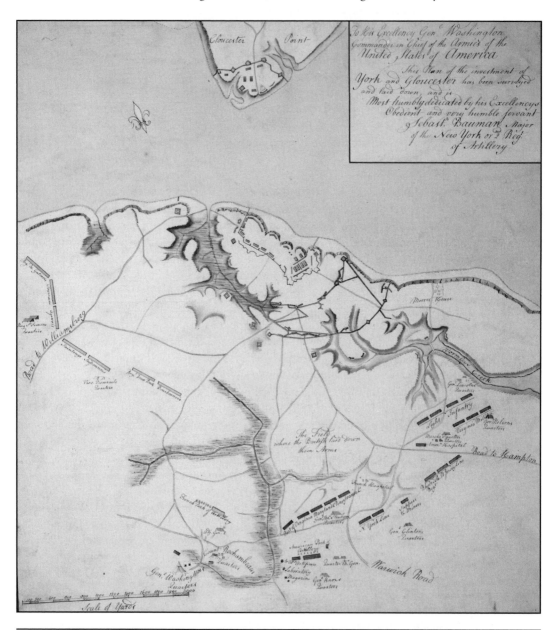

Map 1.3 American map of the Battle of Yorktown, 1781. BL. Add. 57715 no 13. © British Library.

his army led the British government to abandon the war and to acknowledge the independence of the thirteen colonies. In a separate campaign, the Spaniards campaigned successfully in West Florida, culminating with the capture of Pensacola in May 1781.

In the event, elsewhere the British Empire largely held during the war, especially in Canada, Ireland and most of the West Indies. For the British, paradoxically, the war was a clear defensive victory. Once France had come in, it was a global struggle in which Britain was alone. Aside from France, Spain and the Dutch, Britain was also at war with India's two leading military powers: the Marathas from 1778 to 1782, and Mysore from 1780 to 1784. There were serious defeats and blows during the conflict, not only the loss of the thirteen colonies but that of West Florida (the Florida panhandle over to the Mississippi) to Spain (1779–81), the Mediterranean island of Minorca to French and Spanish forces (1782), and, in the West Indies, Dominica (1778), Grenada (1779), St Vincent (1779), Tobago (1781) and Nevis, St Kitts and Montserrat (1782) to the French, and, in India, defeats at the hands of the Marathas at Wadgaon (12–13 February 1779) and by Mysore at Perumbakam on 10 September 1780 and near the Coleroon river (18 February 1782).

Plate 1.3 *The Death of Colonel Moorhouse at Bangalore, 21 March 1791*, by Robert Home. An important episode in the British advance on Seringapatam, capital of Tipu Sultan of Mysore, in southern India. Bangalore had to be seized to secure British communications and the creation of a reliable supply system. Anne S.K. Brown Military Collection, John Hay Library, Brown University, Providence, Rhode Island, Ind B 1791 1f-1.

Yet, the bulk of the Empire was held. The Americans failed to gain Canada, the French and Spanish invasion attempt on Britain was unsuccessful, and Gibraltar withstood a long siege. In India, the British were able to hold their key positions against both the Marathas and Mysore, and to end up with peace treaties that left them with no gains at Britain's expense. Crucially, the French fleet was defeated

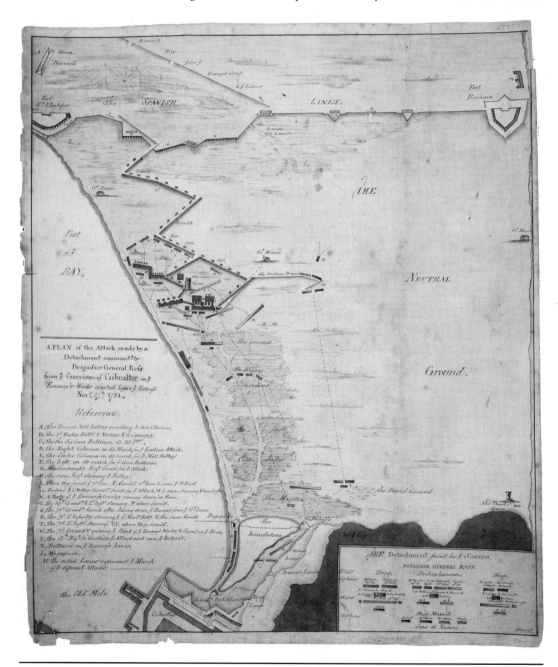

Map 1.4 Siege of Gibraltar, 1781. BL. Add. 69849. © British Library.

BOX 1.1   WAR BETWEEN THE USA AND NATIVE AMERICANS

The Native Americans were not consulted in the peace settlement that closed the American War of Independence in 1783, and it was followed by a major upsurge of American settlement, especially in Kentucky and Ohio. Seen by most Americans as a rightful response to God-given opportunities for expansion, this settlement was resisted by the Natives. In 1790, full-scale war broke out. The small size of the American regular army ensured that the emphasis was on the militia, which lacked the fighting quality of the Natives. Seeking to maximize their opportunity to deliver aimed fire and to minimize the target they offered, the Natives fought in open, not close, order; but the Americans lacked the confidence and training to do so. The Americans also suffered from underrating their opponents, and exaggerating their own capability. In 1790, the Miami (a Native tribe), under their leader Little Turtle, twice successfully ambushed advancing American forces. The Americans, however, were able to fall back on Fort Washington (now Cincinnati). The shelter provided by forts was a major advantage for the Americans, as was the lack of Native capability for major offensives. A largely American advance in 1791 was fatally over-confident, and on 4 November, at the side of the Wabash River, Little Turtle surprised the poorly prepared American camp. Unable to offer an effective response to elusive Natives firing from cover, the Americans were badly shot up, before fleeing with over 600 dead to twenty-one Natives. American/European formations and tactics were clearly not necessarily superior. Better-trained American troops, benefiting from serious divisions among the Natives, reversed the situation at the battle of Fallen Timbers on 20 August 1794. By the Treaty of Greeneville of 1795, the Natives confirmed earlier territorial cessions and made new ones. Victory helped encourage the forward drive of American expansion. It was not just North American settlers who fought indigenous peoples at this time, but also those of Central and South America. Many of these peoples displayed considerable resilience: the Araucanians were not subdued by Chile until the 1880s.

in the Caribbean at the battle of the Saints on 12 April 1782. Britain had failed in the thirteen colonies, but the crisis of empire had been overcome. This was no mean achievement.

The availability of naval support proved a key factor. British initiatives, such as the plan to capture Cape Town from the Dutch in 1781, were thwarted by the arrival of French warships. Likewise, besieged British positions, such as Quebec in 1776 and Gibraltar from 1779, were relieved by the British fleet, while those that were not relieved, such as Pensacola in 1781 and Minorca in 1782, fell. The British were helped by the failure of the most threatening Bourbon naval schemes: the attempted invasion of southern England in 1779, and the deployment of a large fleet in the Caribbean in 1782, which it was feared might attack Jamaica. Furthermore, although they were hard pressed in southern India by the French and their ally, the Sultan of Mysore, the British situation there did not collapse on either land or sea, partly because, in a major deployment of transoceanic strength, ten regiments reached India in the period 1780–82. The British fleet in Indian waters also displayed great resilience in a series of battles with the French.

The deployment of considerable forces at great distances indicated the organizational strength of the European oceanic empires. The growing role of the state in European warfare, replacing the semi-independent military entrepreneurs of earlier days, was readily apparent, not least in terms of a higher level of military preparedness and planning. Aside from the imperial struggle, the American success in winning independence was of great long-term importance. So also was the departure of large numbers of Loyalists to Canada and Britain, which removed what might have been a continual cause of insurgency in the USA.

BEFORE THE FRENCH REVOLUTION

Prior to the outbreak of the French Revolutionary Wars in 1792, the tactics of European armies focused on the deployment of infantry in close-packed, thin lines in order to maximize firepower. Such formations also lessened the problems of command and control posed by the limitations of communications on the battle-field. Soldiers used flintlock muskets equipped with bayonets, and fired by volley, rather than employing individually aimed shots. Despite the bayonets, hand-to-hand fighting on the battlefield was relatively uncommon and most casualties were caused by shot. The accuracy of muskets was limited, and training, therefore, stressed rapidity of fire, and thus drill and discipline. Musket fire was commonly delivered at close range.

The problems caused by short-range muskets, which had a low rate of fire and had to be re-sighted for each individual shot, were exacerbated by the cumulative impact of poor sights, eccentric bullets, heavy musket droops, recoil, overheating, and misfiring in wet weather. As muskets were smooth bore and there was no rifling, or grooves, in the barrel, the speed of the shot was not high and its direction was uncertain. Non-standardized manufacture and wide clearances (windage) diminished the velocity of the shot and meant that the ball could roll out if the barrel was pointed towards the ground, while, at best, the weapon was difficult to aim or to hold steady. Balls were rough-cast, and the balls (spherical bullets) maximized air resistance. The development of iron instead of wooden ramrods was believed to increase the rate of musket fire, but they had a tendency to break or went rusty; and frequent use of the ramrod distorted the barrel into an oval shape. Europeans could produce more sophisticated weapons at this point, but could not make them on a large scale prior to industrialization.

Despite the limitations of the weaponry, casualties could be substantial because the combatants were densely packed and fought at close range. Low muzzle velocity led to dreadful wounds, because the more slowly a projectile travels the more damage it does as it bounces off bones and internal organs.

The infantry was flanked by cavalry units, but the proportion of cavalry in European armies declined during the century (cutting the average cost of soldiers) as a result of the heavier emphasis on firepower. Cavalry was principally used on the battlefield to fight cavalry; cavalry advances against unbroken infantry were uncommon. Unbroken infantry was more vulnerable to artillery, especially because of the close-packed and static formations that were adopted in order to maintain discipline and firepower: discipline was required to maximize the effectiveness of the weaponry.

The ability to mobilize resources for war reflected the nature of society: the combination of a cash economy (which provided a basis for taxation), under-employment and governments that enjoyed great authority over the bulk of the population (although not the social elite), created the context for the major mobilization of manpower for war. This took a variety of forms, including the systems of general conscriptions (with exemptions) in Eastern Europe, but the common element was the assumption that the bulk of the male population would serve if required and on terms that they did not influence, and that their views on the purposes and methods of warfare would not be sought. Command and control systems were hierarchical.

Mutinies were rare. Desertion was far more common and was harshly punished: it was a dangerous protest against often desperate conditions. Training was harsh, discipline could be brutal and the conditions of service in terms of accommodation, food and pay were poor, although not always worse than those in civilian society.

The lack of interest in the views of soldiers and sailors did not mean that rulers, generals and admirals were oblivious to the condition of their troops and to casualties. They were well aware that poor food and accommodation could lead to debilitating diseases, although adequate provision was difficult to secure, especially on campaign. The military were a section of the community which governments needed and therefore cared for, albeit at a basic level. Though pay was generally low and was frequently delayed, troops were the largest group paid by governments. Experienced troops could be difficult to replace, and new recruits were of limited value until blooded. As a result, the fate of battle, as today, was frequently determined by which side had the more battle-hardened men.

Concern about casualties could encourage caution in risking battle, although it is necessary not to exaggerate this. The dangers of casualties and defeat did not prevent leaders from seeking battle. There was certainly nothing inherently cautious about generalship at this time. The ethos of the period placed a great premium on bravery and boldness in command. Although factors such as recruitment and logistics were known to be of great consequence, they did not determine the culture of warfare; just as the character of the domestic rule of kings was not decided by the financial issues that they knew to be important. Monarchs were expected to win glory through victory and conquest.

There is a widely held, but largely misleading, view, deeply rooted in popular military history, that warfare before the French Revolution was inconsequential in its results and limited in its methods, and contrasted with the supposed nature of Revolutionary warfare. This thesis is mistaken, as a consideration of the rise of Russian and Prussian power earlier in the century, and of the heavy casualty rates in battle, indicates. Indeed, the former had important short and long-term implications for European power politics.

THE FRENCH REVOLUTIONARY WARS, 1792–99

In addition to the American War of Independence, the wars that broke out between Revolutionary France and its opponents are also seen as marking and making a major change in the waging of war, and, indeed, as constituting the origins of modern warfare. Becoming steadily more radical, by the winter of 1791–92 the French Revolution was preaching the brotherhood of man in a way that threatened the established interests of neighbouring rulers, and the treaties by which past rulers of France had acknowledged these interests. A failure on both sides to understand the military capability of the other further exacerbated the situation. The Revolutionaries were convinced that *ancien régime* militaries were feeble because of their social composition – unwilling peasants commanded by decadent officers, while, to their opponents, the Revolutionaries' attack on hierarchy, order and deference wrecked discipline and coherence and led to a derisory amateurism. War broke out in the spring of 1792 with France opposed to Austria and Prussia.

The rapid overthrow of the Revolution had been widely anticipated, but, in the event, an invasion of France by the experienced Prussian army under the Duke of Brunswick was checked on 20 September 1792 at Valmy by a larger and more heavily-gunned French force. Brunswick retreated, while the French advanced rapidly, making extensive territorial conquests. The Austrian Netherlands (modern Belgium) was conquered within a month, while other French forces successfully invaded the Rhineland and also Savoy, then part of Italy. Although the French subsequently met with checks at the hands of their opponents, especially in early 1793, they were able to defeat the opposing coalition which, by March 1793, had increased to include Britain, the Dutch and Spain.

The larger French numbers of troops, once organized, told, especially as Allied cohesion was limited. Superiority in numbers was important in both battles and offensives. Numbers came from the large French population, the largest in Europe after Russia, and due to the *levée en masse*, the general conscription ordered in August 1793: the entire population could be obliged to serve the war effort and all single men aged between 18 and 25 were to join the army, where they were deluged with Revolutionary propaganda. The long-term global impact of this *levée en masse* was far greater than the American minute man myth: twentieth-century Chinese, Algerian, Vietnamese and Latin American revolutionaries all drew on the *levée* filtered through a largely Marxist reading of French history. The *levée* indeed had an ambiguous position. It supposedly symbolized spontaneous popular action (and hence was idealized by the left), but in practice it justified a considerable expansion of state power and regulation, leading to American hostility to the idea.

The armies raised were both larger than those deployed by France hitherto, and enabled it to operate effectively on several fronts at once, to sustain casualties, and to match the opposing forces of much of Europe. Feeding and supplying forces on this scale, however, created new logistical and organizational problems. In the period 1793–95, the French fought in the Low Countries, the Rhineland, northern Italy and northern Spain, as well as fielding forces against domestic opponents. The struggle against counter-revolutionaries, particularly in the Vendée in western France in 1793 and 1794, looked forward towards the bitterness of much civil conflict and counter-insurgency warfare in the nineteenth and twentieth centuries, not least with the difficulties of distinguishing between fighters and civilians, and with atrocities against the latter.

The French forces also benefited from pre-Revolutionary developments. Far from being rigid and conservative, the pre-Revolutionary French military had been very open to new ideas, in part as a result of being heavily defeated by Frederick the Great of Prussia at the battle of Rossbach in 1757. There had been a major improvement in the French artillery, not least with a standardization of gun types, while there had also been considerable interest in organizational improvements, especially in the creation of divisions as new structures. An emphasis on military education produced a number of officers who were to rise to prominence in the Revolutionary armies, the greatest being Napoleon.

In the 1790s, divisions about goals and means among France's opponents combined with differences in success and failure to affect their determination to continue the struggle. In 1795, Prussia and Spain agreed terms with France, while the defeated and overrun Dutch accepted satellite status. At the same time, it is important not to underrate the motivation of France's opponents, particularly Austria on land and Britain on the sea, nor the military value of the professionalism of their forces. The Austrians won a series of victories, and denied France control over Germany, although, thanks to Napoleon's leadership of the French, they were far less successful in Italy. The British navy proved particularly successful

BOX 1.2   THE VOICE OF WAR: THE FRENCH REVOLUTIONARY WARS

The Guards[1] marched in excellent order through the wood keeping as good a line as their situation would permit . . . the masked battery of the French (of which the Guards were completely ignorant) commenced the heaviest firing of grape shot . . . within 30 years . . . The fire was so sudden that almost every man by one impulse fell to the ground – but immediately got up and began a confused fire without orders – The second discharge of the French knocked down whole ranks – The officers upon this exerted themselves to make the men come to charge . . . but all was in vain. The soldiers on their knees kept on firing and would have remained so till all were killed [had they not retreated].[2]

The devastating nature of artillery fire, the folly of conventional close-order formations employed in this case by the British, and the impact of battle, especially casualties, on morale and discipline all demonstrated near Tournai.

1   The British Coldstream Guards.
2   R. Williams to Marquess of Buckingham, 11 May 1793, British Library, Additional Manuscripts 59279 folios 23–4.

BOX 1.3 FRENCH REVOLUTIONARY TACTICS

The characteristic battlefield manoeuvre of French Revolutionary forces, and the most effective way to use the mass of inexperienced soldiers, most of whom went into the infantry, was in independent attack columns. This was also best for an army that put an emphasis on the attack. Column advances were far more flexible than those of lines, although frontal attacks by columns led to heavy casualties due to firepower wielded by defending line formations. In contrast, only those at the front of the columns could use their firepower.

Columns were combined with an increased use of cannon, and with large numbers of skirmishers, a successful meshing of tactical elements matched to the technology of the times and the character of the new republican soldiers. Sent in advance of the columns, and deployed in open order so that they were less vulnerable to volley fire or to cannon, the skirmishers were able to use individual fire in order to inflict casualties on the close-packed lines of their opponents; this hit morale and could also disrupt formations. The combination of artillery, skirmishers and assault columns ensured that command and co-ordination skills became more important, and the French benefited from young and determined commanders. Those who failed, or were suspected of treachery, were executed. Talent flourished: French commanders included Jean-Baptiste Jourdan, a former private, Lazare Hoche, a former corporal, and Napoleon Bonaparte. There was also a more 'democratic' command structure, at least at battalion level.

The armies were systematized by Lazare Carnot, head of the military section of the Committee of Public Safety, who brought a measure of organization to the military confusion. Success in forming and training new armies was instrumental in the transition from a royal army to a nation in arms.

If, however, opposing forces maintained their cohesion, then French tactics were not inevitably successful. Indeed, in the 1790s the Austrians won half the battles they fought with the French. Furthermore, with French victories such as Jemappes on 6 November 1792, the key battle that gave them control over the Austrian Netherlands (modern Belgium), it is difficult to know how far this was due to the use of columns and how far to the larger size of the French army.

in inflicting a series of defeats, including the Glorious First of June (1 June 1794) and the Nile (1 August 1798) over the French, Cape St Vincent over the Spaniards (14 February 1797), and Camperdown over the Dutch (11 October 1797). This continued opposition helped deny the Revolutionaries the sweeping victory necessary if they were to dominate Western Europe and demilitarize the Revolution, although the vested interests involved in its military character, especially the generals, also made this difficult.

THE RISE OF NAPOLEON

Far from demilitarization, the opposite occurred in France in 1799 when a general seized power with a coup. A Corsican, who had become a second-lieutenant in the pre-Revolutionary artillery, Napoleon Bonaparte (1769–1821) had made his name in 1793 when his successful command of the artillery in the siege of Toulon played a major role in driving British and Royalist forces from the port, France's leading naval base on the Mediterranean. Military service, especially at the level of generals, was intensely political during the Revolutionary years, and in October 1795 Napoleon came to the aid of the government using artillery firing at point-blank range, the famous 'whiff of grapeshot', to help put down a rising in Paris. As a reward, he was given command of the Army of Italy. In 1796, in this command, Napoleon developed and demonstrated the characteristics of his generalship: self-confidence; swift decision-making; rapid mobility – marching faster than his opponents; the concentration of strength at what was made the decisive point – using the army's divisional structure to advance along many routes with one objective; and, where possible, the exploitation of interior lines. In north-west Italy, Napoleon seized a central position between the Austrians and the king of Sardinia (ruler of Piedmont), defeating both and knocking Sardinia out of the war. Napoleon's tactical genius and ability to manoeuvre on the battlefield brought victory over the Austrians, especially at Arcole (15–17 November 1796) and Rivoli (14–15 January 1797), and associated Napoleon with military success. His siting of the artillery was particularly important.

Napoleon forced Austria to accept peace in 1797, but the French inability to accept restraints led to the resumption of conflict. Napoleon won further glory when he invaded Egypt in 1798, defeating the Mamelukes at the battles of Shubra Khit and Embabeh, the latter known as the Battle of the Pyramids (21 July), although, in fact, his army was cut off by the victory of the British fleet at the battle of the Nile (1 August). In the battles on land, French cannon and musket fire repelled cavalry attacks, inflicting heavy casualties. Napoleon did not use the linear formations common on European battlefields, but instead employed squares, combining the firepower of densely packed infantry with a tactical flexibility of formations that could not be put at a disadvantage by being attacked in flank or rear by more mobile cavalry.

The continuation of the war in Europe helped make the divided Directory ministry unpopular and, having returned to France, Napoleon staged a coup in 1799, becoming first consul and general-in-chief.

ASIAN CONFLICTS

Napoleon's campaign in Egypt and Palestine from 1798 to 1799 had been part of a French attempt to gain a position on the route to India and challenge the British position in South Asia. Indeed, his secretary thought that the general wished to repeat the triumphs of Alexander the Great by marching overland against India. Instead, it was the British who were more successful. Having repeatedly failed in the 1760s, 1780s and early 1790s to defeat the Sultanate of Mysore, the leading power in southern India, they stormed its capital, Seringapatam, on 4 May 1799 at the climax of a well-paced and ably co-ordinated offensive, and then installed a client regime.

Further west, the Russians displayed an ability to defeat semi-nomadic peoples. Having annexed the khanate of the Crimea in 1783, they overran the Kuban to the east of the Black Sea. There, when in 1783 the Nogais resisted being incorporated into the expanding Russian state, they were beaten in battles by a small, determined Russian force under Count Alexander Suvorov. The Russian ability to force battle on semi-nomadic peoples was crucial to the Nogais' defeat. The Russians also won repeated victories at the expense of the Ottomans (Turks) during their war of 1787–92. In 1789, the main Russian army advanced to the Dniester, in 1790 the forts in the Danube delta were captured, and in 1791 the Russians advanced south of the Danube. They were increasingly effective in battle and on campaign, with column formations employing both firepower and bayonet charges; they also introduced more flexible supply systems, which permitted better strategic planning. The Ottomans finally accepted terms that left Russia firmly established on the Black Sea. Allied to the Russians, the Austrians developed tactical formations to counter

Plate 1.4 The storming of Seringapatam, 4 May 1799, colour aquatint. Capital of Tipu Sultan of Mysore, this was a formidable position on an island in the Cauvery river. The artillery on the opposite bank blew a breach in the ramparts, which were then stormed under heavy fire. Tipu was killed in the subsequent fighting. National Army Museum 7102-33-382.

Ottoman cavalry superiority, especially infantry squares arranged in a mutually supporting checkerboard pattern, helping them to defeat the Ottomans in 1789.

Most wars in Asia, however, did not involve European powers, and firearms played a smaller role in them than they did in Western warfare. The leading Asian military power, China, was not involved in any major external conflict in this period, and had mixed success in the wars it fought. Having failed in invasions of Burma from 1766 to 1769, the Chinese did likewise when they intervened in Vietnam in 1788 and 1789: their attempt to capture Hanoi was defeated by Nguyen Hue, who had reunited Vietnam, and the Chinese force was hit hard. The Vietnamese were well familiar with the use of firearms. Further west, however, in 1792, the Chinese advanced to Katmandu, where the Gurkhas of Nepal, whose expansion had begun to challenge the Chinese position in Tibet, were forced to recognize Chinese authority. By the end of the century China was at peace with all its neighbours, and on its own terms. Russia respected China's treaty boundaries, but not those of the Ottoman Empire or Persia. Aside from Russia, China's neighbours were tributary powers. In contrast to the situation a century later, Japan followed a pacific policy and had only a modest military.

Major revolts made the situation less benign within China. The huge millenarian White Lotus rebellion of 1796–1805 in the province of Shaanxi was made more troublesome by the rebels' extensive use of guerrilla tactics and by the extent to which they benefited from the hilly character of their core area.

Plate 1.5 Indian demon attacking fort defended by British troops, 1791. Indian representation of conflict was different from that by Europeans and did not share the latter's sense of European superiority. Ind 0 1791 *sf*-1, Anne S.K. Brown Military Collection.

The government had to mount a formidable and costly military effort, and also employed brutally repressive methods; a marked contrast to the situation in Britain's North American colonies. Similar brutality was used in response to revolts by non-Chinese subjects, especially the Miao revolts in the provinces of Hunan and Guizhou in the period 1795 to 1805, which were similar to the opposition of the Native Americans to American expansion in that they were in opposition to the spread of Han settlement and the attempt to increase government power. The army responded by creating more garrisons, introducing military-agricultural colonists and building a wall.

Assertive rulers helped other Asian states to expand. The Burmese deployed large armies and overran neighbouring Arakan to the west, but, although about 200,000 men were conscripted for the 1785 and 1786 expeditions against Siam (modern Thailand), these failed. India was an area of rapid changes in weaponry and military organization. European-style infantry forces were created by the Marathas and the Nizam of Hyderabad, the major ruler in south-central India. A volatile and pressurized international system was driving the pace of military adaptability. French experts taught Indians to cast cannon in the French style and also played a role in local fortification technique. Thus, Benoît de Boigne, commander of a corps for the Maratha leader Sindhia, constructed French-style fortifications in Aligarh, east of Delhi, after 1788. Sindhia's army itself proved successful in campaigns in Rajputana in the 1780s and 1790s, and his artillery captured the major Rajput fortress of Chitor in a matter of weeks.

Like China, the Ottoman (Turkish) Empire faced both external foes and rebellions. In the first case, aside from the Russians, there was also war with Persia from 1774 to 1779, while serious rebellions included that by Kara Mahmoud, the governor of Scutari, in the 1780s and 1790s. In addition, it proved difficult to maintain authority over the nomadic tribesmen of the Arab borderlands. Yet it also proved possible to counter some of these challenges. In 1786, an Ottoman expeditionary force landed in Egypt, defeating rebels and capturing Cairo. As a reminder, however, of the difficulties that all empires faced, and still face, in maintaining their power and enforcing their authority, the rebel leaders retreated to Upper Egypt and, unable to impose a settlement, the Ottomans had to negotiate terms in 1787.

NAVAL POWER

Significant naval forces with a range greater than war canoes were deployed by only a handful of non-European powers, principally the Ottoman (Turkish) Empire, the Barbary states of North Africa (Algiers, Morocco, Tripoli and Tunis), and the Arabs of Oman. The ships of these powers approximated to European warships, but lacked the destructive power of the latter: the Barbary and Omani ships were commerce raiders that emphasized speed and manoeuvrability, whereas the heavier, slower ships-of-the-line of European navies were designed for battle and stressed battering power. Programmes of naval construction indicated not only the resources of European governments but also the capability of their military-industrial complexes. Fleets were powerful and sophisticated military systems, sustained by mighty industrial and logistical resources, based in dockyards that were among the largest industrial plants, employers of labour, and groups of buildings in the world. The range of European fleets owed much to overseas bases, such as Batavia (modern Jakarta, then Dutch), Bombay (modern Mumbai, then British), Cape Town (Dutch), Halifax (British), Havana (Spanish), and Port Royal, Jamaica (British), and to the supply systems that supported their warships; but navies found it hard to fulfil their potential. Thanks in large part to the combination of dependence on the wind and the poor manoeuvrability of warships, battles frequently did not develop as suggested by fighting instructions, and admirals had only limited control once fighting had begun.

In order, the leading naval powers were Britain, France and Spain. The United Provinces (modern Netherlands, sometimes called Holland), Denmark, Russia and Sweden were also important naval powers. Force structures reflected both the goals pursued and the nature of the waters fought over. The shallow and shoaly waters of the eastern Baltic, especially the heavily indented shoreline of the Gulf of Finland, encouraged a reliance there on galleys, particularly in the war between

Plate 1.6 *The Agamemnon engages four French frigates and a corvette*, by Nicholas Pocock, 1810, showing the capture of the French *Ça Ira* by HMS *Agamemnon* under Captain Horatio Nelson, 1795. Nelson made his name in the Mediterranean where the British sought to use naval power in order to hinder the French on land. In 1796, however, Napoleon's succession in Italy led the British to evacuate the Mediterranean. © National Maritime Museum.

Russia and Sweden from 1788 to 1790, whereas there was no such need or opportunity for galleys in the Atlantic warfare that involved the British, French, Spanish and Dutch fleets. Atlantic warfare required different kinds of ships for line of battle and for commerce raiding and protection. The emphasis in the latter was on speed, and thus on frigates that were too lightly gunned for the line of battle.

The social politics of the British navy is controversial. An emphasis on ferocious discipline (whipping the disobedient with the savage cat o' nine tails), and on forcible service by men pressed into service (seized) by press gangs, has been challenged by a stress on mutual respect between ranks and ships as communities. There was a serious mutiny in the fleet in 1797, mostly over conditions, but the infrequency of mutinies is striking. While firmly disciplined, the sailors were not slaves, nor were the majority pressed. Instead, there was a powerful voluntary dimension to naval service, and this helped make the living conditions bearable. They were cramped and insanitary, and the food was poor, but the situation elsewhere in maritime life was scarcely better.

Plate 1.7 *The Battle of Camperdown*, by Philip de Loutherberg, 1797. Two advancing British lines of warships under Admiral Duncan broke the Dutch line under de Winter into three segments: each fleet had sixteen warships. In the individual ship-to-ship engagements that the battle developed into, British victory owed much to superior gun power. The Dutch lost nine ships of the line and two frigates. © National Maritime Museum.

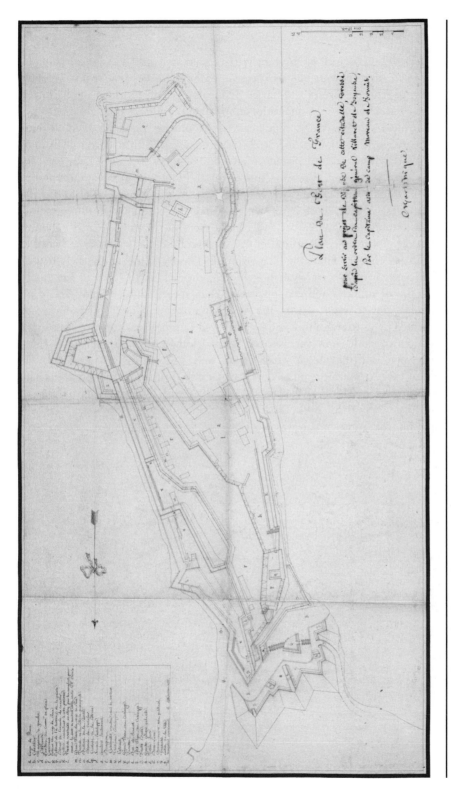

Map 1.5 Plan of the citadel at Martinique. BL. Add. 49362. © British Library.

CONCLUSIONS

The relative importance of Western warfare grew not only because of the global reach of Western powers but also because economic development permitted the support of stronger armies and navies. Industrial growth provided the basis both for the production of large quantities of armaments and for rapidly implementing new advances in weaponry. Significant developments occurred in metallurgy, where the smelting of iron and steel, using coke rather than charcoal, freed an important industry from dependence on wood supplies. Britain led the way, but the technology spread. Buoyant metallurgical industries underlay British and Russian military activity, and the scale of demand was considerable. Supporting the conquest of the French West Indian island of Martinique in 1809, forty-six British cannon fired 4,000 shot and 10,000 shells in five days.

On the global scale, the spread of the Western example frequently provided an impetus for change. Thus, the 'Napoleon of Hawaii', Kamehameha I, fought his way to supremacy in the Hawaiian archipelago from 1791 to 1805, in part thanks to his use of muskets and cannon, rather than spears, clubs, daggers and sling-shots. His power was based on the west coast of the island of Hawaii, a coast frequented by European ships, and he employed Europeans as gunners. Advantages in weaponry alone, however, were of limited long-term (and sometimes short-term) value, and the use to which forces were put has to be considered. The political context put a premium on statesmanship, just as the military dimension put one on generalship. Whether successful, as with Kamehameha or Nguyen Anh, ruler of Vietnam from 1802 to 1820, or, ultimately unsuccessful, as with Napoleon, this combination was crucial.

CHAPTER 2

Empires Rise and Fall, 1800–30

INTRODUCTION

Military history in this period usually centres on Napoleon, dictator of France from 1799 until 1814, and again briefly in 1815, and the leading general in Europe during this period with a series of major victories, such as Ulm and Austerlitz in 1805, to his credit. Napoleon created the largest empire (of direct and indirect control) in Europe prior to that of Hitler's Germany in World War Two. Impressive to his European contemporaries, Napoleon also had a wider impact with his invasion of Egypt in 1798.

Yet on the global scale, and in particular on a longer timetable, it is not Napoleon that dominates the military history of the period, in so far as long-term importance is concerned. Instead, his career ended in failure. This is abundantly clear in Europe, where Napoleon was finally and definitively defeated at Waterloo in 1815, but the Napoleonic Wars also saw the collapse of the French overseas empire. Much of it was conquered by Britain, although the remaining French territories in North America were sold to the USA in the Louisiana Purchase of 1803, taking the territorial claims of the USA to the Rockies (although without consulting the Native Americans). It is two other developments that seem of greater importance: first, Britain's rise to be clearly the strongest power in the world; second, the ability of newly independent states in the Americas to resist attempts to suppress or limit their independence.

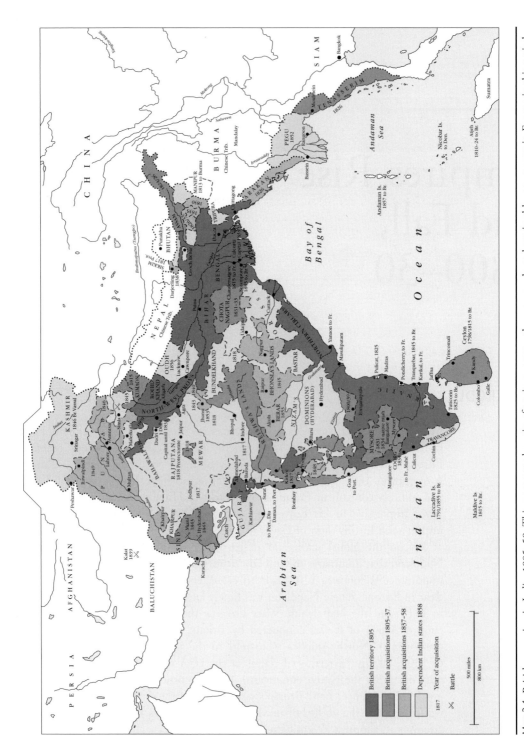

Map 2.1 British expansion in India, 1805–58. This represented a gain of territory greater than any made and retained by any power in Europe in this period.

© George Philip & Son Ltd.

THE RISE OF BRITAIN

At the start of the century, Britain appeared vulnerable. From 1794 to 1798 she had avoided successful invasion by France, and defeated the fleets of France and her Spanish and Dutch allies, but British forces had been driven from the European mainland and her alliance system collapsed during 1800 and 1801 as her allies signed treaties with France. Finally, in the Peace of Amiens of 1802, Britain bought peace, accepting French domination of Western Europe and returning many of her recent colonial gains from France and her allies, including Cape Town, which she had captured from the Dutch in 1795.

By 1830, the situation was very different. Britain's naval position was unchallenged, she was a major player in European international relations, and her position elsewhere was strengthening, especially, but not only, in South Asia. Between 1803 and 1830 the British had defeated the Marathas, their leading rival in India and the kingdom of Burma, and had played the major role in the successful 1816 bombardment of the privateering centre of Algiers (in European eyes, the rogue state of the age) and, on 2 October 1827, alongside French and Russian warships, in destroying the Egyptian fleet in the battle of Navarino Bay. This led to Greece gaining independence in 1830 from the Ottoman (Turkish) Empire, which the Egyptians had been helping.

The strong position Britain secured in this period helped ensure that it was the major global power of the nineteenth century, and thus the state that took the leading role in the process of European imperial expansion, and also in dictating, or at least determining, the terms in which non-European powers that retained independence were made to participate in the world economic system. During the remainder of the century, other European powers, especially France, would try to create empires comparable to that of the British in South Asia and to challenge Britain's naval power, but none would succeed.

BOX 2.1   THE BATTLE OF ASSAYE, 23 SEPTEMBER 1803

The key British victory in India in the early nineteenth century. Arthur Wellesley, later 1st Duke of Wellington, with 4,500 men, seventeen cannon and 5,000 unreliable Indian cavalry, successfully confronted a Maratha army of 30,000 cavalry, 10,000 infantry, and over a hundred cannon. His victory owed much to bayonet charges, scarcely conforming to the standard image of Western armies gunning down masses of non-European troops relying on cold steel. The Maratha cannon moved fast, were well laid and served, disabled the British cannon and inflicted heavy casualties. Repeated attacks were necessary to force the Marathas to retreat. Casualties accounted for over a quarter of the British force. Crucially, the fearsome Maratha cannon were captured. In a subsequent British victory at Argaon on 29 November, the Maratha artillery again was effective. Battles were not the sole factor: the Marathas were weakened by a poor command structure and lack of money: the absence of regular pay destroyed discipline and control.

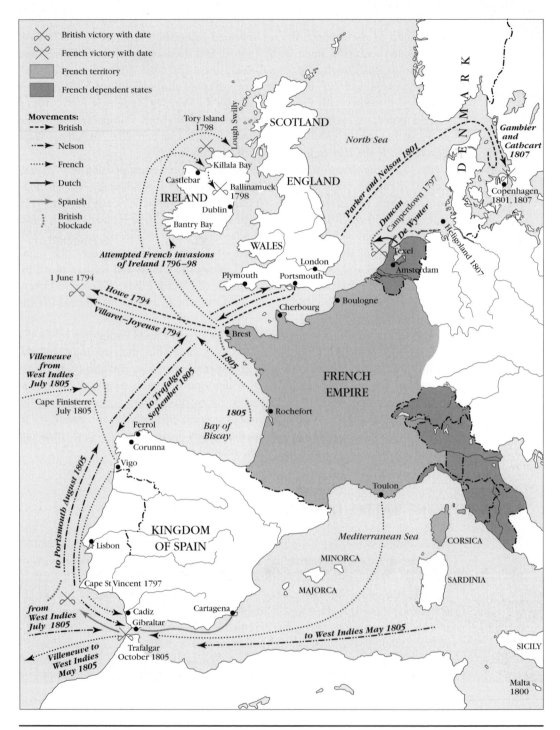

Map 2.2 British victories in home waters, 1794–1805. After *The Times Atlas of World History* (1993), p. 190. © BCA by arrangement with Time Books.

Plate 2.1 Double-headed shot for cutting through rigging, fired at HMS *Victory* from the Spanish *Santísima Trinidad* at the battle of Trafalgar, 1805. © National Maritime Museum.

Plate 2.2 *Capture of the* Chesapeake. On 9 April 1813 the USS *Chesapeake* returned to Boston after a cruise against British commercial shipping. Refitted and remanned she left harbour but was intercepted by HMS *Shannon*, received crippling casualties in an exchange of fire and was taken by the British on 1 June. The British blockade inflicted more damage on the American economy than American privateers did on the British. © National Maritime Museum.

The fundamentals of British strength were an unmatched commitment to naval power, and a skill in employing it to maximize other advantages and forces. British naval hegemony rested on a sophisticated and well-financed administrative structure, as well as a large fleet drawing on the manpower resources of a substantial mercantile marine (although there were never enough sailors), and an ability to win engagements that reflected widely diffused qualities of seamanship and gunnery, a skilled and determined corps of captains, and able leadership. This was true not only of command at sea, especially the innovative tactics and capacity to inspire seen under the leadership of Horatio Nelson, victor decisively over the French and Spaniards off Cape Trafalgar on 21 October 1805, but also of effective leadership of the navy as an institution. Resources permitted, and administrative systems supported, the maintenance both of the largest battlefleet in the world, and of a large number of smaller warships such that a multitude of naval tasks could be executed.

An improvement in naval infrastructure reflected the successful application of resources and also helped sustain the forces available. New naval facilities were developed in Britain, especially at Plymouth, as well as in long-held colonial bases such as Barbados, Bermuda, and Bombay and Madras in India, and in new acquisitions, for example Cape Town and Malta.

Plate 2.3 *The squadron under the command of Sir J. T. Duckworth forcing the narrow channel of the Dardanelles*, from a drawing by Sir W. Parker. Under the command of Sir John Duckworth, a British squadron forced the channel of the Dardanelles on 19 February 1807 in order to sail to Constantinople and put pressure on the Turks. The return under heavy bombardment in March 1807 was less happy. © National Maritime Museum.

Plate 2.4 *Combat du Grand Port*, 1810. Rivalry between the French and the British in the Indian Ocean remained acute after the Battle of Trafalgar. French privateers, operating from Port Louis on the Isle de France in the Indian Ocean, remained a serious threat to British commerce. In 1810 a British fleet was sent to capture the island but was defeated in the Battle of Grand Port off the south-east coast. This indicated the danger of over-confident dispersed British forces being defeated by French squadrons enjoying a local superiority. Later in the year the British were able to mount a close blockade and then to land a force that captured the island, which was renamed Mauritius. Painting, © National Maritime Museum.

Thanks to her naval resources, Britain was able to turn tactical triumphs to operational and strategic advantage. As on land, mobility, firepower and determination were crucial in battle. Successive victories, especially Trafalgar, conditioned British and foreign expectations, and the latter was crucial because it affected French naval strategy, or rather the absence of it, for the remainder of the Napoleonic Wars. Confidence is a vital military resource, and victory both brought it to Britain and denied it to France.

WAR IN THE AMERICAS

British naval power also played a major role in the Americas. It enabled Britain to wage war with the USA and also to cover the newly-independent Spanish colonies from attempts at reconquest. War with the USA started in 1812, in large part because a series of disputes, especially over maritime rights and British policy in frontier regions, had been exacerbated by American bellicosity and a lack of

British finesse. In the subsequent war, poorly-executed American invasions of Canada in 1812 and 1813 were thwarted, thanks, in large part, to Canadian loyalty to the British crown. In 1814 the British riposte came. A large force was sent to North America, and attacks were launched on the Canadian frontier, and in the Chesapeake and the Gulf of Mexico. These expeditions reflected British amphibious capability, as also did the blockade, which harmed the American economy and encouraged disunity among the American states. The expeditions, however, led to no permanent gains. Instead, they were memorable for the burning of Washington on 24 August (a retaliation for American destructiveness in Canada), the unsuccessful bombardment of Fort McHenry at Baltimore on 13 September and, on 8 January 1815, a serious British defeat outside New Orleans. Nevertheless, the British retained and used amphibious capability until the end of the war when they were planning to attack Charleston.

British naval power also helped cover the newly-independent Latin American states from Spanish *revanche*. The Latin American Wars of Independence arose from the disruption caused by Napoleon's conquest of Spain in 1808 and the Peninsular War of 1808–13 which created great confusion in the Spanish Empire. Attempts to re-establish royal authority in Spanish America in the 1810s enjoyed considerable success, but the resistance benefited from the financial and economic weakness of the Spanish Empire. The success of this resistance brought Spain's great-power status to a close.

The willingness of independence forces in South America to travel great distances in order to affect the struggle elsewhere was important to the struggle: after Argentina had gained independence in 1816, forces under José de San Martin crossed the Andes and defeated the royalists (pro-Spaniards) in Chile from 1817 to 1818: at Chacubuco (12–13 February 1817) and Maipó (5 April 1818). San Martin then pressed on to attack Peru. Further north, after repeated failures, Simon Bolívar overran Colombia in 1819, Venezuela in 1821, and Ecuador in 1822. Helped by Antonio de Sucre, Bolívar defeated Spanish forces in Peru from 1823 to 1824, Sucre's victory at Ayacucho on 9 December 1824 being crucial. Mexico declared independence in 1821, while in 1822 and 1823 a successful rebellion ended Portuguese rule over Brazil.

The wars indicated the difficulty both of sustaining a revolutionary struggle and of mounting effective counter-insurgency action. The force–space ratios of conflict in Latin America were different to those in Western and Central Europe, and the problems of political control were greater. The need that both the revolutionaries and the royalists faced to create new armies put a premium on overcoming problems in recruitment and in resisting desertion. The creation and legitimization of government structures were important in providing the context for harnessing resources. Remedies were often brutal. Recruitment was enforced with violence and the threat of violence, desertion punished savagely, frequently with executions, and, faced with major logistical problems, armies raised supplies through force. This looked toward the norm in the independence struggles across the world in the late twentieth century, for example in sub-Saharan Africa. As with them, there was much burning and destruction – of crops, haciendas and towns – in order both to deny resources to opponents and to punish those judged disloyal. As also in the late twentieth century a shortage of arms put a premium on foreign supplies but also ensured that weapons other than firearms were used. The extent to which the wars were civil conflicts led to an emphasis on political factors in strategy; political factors that were different to those seen in the state-to-state conflict of the Napoleonic Wars in Europe. Alongside brutality, there was also a concern with the social order and with the post-war structure of society. This led the South American rebels to endorse a policy of moderation toward loyalists which was ultimately successful; in contrast to the moderate British policies toward the rebellious Patriots in the thirteen colonies from 1775 to 1783.

BOX 2.2   DECISIVE AMERICAN VICTORIES, 1811–14

From 1811 to 1814 a series of decisive victories by the European Americans over the Native Americans greatly weakened the latter east of the Mississippi, and helped ensure that the European Americans encountered only localized resistance over the following decades. From 1805, Native ideas of resistance received new direction from a stress on spiritual revival and a widespread rejection of accommodation with the Americans. This led to significant resistance to westward American expansion. At the battle of Tippecanoe (7 November 1811), Indiana militia under Major-General William Henry Harrison fought off an early morning attack by Natives under Tenskwatawa, the 'Prophet', who had inspired the Shawnee to resist the Americans. He misled the Natives by promising them immunity to American musket fire, but the robust defence exposed that claim. At the battle of the Thames (5 May 1813), Tenskwatawa's brother, Tecumseh, the leading Shawnee warrior, who had tried to unite the Natives against the Americans, was defeated and killed. Harrison was also the victor here, and his fame led to his later election as president, although he died soon after taking up office in 1841.

Like other battles of the period, American victory reflected an improvement in fighting quality due to better training and tactical skill, and to a clearer understanding of Native techniques and their limitations. Further south, the Creek were defeated at Tallasahatchee (3 November 1813), Talladega (9 November 1813) and Horseshoe Bend (27 March 1814). In the last, 800 Natives out of a force of 1,000 died, the largest Native number of fatalities in any battle with American forces. Andrew Jackson, commander at Talladega and Horseshoe Bend, and also later American president (1829–37), was astute not only in his tactics, especially his envelopment of Native forces, but also in his response to the topography and possibilities of particular battlefields. More generally, although tactically adept, the Natives were weakened by division, by their dependence on American/European weaponry, and by the major population growth of the Americans. Although the British provided the Natives with some support, it was inconsistent and, in crucial moments, unreliable.

NAPOLEON

'War is waged only with vigour, decision and unshaken will. One must neither grope nor hesitate.' Napoleon's ability to gain and use the initiative was the most impressive feature of his generalship. In modern terms, he got within the decision loop of his opponents and, as a result, was able to maximize the fighting capability of his forces. The result was rapid and victorious offensives, particularly Napoleon's defeat of the Austrians in Italy at Marengo on 14 June 1800, and his successful command of the Grand Armée against Austro-Russian forces in 1805, and against the Prussians in 1806. In 1805, the Austrians were outmanoeuvred and forced to surrender at Ulm (17 October), before Napoleon successfully pressed on to occupy Vienna and then to defeat an Austro-Russian army at Austerlitz (2 December). In 1806, thanks to his victory at Jena (14 October), the Prussians were also rapidly overthrown, a result that greatly impressed contemporaries, as, thanks to the reputation of Frederick the Great (reigned 1740–86), Prussia was seen as Europe's leading military power. These were impressive eastward projections of French strength, far surpassing anything achieved under the *ancien régime* prior to the French Revolution. It was necessary to go back to Charlemagne (reigned 771–814) to see such range on the part of a French ruler, although the context was very different. Napoleon also exceeded Charlemagne's range with his operations against the Russians in Poland in 1807. Furthermore, his imperial system enabled him to create an integrated European military system. Of the army that invaded Russia in 1812, more than half were French. This enabled Napoleon to draw support from much of Europe while still effectively directing military operations.

It proved impossible, however, to secure decisive victory over the Russians in 1807 and over the Austrians in 1809, while the invasion of Russia in 1812 was a total and devastating failure, only mitigated by Napoleon's ability to ensure that he (and a small portion of the invasion force) returned safely. Furthermore, Napoleon's ability to outmanoeuvre opponents so as to ensure major victories at reasonable cost was no longer in evidence during his major battles. The slogging match of the battle of Borodino en route to Moscow on 7 September 1812, seen in France as a victory, was followed by similar battles at Leipzig (16–19 October 1813) and Waterloo (18 June 1815) that were clearly French defeats.

As so frequently in European military history, a capability gap on land had been swiftly closed. Combined with the widespread reluctance within Europe to accept Napoleonic views, this ensured the end of his unrealistic drive for hegemonic power. Indeed, repeated opposition to French hegemony required a skilful response, both military and political. Napoleon's failure to overcome nationalist resistance following his initially successful invasion of Spain in 1808 had suggested that his ability to provide this was deficient, and his defeat in 1812 left no doubt about this. His retreat from Moscow in October–November 1812, with his army ebbing away into the snows, was a fitting symbol of the folly of his attempt to dominate all of Europe.

This was seen the following year at Leipzig, where, in the Battle of the Nations from 16 to 19 October, the French were outgeneralled and outfought in the most serious defeat in battle Napoleon personally had hitherto faced. At the outset

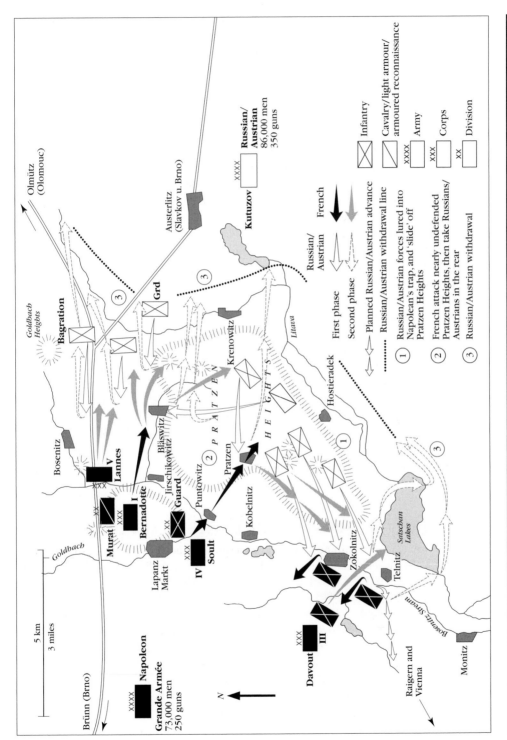

Map 2.3 Battle of Austerlitz, 2 December 1805. From *The Oxford Companion to Military History* (2003), p. 108, edited by Richard Holmes, by permission of Oxford University Press.

of the battle he exploited the advantage of the interior lines on which he was operating, while his mutually suspicious opponents faced the difficult task of co-operation on exterior lines (a demonstration in miniature of Napoleonic grand strategy); but, under pressure from greater numbers, the French were finally defeated, leading to the collapse of Napoleon's position in Germany. Napoleon had been able to defeat greater numbers before, but no longer.

The 1813 campaign clearly indicated that French military hegemony had collapsed in Central Europe. It was possible to defeat the main French field army, and without the benefit of the distances and climate of Russia. The aura of Napoleonic invincibility had been wrecked by the Russian campaign; the Austrians had now learned to counter the French corps system, with its creation of a sub-army integrating all arms, by using one of their own; and the Prussians had improved their army, not least by developing a more coherent and comprehensive staff system. In 1814, France itself was invaded by Austrian, Prussian and, from Spain, British forces. Outmanoeuvred, despite initial successes, such as Champaubert (10 February), that indicated Napoleon's continued operational ability as a commander, and abandoned by many of his generals, Napoleon was obliged to abdicate. This brought to an end not only the struggle in the main sphere of hostilities but also those elsewhere, for example in Italy and Spain. The Napoleonic defeat was total.

Returning from exile on the island of Elba in March 1815, Napoleon, nevertheless, regained power over France from the weak Louis XVIII and invaded Belgium on 15 June, helping to divide and defeat the Allied forces, only to be defeated at Waterloo by Anglo–Dutch–German forces. Their defensive firepower beat off successive, poorly co-ordinated French frontal attacks. The French army was not at its peak; nor was it well commanded: the individual arms were not combined ably, and there was a failure to grasp tactical control. After the battle, France was easily invaded, and Napoleon surrendered to a blockading British warship. He was detained on the South Atlantic island of St Helena until his death in 1821.

BOX 2.3   THE VOICE OF WAR: THE BATTLE OF LEIPZIG

[T]wenty battalions of Russians . . . under cover of a most formidable fire from about fifty pieces of artillery made their attack, the foremost battalions dispersing in small parties, and pushing the enemy at every point where the ground best admitted . . . the enemy firing from the houses (and streets which had been barricaded and filled with obstructions of every kind) and making at every corner and at every house a most obstinate resistance . . . the dead and the dying absolutely obstructed the passage in the gates and streets.

Colonel Hudson Lowe to Colonel Bunbury on the French in Leipzig on 19 October 1813, British Library, Additional Manuscripts 37051 folio 162.

BOX 2.4   BATTLE OF WATERLOO, 18 JUNE 1815

'We dashed them back as coolly as the sturdy rock repels the ocean's foam . . . we presented our bristly points like the peevish porcupines assailed by clamorous dogs.' Writing of the squares which the Duke of Wellington's British troops formed to resist the French cavalry, Ensign Edmund Wheatley captured the defensive nature of Wellington's tactics. With more men and time, however, Napoleon might have won. The British centre was in a dreadful state by late afternoon: Napoleon's costly frontal attacks, greater in scale than any Wellington had hitherto encountered in fighting the French in Portugal and Spain, did have an effect. A veteran also of India, Wellington regarded Waterloo as his hardest battle, and he suffered over 15,000 casualties. With more men and time, Napoleon could also have threatened Wellington's flanks, but he had no more of either because a large Prussian force under Marshal Blücher closed in on Napoleon's right. Blücher's main force had escaped from the dilatory pursuit of Emmanuel de Gronchy's 33,000 men (nearly a third of Napoleon's total strength), who became tied down eight miles away at Wavre by the Prussian rear guard and therefore took no part in the battle.

Napoleon's tactical lack of imagination on the day was in keeping with his earlier failure to obtain a decisive success while his British and Prussian opponents were divided. He was less brave and decisive on the battlefield than Wellington; more a distant commander who lost touch with the progress of the battle and failed to manoeuvre. Wellington had constructed a strong defence in depth which, even under better weather and other conditions, would have proved difficult to overcome. Due to the steady decline in the quality of the French army, ruined by incessant warfare, it no longer had any advantage in fighting calibre.

There was a lot that was familiar in Napoleonic warfare. Much that it is noted for had been anticipated in earlier conflicts: large armies, a strategy of movement, a preference for battles over sieges, a greater emphasis on artillery. In this context, Napoleon was more of a consolidator than an innovator, using yet greater resources of troops, *matériel* and funds to try to overcome opposing coalitions. Yet, the issue of scale did raise important organizational, operational and logistical problems, the command implications of which the French successfully addressed with the use of the corps system: 233,000 troops and 1,227 cannon were deployed at Borodino in 1812 and 560,000 troops in the Battle of Leipzig in 1813. Waterloo was a smaller-scale affair, but still involved 140,000 men aside from the Prussians. The British commander, the Duke of Wellington, indeed had argued that the Allies should not begin their offensive against Napoleon until they could ensure overwhelming superiority by deploying 450,000 troops.

Due to the length of the period of warfare and the escalating competitiveness of military confrontation, the mobilization of a large proportion of national manpower and wealth became more insistent. Napoleon raised 1.3 million conscripts in the period 1800 to 1811, and one million from 1812 to 1813 alone. The conscription instituted across Europe altered the nature of military institutions and systems: this was both a product of the French Revolution and Napoleon, and a reaction to them. Similarly, large quantities of munitions were produced. In August 1813 Napoleon had a reserve of 18 million musket cartridges.

The deployment of these forces created problems, although better roads and improved map-making facilitated swifter movement. In 1805, Napoleon speedily moved 194,000 men and about 300 cannon from northern France, where they were preparing to invade Britain, eastwards to attack the Austrians in south-west Germany. To support their advance, the French requisitioned supplies through contracts with the German rulers. Because their logistical support was often inadequate, however, French forces on other campaigns resorted to ravaging the countryside. This was an aspect of the devastation produced by the wars which led to high rates of civilian casualties. Disease spread by the armies and their own brutality to civilians contributed to these rates, the latter especially, as in Calabria, Portugal, Spain and the Tyrol where guerrilla opposition to the French further alienated them from the population. In 1811, for example, the French retreat from Portugal (after they had failed to break through the Lines of Torres Vedras prepared by Wellington for the defence of Lisbon) led to about 80,000 deaths among Portuguese civilians.

Plate 2.5 *Defence of Hougoumont, 1815*, watercolour by Denis Dighton. The fortified farm complex at Hougoumont anchored Wellington's right flank at the Battle of Waterloo. Repeated French attacks on Wellington were thwarted by a strong defence in depth. National Army Museum 7505-7-1, neg 29985.

EUROPE AFTER NAPOLEON

After the Napoleonic Wars there was a preference among European rulers for long-service regulars rather than large numbers of conscripts. Experienced troops were seen as more valuable both in battle and for irregular operations, as well as being more politically reliable. Combat certainly required a disciplined willingness to accept hazardous exposure, but political reliability appeared more important. This was accentuated because state-to-state warfare seemed less significant for military tasking than counter-insurgency operations. The issue was enhanced by the ideological legacy of the French Revolutionary period, and the sense among most of the powers that developments in the domestic politics of other states could be a threat and had to be suppressed. Such intervention became more common from 1815 as the leading continental powers sought to maintain the internal political, as well as the international, order left by the Congress of Vienna of 1814–15. This was to be enshrined in a number of agreements, including the Protocol of Troppau of 1820 by which Austria, Prussia and Russia agreed on intervention to reverse the overthrow of a government by revolution.

Liberal uprisings during 1820 and 1821 led to a military response. Advancing to Naples and Turin, Austrian forces crushed rebel forces in Naples and the kingdom of Sardinia (often known as Piedmont) in 1821, and restored the previous conservative systems of government. At Rieti (7 March 1821), trained Austrian regulars quickly defeated untrained and poorly disciplined *Carbonari*. The decision to fight a battle had exposed the *Carbonari* in unsuitable circumstances, and Austrian success was decisive: on 23 March, Austrian forces entered Naples. Two years later, civil conflict in Spain between liberals and supporters of King Ferdinand VII was resolved by an invasion by French forces in support of Ferdinand. Assisted by liberal disunity and weakness, the French made rapid progress and overthrew the liberals.

In contrast, in Paris in July 1830 French regulars failed to stop an armed popular rising against Charles X. In part, this was a matter of the deficiencies of regulars in street fighting, but it has to be set in the wider context of a very unpopular government and its attempt to reverse the verdict of recent elections. Much of the army was disaffected. As a result, the lack of training, equipment and discipline that characterized most insurgent forces did not lead to rebel failure in Paris.

Similarly in Brussels, where a rising against rule by the Dutch William I drove out the Dutch garrison that August. In September, a stronger attempt was made to suppress the rising: 10,000 Dutch troops entered Brussels, but street fighting in the face of determined opponents who employed the cover of barricades and fire from windows and housetops proved difficult. The Dutch troops withdrew and the Belgians declared independence. This episode serves as testimony to the variety of warfare in Europe in the early nineteenth century.

DEVELOPMENTS ELSEWHERE

Outside the West there was no metallurgical capacity comparable to that of the industrial sectors of the leading Western powers, and also nothing to compare with their fleets of heavily gunned specialist warships, but there were significant attempts to introduce changes in order to improve military capability. Some of these rested on trying to emulate European armies and navies. At the close of the eighteenth century Selim III attempted to introduce changes in the Ottoman (Turkish) army. He created a new force, the Nizam-i Cedid (new order army), organized and armed on European lines. The overthrow of Selim in 1807, however, when he tried to reform the janissary corps, traditionally the key force in the Ottoman army, the dissolution of the Nizam-i Cedid, and the failure of Selim's successor, Mahmud II, to re-establish control over the janissaries in the 1810s (he only managed to do so in 1826), indicated the deeply rooted ideological, political and social obstacles to Ottoman military reform, as well as the hostility to Western influences.

The Ottomans were no longer a major military force. They were also beaten by the Russians who in the war of 1806–12 advanced south of the Danube, defeated the Turks, and gained Bessarabia at the peace. The war with Persia from 1820 to 1823 also revealed serious deficiencies, and the Ottomans avoided serious defeat only largely as a result of the inroads of cholera in the Persian army. The Russians were victorious anew from 1828 to 1829, forcing the Ottomans in the peace to abandon their position on the Circassian coast on the eastern shore of the Black Sea.

Plate 2.6 *Ras al-Khaimah from the S. W. and the situation of the troops*, by R. Temple, 1809. From their base in the Persian Gulf, the Wahhabi pirates had attacked East India Company ships and British warships in the Arabian sea. The punitive expedition of 1809 resulting in the sacking of Ras al-Khaimah freed British trade from attack until a fresh pirate campaign began in 1816. Painting, National Maritime Museum, PW 4801.

Although military improvements were to play a role, the Ottoman Empire, nevertheless, owed much of its survival to the concern of European powers about the geopolitical consequences of its collapse. In 1807, French advisers helped Ottoman forces to deploy cannon to prevent a British fleet seeking to force acceptance of British mediation of their war with Russia. In those pre-steamship days, the British warships were also held back by contrary winds.

After eliminating the janissaries in 1826, Mahmud II westernized the Turkish military and also used it to reduce the autonomous power of the pashas, bar in Egypt. There, Mehmet Ali, viceroy for the Ottoman sultan from 1805 until 1848, but its real ruler, made a more effective attempt to improve his military. The Ministry of War was the first permanent department of state to be instituted in Egypt. A staff college was established in 1825, while the introduction of conscription in the 1820s enabled him to create a large army 130,000 men strong. This force was used for a series of expeditions. In 1813, Mecca and Medina, the holy Muslim cities, were retaken from the Wahhabis, an orthodox (or fundamentalist) Muslim sect that energized much of Arabia, after an earlier Egyptian expedition launched in 1811 had been ambushed. A fresh rebellion, however, led to initial

Plate 2.7 Turks learning French manual exercise, 1797. The state of the Turkish armed forces led Sultan Selim III to attempt reform, and this entailed seeking French assistance. Anne S.K. Brown Collection, TUH 1797 mf 1a.

disaster for the Egyptians until, in 1814, the Wahhabi forces were defeated. In 1816, the Egyptians resumed the offensive into the deserts of Arabia, seizing the Wahhabi strongholds, culminating with the capture of their capital, Dar'iyya, in 1818, after a six-month siege. The resilience of the Wahhabis was shown by their continued opposition, and, in 1824 the second Sa'udi–Wahhabi state was founded in the interior of Arabia, demonstrating that the regular forces of settled societies could only achieve so much.

The Egyptian army was trained by French officers after 1815 and supplied by France until 1840. To the south of Egypt, Massawa and Suakin on the Red Sea were occupied by the Egyptians in 1818 and Nubia (northern Sudan) in 1820, while relatively well-equipped Egyptian forces operated from 1824 against Greeks revolting against Ottoman rule, reducing the area under Greek control. Egypt seemed the most dynamic state in the eastern Mediterranean and north-east Africa; that is, until its navy was defeated in Greek waters in Navarino Bay on 20 October 1827 by an Anglo-French Russian fleet in a dramatic assertion of Western power.

Further east, in Persia, Crown Prince Abbas Mirza (d. 1833) developed a European-officered, armed and trained new army in response to Russian victories in the wars of 1804–13 and 1826–28. A Russian renegade named Yúsuf Khan, the commander of artillery in the 1810s of Abbas Mirza's eldest brother, established a foundry for casting brass cannon and a factory for manufacturing gunpowder. Aman-Allah Khan, the Vali of Ardalan (*c.* 1800–24), a powerful Kurdish leader, also tried to use European methods in the training of his troops, as did other provincial potentates. Success, however, was limited and the Russians were still victorious over Persia in a war in 1826–28.

Still further east, in the Punjab in north-west India, the Sikh leader, Ranjit Singh established Sikh dominance in 1799, and in 1803 began to create a corps of regular infantry and artillery on the Western model to complement the Sikh cavalry. In 1807 he set up factories in Lahore for the manufacture of guns, and in 1822 he recruited several European officers. They raised a model unit of regular infantry and cavalry, the Fauj-i-Khas, designed to act as a pattern for the remainder of the army. Yet further east, in Nepal, the Gurkhas used British deserters to teach them British drill and how to manufacture European-style muskets. They also learned how to cast cannon, although in battle the Gurkhas did not act tactically like a European force, instead displaying more mobility.

Nguyen Anh, who united Vietnam through conquest from 1788, ruling it as Gia-long (reigned 1802–20), was interested in Western technology, using it in developing his fleet, so that square-rigged galleys constructed in the Western style were built. He also hired French advisers to train his troops in European methods. His successor, Minh-mang (reigned 1820–41), took this further and tried to build steamships. Western models were borrowed for the uniform, arms and discipline of the Vietnamese army, as well as for fortifications. As with other instances of Westernization, however, it proved difficult to translate form to substance. Tactically and technologically, the Vietnamese did not match leading-edge Western developments and, more seriously, did not embrace the process of continuous change that was increasingly powerful in European armies and navies. This difference owed something to cultural preferences, especially the conservative nature of Confucianism and its role in 'tasking' (the setting of military goals): the army was largely designed to cope with peasant uprisings, of which there were 307 during Minh-mang's reign.

The spread of gunpowder weaponry was the expression and cause of change across much of the world. This had been the case for centuries, but Western traders took their weapons to peoples and polities across much of the world. In Madagascar, Andrianampoinimerina, ruler of Ambohimanga (reigned *c.* 1783–*c.* 1810) in the centre of the island, used slaving to acquire guns and gunpowder from the coast where Europeans traded: he seized slaves from other Malagasy territories and exchanged them for these weapons. Having conquered part of the interior, he left his son Radama (reigned *c.* 1810–20) with the idea of extending the kingdom over the whole island. This proved a formidable task, not least because the army lacked adequate training, discipline and armies. Radama, however, transformed it with the help of three sergeants who had served in Western armies. Drill, discipline and firearms proficiency were introduced in a smaller, 15,000-strong, force armed with modern European firearms. This force was far more effective than the spears and old guns that its rivals possessed, although disease, hunger and fatigue were major hindrances to operations, especially in the dry lands of the south. Much of the island was conquered from 1822 to 1827, although rebellions inspired by demands for tribute and forced labour had to be suppressed. This was one of the most impressive conflicts of the decade, but it is one that is largely obscure, mainly because of a lack of sources, but also due to insufficient attention. War in Madagascar, as in many other parts of the world, was linked to state building, with the lack of alternative means for political cohesion leading to a ready reliance on conflict.

In New Zealand, as a result of trade with Westerners, the use of muskets spread from the 1810s. Their high value was such that in 1820 one musket was worth 200 baskets of potatoes or fifteen pigs. Maori raiders armed with muskets became increasingly active in New Zealand from 1820. The Nga Puhi from the northern tip of the North Island raided to the southernmost tip of the island, using their muskets to win victories – for example at Nauinaina in 1821 and Totara in 1822. These raids helped lead to a series of migrations and conflicts that were similar to (although smaller in scale than) those in southern Africa during the period in which the Zulu took a major role.

Firearms were not, however, the key everywhere. The complexity of warfare in Africa brings out the dangers of assuming any such pattern. The successful forces in the *jihad* (holy war) launched by Usuman dan Fodio and the Fulani against the Hausa states in modern northern Nigeria in 1804 initially had no firearms and were essentially mobile infantry forces, principally archers, able to use their firepower and to defeat the cavalry of the established powers, as at the battle of Tabkin Kwotto in 1804. Their subsequent acquisition of cavalry (not firearms) was crucial in enabling them to develop tactics based on mobility, manoeuvre and shock attack. The powerful Hausa-fortified positions were isolated and fell to the irregular insurgents, so that by 1808 all the major Hausa states had fallen. In 1808 the Gobir capital of Alkalawa fell to a co-ordinated three-pronged pincer attack, indicating that firearms were not prerequisites for sophisticated offensive strategies. The *jihad* resulted in the creation of a new state, the Sokoto Caliphate.

In southern Africa the Zulus, under Shaka, their chief from 1816 to 1828, proved both aggressive and expansionist, leading other peoples to migrate in the *Mfecane* (Time of Troubles). Shaka changed Zulu tactics, replacing light throwing *assegais* (javelins) by the *i-klwa*, a heavier, thrusting spear, and emphasizing speedy assault and shock tactics. The success of the Zulu crescent formation was made possible by brave and disciplined troops led by effective soldiers. Shaka forced defeated peoples to become Zulus: their clans were absorbed.

CONCLUSIONS

Creating a chapter divide at 1830 serves deliberately to break with the usual pattern of treating the nineteenth century, or at least the century from the battle of Waterloo (1815) to the outbreak of World War One (1914) as a whole. To do so underlines the extent to which there was more than simply a difference in scale, although many of the themes obvious later in the century, such as European imperial conquest and the increased mechanization of war were already apparent. In the period 1800 to 1830, non-Western powers expanded (Egypt) or remained undefeated, and were scarcely affected by the West (China, Japan, Siam/Thailand, Abyssinia/Ethiopia). Western control was far more obvious on the seas than on land. The British victories over the Marathas (1803–6, 1817–18), Gurkhas (1814–15) and Burma (1824–25) had not yet been repeated at the expense of China and the Sikhs, as they were to have been by 1850; and in West Africa a British force under the governor of Sierra Leone was destroyed by the Asante in 1824. The Dutch found it difficult to prevail in warfare in Sumatra from 1819 to 1838 and in Java from 1825 to 1830, although they finally did so.

Within the West itself, the naval hegemony of the British was not matched by any power on land. Napoleon had failed to sustain such a hegemony in Europe, and his position was taken not by another hegemon but by a system of collective power in which Austria and Russia played major roles, each, also, dominating part of Europe: Austria, Italy, southern Germany and part of the Balkans, and Russia, Eastern Europe. In the New World, Spanish control over most of Latin America had been destroyed, Spain being left only with Cuba and Puerto Rico, while the War of 1812 had ensured that in North America there would be an uneasy duality of an expanding United States and a Britain that controlled Canada and was dominant at sea.

Multipolarity in Latin America and Europe, the USA as an expanding power in North America, and rulers in Asia, Africa and Oceania seeking to acquire Western military technology and to organize their forces on Western lines. Much of the period appears very familiar from the perspective of the early twenty-first century.

CHAPTER 3

Moulding States, 1830–80

INTRODUCTION

While military commentators digested the apparent lessons of the Napoleonic Wars, rulers and politicians considered how best to use force to achieve their purposes. The building of overseas empires was a major theme for Western powers, which will be addressed in the next chapter, but struggles over the identity and character of states were also important. In some cases, such as France, these were short term, more seizures of power than conflicts, but in many states there were protracted civil wars. In part, this was a consequence of the politicization of an age of spreading nationalism, with the volatility of major social changes including large-scale urbanization and industrialization, but this politicization was also focused by specific differences over the policies of states. These differences in some cases included questions about whether the states should continue unchanged, be divided to create new territories (the central issue in the American Civil War), or be united by force to form new powers (the key question in the Wars of German and Italian Unification).

These political issues were made more complex by developments not only in military technology but also in wider industrial capability. In particular, advances in technology and its application in transport and communications, in the shape of railways, steamships and the telegraph, changed and potentially revolutionized military force and warfare. The armies and navies of 1830 were still in most respects fighting like their late seventeenth-century predecessors, with close-packed formations of troops on land using low-accuracy, slow-firing weapons at short range, and wooden warships totally reliant on wind power at sea, but those of

1880 seemed and, in many respects were, very different. Industrial development helped provide not only the means but also the resources for greater military activity. This was true not only of the industrial world, particularly Western Europe and the USA, but also of those areas that sold it raw materials, for example Latin America. The sale of arms from the industrial world increased its impact.

THE AIMS OF CONFLICT

The wars of 1775–1830 had disrupted the state system across much of the world, especially in Europe and the Americas but also in South and South-East Asia and the Middle East. Although attempts were made to restore and reinforce stability, especially in Europe, by sustaining the 1814–15 Congress of Vienna peace settlement, and in Latin America by applying the Monroe Doctrine, these faced considerable difficulties. In part, this was due to rising nationalism and to practices of popular political activism that reflected the revolutionary legacy of the American, French, Latin American and other revolutions. In part, however, the problem was one of political leaders who faced the fluidity of recent and apparent circumstances by regarding existing arrangements as unlikely to last. This was linked to a sense of competition, both between states and, within states, between political groups, in which compromise did not appear a valid option. In Europe and Latin America an ideological clash between radicals and conservatives stemming from the wider impact of the French and Latin American revolutions added a powerful dimension to disputes.

The difficulty of securing compromise was to lead to civil war, not only in the USA but also across much of Latin America. Thus, liberals and conservatives fought in Argentina, Mexico, Uruguay and other countries, helping make the 1860s in particular a bloody decade across the Western hemisphere. A different form of civil conflict was that seen in Germany and Italy, as successful efforts were made to create a common state out of a number of territories. In addition, there were major rebellions in a number of European states, including Poland from 1830 to 1831 and in 1863, France in 1848 and Hungary from 1848 to 1849; while the French army proved more successful in suppressing the violently radical Paris Commune in 1871 than in defeating Prussia from 1870 to 1871. Rebellions themselves were very varied in intention: those in Poland and Hungary involved nationalist opposition to foreign rule – by the rulers of Russia and Austria respectively – while that was not the issue in France, or in the German states where there were also rebellions in 1848.

Whatever the type, the common theme of civil conflict was a degree of commitment frequently not seen in international conflicts. Thus, the American Civil War of 1861–65 was far more intense than say the Mexican–American war of 1846–48, or the Crimean War of 1854–56 between Russia and an alliance headed by Britain and France. This intensity took a number of forms, including a willingness to accept a large number of casualties and yet fight on. There was also a degree of mobilization of resources for conflict that looked towards what would be termed total war.

THE IMPACT OF TECHNOLOGY

The mobilization of resources appeared both necessary and possible because of a major shift in the material culture of war: the world of things. This was in part a matter of weapons, although, on land, these changed less than they were to do over the following half-century: 1880–1930 was to bring the tank, as well as mechanized road transport and the large-scale use of accurate, high-speed machine guns, as well as the need to respond to air attack.

Instead, it was the technologies of transport and communications that altered greatly in the period 1830–80, with all that this entailed in a number of spheres including logistics and command. The particular shift was in force projection, prefiguring the situation during the so-called Revolution in Military Affairs of the 1990s and 2000s (see pp. 254–7). Railways and steamships could not, on the whole, take troops to the battlefield, but they could move them towards the zone of conflict, and then sustain their presence in large numbers and over a long period. Railways were to play a major role both in the American Civil War (1861–65) and in the Wars of German Unification (1864, 1866, 1870–71). In addition, improvements in medical knowledge and application, in mechanical water distillation, and in the preparation and storage of provisions – for example canned meat, dried milk powder and margarine – made it easier for units to operate with lower non-combat casualties.

This applied technology in turn rested on a wider industrial capability that reflected the economic expansion of the period. Rates of increase varied greatly, with Britain enjoying a tremendous industrial and technological lead early in the period. Demographic (population) and economic growth helped fuel not only each other but also the war-making capacity of societies across the world, although this growth was most pronounced in Europe and the USA. Without this growth and capacity the specific technological improvements would have made far less of a difference, but, thanks to this background, it was possible to apply and afford the large-scale use of what were judged advances. Thus, the use of, first, steam power and, then, even more clearly, construction with iron were applied rapidly by leading navies, and, indeed, their demands helped drive forward the process of technological innovation. Wind and wood, the dynamics and properties of which had dominated naval power for millennia, became redundant within decades in what truly was a revolution in means and capability. Furthermore, this shift occurred across the world. Beginning in Atlantic Europe and the USA, it was copied in East Asia (China and Japan), the Islamic world (Turkey), and Latin America (especially Brazil and Chile), all of which purchased warships built in Britain and sought to use them as the Western powers did.

In part, in what was an increasingly common action–reaction cycle, these changes were driven not simply by a sense of what was possible but also by the needs created due to other advances. Thus, the growing power of naval armament, as a result of the development of guns firing shells, encouraged the improvement in defensive armament seen with the use of iron and then of compound armour.

This makes the interacting process of technological development sound easier than was in fact the case. In practice, a constant process of speculation and experiment, trial and error, matched debate over how best to use, respond to and shape the changes in weaponry. What is clear, and this helps mark the period as the real birth of modern warfare, in so far as such a concept is helpful, was that a continual process of change now seemed a reality, and, as such, made all existing arrangements, and even ideas, seem tentative and open to revision. It was still possible to write of immutable principles in warfare, but this seemed less helpful an approach, or one that had to be more abstract, given the pace of change.

The first clash between ironclads in history, the inconclusive duel between the *Monitor* and the *Merrimack*, occurred in Hampton Roads on 9 March 1862 during the American Civil War as Union warships sought to strengthen their blockade of the Confederacy, although there was none earlier only because the three European navies that already had commissioned ironclads (Britain, France and Italy) had not fought one another. In this duel in Hampton Roads, cannon shot could make little impact on the armoured sides of the two ships, even though they fired from within 100 yards.

The capability of ironclads increased rapidly during the war. Whereas the *Monitor* had two guns in one steam-powered revolving turret, the Union, in 1863, laid down its first monitor with two turrets. Less powerful than the British navy, the Union navy still became the second largest in the world, with over 650 warships, including forty-nine ironclads – although after the war most of it was rapidly decommissioned as the Americans returned to imperial expansion against Native Americans, rather than overseas power-projection. Indeed, as a result, in the late 1860s, the Brazilian navy took the role of the most active in the New World.

The transformation of conflict on the battlefield did not match those in force-projection and naval capability, but the greater firepower wielded by armies both ensured high casualty rates, as in the American Civil War and the Wars of German Unification, and also challenged equations between attack and defence. Advances in artillery and infantry firepower appeared to make particular tactics more or less viable and could also be seen as responsible for victory or defeat, although a simple attribution risked underrating the role of other factors. Generals and commentators struggled to come to terms with weapons and casualty rates. This again looked forward to the conflicts of the twentieth century and, indeed, within the Western world, those of 1861–71 were the last major wars until World War One broke out in 1914.

THE TAIPING REBELLION

To turn to China is to be reminded that the analysis of conflict should not only be located within that Western world. Indeed, in terms of number of combatants, the rebellion was the largest-scale war in the world in this period. Furthermore, the defeat of the rebellion was crucial to the course of nineteenth-century Chinese history, just as, although cause, course and consequences were different,

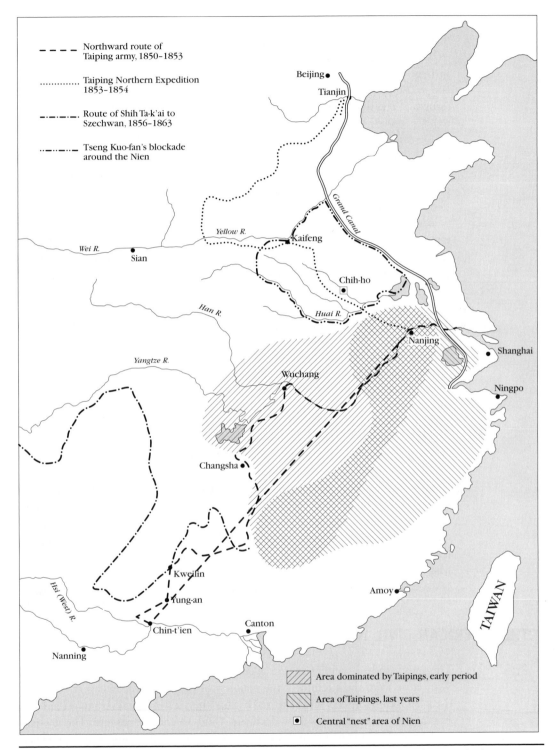

Map 3.1 The Taiping rebellion, 1850–64. After *East Asia: The Modern Transformation*, by John K. Fairbanks, Edwin O. Reischauer and Albert M. Craig (1967), p. 160. © Allen & Unwin.

the crushing of the rebellious attempt to resist modernization was very important to that of Japan.

The Taiping rebellion did not attract much foreign attention during the period, in large part because its details were obscure but also because, due to a cultural and racist ranking of societies by Western commentators, China seemed in the slough of reaction. As a consequence, its military history appeared to have little to offer foreign commentators. This view indeed was accentuated both because the Chinese sought Western advisers and weaponry, and because China was defeated by Western forces in this period, particularly by the British in the Opium War of 1839–42 and then by the British and French from 1858 to 1860, a conflict that culminated in 1860 with the occupation of the capital, Beijing, the first by Western troops.

In practice, the Taiping rebellion prefigured the American Civil War in showing what could be unleashed by an attempt to remould a state. The quasi-Messianic search for Chinese revival launched by the Taiping was bitterly resisted. The rebellion began in 1851 as a reaction against Manchu (imperial) rule that included an attempt to create a new Han Chinese dynasty that would unite Christianity and Confucianism. Unlike the American Civil War, this was not a separatist struggle. Their ideological conviction made the Taiping reckless of their lives and thus formidable in battle, although the leadership was flawed and seriously divided. Taiping armaments were not modern, and the Taiping relied heavily on spearmen, halberdiers and matchlock muskets, but Taiping numbers were considerable. About three-quarters of a million troops took the major city of Nanjing in 1853: mines created breaches in the wall, through which the outer city was stormed, and human wave attacks carried the inner city's walls.

That winter, a Taiping expedition advanced to within seventy miles of Beijing, but it was insufficiently supported, retreated in 1854, and was destroyed the following year. Their westward advance was also stopped after bitter fighting from 1854 to 1855, while the Taiping were affected by civil war in 1856 and by the serious shift of foreign support to the Manchu in 1860: Taiping attempts to take Shanghai were blocked by Anglo-French firepower, then and in 1862. In 1860 the imperial siege of Nanjing was broken by the Taiping, but in 1864 the city was captured, and in 1866 the last Taiping force was defeated. Rebellions elsewhere against Chinese rule, especially in frontier areas, were suppressed in the late 1860s and 1870s, particularly in Yunnan in 1873 and Xinkiang in 1879.

THE AMERICAN CIVIL WAR, 1861–65

The most studied conflict in pre-twentieth-century history, the American Civil War, arose from the attempt of the majority of the states where slavery was practised (all located in the South) to resist what they feared would be an attempt by Abraham Lincoln, the president elected in 1860, to end this slavery. The decision in the North to maintain the Union by resisting the declaration of independence by the Southern states completed the process by which the divisive elections of 1860 led to civil war: the Confederate states of the South were opposed to the

Union states of the North. The war was a bloody one with over one million dead or wounded. These casualties reflected the degree to which the popularly grounded determination of the two sides, based on a conviction of righteousness, was underlined by military and political factors. In part this was a matter of the use of new firearms, especially the percussion-lock rifle, but the attritional quality of the fighting, and the signs of what were to be seen as total war, was also crucial. These included a willingness to take heavy casualties and to employ large quantities of resources.

The North's task was great not only because of the size of the area contested but also because its goal was to end the Confederacy as an independent state. In contrast, in the Wars of German Unification (1864–71) the Prussian goals were, although ambitious (to establish a new order of power in central Europe), also more modest (to defeat Denmark, Austria and France, not to annex them). Although the Napoleonic Wars had been lengthy, subsequently Western commentators had become used to short wars, and it was expected that in future conflicts there would be a major battle that would prove a decisive encounter. The American Civil War could have gone that way: there might have been a Union victory in a war of the frontiers from 1861 to 1862, leading the Confederacy to abandon the struggle to maintain independence. Had Union forces been successful at First Bull Run/Manassas on 21 July 1861 then they might have gained an impetus leading to rapid success, while there was an opportunity for Union forces to seize the Confederate capital, Richmond, Virginia in April–June 1862, but it was thrown away because of the caution of the Union commander George McClellan.

Not only was it the more poorly commanded army, that of the Union, that had to mount the strategic offensive – in contrast to the Prussians in 1866 and 1870 (against Austria and France respectively) – but, in addition, a war of the frontiers was a more formidable challenge in America. Union operations in early 1862 were so far-flung and extensive that the 'frontiers' have to be understood in different terms to those of, say, the Franco-Prussian war. There were long advances in Europe, but they did not match the distance across which the Union forces had to fight.

The scale of resources used and means employed to tap them were particularly apparent and impressive on the wealthier and more populous Union side, which was presided over by President Abraham Lincoln, a politically-astute, civilian commander-in-chief. The Union raised a total of 2.1 million troops, as well as mobilizing its resources by creating a National Bank and introducing income tax and paper currency. The North also had a formidable advantage in naval strength, bullion, manufacturing plant, railway track and agricultural production. The railways helped the Union mobilize and direct its resources, although they took troops to the battlefield rather than giving them mobility on it. The relationship between the telegraph and communications was similar, and battlefield communications proved especially problematic, a situation that persisted until the widespread use of radio in World War Two.

The willingness of the more industrialized North to seize and, even more, destroy civilian property was also very marked. Ulysses Grant, from 1864 the

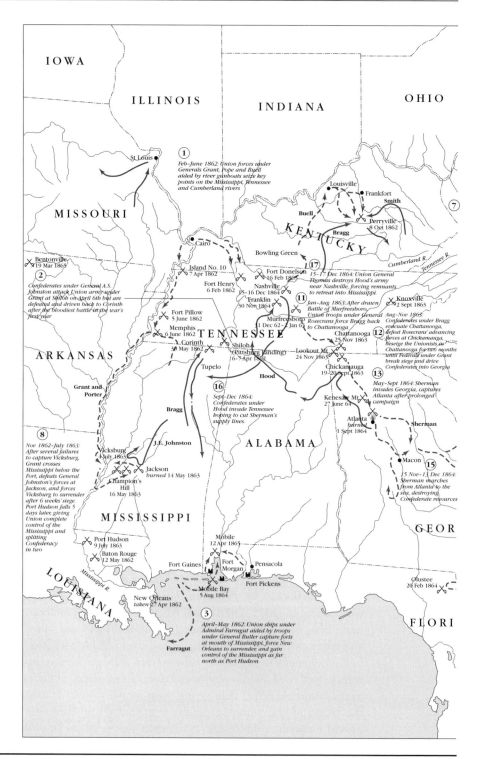

IOWA

ILLINOIS

INDIANA

OHIO

MISSOURI

MISSISSIPPI R.

St Louis

① *Feb–June 1862: Union forces under Generals Grant, Pope and Buell aided by river gunboats seize key points on the Mississippi, Tennessee and Cumberland rivers*

Louisville

Frankfort

Smith

⑦

KENTUCKY

Buell

Perryville
8 Oct 1862

Bragg

Bentonville
19 Mar 1865

Cairo

Bowling Green

Cumberland R.

Tennessee R.

② *Confederates under General A.S. Johnston attack Union army under Grant at Shiloh on April 6th but are defeated and driven back to Corinth after the bloodiest battle in the war's first year*

Island No. 10
7 Apr 1862

Fort Henry
6 Feb 1862

Fort Donelson
16 Feb 1862

⑰

15–17 Dec 1864: Union General Thomas destroys Hood's army near Nashville, forcing remnants to retreat into Mississippi.

Nashville
15–16 Dec 1864

Franklin
30 Nov 1864

Knoxville
2 Sept 1863

⑪ Jan–Aug 1863: After drawn Battle of Murfreesboro, Union troops under General Rosecrans force Bragg back to Chattanooga

Fort Pillow
5 June 1862

Memphis
6 June 1862

TENNESSEE

Corinth
30 May 1862

Murfreesboro
1 Dec 62–2 Jan 63

Chattanooga
25 Nov 1863

⑫

Aug–Nov 1863: Confederates under Bragg evacuate Chattanooga, defeat Rosecrans' advancing forces at Chickamauga, besiege the Unionists in Chattanooga for two months until Federals under Grant break siege and drive Confederates into Georgia

ARKANSAS

Shiloh
(Pittsburg Landing)
6–7 Apr 1862

Lookout Mt
24 Nov 1863

Chickamauga
19–20 Sept 1863

⑬

May–Sept 1864: Sherman invades Georgia, captures Atlanta after prolonged campaign

Tupelo

Hood

Grant and Porter

⑯ Sept–Dec 1864: Confederates under Hood invade Tennessee hoping to cut Sherman's supply lines.

Kenesaw Mt
27 June 64

Bragg

Atlanta
burned
1 Sept 1864

Sherman

⑧ Nov 1862–July 1863: After several failures to capture Vicksburg, Grant crosses Mississippi below the Fort, defeats General Johnston's forces at Jackson, and forces Vicksburg to surrender after 6 weeks' siege. Port Hudson falls 5 days later, giving Union complete control of the Mississippi and splitting Confederacy in two

Vicksburg
4 July 1863

J.E. Johnston

Jackson
burned 14 May 1863

ALABAMA

Champion's Hill
16 May 1863

Macon

⑮

15 Nov–13 Dec 1864: Sherman marches from Atlanta to the sea, destroying Confederate resources

MISSISSIPPI

Port Hudson
9 July 1863

Baton Rouge
12 May 1862

Mobile
12 Apr 1865

Fort Gaines

Fort Morgan

Pensacola

GEOR

Olustee
20 Feb 1864

LOUISIANA

Mississippi R.

New Orleans
taken 27 Apr 1862

Mobile Bay
5 Aug 1864

Fort Pickens

③ *April–May 1862: Union ships under Admiral Farragut aided by troops under General Butler capture forts at mouth of Mississippi, force New Orleans to surrender, and gain control of the Mississippi as far north as Port Hudson*

FLORI

Farragut

Map 3.2 The American Civil War, principal campaigns. After *The Times Atlas of World History* (1993), p. 219. © BCA by arrangement with Time Books.

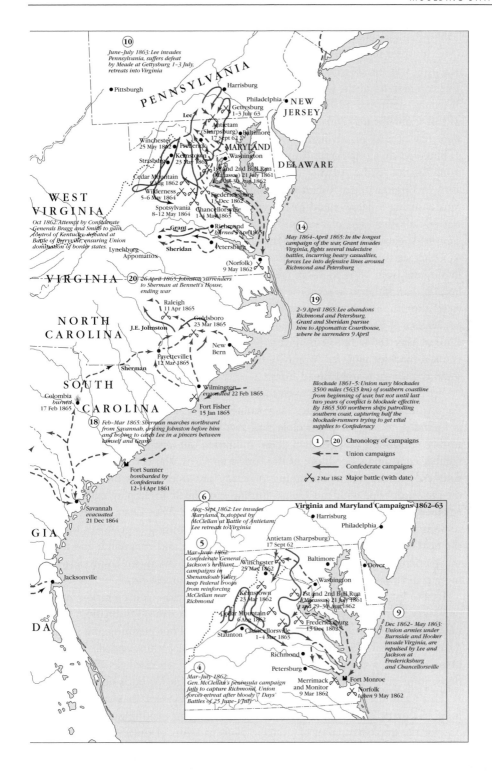

(10) *June–July 1863: Lee invades Pennsylvania, suffers defeat by Meade at Gettysburg 1–3 July, retreats into Virginia*

PENNSYLVANIA

● Pittsburgh

Harrisburg ●

Philadelphia ● ● NEW JERSEY

Lee

Gettysburg
1–3 July 63

Antietam
(Sharpsburg) ● Baltimore
17 Sept 62

Winchester
25 May 1862 ● Frederick ● MARYLAND

Strasburg ● Kernstown
23 Mar 1862 ● Washington ● DELAWARE

Cedar Mountain
9 Aug 1862 1st and 2nd Bull Run
(Manassas) 21 July 1861
and 29–30 Aug 1862

Wilderness
5–6 May 1864 Fredericksburg
13 Dec 1862

Spotsylvania
8–12 May 1864 Chancellorsville
1–4 May 1863

WEST VIRGINIA

Oct 1862: Attempt by Confederate Generals Bragg and Smith to gain control of Kentucky, defeated at Battle of Perryville, ensuring Union domination of border states.

Lynchburg ●
Appomattox Grant

● Richmond
burned 3 April 1865

Sheridan Petersburg ●

(Norfolk) ●
9 May 1862

(14) *May 1864–April 1865: In the longest campaign of the war, Grant invades Virginia, fights several indecisive battles, incurring heavy casualties, forces Lee into defensive lines around Richmond and Petersburg*

VIRGINIA (20) *26 April 1865: Johnston surrenders to Sherman at Bennett's House, ending war*

(19) *2–9 April 1865: Lee abandons Richmond and Petersburg. Grant and Sheridan pursue him to Appomattox Courthouse, where he surrenders 9 April*

NORTH CAROLINA

Raleigh ●
11 Apr 1865

J.E. Johnston Goldsboro
23 Mar 1865

New Bern ●

Fayetteville
12 Mar 1865

Sherman

SOUTH

Columbia
burned
17 Feb 1865 CAROLINA

Wilmington
evacuated 22 Feb 1865

Fort Fisher
15 Jan 1865

(18) *Feb–Mar 1865: Sherman marches northward from Savannah, driving Johnston before him and hoping to catch Lee in a pincers between himself and Grant*

Blockade 1861–5: Union navy blockades 3500 miles (5635 km) of southern coastline from beginning of war, but not until last two years of conflict is blockade effective. By 1865 500 northern ships patrolling southern coast, capturing half the blockade-runners trying to get vital supplies to Confederacy

Fort Sumter
*bombarded by Confederates
12–14 Apr 1861*

(1)—(20) Chronology of campaigns

◀--- Union campaigns

◀— Confederate campaigns

⚔ 2 Mar 1862 Major battle (with date)

GIA

Savannah
*evacuated
21 Dec 1864*

Jacksonville ●

DA

(6)

Virginia and Maryland Campaigns 1862–63

Aug–Sept 1862: Lee invades Maryland, is stopped by McClellan at Battle of Antietam, Lee retreats to Virginia

Harrisburg ●

Philadelphia ●

Antietam (Sharpsburg)
17 Sept 62

(5) *Mar–June 1862: Confederate General Jackson's brilliant campaigns in Shenandoah Valley keep Federal troops from reinforcing McClellan near Richmond*

Winchester
25 May 1862 Baltimore ●

Dover ●

Washington ●

Kernstown
23 Mar 1862 1st and 2nd Bull Run
(Manassas) 21 July 1861
and 29–30 Aug 1862

(9) *Dec 1862–May 1863: Union armies under Burnside and Hooker invade Virginia, are repulsed by Lee and Jackson at Fredericksburg and Chancellorsville*

Cedar Mountain
6 Aug 1862 Fredericksburg
13 Dec 1862

Staunton ● Chancellorsville
1–4 May 1863

Richmond ●

(4) *Mar–July 1862: Gen. McClellan's peninsula campaign fails to capture Richmond, Union forces retreat after bloody 7 Days' Battles of 25 June–1 July*

Petersburg ●

Merrimack and Monitor
9 Mar 1862 Fort Monroe

Norfolk
taken 9 May 1862

leading Union general, pressed for attacks on private property from the spring of 1862 in order to hit Confederate supply capacity and thus war-making; in effect declaring war on an entire people, an aspect of what has been termed total war. The commander of the leading Union field force in the south, William Tecumseh Sherman, destroyed $100 million worth of property as he set out to wreck the will of Confederate civilians in 1864 by making 'Georgia howl', although there were few attacks on civilian property. Indeed, his ability to spread devastation unhindered by Confederate forces across the southern hinterland as he advanced from Atlanta to the Atlantic undermined the position of the main Confederate army in Virginia under Robert E. Lee and helped to lead to Confederate surrender, thus ensuring a decisive end to the war. As a reminder of the variety of modern warfare, another sign of modernity was provided by the bitter guerrilla warfare seen in Appalachia, Kansas and Missouri.

Other signs of modernity included the development of trench tactics, especially in Virginia from 1864 to 1865: creating field entrenchments in a more systematic fashion than hitherto in response to the lethal nature of offensive firepower. There were also important developments in weaponry. The first recorded battlefield appearance of barbed wire (originally designed to pen cattle) occurred at Drewry's Bluff in May 1864. The Gatling gun, patented in 1862, brought an effective hand-cranked machine gun, fed by gravity from its magazine, onto the battlefield; while some cannon now used timed fuses.

Yet it is important not to overestimate the weaponry nor the sophistication of the organization on either side. They cannot be described as war machines, if that is intended to suggest predictable and regular operating systems that could be readily controlled and adapted. Few militaries can operate in that fashion in combat conditions, but those of the American Civil War certainly did not. Both sides experienced major limitations in raising resources and in their effective use on the battlefield, with the Union finding it difficult to employ extensively the advantage it had in overall resources. As in World War One, which in many respects the Civil War anticipated on land, rapidly raising large forces for use in the field created serious problems of supply, training and command; and training was particularly deficient in infantry–artillery co-ordination. An emphasis on will, morale and character as a means to victory proved no substitute.

It also proved difficult to secure adequate tactical concentration and co-operation on the battlefield, and too many assaults lacked co-ordination: between units, or between arms (infantry, artillery, cavalry). Poor planning and an inability to implement plans, especially the co-ordination of units, and the interaction of moves with a planned time sequence, repeatedly emerged, as did command flaws. Joint army–navy operations also proved difficult for both sides.

This was more than a matter of inadequate commanders. In addition, the basis for a systematic process of effective and rapid decision-making was absent, as was one for the implementation of strategic plans in terms of timed operational decisions and interrelated tactical actions. This encouraged incoherent strategies and piecemeal tactics that led to battles without overall direction. Co-ordination was handicapped by the role of the individual states in raising and officering units on both sides. On the Union side, the regular establishment was increased, but the bulk of the army was comprised of volunteer units organized by the states. Their officers frequently had uneasy relations with those who served, or had served, in the regular army. Compared to Prussia, there was very limited background in staff training and doctrine, and no attempt was made to standardize the situation during the Civil War. Most generals failed to develop staffs up to the challenge of moving and controlling large forces and providing reliable operational planning, and each side lacked an effective high command.

Furthermore, the strength of entrenched troops was accentuated because the opposing artillery did not find an effectual way of suppressing them. Use of the machine-gun, in addition, was limited. Aside from mechanical problems, high rate of ammunition usage and expense, the Gatling gun suffered from being considered eccentric to battlefield dispositions and tactics. Assaults on prepared troops caused heavy losses, blunting Confederate attempts to win victory at Antietam (17 September 1862) and Gettysburg (1–3 July 1863), and thus ending the northward advances of Robert E. Lee's Army of Northern Virginia. At the same time, by showing that they could fight on and launch offensives into Union territory, the Confederates hoped to create the impression that they could not be crushed and to induce war-weariness in the Union camp. Had Lincoln lost the 1864

Plate 3.1 *Bringing Up the Guns*, lithograph by Gilbert Gaul. The battlefield effectiveness of cannon was dependent on the difficult task of deploying both them and their munitions. Because railways were not yet complemented by internal combustion engines, the absence of mechanized transport in the field ensured a heavy dependence on draught animals. Anne S.K. Brown Collection.

presidential election then their strategy would have not been without value. This is an instance of the need to consider campaigns in light of political objectives, the context within which strategy should be evaluated. To have rested on the defensive might have been more appropriate for the Confederates militarily, as they would have conserved their forces, but an offensive strategy was the best way to force a political verdict on the Union.

In the end, Ulysses Grant, general-in-chief of the Union army from 1864, defeated Robert E. Lee, the commander of the leading Confederate army, with an attritional pounding. Grant worked through the experience of the war and added a strategic purposefulness and impetus to Union military policy. He subordinated the individual battle to the repeated pressure of campaigning against the Confederates and inflicting cumulative damage. For example, after the battle of the Wilderness (5–6 May 1864), the Union forces pressed on towards Spotsylvania Court House, where the two sides fought it out around the Confederate entrenchments from 8 to 21 May. On 3 June, Grant attacked again, against Cold Harbor. A high tempo of attack was not unprecedented – the 1813 and 1814 Napoleonic campaigns had been characterized by a high rate of conflict – but the multiple of high-tempo fighting, numbers of troops and weaponry ensured high casualties. Whereas Lee exemplified the Napoleonic focus on battlefield victory, Grant

BOX 3.1   THE VOICE OF WAR: THE AMERICAN CIVIL WAR

[T]he enemy promptly built a strong line of rifle pits, all along the edge of the dead space with elaborate loop holes and head logs to protect their sharp-shooters, and they maintained from it a close and accurate fire on all parts of our line near them . . . We soon got our lines at most places in such shape that we did not fear any assault, but meanwhile this mortar firing had commenced and that added immensely to the work in the trenches. Every man needed a little bombproof to sleep in at night, and to dodge into in the day when the mortar shells were coming.

Edward Porter Alexander, chief of ordnance for the Confederate Army of Northern Virginia, of the trenches near Petersburg, Virginia, where he served from 1864 to 1865: G. Gallagher (ed.), *Fighting for the Confederacy. The Personal Recollections of General Edward Porter Alexander* (Chapel Hill, N.C., 1989), pp. 435–6.

It shows the danger, which seems to be daily increasing, that the present war may degenerate into a context, in which, under the guise of retaliation on both sides, the usages of civilized warfare will no longer be observed.

Lord Lyons, British envoy in Washington, February 1863, on threats by a Union commander to kill prisoners if the Confederacy tried a Union prisoner for inciting slaves to rebel, Public Record Office, Foreign Office papers 5/877 folios 139–41.

displayed a greater understanding of campaign and grand strategy. While Grant may not have bested Lee in any particular battle (although he certainly bested others at Fort Donelson, Vicksburg and Chattanooga among other battles), he held Lee while other Union forces pounded their way to victory, overrunning key areas of the Confederacy.

The political context of victory was more complex, however, than the simple military verdict might suggest. The Confederate forces surrendered in 1865, Lee at Appomattox on 9 April, but at another level the conflict continued because the Southerners did not surrender their belief in White supremacy. This led not to guerrilla operations against Federal forces but to the large-scale intimidation of African-Americans by nightriders and other means. Whites clashed with the black militias recruited by Radical Republican state governments. In the end, the Federal troops were withdrawn in 1876 and White supremacist state governments estab-lished so that, having lost the main-force civil war, the South won the supremacism they had sought to sustain. Meanwhile, in the aftermath of the Civil War, the Union army and navy were largely dismantled. Public support for a substantial military was absent.

THE WARS OF GERMAN UNIFICATION

Sweeping Prussian victories over Denmark in 1864, Austria in 1866 and France from 1870 to 1871, gripped the attention of contemporaries, ensuring that Western and Japanese war-planning thereafter until 1944 took place largely under the shadow of Prussian models and strength. The Prussians sought to apply rigorous and comprehensive analysis and planning in order to reduce the element of risk and, instead, to control conflict as a process in which the systematized appli-cation of planned pressure led to predicted results. Furthermore, this planning interacted with attempts to take advantage of specific changes in the nature of war at different levels. Helmuth von Moltke, the chief of the Prussian General Staff from 1857 until 1887, adapted Napoleonic ideas of the continuous offensive to the practicalities of the industrial age, including railways. At the tactical level, in place of frontal attack, he sought to envelop opposing forces, and to oblige them to mount such attacks themselves in an effort to regain freedom of manoeuvre. Thus, he sought by operational advantage to counter the benefits that rifled weapons and the scale of conflict had given the defence. The Prussians also bene-fited from the adaptability with which they responded to new weaponry. The Dreyse 'needle' rifle could be fired four to seven times a minute and had an accu-racy rate of 65 per cent at 300 feet, causing disproportionately heavy Austrian casualties in the Seven Weeks War of 1866. Alongside tactical flexibility came operational skill, reflecting effective staff work. Whereas Napoleon had used separ-ately operating corps within his army, Moltke employed independently operating armies; that is, much larger forces. Furthermore, unlike Napoleon, who concen-trated his forces prior to the battle, Moltke aimed for a concentration of his armies in the battle. Heavily defeated at Sadowa/Königgrätz on 3 July 1866, Austrian morale collapsed, and peace was conceded with Prussia left dominant in Germany. The Prussians, crucially, did not have to conquer Austria: victory in part of its empire sufficed to secure Prussia's goals.

Hostile to growing Prussian power, Napoleon III of France declared war in 1870, but, having mounted an ineffective invasion of Germany on 1 August, the outnumbered French rapidly lost the initiative and the Prussian advance became the key development. The Prussian use of dispersed forces outmanoeuvred the more concentrated and slower moving French armies. In part, this reflected Prussian superiority in command and control, but a fixity in purpose and a clearly planned strategy were as important. Whereas the French essentially sought to muddle through, the Prussians operated a co-ordinated command system in which staff officers had a major role, with officers from the General Staff expected to advise commanders. This helped the management of risk and error. So also, at the micro level, did an emphasis on professionalism, including the training of officers to take their own decisions at all levels within the constraint of the command plan. A dynamic interaction between hierarchy and devolved decision-making meant that small unit operations supported and harmonized with those of large forces. At the tactical level, the more dispersed formations favoured by the Prussians were less dense than columns or lines, reducing the target for French firepower. This reflected a tactical adaptation to new technology that represented an end to Napoleonic warfare.

Rapid Prussian victories near the French frontier, especially the envelopment of French forces that surrendered at Sedan on 2 September, were followed by a Prussian advance on Paris, which was besieged from 19 September, and also across much of northern France. Defeated and divided, the French accepted an armistice on 28 January 1871, and then terms that left most of Alsace and much of Lorraine annexed by Prussia.

Yet Moltke himself warned of the hazards of extrapolating a general principle of war from Prussian successes, and was increasingly sceptical about the potential of the offensive. Prussian skill at the operational and tactical levels had not prevented many difficulties from arising, not least at the hands of Austrian artillery and French rifles. Furthermore, deficiencies in leadership and strategy on the part of Austria and France had played into Prussian hands, enabling them to outmanoeuvre their opponents. Napoleon III proved a particularly maladroit leader for the French, but the calibre of his generals was also poor. These prefigured German successes in 1914 or, even more, 1939–41. As then, it was necessary to focus on relative capability and the extent to which offensives were (or were not) countered by defensive skills, not least by the availability and use of reserves. The success of 1866 and 1870–71 also prefigured eventual German failure in the two world wars, as the German military was better prepared for quick victory than long struggle. In the closing stages of the Franco-Prussian war, *francs-tireurs* (civilian irregulars) disrupted German operations far more than their numbers might suggest. Their presence triggered a debate on the status of combatants that looked forward to subsequent disagreements on the subject.

LATIN AMERICA

The general focus on European warfare and the American Civil War leads to an underrating of conflict, not only in China and Africa but also in Latin America. The latter tends to be neglected in military history after the Wars of Independence of the early nineteenth century, but this is mistaken, not only because of the importance of conflict for the history of the continent but also because of the more general interest of these conflicts for military history. In part this arose from their range which encompassed rebellions, wars between states, and foreign intervention. The first type tends to be underrated, but was important to the politics of the period. Rebellions frequently stemmed from regional opposition to the central government, for example that of 1835–45 by the Farrapos of the Brazilian province of Rio Grande do Sul, and by the millennium rebels based in Canudos in north-eastern Brazil in 1897, or the successful rebellion in Texas against Mexican rule from 1835 to 1836, culminating in the victory at San Jacinto on 21 April 1836. Having defeated provincial leaders in 1861, in 1862 Bartholomé Mitre established a centralist government in Argentina, only to be faced with federalist revolts from 1866 to 1867.

The instability of a number of countries and the rivalry between them ensured that rebellions could overlap with wars between states. From 1851 to 1852 Brazilian troops intervened in divided Argentina and played a major role in overthrowing its dictator, Juan Manuel de Rosas. In 1854 they intervened in Uruguay at the request of the government, and from 1864 to 1865, intervened again, this time overthrowing the government. President Francisco López of Paraguay determined to strike back, and invaded Brazil, following up with an invasion of Argentina, launching the War of the Triple Alliance (1864–70) in which Paraguay was opposed by Argentina, Brazil and Uruguay.

This was a bitter war, characterized by logistical problems, that indicates the variety of warfare in the 1860s. Disease, especially cholera, hit the combatants hard, affecting operations. Once their opponents, especially Brazil, had mobilized their forces, the war led to the loss of about 70 per cent of the population of Paraguay. The outnumbered Paraguayans were defeated in the field from 1868 to 1869, but the war then became a guerrilla struggle as the Brazilians tried to hunt down López in the barren vastness of northern Paraguay. In the end, as with other counterguerrilla struggles, this required the adoption of more flexible operational units, specifically flying columns, and the development of a successful intelligence system. The combination of the two led to López being surprised in his encampment in March 1870, defeated, and killed.

Civil warfare overlapped with foreign intervention in Mexico, again indicating the variety of warfare in the 1860s. French forces landed in Vera Cruz, Mexico's leading port, in 1861. After an initial advance on the capital had been checked in May 1862, in 1863 the French advanced to capture Mexico City on 10 June after the Mexican army besieged at Puebla had surrendered on 17 May. Napoleon III of France encouraged opponents of the republican government of Benito Juárez to offer the throne to Archduke Ferdinand Maximilian, the brother of the Austrian emperor. Maximilian's attempt to take over the country was mishandled, however, and met a strong nationalist response. There was a long guerrilla war, led by Juárez, with few conventional battles, and French backing for Maximilian, although 40,000 troops at the peak, was both insufficient and unsustained. The French benefited from naval support on both coastlines, and on land were able to seize positions; but they could not stabilize the situation, a situation that prefigured the position with many counter-insurgency forces in the twentieth century. Following the conclusion of the American Civil War, American pressure, and concern about Prussian schemes in Europe, led the French to withdraw in March 1867. Refusing to go, Maximilian was defeated by the Mexicans at Queretaro in 1867 and executed on 19 June.

In part because the civil war dimension was absent, Chile was far more successful in the War of the Pacific of 1879–83 with Bolivia and Peru, defeating them thanks to the flexibility stemming from successful amphibious operations against first the Bolivian Pacific coastline and then Peru.

Plate 3.2 *Execution of Maximillian*, emperor of Mexico, 1867. Intervening in the Mexican civil strife, Napoleon III of France supported the offer of the Mexican throne to an Austrian archduke. After the American Civil War American pressure led Napoleon to withdraw his forces. Maximilian, who refused to leave, was defeated at Queretaro and shot. Unknown Mexican artist, nineteenth century, Philadelphia Museum of Art, Louise and Walter Arensburg Collection, 1950-134-827.

CONCLUSIONS

The period saw a move towards what was to be termed total war, although at the same time developments in international law represented a European attempt to civilize war at a time when weaponry was making it more destructive. Europeans did not extend these rules to their conflicts with other peoples. The Franco-Prussian War was total in that Moltke's systematized warfare offered a hitherto unprecedented degree of methodical effectiveness, although there were serious logistical problems for the Prussians in 1870, with confusion on the railways and, ironically, a return to dependence on horses. The scale, duration and mobilization of resources of the American Civil War provided a different type of totality to anything seen hitherto in American warfare.

Furthermore, the difficulties of co-ordinating units and also arms (infantry, cavalry and artillery), looked forward to the practical issues that were to be

BOX 3.2   CLAUSEWITZ, JOMINI AND MILITARY THOUGHT

The two most influential writers, as far as war on land in the nineteenth century was concerned, were Antoine-Henri de Jomini and Carl von Clausewitz. Although contemporaries chronologically, Jomini reflected the intellectual framework of the Enlightenment (emphasizing a rationalization or systematization of warfare), whereas Clausewitz reflected the ideas of the subsequent Romantic era in stressing the unpredictable and irrational nature of warfare.

The Swiss-born Jomini (1779–1869) rose into French service through the army of the Helvetic Republic (a French client state) and became chief of staff to Marshal Ney. He subsequently served in the Russian army. Jomini's influential works, which included the *Traité des Grands Opérations Militaires* (1804–9) and the *Précis de l'Art de la Guerre* (1838), sought to find logical principles at work in warfare, which was seen as having timeless essential characteristics, and, in particular, to explain Napoleon's success, the central theme of his *Vie Politique et Militaire de Napoléon* (1827). For Jomini, the crucial military point was the choice of a line of operations that would permit a successful attack. Napoleonic operational art was discussed in terms of envelopment – the use of exterior lines, or of interior lines, and the selection of a central position that would permit the defeat in detail (separately) of opposing forces. This, however, was an emphasis on battle-winning, rather than on the wider military and political mobilization that Napoleon had secured. Furthermore, Jomini failed to make sufficient allowance for changing aspects of war-making, not least the tactical and wider consequences of social, economic and technological change. He offered little guidance on what was to be seen as 'total war'. Jomini's influence was not restricted to Europe. His *Summary of the Art of War* was published in New York in 1854 and in Philadelphia in 1862, and he was much studied at West Point, influencing many of its graduates.

continued

Clausewitz (1780–1831) was a Prussian officer who had also seen service in the Russian army, and, from 1818, was director of the War Academy in Berlin. His posthumously published *Vom Kriege (On War)* of 1832 was initially less influential than Jomini's works, in part because it was (and is) less accessible. In addition, French war-making had greater prestige until Prussia's defeat of France (1870–71), while *Vom Kriege* was not translated into English until 1873. Clausewitz, however, understood better than Jomini the need to relate war to the socio-political context, and thus to assess military capability and skill in terms of political objectives, and was ready to engage with these objectives. Furthermore, Clausewitz offered a more appropriate description of conflict. He emphasized uncertainty, and therefore risk, rather than Jomini's controllable environment, and thus pressed the need for a continuous process of planning that could take account of the dynamic and unpredictable character of events, and the importance of an individual of genius as commander. Clausewitz saw the French Revolution as having changed war. He regarded the direction of a national will, and the mobilization of a nation's resources that it made possible, as truly potent.

As the prestige of German war-making rose with Prussian victories from 1864 to 1871, so interest in Clausewitz increased, and this was important to the development of a canon of 'classic' texts in military affairs that were not simply those of the ancient world. The place of formal education in the military was increasingly seen as important to professionalization, and this also encouraged the development of the canon.

encountered in campaigning in World War One. The smaller battlefield role of cavalry also prefigured that conflict. At sea, the role of the Union blockade in creating economic pressures for the Confederacy also prefigured the British blockade of Germany in World War One: both indicated a primacy of the strategic use of sea power in pursuit of total war goals over the goal of seeking battle.

If a greater Prussia, but in contrast a defeated Paraguay (see p. 65), was one of the results of the warfare of the period, this reflected the superior leadership and resources of the former, as well as the range of opponents simultaneously facing the latter. Comparative issues help highlight the factors that played a key role in success and failure, but also the uncertainties of the period. Once victories had been won there was a tendency to see them as inevitable and, in particular, as the culmination of a national destiny. Indeed, this was to be pushed hard not only in the monarchies of Germany, Italy and Japan but also in the confident expanding American republic. This encouraged an emphasis on will as a crucial factor in success, an emphasis that was to help mould the strategies, operational doctrines and tactical methods of World War One.

In practice, a careful reading of the conflicts of 1830–80, and, indeed, of those between then and World War One, suggested that there was no such easy analysis. Instead, the difficulty of ensuring victory in battle, or of turning such victory into triumph in war, emerged, as, more specifically, did the problems of assessing the consequences both of particular weapons and of rival combinations of weapons and tactics. The American Civil War and the Taiping rebellion provided clear indications of the difficulties of ensuring that a weaker and/or defeated side yielded, and these were to be more appropriate as lessons than the swift success of the Prussians in the Austro-Prussian War and in the early stages of the Franco-Prussian counterpart.

CHAPTER 4

Building Empires 1830–1913

INTRODUCTION

In the nineteenth century, particularly the last two decades, Western power was territorialized, as control over large tracts of the world, and a significant portion of its population, changed hands. Native polities were overthrown in a competitive rush by the Western states to seize territory. This was seen as a source of prestige, a fulfilment of destiny, an area for Christian missionary activity, and a valuable economic resource, providing both markets and resources, such as, in the case of three British colonies, the tin of Malaya, the timber of Burma, and the cocoa of Ghana. The pace of conquest dramatically increased in the second half of the century and, even more, in its last fifteen years, especially in Africa, South-East Asia and Oceania. Whereas for centuries the French had made little headway in Madagascar, where they had first established a position in 1643, the island was rapidly conquered in 1895, although French forces suffered heavy casualties from yellow fever.

EUROPEAN IMPERIALISM

The flexibility of Western military imperialism was both notable and necessary for the fulfilment of its goals. Along with the benefits derived from the use of modern armaments and means of communication, it was important for imperialists to be able to adapt to different physical and political environments. Attitudes were crucial. Expansion was normative, seen as both desirable and normal, an attitude that increasingly drew on triumphalism, racialism and cultural arrogance. What were believed to be divine purpose, natural right, geographical predestination, the appropriate use of natural resources, and the extension of the area of freedom and culture, all apparently combined to support the cause of territorial expropriation. The sense of mission that underlay late nineteenth-century Western imperialism led to a determination to persist even in the event of setbacks, as with the British against the Zulus in southern Africa in 1879.

Western expansion also owed much to an ability to exploit native divisions and to win local support, as with the British use of their large Indian army for operations in China, East Africa, south-western Asia (both Aden and the Persian Gulf), and on the lands seen by Britain as the North-West Frontier of India. Other imperial states benefited from the same process. The French used soldiers recruited in Senegal to conquer the interior of what became French West Africa: the modern states of Niger, Mali, Burkina Faso and Chad. Thus imperial gains in turn provided the basis for fresh conquests. When Italy successfully invaded Ethiopia in 1935 it benefited not only from the use of local troops from its neighbouring colony of Eritrea but also from the extent to which some prominent Ethiopians defected to the Italians.

Winning support was also important when rebellions had to be confronted. From the Mediterranean city of Algiers, which they had captured in 1830, the French expanded their power into the interior of modern Algeria. In the 1840s they sought to build up a network of favourable tribes; and when there was a major rebellion there in 1871 much of the population did not take part. Combined with the failure of those who did rebel to co-operate effectively, and with the arrival of French reinforcements after the end of the war with Prussia in 1871 (a reminder of the need to locate operations in their wider context), this ensured that the rebellion was overcome by January 1872.

BOX 4.1   THE VOICE OF WAR: IMPERIAL ENTHUSIASM, 1879

The patriotic spirit of the inhabitants, already kindled by the fact that they were to bid farewell to the first reinforcements for the Cape [Cape Town] was thoroughly aroused by an address issued by the Mayor calling upon them to assemble at noon on the Castle to give the departing soldiers a hearty Devonshire cheer . . . When at length the steamer passed she was greeted with hearty and continued cheers from the crowded shore. The band on the shore played 'The British Grenadier', 'Auld Lang Syne', and 'God Save the Queen'.

Western Times, 25 February 1879, recording the departure of the 2nd battalion of the 60th Rifles on the steamer *Dublin Castle* to reinforce British forces struggling against the Zulus in southern Africa.

BOX 4.2   THE VOICE OF WAR: THE INDIAN MUTINY, 1857

[V]illage fighting ... desperate ... we took two sepoy prisoners the other day and they were blown away from the guns: the stink of fresh flesh was sickening in the extreme, but I have seen so many disgusting sights and so much blood-shed that I have grown quite callous.

Suppressing the Indian Mutiny: Lieutenant Hugh Pearce Pearson to his parents, 1 August 1857, British Library, Indian Office MSS Eur. C 231 p. 56.

Similarly, much of India did not support the Indian Mutiny of 1857–59 against British control. Indeed, loyal Indian forces, especially Sikhs and Gurkhas, helped in its successful suppression, as did British units transported from other colonies: a benefit of Britain's dominant maritime position. Had all of India rebelled then (unlike in the case with North America from 1775 to 1783) the British would have been unable to translate their ability to use maritime power to move troops there into success on the ground.

In addition to the use of local support there was also the issue of relative military capability. Technology definitely enhanced the capability of Western forces. This was a matter in part of weaponry, such as the mobile light artillery employed by the French to blow in the gates of positions they attacked in West Africa, and, eventually, of machine-guns. In the well-organized and successful British punitive expedition of 1873–74 against one of the more militarily powerful of all African peoples, the Asante of West Africa, Garnet Wolseley used Gatling guns (a repeating rifle) and seven-pounder artillery. Irrespective of these weapons, British breech-loading rifles outgunned the Asante whose muskets only inflicted minor wounds. In 1889, the British adopted a fully automatic machine-gun developed by Hiram Maxim that could fire 600 rounds per minute, using the recoil to eject the empty cartridge case, replace it, and fire.

Alongside weapons, other aspects of Western technology were also important in aiding and encouraging imperial expansion. Communications were greatly enhanced by steamship, railway and telegraph. Thus, steamships carried British troops to New Zealand in the 1860s and 1870s to help overcome Maori (native) resistance, while the building of a railway was crucial to the logistics of Britain's successful campaign in Sudan from 1895 to 1899.

In the field of Western medical science some progress was made in understanding and counteracting tropical diseases. The British established the Royal Army Medical Corps in 1898, and, in the Boer War of 1899–1902 in South Africa, the death rates among non-battle casualties were lower than in earlier imperial operations; although, thanks to cholera, dysentery and typhoid, more British and imperial troops still died from disease than in battle. The same was true of American operations in the Philippines during their conquest from Spain in 1898, and subsequently against Filipino resistance.

Most of Africa, much of Asia, and all of Oceania were partitioned by Western powers. Britain, Russia and France made the largest gains, and the British Empire became clearly the largest in the world. The Russians meanwhile advanced in the Caucasus, Central Asia and the Far East. The centres of once-great Central Asian empires were brought under Russian control: Tashkent was captured in 1865 and Samarkand in 1868. This, however, makes the situation appear easier for the Russians than was in fact to be the case. For example, the suppression of the Caucasus proved very costly, despite major commitments of troops, supported by naval blockades and the building of forts, and attempts both to pursue pacification and to adopt more brutal tactics. The Russians suffered serious defeats in the 1840s, and, although helped by ethnic and religious divisions among the local people, did not conquer Chechnya and Daghestan until 1859 and Circassia until 1864. This looked towards problems Russia was to encounter in the region in the 1990s and 2000s (see pp. 243–4). In the Far East, Russia made gains at the expense of China from 1858 to 1860, overturning the Treaty of Nerchinsk of 1689 which had left China dominant in the Amur Valley. The port of Vladivostok was founded in the newly acquired Ussuri region in 1860.

The British feared that the Russians would seek to press on from Central Asia to dominate Afghanistan and threaten India, and this encouraged their own interventions in Afghanistan in the 1830s and 1870s. As later, however, with foreign intervention there from 1979 (Russian from 1979 to 1988 and American-led Western from 2001), lasting success proved elusive. British support for an unpopular client ruler whom they installed in 1839 was swiftly challenged. A general revolt was mishandled and, when the poorly led British force retreated from the capital, Kabul, towards India in January 1842 it was delayed by snow and destroyed in the mountain passes. A British army reoccupied Kabul that autumn, showing that the British had retained their ability to strike into Afghanistan, but it was deemed prudent to withdraw.

The British intervened in Afghanistan again from 1878 to 1880. A successful advance on Kabul and Kandahar in 1878 was followed, on 27 July 1880, by the defeat of an outnumbered, outgunned and poorly commanded British force at Maiwand and the siege of the British garrison in Kandahar. A relief expedition under Frederick Sleigh Roberts defeated the Afghans on 1 September but, again, it was thought sensible to withdraw from Afghanistan. Both expeditions showed the difficulty of translating battlefield success into a lasting settlement, prefiguring the situation for Western warfare over recent years, in which force projection has not proved the same as control. There was no lasting political solution on offer for the British in Afghanistan bar withdrawal.

The pre-emptive character of British action in Afghanistan, designed to block expansion by Russia, another Western power, was also seen elsewhere. For example, Spanish concern about British interest in the sultanate of Sulu in the southern Philippines led to a Spanish expedition to Sulu in the 1870s, and to an agreement with Britain in 1885. The Americans were to take over the Spanish position when they conquered the Philippines in 1898 and also to employ force to subjugate the sultanate. Further south, German interest in New Guinea led the British and Dutch to assert claims, so that by 1895 boundaries on the island had been settled; however, control of the Western powers over the mountainous interior was limited.

The pace of conquest continued into the early twentieth century. Then it tends to be overshadowed in most work on military history both by conflicts between Western or Western-style forces (Spanish–American War 1898, Boer War 1899–1902, Russo-Japanese War 1904–5, Balkan Wars 1912–13), and by the build-up towards World War One which broke out in 1914. While understandable, this approach neglects the significance of the Western expansion of the years from 1900 to 1914 for the people of much of the world and for the later political development of large areas. This was especially so in Africa and in what became Indonesia.

In Africa, the French made major gains in both Morocco and the Sahara. In the latter in 1900, the fall of In Rhar, after French artillery had breached its walls, had broken the resistance of the Tidelkt, and the submission of the Ahaggar Tuareg in 1905 ended effective resistance to the French. In West Africa, the British established the protectorates of northern and southern Nigeria in 1900, annexed Asante in 1901, and destroyed the army of Sokoto at Burmi in 1903, with vastly disproportionate casualties, ending resistance in northern Nigeria. The Italians captured the major coastal positions of Libya from the Ottoman Turks in 1911, although the Senussi tribesmen in the interior mounted a successful resistance to the Italians, again indicating the difficulty of establishing and consolidating control. This was the first war in which armoured cars and aeroplanes were used: hand grenades were dropped by an Italian plane on an Ottoman army camp in 1911.

Across much of Africa, however, the suppression of what were termed rebellions by the colonial rulers was important in consolidating control. Anti-French revolts in Madagascar from 1898 to 1904 and Morocco in 1907 were suppressed, as was an anti-British Zulu revolt in Natal in 1906, the Maji Maji rising in German East Africa (Tanzania) in 1905, and the Nama and Herero risings in German South-West Africa (Namibia) from 1904 to 1907. The Germans used particular brutality, their scorched-earth policy against guerrilla resistance leading to hundreds of thousands of deaths, mostly of civilians denied water, in what was later to be seen as a policy of genocide. In Natal, the less bloody, more rapid defeat of the Zulus, who were protesting in particular against a new poll tax, led to a further establishment of white control. The Natal militia had been the crucial force in defeating the Zulus. After the war, most of the Zulus became a more malleable labour force, much of it used in the gold mines of the Transvaal, which, after Britain's eventual success over the Boers in the Boer War, were a crucial economic resource for the British Empire.

In Asia, a British force, overcoming resistance en route, advanced to Lhasa, the capital of Tibet, in 1904, the sole European force to do so in the history of Tibet. Meanwhile the Dutch consolidated their control over more of the East Indies, bringing recalcitrant areas of Bali, Sumatra, Sulawesi and Borneo under their power. Further east, Portugal and the Dutch imposed control on their parts of the island of Timor. Thus, a major effort was made to match authority on the ground to newly drawn lines on the map, fixing territorial boundaries that have largely remained unchanged today.

Individuals even sought to create an imperial presence of their own. With British governmental support and that of the local power, the sultan of Brunei, James Brooke created an independent position for himself in Sarawak in northern Borneo in 1863. In contrast, crucially lacking local and international support, William Walker, an American adventurer who tried to seize Nicaragua and Honduras in the 1850s and 1860, eventually failed and was shot. After the American Civil War, ex-Confederates also played an important role in both Mexico and Cuba.

AMERICAN EXPANSION

The consequences of the conquest of the Native Americans are still very much with us today, helping shape the USA and thus the modern world. They are also irreversible and have had more lasting consequences than most European imperialism. The Native Americans suffered from being heavily outnumbered and divided, as well as from an unhelpful international context: no foreign power provided support. The demographic weight of the (European) Americans and their willingness to migrate and force their way into regions already settled by Native Americans was crucial: rapid American population growth led to significant levels of migration within America. The Americans, therefore, did not need to go overseas in order to fulfil what they saw as their national purpose and to seize land, and this had an important long-term consequence in terms of the character of American power and of Western imperialism. The thinly settled nature of the West also helped: the Americans faced no resistance from a large and resilient population comparable to that encountered by the French in Algeria or the Russians in Central Asia.

East of the Mississippi, the Native presence in North America was dramatically lessened by the policy of removal of Natives to west of the river pursued from 1815 and, more explicitly, from 1830, when the Indian Removal Act was passed. Removal completed the total disruption of Native society, destroying any sense of identity with place. The rapid defeat, in the Black Hawk War of 1832, of Black Hawk and his band of Sauk and Fox by regulars and Illinois militia underlined American dominance of the Mississippi valley.

The Louisiana Purchase of lands from France in 1803 had led to an unprecedented westward extension of American sovereignty to the Rocky Mountains, and this was followed by major annexations from Mexico in 1848. American expeditions were followed by roadbuilding and the establishment of forts, as the frontier of effective control moved west. The advance beyond wooded terrain into the Great Plains led the American army to introduce mounted regiments in 1833 and 1836: cavalry was more expensive, but it permitted a lower density in fortifications. Forts could be bypassed by Native raiders, but were difficult for them to take. They therefore helped to control communication routes and were a solid sign of American power. Forts were built along the edges of settlements to deter raids; but strategic thinking developed in favour of using forts as bases for offensive campaigns against Native homelands.

From the 1840s the Americans were no longer only interested in pushing the Natives back in a piecemeal fashion. Instead, fired by a conviction that they were bringing civilization to the Natives and to the lands of the West, the authorities in Washington sought total control of the whole of America: from ocean to ocean. Widespread military operations in the 1850s were characterized by a greater willingness to massacre Natives and by the use of far more violence against women and children than in earlier conflicts. In a similar vein in Argentina, Native peoples were brutally subjugated in the 'Conquest of the Desert', and then of Patagonia. Advances there and in the USA were consolidated by the building of forts.

BOX 4.3   THE MEXICAN–AMERICAN WAR, 1846–48

American victory in this war defined the geopolitics of North America, leading to confirmation of Texas's union with the USA in 1845, the major cause of the conflict, and also to the annexation of what were to become the states of California, Nevada and Utah, as well as most of Arizona and parts of New Mexico, Colorado and Wyoming. In 1846, an American force under Zachary Taylor successfully invaded northern Mexico, capturing Monterrey (24 September) after difficult street fighting. Distance and logistical problems, however, discouraged an advance from there on to Mexico City, and, instead, in 1847, an American amphibious force under Winfield Scott landed near Vera Cruz (9 March), advanced inland, defeated larger Mexican forces in a series of battles, including Cerro Gordo (18 April), Contreras and Churubusco (19–20 August), Molino del Rey (8 September) and Chapultepec (13 September) and captured Mexico City (14 September). Further afield, American forces had overrun Mexico's northern possessions, greatly assisted in California by a revolt by American settlers and by the support of the American Pacific Squadron.

American campaigning was what would be subsequently described as 'high tempo'. Its aggressive and fast-moving character was necessary for political as well as military reasons. The Americans were helped by naval superiority as well as better artillery. Although criticized by the elderly Duke of Wellington, Scott's generalship displayed strategic insight and daring, a skilful transfer of this into effective operational planning and direction, and an ability to gain and retain the initiative. The Mexicans benefited from numbers, but their army was poorly armed and supplied, outgeneraled and outfought. By not trying to annex any real core parts of Mexico, the Americans also ensured the possibility of an exit strategy that limited their commitments. The absence of foreign intervention on behalf of Mexico was also useful to the USA. In the 1860s, the Americans were to be concerned about French intervention there, which was seen as a clear breach of the Monroe Doctrine; but that was not an issue in the 1840s.

The railway played a major role in fostering American power, not only in supporting the military but also in developing economic links between coastal and hinterland America, and thus making the frontier of settlement profitable. This was important in the spread of ranching, with the cattle being driven to railheads, and also in the development of mining. Again, the same was true in Latin America, especially Argentina and Brazil.

After the Civil War finished in 1865, the American army developed techniques for Native warfare that focused on winter campaigning and on the co-ordination of independently operating columns advancing from different directions. Native villages were attacked, crops destroyed and horses seized, while the bison the Natives relied upon for food were slaughtered. This was more than an application of the devastation meted out to parts of the Confederacy from 1864 to 1865, for now there was also much slaughter of those depicted as pagan savages.

The Natives could mount effective resistance, as in the war against the Bozeman Trail from 1865 to 1868, and win clashes, most famously Crazy Horse's triumph over Custer and his over-extended cavalry force at Little Bighorn on 25 June 1876, but they could not match the inexorable American pressure, a product of resources, determination, and increased skill. Pursued hard, and defeated at Slim Buttes (9 September 1876), Crazy Horse was forced to surrender in May 1877; that October Chief Joseph's Nez Percé were forced to surrender, and Geronimo, the leader of resistance among the Apache in the south-west, followed in September 1886. In 1890, the year in which the outgunned Sioux Ghost Dance revival was defeated at Wounded Knee (29 December), the frontier was declared closed.

Aside from expanding power in North America, including purchasing lands from Mexico in 1853 (the Gadsden Purchase), and Alaska and the Aleutian Islands from Russia in 1867, the USA also projected its power abroad, using naval force to support its interests. The Mediterranean Squadron made a demonstration along the coast after foreigners, including Americans, were killed at Jaffa in 1851. The protection of American interests led to the landing of forces in Buenos Aires in 1852 and 1853, Nicaragua in 1853, Shanghai in 1854, 1855 and 1859, Fiji in 1855 and 1858, Uruguay in 1855 and 1858, Panama in 1856 and 1865, and Canton in 1856, as well as to a show of force off Japan in 1853 (see pp. 82–3). From 1858 to 1859, in order to overawe a hostile dictator, Carlos Antonio López of Paraguay, whose forces had fired on an American survey ship, the Americans deployed a powerful squadron on the rivers Paraná and Paraguay and made the dictator pay an indemnity. In the 1890s, the USA became a major force in the Pacific. After overthrowing the Hawaiian monarchy, Hawaii was annexed in 1898. The defeat of Spain led to the annexation of the Philippines and Guam in 1898 and Wake Island in 1899, while control of American Samoa was established in 1899.

NON-WESTERN STATES

The counterpart to Western imperialism was the response of others. Divisions that led to co-operation from some of the population were important in Asia,

Africa and among Native Americans. So also was the fate of attempts to develop the militaries of potentially rival non-Western states. Thus, it is instructive to consider what happened to the Egyptian, Sikh and Persian forces mentioned in Chapter 2.

Mehmet Ali of Egypt continued his military expansionism in the 1830s, building a battle fleet with French technical support, making major gains in Yemen, and, after turning on his Ottoman overlord, winning victories in Syria in the 1830s, especially at Nezib in 1839. Asia Minor was invaded in 1840 and the Ottomans were defeated at Konia. Mehmet Ali was unable, however, to sustain his position, in large part because key Western powers saw his gains from the Ottoman Empire as a cause of instability. In 1840 a British squadron blockaded the Egyptian fleet in Alexandria, while British and Austrian warships and marines helped overthrow the Egyptian position in Lebanon and Syria. The port of Sidon in Lebanon was stormed, the marines joined the Ottomans in defeating the Egyptian army at Boharsef, and the port of Acre was heavily bombarded, leading to the departure of Egyptian forces. Mehmet then agreed to evacuate Syria.

Further south, the British occupied Aden in 1839, and in 1840 they were able to press the Egyptians to leave Yemen: occupation of Aden gave the British control over the route between the Red Sea and the Indian Ocean, and this was to become more important after the Suez Canal was opened (1869), shortening and altering the sea route from Britain to India. By 1880, three-quarters of the ships using the Suez Canal were British.

Western pressure on Egypt culminated in 1882 when anti-European action led to British intervention in which the British fleet devastated coastal defences at Alexandria, before an army was landed and the less well-trained Egyptians were defeated by Garnet Wolseley at Tall al-Kabir on 13 September. The route to India now seemed secure, not least because in the Mediterranean the British also had military bases in their colonies of Gibraltar (acquired 1704), Malta (acquired 1800) and Cyprus (acquired 1878). In 1878, when Russian forces had overrun much of European Turkey and advanced to near Constantinople, the British thwarted their

BOX 4.4   THE VOICE OF WAR: THE ANGLO-SIKH WAR, 1849

The havoc they [Sikh cannon] committed was fearful . . . At one time the grape and round shot were flying so thick that the ground was actually covered with them; and every bush you passed out rushed a Sikh and tried to cut you down. Of course we never thought of looking into every bush we passed and thus they got in our rear.

Unidentified British officer reporting on hard-won victory over the Sikhs at the battle of Chillianwalla in January 1849, a key episode in the Second Anglo-Sikh War which was won by the British. British Library, Indian Office MSS. Eur. C 605 folios 1–2.

pressure on the Turks by moving six ironclad battleships to within sight of the Russian army, an impressive display of naval capability.

Egypt and Ottoman Turkey were not the only non-European powers to be defeated. Further east, the Sikhs had been overthrown. By 1835, Ranjt Singh's army was organized on brigade lines and armed with flintlocks, and, when he died in 1839, it was about 150,000 strong, including 60,000 to 65,000 regulars. Many of the officers were Sikhs trained in European drill and tactics. In the Anglo-Sikh Wars of 1845–46 and 1848–49, the Sikhs fought well, making effective use of their firearms and cannon, but they were defeated by the British. Vietnam's more limited military Westernization did not save it. Action against missionaries led to a Franco-Spanish expedition that seized Danang in 1858 and Saigon in 1859. Later in the century, Vietnam became a French colony, in stages: Cochin China followed by Annam and Tongking. Neighbouring Cambodia became a French Protectorate in 1863 and Laos a colony in 1893.

In Persia, Thailand and Ethiopia, independence was preserved, although in very different ways. In Persia, the new units introduced by 'Abbas Mirza had not transformed the situation. In 1838, the Persian siege of Herat in Afghanistan, a traditional goal for Persian expansion, was poorly handled and unsuccessful. The new units were regarded by observers as less impressive than traditional-style mounted levies led by Persian commanders. These continued to have a role in a military environment largely framed not by confrontation with neighbouring Russia but by the need to suppress regional risings, for example in 1832 and 1838, to overawe hostile royal princes and provincial governors, and to campaign against nomadic Türkmens as in 1836.

After the death of 'Abbas Mirza in 1833, few attempts were made to continue the Westernization of the Persian armed forces. The army remained poorly organized and the sale of commands to unqualified individuals, who used positions for personal profit and took no interest in training, further weakened cohesion and quality, as, indeed, was to be the case with some Third World armies in the late twentieth century and the 2000s. As in Ethiopia, the small regular army was greatly outnumbered by tribal forces that fought in a largely traditional fashion. The Persian government relied heavily on the powerful and well-armed tribal forces that continued to focus on cavalry, which provided mobility in a country lacking roads and railways. The Persian forces did not distinguish themselves in a brief conflict with Britain in 1856 and 1857. The development of a large Western-style force appeared unviable, and yet also unnecessary. Instead, the manipulation of tribal politics was seen as the route to domestic security, while, externally, there was an attempt to secure British protection against Russian expansion. A strong conservatism restricted reform initiatives and, unlike in China, Ethiopia and the Ottoman Empire, there was only limited conflict with foreign enemies to inspire change.

Nevertheless, visiting Russia in 1878, Shah Nazir al-Din Shah, the ruler of Persia, was impressed by Russian Cossack forces and, thereafter, he used Russian officers to command and train the Persian Cossack Brigade founded in 1879. His eldest son, Zill al-Sultan, a provincial governor, also built up a personal force of Western-trained troops in the 1880s and early 1890s. By the 1890s 2,000 strong, and the sole well-trained force in the army, the Cossack Brigade was a crucial support to the Shah, being used by Muhammad 'Ali Shah when he suppressed the popular national government in 1908. However, the city of Tabriz, which had an effective popular guard, successfully resisted the army. In 1909, revolutionary and tribal forces advanced on Tehran, and the Shah abdicated. As an example of its weakness, and of the Western tendency to divide up the world, Persia had been neither consulted nor informed when it was divided in the Anglo-Russian Treaty of 1907 into regions of Russian and British influence and a neutral sphere.

In Siam (Thailand), in contrast, there was more Westernization. Under Rama IV (reigned 1851–68), and especially Rama V (reigned 1868–1910), a degree of modernization included significant changes in the army, communications and finances. Siam also benefited from its location as a buffer state, lying between spheres of British (Burma, Malaya) and French (Indo-China) expansion – although it lost territory to both powers in the 1900s. A Department of the Army was created in 1888, and conscription was introduced in 1902. The Siamese forces did not match those of Western powers, but they fought effectively against the French in Laos in 1893, and also used modern weapons to suppress revolts that owed much to policies of modernization and centralization. These revolts included the Raja of Pattani's rising in the south in 1902, and the Holy Man's Rebellion of the same year: a messianic rebellion that reflected regional opposition in the north-east.

Sub-Saharan Africa is generally presented in military history for this period in terms of conquest by Western powers (the British focusing on conflict with the Zulus in 1879) and of rivalry between Europeans, particularly the Boer Wars of 1881 and 1899–1902 between the British and the Afrikaner settlers of Dutch descent in southern Africa. While understandable from the perspective of Western control over most of Africa by 1914, this not only leaves out much of the military history of the period but also seems less relevant as the relatively brief period of Western territorial control (largely over by 1975) and the subsequent history of the continent draws attention to earlier conflict between African polities.

Furthermore, it is unclear that the military history of Africa in the nineteenth century should be presented largely in terms of the adoption of European weaponry. There were important instances of such adoption. In West Africa, Gezo, the ruler of Dahomey, whose troops were armed with firearms, expanded Dahomey to its furthest limits in the 1830s and 1840s, conquering the Mahi to the north-east: their warfare was based on bows and arrows, as Dahomey prevented the sale of European firearms to the peoples of the interior. Further north, Toure Samory, leader of the Mandinke people and the Napoleon of the Sudan according to the French, who established a state on the upper Niger in the 1870s and 1880s, relied on the *sofa*, professional troops trained along European lines and equipped with modern firearms bought in part from British traders in Sierra Leone, but also manufactured in Samory's own workshops: he had placed agents in the French arsenal in Senegal to learn how to make rifles and cannon. Samory was obliged to accept French terms in 1886, but he resumed war with them in 1891 and was not captured until 1898.

By the mid-1870s the Egyptian army was equipped with modern Western weaponry: Remington rifles, Gatling machine guns, and 80-mm Krupp artillery; while Muhammad Ahmad-Mahdi, who took over much of Sudan from Egyptian control from 1881–1885, had an infantry force armed with Western rifles: the *jihadiyya*.

Yet, the extent and impact of such adoption of weaponry should not be exaggerated, and this is even more the case if tactics in African warfare are considered. Although firearms were eagerly adopted in many cases, wheeled gun-carriages made little impact. Furthermore, weapons that were received or copied from Europeans were not always employed for military purposes, or used effectively by European standards. For example, King Tenimu of Zinder (1851–84) developed the local manufacture of cannon, powder and shot, and constructed wheeled gun-carriages, but the latter were not put to practical use and the cannon were only employed to fire salutes. Hadji Omar, who created the Tukolor empire in West Africa from 1848, did so with cavalry, while although Samory used firearms, his tactics and operations relied not on European-style formations and manoeuvres but on mobile and, frequently, guerilla warfare.

In southern Africa, the Zulus did not want rifles and referred to the British as cowards because they would not fight hand to hand. The Zulus were eventually heavily defeated in 1879 in a series of battles by defensive infantry fire from prepared positions. On 4 July, the British force at Ulundi used breech-loading rifles, Gatling machine-guns, and cannon, and burned down the Zulu capital.

In Sudan, the Mahdists put a heavy emphasis on spearmen. They destroyed an Egyptian army under the command of Colonel William Hicks, a British officer with experience of India, at the battle of Shaykan on 5 November 1883, and another Egyptian army outside Suakin on 6 November 1883; they also defeated the Ethiopians in 1887 and 1889. The conflict in this region was to draw in the British, who defeated the Mahdi's successor, Abdullahi, at Omdurman (2 September 1898) and Um Debreika (1899), but it is important not to neglect the campaigns fought earlier by Egypt, Ethiopia and the Mahdists. These were of some scale: at al-Qāllabāt in 1889 a Mahdist army of about 100,000 men defeated an Ethiopian force of comparable size after the emperor, Yohannis IV, was shot dead. The Ethiopians themselves had defeated the Egyptians at Gundet on 16 November 1875 and Gura on 7 March 1876: religion fused with patriotism in Ethiopian (Christian) resistance to Egypt and to the Mahdists, both Islamic forces. These wars receive even less attention than the contemporary conflicts in Latin America (the War of the Triple Alliance, 1864–70, and the War of the Pacific, 1879–83), but, like them, were major and costly struggles.

In Ethiopia, the process of Westernization ironically led to a spectacular triumph over a Western force. Thanks to the leadership of three emperors, Tewodros II, Yohannis IV and Menelik II, a numerous and successful army was developed, with an increase from fewer than 15,000 men in the 1860s to 150,000 in 1896, by when nearly half were armed with modern weapons. By 1880 a force of Ethiopian artillerymen had been trained, and in the 1890s French and Russian advisers improved the artillery, helping Ethiopia to a notable triumph over Italy at Adua on 1 March 1896. The Ethiopians used Hotchkiss machine-guns in the battle, although victory over the far smaller Italian army owed more to poor Italian tactics, not least the failure to ensure co-ordination between units. In the Ethiopian army review in 1902 elite units demonstrated the use of machine-gun and artillery fire. Ethiopia was not to be conquered by Italy until 1936.

Ethiopia's expansion under Menelik II, who, prior to his death in 1911 had greatly expanded his territorial sway, especially to the south and south-east, is a reminder of the vitality of some non-Western powers. International competition, however, led to serious political strains for such powers, not least because it produced pressure for a consolidation of state authority to pre-empt foreign territorial claims. This consolidation opposed government power to tribal and other opponents, especially in border areas.

Thus in what is now Jordan, the Ottomans established forts and outposts in the second half of the century, and in 1867 forced the submission of the Balqa Bedouin with an armed expedition, collecting unpaid taxes, and ended the extortion of tribute from the villagers who were the source of Ottoman revenue. The Ottoman presence was consolidated with agrarian settlement, and, subsequently, with the building of the Hijaz railway from Damascus to Arabia in the 1900s. The accession of the reformist Young Turks to control over the Ottoman Empire in 1908 brought new energy to Ottoman government. In Jordan, the Jabal Druze was subjugated in 1910, and, further south, the Ottomans suppressed a revolt in Karak. Ottoman control was defended by military force, fortification and bribery. This is a part of the world whose military history is generally ignored, but these events, like those in China, Ethiopia and Persia, indicate the degree of volatility and extent of conflict around the world, including in areas not under Western control.

CHINA AND JAPAN

The contrasting nature, but common pressures, of military and political developments was shown in East Asia, in the case of China and Japan. China, the largest non-Western state, suffered defeat at the hands of Britain in the Opium War of 1839–42, as amphibious forces seized Amoy, Canton, Shanghai and other coastal positions. The British made effective use of new technology in the shape of paddle-wheel iron gunships, which were able to steam up rivers such as the Yangzi. Advancing to the walls of Nanjing, the British obliged the Chinese to negotiate and to cede Hong Kong, providing Britain with a valuable naval and commercial base that became part of the worldwide structure of Britain's global power. In 1860, during the Arrow War, British and French forces fought their way to Beijing and captured the city, forcing the Chinese to accept greater Western commercial penetration, while in 1884 and 1885 China failed to block French ambitions in neighbouring Vietnam, traditionally an area in which the Chinese had sought to exercise hegemony.

Western pressure was also brought to bear on Japan. On 8 July 1853, a squadron of four American ships, under Commodore Matthew Perry, entered Tokyo Bay in order to persuade Japan to inaugurate relations. After presenting a letter from President Fillimore, Perry sailed to China, wintering on the coast (rather than sailing back to the USA), an important display of naval capability. Having made naval demonstrations in the Ryuku and Bonin Islands, which secured a coaling concession from the ruler of Naha on Okinawa, Perry returned to Japan with a larger squadron and negotiated the Treaty of Kanagawa.

Western pressure on China was greater, and some regional officials tried hard to improve their forces. Western-officered units, especially the 'Foreign Rifle Company', which in 1862 was renamed the Ever Victorious Army, as well as the Ever-Triumphant Army, were used successfully against the Taiping rebels in the early 1860s, and these forces served as an inspiration and a challenge to a number of Chinese leaders, encouraging the formation of Western-style armies towards the end of the century. The first modern Chinese attempts to start military industries using Western technology were the 'self-strengthening enterprises' which began in about 1860. The initiative was taken by leading provincial officials, but their options were restricted by the determination to preserve unchanged traditional or Confucian Chinese culture and only bolt-on Western technology.

In contrast, from 1867 the Tokugawa shōgunate in Japan began a serious effort to remodel its army along French lines: prior to defeat by Prussia in 1870 the French army had the highest international reputation. Already opposition domains in Japan, such as Choshu, had begun to introduce military reforms. As a consequence of the strengthening of the emperor in the so-called Meiji Restoration, further and yet more radical military changes followed. The domestic conflicts of the period had demonstrated the superiority of Western weaponry, and the political shift of 1868 made it easier to advocate and introduce a new military order. The privileged, caste nature of military service monopolized by the samurai was replaced by conscription, which was introduced in 1872.

The two Japanese systems, one traditional, one Western and modern, were brought into conflict in 1877 with a samurai uprising in the domain of Satsuma. The large samurai force, armed with swords and matchlock muskets, was defeated by the new mass army of conscripted peasants: individual military prowess and bravery succumbing to the organized, disciplined force of an army that, on an individual basis, was less proficient. This episode served as the basis for the 2003 film *The Last Samurai*. In Japan, conscription broke down the division then still seen in Persia and Ethiopia between a small Westernized force and very differently armed levies that were often tribal or clan-based in character.

Japanese military development was supported by policies of military education and by the institutionalization of planning. In 1874, the Sambōkyoku, an office to develop plans and operations, was created within the Army Ministry. This became, first, the Staff Bureau and, subsequently, the General Staff Headquarters. The organizational transformation of the Japanese army was linked to an institutional professionalization and, also, to the creation of a capacity for overseas operations. In the 1880s, not least due to the creation of a system of divisions, the army was transformed from a heavily armed internal security force, reliant on static garrison units, into a mobile force.

Thanks to the progress of both army and navy, the Japanese developed an amphibious capability. While French and, later, German models and military missions influenced the army, the navy looked to Britain for warships and training. Power-projection gathered pace. In the 1870s and 1880s, effective sovereignty was established over the nearby Bonin, Kurile and Ryukyu Islands, although an attempt to seize the island of Taiwan from China in 1874 was unsuccessful and led to heavy losses of troops to disease.

From 1894 to 1895 China and Japan clashed more seriously. Despite problems with logistics and transport, Japanese forces advanced speedily through Korea, driving the Chinese, who they defeated at Tangijn on 29 July, before them, and then crossed the Yalu river into Manchuria (the bordering province of China) and captured the major base of Port Arthur in November 1894, as well as Weihaiwei on China's north-east coast the following March. The Japanese fleet had won the battle of the Yalu river (17 September 1894) over the less speedy and manoeuvrable Chinese warships. Another force seized the Pescadores Islands. However, in the eventual peace, the Japanese were obliged to limit the gains China had ceded under the Treaty of Shimonoseki on 17 April 1895 owing to pressure from Russia, Germany and France; Japan kept Taiwan and the Pescadores but was forced to return Port Arthur. This showed that industrial armaments and Western-style organization and thought were not in themselves sufficient; the new scale of war and its geopolitical consequences gave a far greater weight to alliances, and Japan needed to win support, or at least acceptance, if it was to make further gains, a lesson learned more successfully in the 1900s and 1910s than in the 1940s. Conquest brought its own problems on Taiwan, where the Japanese suppressed a popular resistance movement, although in the mountainous forests of the interior tribesmen continued guerrilla resistance for over three decades.

Plate 4.1 Japanese woodblock triptych print depicting an attack during the Sino-Japanese War of 1894–95. The contrast between the Western-style uniforms of the Japanese and those of the Chinese troops is readily apparent. Anne S.K. Brown Collection.

A further instance, both of the strength of China's foreign opponents and of the capacity of their forces to mobilize quickly, was provided by the suppression of the Boxer movement in China. This anti-foreign movement began in 1897 and became nationally significant in 1900 when the Manchu court increasingly aligned with the Boxers against foreign influence. Converts to Christianity were killed, hostilities between Boxers and foreign troops began, the government declared war on the foreign powers, and the foreign legations in Beijing were attacked on 20 June and then besieged. In response, international relief expeditions were mounted. The first was blocked by the Chinese and forced to retreat to Tianjin, which was unsuccessfully besieged by the Boxers whose swords and lances provided no protection against the firearms of the Western garrison. After Tianjin had been relieved, a second force was sent to Beijing, defeating opposition en route, breaching the walls of the city and relieving the legations on 14 August. The alliance of Western and Japanese troops paraded through the Forbidden City, a powerful sign of Chinese loss of face, as earlier was the failure of far larger forces to defeat the defenders of the legations in a siege of fifty-five days.

The subsequent treaty with China, signed on 7 September 1901, decreed very large reparations, as well as twelve foreign garrisons between the coast and Beijing, and the prohibition of imports of foreign-made weapons for two years. The Boxer failure had made it clear that Western-type weapons were indeed required. Whereas earlier peoples might have boasted of their invulnerability to Western bullets, and, in practice, had been protected in part by the inaccuracy of firearms, now the Boxers had been made to pay for their trust in magic. Similarly, in suppressing the Zulu rising of 1906, the Natal militia showed that Bambatha, the Zulu chief, could not make his followers invulnerable to bullets. Instead, about 3,000 Zulu died as opposed to only thirty-three militiamen.

At the same time, at the expense of non-Westerners, the Manchu government, like the Ottomans in Jordan, continued its policy of trying to consolidate control over border areas, a policy that was to characterize states not only during the age of imperialism but also thereafter. A good example of this general process was presented in the area of Kham, part of eastern Tibet that had been an autonomous section of China since the eighteenth-century expansion of the latter. Attempts in 1903 and 1904 to increase control, not least by appointing Chinese officials, led to a rising in Kham in 1905 that was crushed when troops were sent from Sichuan, the south-western region of China. As a result, the pace of establishing Chinese administration (and language education) was stepped up. In 1910, this was taken further when the Chinese invaded neighbouring Tibet. The new order, however, was overthrown in both Tibet and Kham when the Manchu dynasty itself fell as a result of a large-scale revolt in China that broke out on 10 October 1910, leading the emperor to abdicate on 12 February 1912. In turn, the new republican government in China regained control of Kham from 1912 to 1914.

NAVAL POWER

The deployment of Western and Japanese troops to China in 1900 was a clear sign of the amphibious capability of these powers. This rested on a naval strength that had been enhanced by technological and organizational development. Ship designers sought to juggle the desirable qualities of speed, armament and armour, while responding to new hull materials such as nickel-steel, and to changes in gunnery, not least the replacement of muzzle-loaders by breech-loaders. Improved gunnery led to an increase in the strength per ton of armour which, in turn, led to pressure for still more powerful gunnery.

Changing technology interacted with differing and developing views on the most effective form of naval strength. The development, from the 1860s, of submerged torpedoes driven by compressed air and, eventually, equipped with gyroscopes to provide an automatic means of steering, and, from the 1880s, of electric-powered submarines, made the situation at sea more volatile. This encouraged debate about tactics, strategy and force-structure.

Rather than focusing on conflict between battle fleets, the French naval thinkers known as the Jeune École, especially in the 1880s, argued that France should respond to the combination of Britain's global maritime power and its unparalleled naval strength by emphasizing commerce raiding, a strategy that required fast cruisers, while the torpedo was seen as a way to challenge British battleships. Towards the close of the century, however, command of the sea through battle was emphasized by theorists, especially an internationally influential American, Alfred Thayer Mahan. This led to a stress on battleships, and from the 1890s the leading powers, including states such as Japan and the USA that had not hitherto had a fleet of this type, all developed strong battleship navies. The impact of victories at sea – of Chile over Peru off Punta Angamos on 8 October 1879 and Japan over China in the battle of the Yalu on 17 September 1894 – appeared to confirm Mahan's doctrine.

CONCLUSIONS

The humbling of China from 1900 to 1901 was an abrupt demonstration of Western power over non-Western states, and a marked contrast with the situation a century earlier. There were, however, also signs of the precariousness of Western control and military methods. In the Philippines in 1898, the Americans easily beat Spain, the colonial power, not least due to a total naval victory in Manila Bay, but then encountered bitter resistance from Filipinos, who had, in the Katpunan revolt, struggled for independence from Spain from 1896 to 1898, using guerrilla methods. Thwarted of their hope for independence by American annexation of the Philippines, the Filipinos under Emilio Aquinaldo resisted the new order from February 1899. Defeated in conventional warfare by the Americans in 1899, the Filipinos turned to guerrilla warfare, leading the Americans to increase the size of their force to 70,000. Their resistance to the Americans was longer-lasting than that of Spain, although eventually it was also overcome in part by tough anti-insurgency methods, including the use of detention camps. Divisions among the population were also important. Aquinaldo was captured in 1901, but resistance continued. In Cuba, in contrast, the Americans made no attempt to retain control after they rapidly defeated the Spaniards in 1898.

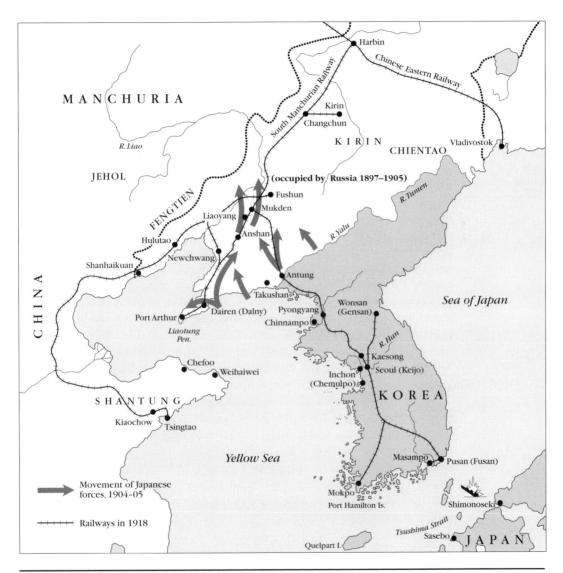

Map 4.1 The Russo-Japanese War, 1904–5. After *The Times Atlas of World History* (1993), p. 238. © BCA by arrangement with Time Books.

More arrestingly for contemporaries was the first major defeat of a Western power by a non-Western state able to rely on similar military methods; that is, taking part in what is now termed 'symmetrical warfare'. Japanese influence in newly conquered Korea had been challenged by that of Russia, and the self-confident and racialist Russians, unwilling to accept the Japanese as equals, refused to agree to a Japanese offer of a recognition of Russian dominance in Manchuria, occupied by Russia in 1900, in return for Japanese control of Korea. In the sub-sequent war of 1904–5, the Japanese were victorious not only at sea, especially in a crushing fashion at the battle of Tsushima (27–28 May 1905), but also on land, defeating the Russians in the Liaotung peninsula and Manchuria, while a Japanese amphibious force landed in Sakhalin. The Japanese had attacked on 8 February 1904 before declaring war.

On land, the Japanese took very heavy casualties in a conflict that showed the strength of entrenched positions supported by quick-firing artillery and machine-guns, and found it difficult to sustain the struggle, but, hampered by insurrection in European Russia from January 1905, and operating at the end of very long supply lines, the Russians, who were not ready for war in the Far East, weakened first. The cautious generalship of Aleksey Kuropatkin ensured that the Japanese dominated the tempo of operations. They were able to gain the central position between the Russian garrison at Port Arthur and the main Russian army in Manchuria. This enabled them to move their forces between the fronts, until the siege of Port Arthur ended with its surrender on 2 January 1905. In the subse-quent peace, the Treaty of Portsmouth of 5 September 1905, Japan gained Russian rights and privileges in South Manchuria, not least the lease on the Liaotung peninsula. The course of operations was carefully followed by Western observers who came away from the war convinced that the Japanese had won because they had taken the initiative, and that frontal assaults were still feasible. These lessons influenced planning for what was to become World War One.

Victory enabled the Japanese to create a protectorate over Korea in 1905. A rebellion there from 1908 to 1910 was brutally suppressed, and in 1910 Korea was formally annexed, with a tough general becoming the first governor-general.

This was the sign of a very different century than the one that usually commands attention. The struggle for hegemony in East Asia, the largest concen-tration of people in the world, tends to attract less discussion than that for control over Europe, but from the perspective of the early twenty-first century it is a key issue that repays consideration.

CHAPTER 5

World War One, 1914–18

INTRODUCTION

World War One dominates the public perception of twentieth-century conflict to a disproportionate extent, and the impression created focuses on the heavy casualties of the war on the Western Front in France and Belgium and the impasse of trench warfare. This underrates the extent to which the war ended with victory, the total defeat in 1918 of Germany and its allies by Britain, France, the USA and their allies. Given the difficulties of applying strength effectively, this was a more impressive outcome than is generally appreciated.

BACKGROUND

Prior to the outbreak of the war, the General Staffs of all the European belligerents had pre-planned and executed manoeuvres on a massive scale in war games and staff rides. With these, staff officers convinced themselves that they could knock out their opponents before their own resources ran out. Although the defensive advantages resulting from the new breech-loading, smokeless, quick-firing firearms were understood, and the benefits of field fortifications, especially trench lines, had been shown in the Russo-Japanese War of 1904–5, there was a firm conviction within the General Staffs that sooner or later the supply of artillery firing high-explosive shells, combined with the élan of (their) infantry advances, would overcome trenches, barbed wire and automatic weaponry. In the Spanish–American

War of 1898, the Russo-Japanese War of 1904–5, and the Balkan Wars of 1912–13, the attacking power had won.

On the eve of World War One, observers saw the Balkan Wars as confirming their faith in massed infantry assaults. This lesson was taken in particular from the Bulgarian victories over the Turks in 1912, such as Kirkkilese and Lyule Burgas, which appeared to show the effectiveness of high morale and of infantry charging in to the attack. There was a general failure to note the degree to which rapid-firing artillery and machine-guns might blunt such attacks. Indeed, the power of entrenched positions supported by artillery when neither had been suppressed by superior offensive gunfire was shown in the failure of the Bulgarian attack on the Turks at Chataldzha in 1912.

In the run-up to what became World War One, the arms race escalated in Europe. The pace of the change in military capability owed much to the size, growth and flexibility of the industrial base of the major powers, while the very process of industrialization exacerbated social divisions and created a situation in which war appeared as a viable solution to domestic crisis. It was possible for industrial sectors to take new concepts and turn them relatively rapidly into new or improved weapons. It was also possible, thanks to mass-production, to have such weapons adopted in large quantities. In 1900, the Russians ordered 1,000 quick-firing field-guns from the Putilov iron works, while Prussia doubled the complement of field-guns to 144 per infantry corps between 1866 and 1905, and the guns themselves were more powerful. Workshop space in Krupp's great Essen works in Germany grew by an average of 5.2 acres per annum in the five years to 1908 and thereafter, up to 1914, by 6.4 acres per annum. Even before the outbreak of war, Krupp was producing 150,000 shells of all calibres monthly, while already in 1909, only six years after the Wright brothers took to the air, launching powered flight for humans, Hiram Maxim predicted raids on cities launched by bombers, as were indeed launched by the Germans against London during World War One. Aerial reconnaissance was to play a role in the opening campaign on the Western Front in 1914.

At sea, the Japanese victory over the Russians at Tsushima on 27–28 May 1905 appeared to vindicate an emphasis on battleships and on Mahan's ideas about naval power: a high seas encounter had occurred, had been a decisive battle, and had then greatly affected the course of the war. Thirty-one out of thirty-nine Russian warships had been destroyed or captured. Tsushima saw hits scored from unprecedented distances, which led to pressure for the development of big-gun battleships. Ironically, Tsushima was in fact to be the only example of a clash between modern battleships in the twentieth century that led to the destruction of one of the fleets. The Russo-Japanese War also saw the use of mines, torpedoes and destroyers, although not submarines, the potential of which was greatly underestimated by most naval commanders.

There was a major pre-war naval race for predominance between Britain and Germany, with both sides equally adopting a new class of battleship called, after the first one, dreadnoughts. These represented a new stage in the industrialization of military capability. The *Dreadnought*, launched in 1906, was the first capital ship in the world to be powered by the marine turbine engine. Completed in

14 months, her construction reflected the industrial and organizational efficiency of British shipbuilding. Other states rushed to follow. Benefiting from their economic growth, the Japanese laid down their first dreadnought in 1909.

A command and control revolution built on new technology in the shape of the radio was important in deciding how these new warships were to be employed. Instead of deploying ships on fixed distant stations, they could now be deployed more flexibly, many being kept in home waters and sent to handle tasks rapidly in response to radio messages.

War broke out in 1914 as a result of the interaction of instability in the Balkans with great power rivalries within a context in which militarist attitudes were dominant in Germany, Austria and Russia, while Britain and France were willing to fight to defend their interests. The assassination on 28 June of Archduke Franz Ferdinand, the Austrian heir, in Sarajevo, capital of Austrian-ruled Bosnia, by Slav nationalists supported by the Serbian secret police, was used by Austria as an opportunity to end what it saw as the Serbian threat to its control over neighbouring Slav territories. Despite the fact that Franz Conrad von Hötzendorf, the chief of the Austrian General Staff, feared that war with Serbia would lead to a widespread war for which Austria was not ready, he pressed for intimidation, and on 23 July an ultimatum was delivered to Serbia that it was correctly believed her government could not accept.

The focus of international relations on two competing alliance systems, centred on the rival alliances of France–Russia and Germany–Austria, ensured that a breakdown in a particular area, in this case between Serbia and Austria, rapidly expanded, with states acting because they thought that not to do so would lead to a weakening of their relative position. Russia feared that the defeat of its Balkan protégé Serbia would leave Austria too powerful in the Balkans, and thus endanger Russia's overall ability to compete with Austria and Germany. The initial combatants were Serbia, Russia, France, Belgium, Britain and Japan, against Germany and Austria. The former were to be joined by Italy (1915), Romania (1916) and the USA (1917), and the latter by Turkey (1914) and Bulgaria (1915). Had Italy, which was allied to Germany and Austria, joined them in 1914, then the situation for France would have been far more serious, but it switched alliance system. By attacking neutral Belgium on 4 August 1914, Germany brought Britain, which had guaranteed Belgian neutrality, into the war.

OPENING CAMPAIGN

In 1914, the Germans sought to repeat the success of Napoleon and Moltke the Elder by mounting and winning a war of manoeuvre. Owing to the alliance between France and Russia, however, there was now the need for Germany to plan for a two-front conflict: the war could not be like the Franco-Prussian War of 1870 to 1871. The strategy of first strike underlay German planning, and it was influenced by Moltke the Elder's preference for the envelopment of opposing forces, rather than relying on frontal attack. Concerned about the ruinous consequences of a lengthy positional conflict, Count Alfred von Schlieffen, chief of the

German General Staff from 1891 to 1906, instead left his successor, Helmuth von Moltke (Moltke the Younger), a plan for an attack on France, through neutral Belgium, designed to permit flank attacks on the French, which was to be the basis of German strategy in 1914. Moltke, however, failed to adapt his plan to changing circumstances, not least Russian recovery from defeat at the hands of Japan in 1904–5 and her build-up of an army that was more powerful than that of Germany's ally, Austria. Furthermore, Russia was to mobilize more rapidly in 1914 than had been anticipated. Moltke's changes to the earlier plan – the proportional strengthening of the left-wing of the advancing German forces in the West, and the abandonment of the invasion of the Netherlands' Maastricht salient, did not alter the plan's essentials.

Moltke and his colleagues in the General Staff wanted war and, by emphasizing future threats – not least faster Russian mobilization once Russian railways improved, and stating that victory was still within grasp in 1914 – helped to push civilian policy-makers towards conflict. No alternative scenario to that of all-out war was offered to the politicians. Schlieffen had excluded non-military problems from General Staff thinking, ensuring that planning failed to devote due weight to political consequences such as British entry into the conflict. Moltke planned for a short and manageable war, but, paradoxically, feared that it could be a long struggle, for which Germany was not prepared.

In the event, the 1914 campaign showed that German war-making, with its emphasis on surprise, speed, and overwhelming and dynamic force at the chosen point of contact, was not effective against a French defence that retained the capacity to use reserves by redeploying troops by rail during the course of operations. Aside from serious faults in German planning and execution, there were also problems with German equipment and discipline that qualify the usual picture of total German competence. The 'fog of war' discerned by Clausewitz – the distorting impact of circumstances and events on plans – was much in evidence.

The French success in saving Paris and stopping the over-extended, exhausted and poorly-deployed Germans in the battle of the Marne in September 1914 ensured that there would be no speedy end to the war. Unlike in 1870 and 1871, the French also benefited in 1914 from being part of a powerful coalition.

After the battle of the Marne, both sides, in the 'Race to the Sea', unsuccessfully sought to turn their opponent's line, which in the event left a front line now extending from the Alps to the English Channel, the Western Front. France was saved, and Germany was thereafter committed to a two-front war. This made it difficult to shift forces to the east in order to defeat the Russians rapidly, as had been planned. This is a reminder that the German army was more effective at the operational and tactical than at the strategic level, which underlines the questionable character of the customary praise of the German General Staff.

Equally, the French and Russian attempts to mount offensives in 1914 in order to gain the initiative and to seize territory were both heavily defeated by Germany, the Russian invasion of East Prussia being brought to an end by a crushing defeat at Tannenberg on 27–28 August and another defeat at the battle of the Masurian Lakes (7–14 September). German generalship proved superior in benefiting from the flow of the campaign and specifically from the deficiencies of Russian commanders, although these were less acute than are sometimes suggested. As a consequence of the Russian failure, and of the failure of the French offensive in Lorraine, the two-front war did not lead to serious defensive problems for Germany in 1914. The difficulties of mounting offensives successfully were also shown by the failure of the Austrian attack on Serbia.

CONFLICT WITHIN EUROPE

World War One is recalled as a brutal struggle in which millions died in trench warfare to little apparent point. Casualties and casualty rates could indeed be very high. Nearly nine million troops died in the war, including 27 per cent of all Frenchmen between the ages of 18 and 27, while of the 8 million soldiers mobilized by Austria, 1,106,000 died. Of the 332,000 Australian troops who served overseas, many in the unsuccessful Gallipoli operation in 1915, 58,460 were killed and 212,000 were wounded. The greatest killer on the battlefield was artillery – possibly up to 70 per cent of battlefield deaths, followed by machine-guns and rifles. The French 75mm field-gun could fire over fifteen rounds a minute, while German 150mm field howitzers could fire five rounds per minute. Air-burst shrapnel shells increased the deadly nature of artillery fire against which the spread of steel helmets offered little protection.

The stress in much discussion of the war is on impasse and indecisiveness; there are frequent complaints about incompetent commanders and foolish command cultures, and the abiding image is of machine-guns sweeping away lines of attackers. Battles such as Verdun (launched on 21 February 1916), the Somme (launched on 1 July 1916), and Passchendaele (launched on 31 July 1917) are seen as indictments of a particular way of war. In fact, the terrible casualties of the war have made it appear more attritional than was the case (although there were specific engagements such as Verdun, where the Germans attacked largely in order to inflict heavy casualties on the French, that were like this). Once the Germans, after the French counter-attack in the battle of the Marne in September 1914, lost the ability to mount a victorious campaign of manoeuvre on the Western Front, this does not mean that their opponents simply wore them down. Instead, like the Confederates in the American Civil War, the Germans were, in 1918, eventually outfought and defeated, both in offensive and in defensive warfare.

There were significant political reasons why the Western Allies (Britain and France) felt it necessary to attack. As the Germans had ended the 1914 campaign in command of economically important parts of France, it was important for the Western Allies to drive them out. It was also felt necessary to reduce German pressure on Russia in order to prevent the latter from being knocked out of the war, and thus enabling the Germans to concentrate all their forces on the West Front.

The heavy casualties owed much to the war being waged by well-armed industrial powers that were willing and able to deploy much of their young male populations. Despite the repeated failure of military operations on the Western Front to secure their objectives from 1914 to 1917, and the heavy costs of the conflicts, both sides showed the adaptability and endurance of modern industrial societies in continuing a large-scale, long-term war; although the costly failure of the Nivelle offensive, the battle of the Chemin des Dames (16 April–5 May 1917) led about 40,000 French soldiers to mutiny. Had the campaigns been waged in a different manner to trench warfare – been for example more manoeuvrist and less static – there is no reason to assume that casualties would have been lower. Instead, troops would have been more exposed to both offensive and defensive fire.

BOX 5.1 REPORTS ON CONFLICT, 1916

The need to retain domestic support encouraged the censorship of war news, although much of this was self-censorship by the journalists. On 1 July 1916, the first day of the battle of the Somme, the British suffered 38,000 casualties, the heaviest of any one day of their military history, as they launched attacks on a German trench line whose defences had not been suppressed by artillery fire. Dependent on official information which they failed to question, the press provided scant clue to the heavy cost at which limited success had been obtained. John Irvine in the *Daily Express* of 3 July claimed:

> The taking of the first-line trenches . . . was in some places comparatively easy – almost a walkover. It was only when our men bit deeper into the enemy's defences that they were brought face to face with difficulties; but their indomitable pluck and perseverance have triumphed . . . One word of caution . . . it would be altogether premature . . . to assume that the offensive on which the British army has now embarked is a movement which is going very soon to end the war.

He wrote of 'British lions . . . let loose on their prey'.

On 3 July, the *Daily Mail* referred to 'going over the top' as a 'gay, impetuous and irresistible leap from the trenches'. Its correspondent, Beach Thomas, wrote:

> The toll of blood today [1 July] has been fairly heavy, but I am glad to be able to state from reports received that it is by no means excessive, having regard to the magnitude of the day's operations – it is and for many days will continue to be siege warfare, in which a small territorial gain may be a great strategical gain; and the price we must pay is to be judged by another measure than miles or furlongs or booty. We are laying siege not to a place but to the German Army.

John Irvine struck a more candid note in the *Daily Express* of 5 July: 'we are learning gradually how terrible this machine gun fire has been . . . a hail of machine gun bullets which were simply terrific . . . casualties were considerable on the first day of the advance'.

Trench systems served to stabilize the line and protect troops, but once they had been constructed it proved difficult to regain mobility, although the combatants sought to mount decisive attacks that would enable them to do so. In large part, the inability to do so was due not so much to the inherent strength of trench systems as to the force–space ratio on the Western Front. As a result, generals confronted the problems of the strength of the defensive. The available manpower made it possible to hold the front line with strength and to provide reserves, the classic need for all linear defence systems. For the offensive, although they were supplied with plentiful troops which could be sustained in the same area for long periods, generals faced the difficulty of devising an effective tactical system that would not only achieve breakthrough through the opposing trench line but also then be able to sustain and develop it. This was far from easy, not least because of the problem of advancing across terrain badly damaged by shellfire, as well as the difficulties of providing reserves in the correct place, of maintaining the availability of shells for the all-crucial artillery, and of providing adequate information to commanders about developments. Deficiencies in communications fed directly into command problems: the potential of radio was inadequately grasped.

Plate 5.1 *A Night Bombardment*, oil painting by Paul Nash, 1918–19. Conflict at night was a feature of twentieth-century warfare. Seen in the Russo-Japanese War in 1904 and 1905, it was large-scale during World War One. Photo © National Gallery of Canada. Transfer from the Canadian War Memorials, 1921. Image no. 8640.

The same problems were the case on the Isonzo front, where the Italians launched eleven offensives from 1915 to 1917, taking very heavy losses to push the Austrians back only six miles, although at the same time they inflicted serious casualties on their opponents. The Austrians benefited from the defensive potential of the terrain, and from the failure of Italian artillery fire to suppress Austrian defences. These problems were also seen at Gallipoli where, in 1915, British, Australian and New Zealand forces failed to break out from their landing zones in order to clear the Dardanelles and make possible an attack on Constantinople. There were times when Allied breakthrough was possible at Gallipoli, but the failure of Allied tactics helped doom the strategy. The intensity of fire was indicated by General Birdwood who wrote on 18 May: 'We have daily and nightly fights with the Turks, and, indeed, I do not think there has been a single half hour since we landed without a rattle of musketry or shrapnel fire. At night, the former constantly grows into a regular roar, the Turks expending thousands of rounds of ammunition' (AWM 3 DRL/3376, 11/4).

The Allies also suffered in the Gallipoli operation from the degree to which the concentration of troops and munitions on the Western Front ensured that insufficient munitions and high-quality troops were sent to Gallipoli. The flawed assessment of Turkish fighting quality was also an issue, not least as it led to an underrating of a resilience that drew in part on a strong nationalism. A similar operational impasse, rather than the anticipated rapid advance, followed the Allied landing at Salonica in Greece in 1916.

Where the force–space ratio was lower it was harder to ensure concentration and mass to mount offensives on the scale of the Western Front, but, at the same time, weaker defences (especially defences in depth) ensured that it proved possible to achieve breakthroughs, to make major gains and to achieve decisive results. This was particularly the case on the Eastern and Balkan Fronts, on which from 1915 to 1917 the Germans and Austrians captured large swathes of territory and defeated large enemy armies in campaigns of manoeuvre. This was seen for example with the Austrian and German breakthrough against the Russians near Tarnow and Gorlice in Galicia in May 1915: artillery and gas proving more effective than on the Western Front that year. Nevertheless, the Russians were able to fight on and by 1916 the supply problems that had characterized the 1915 campaign had diminished. The Russians fought particularly well against Austria that year, gaining much territory with the Brusilov offensive in June, before German reinforcements stiffened the Austrian resistance.

Several powers were knocked out in the war. Serbia was conquered by attacking Bulgarian, German and Austrian forces in 1915, as was Romania in the autumn of 1916. Russia was knocked out in 1917 as a consequence of the combination of defeat by the Germans and internal problems in sustaining the war; these interacted to create a crisis in support for Tsar Nicholas II (who had assumed personal command of the army) and his replacement by a republican government. Instead of suppressing rioters in the capital, St Petersburg, troops had fraternized with the rioters whose action had supported the formation of an interim government. The Soviet of Workers' Deputies pressed soldiers to take control of their units from the officers and to send representatives to the Soviet. In the face of widespread opposition, the Tsar abdicated on 15 March 1917.

The new government sought to continue the war in order to maintain its treaty obligations, and launched another offensive in Galicia on 30 June 1917, but the Germans maintained their pressure, capturing Riga in August, and the continuation of the war was unpopular and led to a growth in support for the Communists. Large-scale Communist disturbances in July were suppressed by force, but, unable to rely on military support, the government was overthrown by a Communist coup in St Petersburg in November 1917. The new leadership, under Lenin, negotiated the Peace of Brest-Litovsk with Germany the following year, accepting major territorial cessions. This hardly demonstrates the indecisiveness of conflict in this period; indeed, Russia had to accept territorial losses greater than those inflicted on her in any previous war.

Italy was nearly knocked out of the war by the surprise Austro-German Caporetto offensive of October 1917, and might well have fallen but for the dispatch of British and French reinforcements which helped stop their opponents at the Piave Valley. In 1917, German strategy entailed going on the defensive on the Western Front, indeed retreating to a straighter line to free up some forces, knocking out Russia, using unrestricted submarine warfare to weaken Britain, as well as testing new infantry tactics of surprise attack and infiltrating opposing defences against Italy in the Caporetto offensive. This was a gamble, as unrestricted submarine warfare led to America's entry into the war on 2 April 1917, but the Germans hoped it would weaken Britain, and that defeating Russia would enable them to transfer forces to the Western Front, defeating France in 1918 before the USA could make its military might felt. Bringing the USA into the war was a calculated risk that failed, but German military leaders feared the collapse of their allies or of the German homefront, so desperate measures were necessary.

WARFARE OUTSIDE EUROPE

The Allies demonstrated their range with the successful overrunning of the German overseas empire. The one exception here was German East Africa (modern Tanzania), which proved an intractable problem. The war in Africa was very different to that in Europe. The ability to cope with disease was critical, while, given the distances and the nature of transport links, the movement of supplies played a major part. Operationally and tactically, manoeuvre and surprise were crucial in Africa, while firepower was less important than in Europe.

Mobility was also the characteristic of the conflict between the Ottomans (Turks) and the British in Mesopotamia and Palestine, the Russians in the western Caucasus, and the Arabs in Arabia. These conflicts in part related to the German hope that it would be possible to destroy the empires of Germany's competitors, and to the Allied expectation that the Ottoman Empire was the weakest of their opponents. The German leadership planned through war, rebellion or revolution to extend the war, particularly to challenge Britain in Egypt and India, and Russia in the Caucasus. The Ottomans were expected to fight both Britain and Russia, and to provide the leadership for pan-Islamic revolts. In the words of the German diplomat Rudolph Nadolny, these were 'to light a torch from the Caucasus to Calcutta'. Within the Muslim world, however, Ottoman pan-Turkism was widely considered an unacceptable part of pan-Islamism. This was readily apparent in Egypt where German promises of independence required Ottoman troops, and they, in turn, were repelled. The Ottomans were less effective on the offensive than in defence, but even in the latter they were eventually overcome. In Palestine, the Ottomans were defeated by the British from 1917 to 1918, primarily as a result of effective infantry–cavalry co-ordination and a skilful strategy, although tanks and aeroplanes were also used, while cavalry played a major role in the breakthrough.

Warfare outside Europe in this period was not simply between the combatants in World War One, although other conflicts, for example the combination of banditry and regional discontent in the Contestado in Brazil in 1915, tend to be ignored. Some of these conflicts looked towards patterns of warfare that were subsequently to become more prominent. In certain areas there was a continuation of resistance to European imperialism that had begun in response to the original attempts to extend European control. This could be seen with the 1915–16 Volta–Bani War in modern Burkina Faso, then part of French West Africa, the largest military challenge the French had faced in the region since they had conquered it, and one that led to the mobilization of a substantial French force. Although lacking comparable firepower, with consequences seen in battles such as Boho (1916), the rebels sought to develop tactics in order to weaken the French columns, to reduce support for the French, and to limit the impact of their firepower. The French themselves employed 'anti-societal' warfare, targeting their opponents' farms, herds, wells and families in order to destroy the human environment among which they operated. Once the rebels' centres had been subjugated, organized opposition ceased. France also suppressed a revolt in Tunisia from 1915 to 1916, while Britain overran the Sultanate of Darfur in west Sudan in 1916.

The Italians proved less successful in Libya. Their firepower had defeated Libyan forces at Asaba in 1913, but the Libyans then resorted to guerrilla tactics. In 1915, an Italian force of 4,000 troops was largely destroyed after its local auxiliaries turned against it, and the Italians were driven back to the coast. It was not only European resistance that was at stake. The Japanese faced a similar position in the mountained forests of the interior of Taiwan: having been ceded the island by China in 1895, tribesmen continued guerrilla resistance for over three decades. In Tibet, the Dalai Lama responded to the imposition of Chinese control in neighbouring Kham (see p. 85) by sending forces, armed with new rifles from Britain, to the frontier. In 1917 and 1918, they clashed with the Chinese, defeating them. This led to a rising in Kham, but, in the summer of 1918, Tibet and China negotiated a truce leaving Kham under Chinese control.

BOX 5.2 WAR AT SEA, 1914–18

British naval superiority led the German surface fleet to take a cautious position. Within Europe, the German fleet was confined for most of the war to German waters. The major naval battle, Jutland in the North Sea on 31 May 1916, was to be the largest clash of battleships in history. Although outnumbered, the Germans inflicted heavier casualties, with more than 8,500 killed on both sides in just one day. The British suffered from inadequate training, for example in destroyer torpedo attacks, and from command and communication flaws, but, in the big-gun exchange, they avoided the devastating damage suffered by the Russians at Japanese hands at Tsushima in 1905. The damage inflicted on the Germans at Jutland, combined with the maintenance of British naval superiority, led the German surface fleet to follow a very cautious policy for the remainder of the war.

German squadrons and warships outside Europe at the outset of the war were hunted down. By the end of 1914, foreshadowing events in World War Two, the Allies, working in unusual concert, had cracked the three German naval codes. While the Germans seemed oblivious to this, the British navy repeatedly, through slovenliness or mistrust, failed to exploit this advantage to its full potential.

German submarines, not surface shipping, posed the greatest challenge to the Allies. Although these submarines had a limited range compared to those in World War Two, they had a tactical, operational and strategic impact, discouraging operations by surface ships and, more worryingly, threatening the supply routes across the Atlantic on which Britain depended for food and supplies. It was very difficult to detect submerged submarines, and depth charges were only effective if exploded close to the hulls. More seriously, the British had failed to take sufficient precautions to protect merchant shipping, and, by the spring of 1917, the Germans were inflicting very heavy losses on it. Finally, after much resistance from the British Admiralty, convoys were introduced from May 1917, leading to a dramatic reduction in losses: the escorts were able to respond to attacks. By 1918 the rate of tonnage sunk per German submarine lost had fallen. In political terms, the submarine was also disastrous for the Germans: their resumption of unrestricted submarine warfare in 1917 helped bring the USA into the war that April, and the submarines were unable to thwart the consequences: American troops crossed the Atlantic to Europe in 1918.

In contrast, the Allied blockade of Germany, in which the British navy played the key role, undermined the German economy and made it difficult for planners in Berlin to realize schemes for increased industrial production. The blockade also increased the economic importance of Britain to the USA.

CLOSING CAMPAIGN

The general view gives credit for victory to the invention of the tank by the British for helping overcome the impasse on the Western Front, while the Germans are seen as succumbing to domestic dissatisfaction and related problems that owed much to the socio-economic strains arising from the British blockade of Germany.

BOX 5.3 TANKS

Like other new weapons, tanks commanded attention, and indeed they had a capability that other weaponry lacked, especially for flattening barbed wire, the essential accompaniment to trenches. In the first use of massed tanks, near Cambrai, on 20 November 1917, the British made significant advances at the expense of prepared German positions, although, thanks to German artillery fire, 179 of the 378 fighting tanks were destroyed. Furthermore, the British success owed much to a heavy, well-planned artillery bombardment. The following day, when the attack resumed, more tanks were lost as a result of inadequate infantry support. On 8 August 1918 no fewer than 430 British tanks broke through the German lines near Amiens. Tanks could be hit by rifle bullets and machine-guns without suffering damage. A memorandum on the characteristics of new tanks from the headquarters of the British Tank Corps, written on 27 June 1918, noted:

> Trench warfare has given way to field and semi-open fighting . . . the more the mobility of tanks is increased, the greater must be the elasticity of the co-operation between them and the others. The chief power of the tank, both material and moral, lies in its mobility, ie. its pace, circuit, handiness, and obstacle crossing power . . . demands an increased power of manoeuvre on the part of the infantry . . . Though the effect produced by tanks leading forward infantry may be compared to that of the artillery barrage, the infantry should not look upon it as such, but should regard the tanks as armoured fighting patrols or mechanical scouts thrown out in front of them.
>
> (AWM. 3 DRL/6643 5/27)

As was only to be expected of a weapon that had not had a long process of peace-time development and preparation, however, there were major problems with its reliability; these were exacerbated by the shell-damaged terrain across which tanks had to operate. Some of the statements subsequently made on behalf of the wartime impact of the tank, as of aircraft, reflected the competing claims about weapons systems made by their protagonists in the 1920s and 1930s, rather than an informed critical assessment of operations in the war. In 1918, indeed, artillery played a greater role in the Allied success than tanks, although the Allies, unlike the Germans, appreciated the potential of the latter. The Germans deployed tanks in smaller numbers and to less effect than the Allies.

This explanation underrates the importance of the development of tactics able to restore mobility to the Western Front. The balance of resources was also important: the Germans ran out of reserves of troops in 1918, while the Allies had a fresh source of troops as a result of American entry into the war in 1917.

The rise in effectiveness had two major components: first, the Germans developed stormtrooper techniques, using them with considerable success in their spring 1918 offensive. These stormtrooper techniques relied on carefully planned surprise assaults employing infiltration, and focusing on opponents' strong points in order to destroy their cohesion. As a consequence, the Germans won tactical breakthroughs, only to lose the advantage because, due to poor military leadership, they had not thought out how to exploit success militarily or politically. Instead, the Germans assumed they could use shock to force an Allied collapse. In practice, Allied defences in depth helped thwart the Germans, while the offensive also led to heavy German losses which could not be replaced, and to a new extended front line that left them vulnerable to attack.

Secondly, the British focused on improving artillery firepower and accuracy and, more importantly, artillery–infantry co-ordination so that they could dominate the three-dimensional battlefield and apply firepower more effectively than in earlier attacks. In place of generalized firepower there was systematic co-ordination, reflecting precise control of both infantry and massive artillery support, plus improved communications. Their 1918 campaign on the Western Front was a great success in this respect. Wilhelm II abdicated on 9 November and two days later an armistice ended conflict on the Western Front. At the same time, having checked an Austrian attack in June, the Italians advanced anew, driving back the Austrians, who surrendered on 4 November.

CONCLUSIONS

World War One was not the first conflict waged around the world, but it was the first in which speedy communications made it possible to integrate operations rapidly and to plan and deploy resources accordingly. The development of the radio and its use was crucial. In 1899, Guglielmo Marconi transmitted by radio across the English Channel and in 1901 across the Atlantic. Radio networks were created and from 1912 to 1914 the Germans built a network of radio stations in their colonies, only for these to be seized in the opening stages of the war. Instead, it was the Allies who made the most effective use of radio, in particular in order to co-ordinate shipping. The global character of the conflict was also underlined by Japanese participation, and by the major economic and, eventually, military role of the USA. This was very different to the last comparable struggle in Europe: the attempt to resist and, eventually, overcome Napoleonic hegemony.

World War One had major and largely unexpected consequences. The profound political consequences included the fall of the Austrian, German, Russian and Ottoman empires. This created long-term instability across much of Eurasia, as successor regimes sought to benefit from opportunities. The collapse of the Austrian and Ottoman empires led to long-term political problems in the Balkans and the Middle East respectively, while the Communist Soviet Union helped create a bitter ideological struggle across the world.

In addition, the unprecedented mobilizations of resources during the war had serious economic and financial consequences: the costs of the war caused levels of inflation and government debt that challenged the middle classes, as well as the public finances. Social consequences were also important: established ideas and practices were affected by a decline of deference and by the rapidly shifting role of women in the militarized wartime societies. There was a major loss of confidence in political orders, Providence, and the future of mankind. Anti-war feeling developed as just one of the far-reaching consequences. The industrialized mass slaughter of much of the conflict led to a concept of total war that contributed to this anti-war feeling.

CHAPTER 6

Between Two World Wars

INTRODUCTION

The inter-war period is generally underrated in accounts of military history. The focus, in so far as there is one, is on the two world wars, with the inter-war period seen as the sequence to World War One and the preparation for World War Two. Both of these are understood primarily in terms of the major Western powers and the ways in which they sought to overcome the impasse of trench warfare. This is misleading, as the prospect of a resumption of symmetrical warfare between the major powers appeared limited until the 1930s. As so often, the standard approach also neglects the role of conflict outside the West, both by Western and by non-Western powers, as well, more specifically, as the military-political tasks of the Western and non-Western militaries in the shape of civil wars and counter-insurrectionary struggles.

POST-WAR CONFLICT

Far from being the war to end all wars, as was hoped, World War One led into a series of struggles, many of which were large scale. Some of these conflicts related to attempts to implement or affect the peace terms; for example, the Greek intervention in Turkey, which led, in 1922, to the victory of the latter, the expulsion of Greek forces and the flight of ethnic Greeks. The drawing of new state boundaries after World War One led directly to violence as efforts were made to affect the course of these boundaries or as new states were challenged. Thus, the city of

Wilno (Vilnius) was seized in 1920 from the new state of Lithuania by Polish forces, while the Polish attempt to control their Ukrainian minority was challenged by the terrorism of the Organization of Ukrainian Nationalists. Other conflicts were of different origin – for example, the struggle between Irish republicanism and British forces.

The widest-ranging post-war struggle, the Russian Civil War, stemmed from World War One, the pressures of which had led to the revolutionary overthrow of the ruling Romanov dynasty in 1917. The subsequent civil war between the Bolsheviks (Communists) and their opponents was complicated by international intervention against the former, particularly by Britain, France, Japan, Poland and the USA. These interventions, however, were by states exhausted by the recent world war, and many of their troops, especially the British and the French, were keen to be demobilized. Furthermore, the international forces hit at the peripheries of Russia and were not deployed against the centres of Bolshevik power. This was particularly true of the large Japanese force sent to the Russian Far East.

The Civil War was won by the Bolsheviks, who benefited greatly from the divisions among their opponents and from the unpopularity of the 'White', or anti-Bolshevik, cause with the peasantry, who saw scant reason to welcome

Plate 6.1 Red Army troops during the Russian Civil War remove a portrait of the deposed Tsar Nicholas II. The Red Army gave force to internal transformation. I. Vladimiroff watercolour, Anne S.K. Brown Collection.

counter-revolution. The White generals did not understand how to win popular support and therefore could not mobilize the anti-Bolshevik majority. The Whites also suffered from serious supply difficulties for which help from the foreign interventionist powers could not compensate. Furthermore, the Bolsheviks held Moscow and St Petersburg and, with them, the central position in Russia and the industrial centres and communication nodes. Furthermore, their position was a compact one. In contrast, the White generals, Kolchak from Siberia, Denikin and later Wrangel from the Crimea and Ukraine, and Yudenich from Estonia, failed to co-ordinate their advances on Moscow.

Like the French revolutionaries from 1792, the Bolsheviks overcame their oppositional tendencies and created a new state and military system reliant on force and centralized control in order to direct resources ruthlessly. Terror, deployed by the All-Russian Extraordinary Commission for Struggle Against Sabotage and Counter-Revolution, or Cheka, established in December 1917, helped greatly in suppressing real or potential opposition to requisitioning and other measures. At the same time, Bolsheviks showed an expedient willingness to compromise in order to achieve their goals: far from rejecting hierarchy, the Red Army restored it alongside conscription and the death penalty. Indeed, about 30,000 ex-Tsarist officers were employed.

Opposition to the Bolsheviks was encountered not only from the Whites but also from the left, and from the peasantry – the Greens. A left-wing rising in Moscow in July 1918 was suppressed, and in early 1921 the sailors and workers on the Kronshtat island naval base outside St Petersburg rose against the government: troops advancing across the ice restored state control. Peasant opposition to the Bolsheviks reflected the burden of the war, the exactions of the new regime, and opposition to its determination to control rural life. Much of this opposition, especially in the Volga valley, was large scale, and its repression involved a significant deployment of government forces. They also compromised by introducing the New Economic Policy in 1921: allowing the peasants to trade in food.

The Russian Civil War also entailed efforts by the Bolshevik government, thwarted in their hopes of world revolution, to regain control by force of regions where non-Russian ethnic groups had sought to win independence. Russian control was reimposed in the Caucasus, Central Asia and the Ukraine, but not in the Baltic states (Estonia, Latvia, Lithuania), which were not conquered until 1940, nor in Finland or Poland. In Finland and the Baltic states, local Bolsheviks were defeated in civil wars. Russia signed peace treaties with the new republics in 1920.

The Russo-Polish war in 1920 demonstrated the characteristics of the warfare of the period: it was very mobile, both militarily and politically, and this type of warfare was to be as common as the fixed sides that tend to dominate modern conceptions of twentieth-century warfare. Attacking in April, the Poles overran western Ukraine, capturing Kiev, but a Soviet counter-attack led to an advance to close to Warsaw, before a successful Polish counter-attack drove the Soviets back in August. Lenin had hoped that the Polish working class would support the Red Army and lead to an advance that would secure revolution in Germany, but this proved as much wishful thinking as the hopes of the French Revolutionaries in the 1790s.

Where it occurred, the imposition of Russian control was accompanied and followed by large-scale violence against groups judged hostile to the Communist cause which, in Ukraine, led to genocidal policies in the early 1930s. The 1924 constitution of the Soviet Union gave nationalities the right of secession, but there was to be no chance of exercising this.

The victorious powers of World War One were challenged not only in Russia but also in their colonies. The world war took Western imperialism to unsurpassed heights, but also helped foster the dissolution of the empires as it weakened them in both metropole (home bases) and colonies, and also fostered the spread of ideas, both nationalism and Communism, that were to be the cause of major weakness. The colonies of the victorious powers had expanded as a result of the allocation of German and Ottoman territories in the peace settlement, a distribution of colonies that reflected the determination of the victorious imperial powers to expand their territorial control of the world. The German territories in Africa and the Pacific were granted as mandates, in the first principally to Britain and France, and the latter largely to Japan. Britain gained mandates over German East Africa and parts of Togo and Cameroon, France over most of Togo and Cameroon, Japan over the Caroline, Mariana and Marshall Islands, Australia over German New Guinea and the Bismarck Archipelago, New Zealand over Western Samoa, and South Africa over South-West Africa (now Namibia). Mandated territories meant that rule was answerable to the League of Nations, a permanent body for international arbitration set up after World War One in order to prevent future wars – but, in practice, they were colonies.

Similarly much of the Ottoman Empire was allocated to Britain (Iraq, Palestine, Transjordan) or France (Lebanon, Syria). There was resistance, but much of it was overcome. Arab rule in Damascus was brought to an end in July 1920 as a French army advanced on it from Beirut. In Transjordan, the British found themselves faced by internecine tribal conflict and having to adopt the Ottoman role of defending settled areas against nomadic raiders. As a result, a force of cavalry and machine-gunners recruited from Circassians used by the Ottomans to this end was established by the British in Amman, and this became what was known as the 'Reserve Force'. This was an instance of the extent to which Western powers found themselves inheriting a difficult legacy. This continues to be the case today, as the Americans and British discovered in Iraq in 2003 and 2004.

It proved harder than anticipated to control the situation in the Middle East in the 1920s. A combination of already-established anti-Western feeling and the spread of a new impulse of reaction against imperial authority affected large portions of the colonial world. This was particularly intense in the Muslim world. Opposition had varied causes and consequences. It included hostility to British hegemony in Egypt, Iraq and Persia (Iran), a rising against French rule in Syria, the continuation of resistance in Libya to the rule Italy had sought to impose since 1911, an upsurge from 1921 in action against Spanish attempts to dominate the part of Morocco allocated to it (an opposition that spread into French Morocco), and the Turkish refusal to accept a peace settlement that included Greek rule over the Aegean coast and European troops in Constantinople.

The Western powers were willing to use considerable force to maintain their imperial challenge. In Syria, the French shelled and bombed Damascus in 1925 and 1926, while the British used the air power they had developed in World War One to strike at opponents and to overawe dissidence in Afghanistan, Iraq, South Yemen and British Somaliland. Anticipating arguments made by American advocates of air power in the 1990s and 2000s, air attack was seen as a rapid response combining firepower and mobility; it did not entail the deployment of large forces. In northern Morocco, the Spaniards used large quantities of mustard gas, dropped by air on civilians and fighters alike; heavy casualties resulted. Albeit after considerable difficulties, and largely due to French intervention, opposition to the Spaniards was brutally suppressed from 1925 to 1927. So also was the anti-French rising in Syria, and, in the East Indies, that against the Dutch in Java. In Libya, the Italians expanded their control, while in the Italian Somaliland the Sultanate of Obbia was overrun.

Elsewhere there was failure. The Turks under Kemal Atatürk, their commander-in-chief, were able to impose their will after defeating the poorly equipped and supplied French in south-east Turkey from 1921 to 1922 (one of the most conspicuous forgotten conflicts of the century) and the Greeks in west Turkey in 1922 (capturing Smyrna/Izmir in September), and facing down the British in Constantinople in September and October 1922. Indeed, Britain, the world's leading imperial power, decided that it had exceeded its grasp. Commitments in Egypt, Iraq, Russia and Persia were abandoned, Egypt being acknowledged as an independent kingdom in 1922, and the British prepared for more self-government in India. Similarly, France found that it was confronting too many problems. It had relatively few troops available for service in Turkey because of its commitments in Morocco.

This abandonment of aspirations and positions was more than the usual situation of needing to assess commitments carefully. Instead, it marked the start of the ebb of European empire. As with many other important shifts in global power, this was a recognition of military capability, both absolute and relative, that did not essentially arise from the results of conflict, and certainly not large-scale conflict, but that was as important as any war. Emphasis on the weaknesses of imperial power in the inter-war period both serves as a valuable corrective to any focus largely on military developments within Europe and on preparations for World War Two, and also looks towards the situation after 1945.

Failure was also seen closer to home. The Versailles peace settlement had included provisions for Germany to pay reparations to the Allies, but a refusal to do so led France and Belgium to send troops into the industrial Ruhr region from 1923 to 1924 in order to pursue the unilateral option of collecting the money directly. Unable to resist formally, the Germans did so passively, ensuring that the occupiers failed to derive the benefits they sought and, instead, withdrew. Their need to rely on German co-operation emerged clearly from the crisis, and led to the Locarno settlement in 1924.

The military difficulties Britain faced in its colonies varied, but a common theme was the problem posed by irregulars who could not be readily differentiated from the civilian populace. Ireland in 1921 provides a particularly instructive example of the difficulty of suppressing such a force, because it was the part of the empire that had been longest under British control and the sole part represented in Parliament. The Irish Republican Army (IRA), a violent nationalist force, drawing its support from much (but by no means all) of the Catholic majority, organized its active service units into flying columns that staged raids and ambushes in order to undermine the stability of British government. Assassinations and sabotage were also employed. The IRA was short of arms (many of which were gained by raids on the British, while the Thompson submachine gun came from the USA), and was outnumbered by the army and the police, but it was able to take the initiative and to benefit from the limited options available to those trying to restore control. The murder of about a hundred Protestants in the south helped terrorize the bulk of the Protestant community, many of whom fled. British reprisals against Catholic civilians were limited, but sapped support for British rule within Ireland among the Catholic majority, and most of the island was granted independence in the Anglo-Irish treaty of December 1921.

Ironically, the IRA then divided, leading to a civil war in the new Irish Free State that was won by the pro-treaty forces, in part because the government was willing to take a firmer line than the British had done, not least with the trial and execution of prisoners. In the North (most of the former province of Ulster), which remained part of Britain, the application of force helped entrench the Protestant establishment.

Irregulars also played a major role in the post-war instability of the defeated powers. This led to violence on the streets of Berlin in January 1919 as right-wing veterans in the Freikorps smashed an attempt by the pro-Communist Spartacist League to seize power. That year, there was civil warfare in Hungary with the fall of the Communist government of Bela Kun accompanied by a Romanian invasion.

CIVIL WAR IN CHINA

Consideration of the scale of conflict in China in the 1920s and 1930s serves again as a corrective to any focus on the contemporary situation within Europe. Much of this conflict appears obscure from the latter perspective, but, from the viewpoint of the early twenty-first century, the history of China seems of much greater relevance, while, in terms of the scale of conflict, these were the largest wars of the 1920s. In the inter-war period, the defeat of regionalism, in the shape of the warlords, was a key development in Chinese history, as it left the Guomindang (Chinese Nationalists) and Communists to battle for control over a country that both wished to keep united.

The role of the warlords is a reminder of the folly of considering modern warfare in terms of modern states. Instead, the divisive tendencies seen in countries such as Lebanon, Afghanistan, Angola and Congo towards the close of the twentieth century were also present earlier and helped to provoke civil conflict. The Chinese warlords were an echo of long-standing regionalism within China, especially tensions between north and south, as well as of developments prior to the Republican uprising of 1911–12 that overthrew the Manchu Imperial dynasty when regional military units had gained greater autonomy. Purchasing modern weapons from Europe in the 1920s, especially from France and Italy, the warlords had plenty of artillery and other arms, including aircraft. Despite the absence of traditional stable state structures, the warlords were able to raise and maintain large armies: that of Wu Peifu was 170,000 strong in 1924, while in 1928 Zhang Zuolin, the Manchurian warlord, and his allies deployed 400,000 men against the Nationalists' 700,000.

Like the Russian Civil War, conflict in China in this period indicated that mobility had not been lost due to increases in firepower, as was suggested by the Western Front in World War One. Politics was also crucial: again, unlike World War One, combat was supplemented by negotiations, and the latter, especially defections by generals, played a major role in ensuring success. Thus, it was necessary to create an impression of victory in order to win.

As commander of the Nationalist forces, Jiang Jieshi (Chiang Kai-shek), who had been trained in the Soviet Union, commanded the Northern Expedition: this was a drive north from Guangshou (Canton) against independent warlords that began in 1926, and that benefited from Soviet military advisers, money and equipment. Jiang reached the Yangzi river that year, defeating Wu Peifu in Hunan and Sun Chuanfang in Jiangxi. In 1927 he captured Nanjing and Shanghai, and defeated Zhang Zuolin. Jiang's forces occupied Beijing in 1928, agreed terms in Manchuria, and, from 1929 to 1930, defeated two powerful warlords, Yan Xishan of Shanxi and Feng Yuxiang of Shaanxi. Excluding Manchuria, most of China was now under the Nationalists. Japanese interventions against the Northern Expedition in 1927 and 1928, the two Shantung interventions, had failed to prevent this consolidation. Jiang's success, however, had depended in part on the co-operation of other warlords, and tension with them continued. Indeed, from 1935 to 1937 the government suppressed those in the south and south-west.

The Communists proved more intractable foes for the Nationalists, both militarily and politically, and China witnessed the ideological conflict that was so important to the nature of war during the century, and that was far from being a 'cold war' (confrontation short of large-scale conflict) in East Asia, either before or after World War Two. The challenge from the Communists was affected by serious divisions over strategy among the latter, while these divisions were in turn influenced by military developments. Urban Communists followed the traditional interpretation of Marxism-Leninism, seeking to exploit the revolutionary potential of urban workers, while Mao Zedong more correctly perceived that the real exploited class were farm labourers. In 1927, the Chinese Communists formed the Red Army. Initially, it suffered from a policy of trying to capture and hold towns, which only provided the Nationalists with easy targets. In 1927 the Communists were swiftly driven out of the port of Shantou after they captured it, and were defeated when they attacked the city of Changsha. They captured the latter in 1930, only to be rapidly driven from it with heavy losses.

The Red Army was more successful in resisting attack in rural areas. There it could trade space for time and harry its slower-moving opponent, especially as the Nationalists lacked much peasant support. This led to the failure of Jiang Jieshi's 'bandit extermination campaigns', launched in December 1930, February and July 1931, and March 1933, to destroy the Communist control of much of Jiangxi province. These were major operations: in the fourth campaign, Jiang deployed 250,000 men. In 1933, he was persuaded to modify his strategy by German military advisers provided by Hitler: in place of the frontal attacks, which had proved so costly in the spring, there was a reliance on blockade in the fifth campaign, which began in October 1933. The Communists tried, and failed, to thwart this strategy by conventional warfare and, instead, in October 1934, decided to abandon Jiangxi in the famous Long March to Shaanxi in the north of China.

The Western European powers had less of an impact on China in the 1920s and 1930s than they had during the Taiping rebellion in the 1850s and 1860s. Unlike during the Opium Wars, Britain now could do little to protect its extensive commercial interests in China. Instead, the principal foreign intervention was by Japan and the Soviet Union. Whereas in 1860 British and French forces had occupied Beijing, in 1929 Soviet forces invaded Manchuria. Well-trained, and using modern artillery, tanks, and, in particular, planes, they defeated Zhang Zuolin's son and successor Zhang Xueliang, inflicting heavy casualties. In turn, in the 1930s, the Japanese made the key moves in Manchuria and then in China.

ELSEWHERE IN THE THIRD WORLD

Other 'Third World' states also found that their principal challenges in the 1920s were internal divisions rather than international conflicts, although the Chaco War between Bolivia and Paraguay from 1932 to 1935 was the leading conflict in Latin America. Elsewhere in the continent, armies tended to support authoritarian regimes, as with the establishment of the *Estado Novo* in Brazil in 1937. To face problems, governments built up their armies and also sought to adopt Western technology. In Persia, in 1921, Riza Khan, a Russian-trained colonel in the Persian Cossack Brigade, suppressed internal rebellions and seized power. He created a new and disciplined national army, 40,000 men strong, the loyalty of which he gained by better equipment, regular pay, and success, and used it to crush opposition. Campaigns from 1922 to 1925 spread governmental power throughout Persia, and the disunited tribes were defeated. Dissidence in Mashhad, Tabriz, Gilan and Kurdistan was crushed, and Khuzistan in the south-west was occupied in 1924. Riza Khan was crowned shah in 1926.

Thereafter, the position of the Persian tribes was further weakened by disarming them and forcibly introducing taxation and conscription, so that conscripted tribesmen could be used against other tribesmen. With these advantages, major tribal rebellions were crushed in 1929 and 1932. The tribesmen suffered heavily from the improved mobility of their opponents. Armoured cars and lorries operated on new roads and were supported by the automatic weapons and observation planes of government forces. The combination of technology, organization and political skill shifted the historic balance between the tribes and regular forces, a particular instance of the more general tension between periphery and centre.

Inside neighbouring Iraq, army expansion was supported by nationalists as a way to integrate the new state, which had emerged from the ruins of the Ottoman Empire. In 1933, the tribes had about 100,000 rifles, the army only 15,000, but conscription was introduced in 1934 and the army was able to break the military power of its disunited opponents. In 1933 the Assyrians (Nestorian Christians) were defeated, and in 1935 tribal uprisings were suppressed.

New technology played a role in 'Third World' conflict. In Ethiopia, a tank was employed to help thwart a coup in 1928 while, the following year, bombing runs with a triplane flown by a Frenchman over a terrified rebel army helped to cause it to flee in disorder. In Saudi Arabia, Chevrolet trucks equipped with machine-guns were used to provide mobile firepower, while in Afghanistan, in the late 1930s, British-supplied light bombers were employed to help the ground forces of the ruler, Mohammed Zahir Shah, suppress rebellions. Nevertheless, most of these forces were poorly armed. Ethiopia had a large army, but most of their rifles and artillery were antiquated and there was a lack of standardization.

The limitations of the Ethiopian military were to be cruelly exposed in battles with invading Italian forces in 1935 and 1936. The Italians deployed over 200,000 troops to attack in 1935. The conquest of Ethiopia from 1935 to 1936, however, led not to ready control but to a resistance movement that in part was a product of the harshness of Italian occupation in 1936 and 1937. This was a resistance of ambushes and surprise attacks on precarious Italian supply routes, which the Italians countered by building forts and by the recruitment of local troops.

THE BRITISH EMPIRE IN THE 1930s

It was not only 'Third World' states that faced opposition. Britain, the leading imperial power, also faced a series of problems, including an Arab rising in Palestine from 1936 to 1938, and serious opposition in Waziristan on the North-West Frontier of the British Empire of India. Yet, the British were able to deploy substantial forces to meet both these challenges. The British were helped greatly by the size of the Indian army. As a result, they did not need to raise large numbers of troops in Britain, and thus could do without conscription. Although the severe worldwide economic depression of the 1930s exacerbated political strains within the British Empire, helping, for example, to cause a rebellion in the Irrawaddy delta region of Burma, based on a politico-religious rejection of British rule, it did not lead to a breakdown of imperial control. Signs of imperial vitality included the building of a major naval base at Singapore designed to provide a support for British power and influence in East Asian waters, and to protect the axis of British imperial power across the Indian Ocean from the Suez Canal via India to Australia, and, specifically, to provide a check on Japanese naval strength.

Far from empire being dead, the demands of imperial protection and policing helped determine the military tasking of the imperial powers, especially Britain, and, therefore, their planning and force structures. Partly for that reason, subsequent criticism that not enough was done to prepare for a major war with another Western power, as it turned out Germany in World War Two from 1939, is

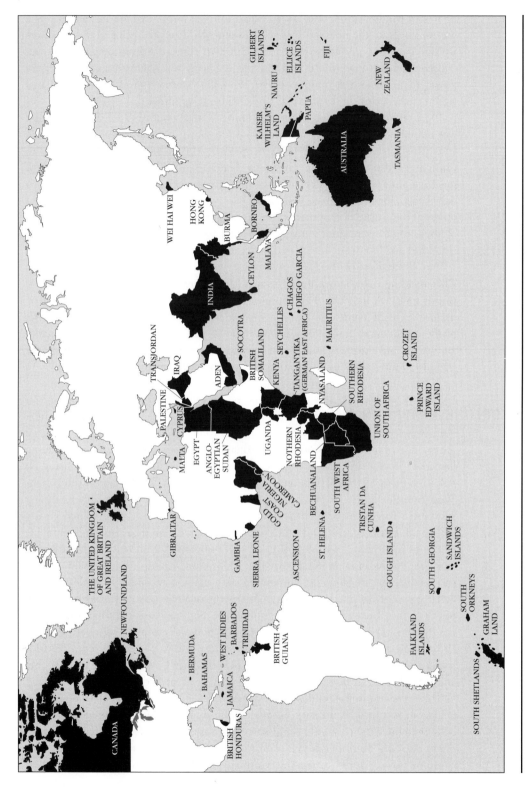

Map 6.1 The British Empire in 1920. In 1919 Britain acquired as Mandates the former German Colonies of Togo, Cameroon, Nauru, Tanganyika, German South West Africa (to South Africa) and Kaiser Wilhelm's land (to Australia). From *The Routledge Atlas of British History* (2003), 3rd edition, by Martin Gilbert, p. 103. © Routledge/Taylor & Francis Informa.

somewhat misplaced. In the 1920s there appeared scant likelihood of this, and the major danger to British interests seemed the improbable one of the Soviets advancing through Afghanistan against India. In the early 1930s the leading power that was the most aggressive, Japan in Manchuria, was one that could only have been influenced by Britain by naval pressure, and, without American support, this was not viable. In contrast, the British army took little role in planning for confrontation with Japan. It was not until the obvious rise of the power and aggression of Nazi Germany under Adolf Hitler from the mid-1930s that the situation changed, and that the British focused on the possibility of another war in Europe. France had prepared earlier, with the construction of a major system of fortifications, the Maginot Line, designed to resist German attack, but was also concerned about the imperial situation.

THE USA

The same was true of the USA. Having fought in World War One, and intervened unsuccessfully in the Russian Civil War, the Americans deployed their power in the 1920s and early 1930s in order to further their interests in Central America and the West Indies, both part of the 'informal' American empire. American forces occupied the Dominican Republic and Haiti for much of the period. The marines sent to support American interests in Nicaragua from 1928 to 1933, in a struggle with rebels using guerrilla tactics, benefited from close air support, although it proved impossible to defeat the rebels. Tasks in the region did not require the development of the tank forces that were to be used against Germany in World War Two; nor did concern about Japan and, in particular, its potential challenge to the American position in the Philippines. This was seen as best protected by naval strength, although air power played a part both in plans for the defence of the Philippines and in operations in the Western hemisphere.

NAVAL DEVELOPMENTS

The rise in American and Japanese naval power and growing concern about strength in East Asian and Western Pacific waters were part of a major shift in maritime capability and priorities away from confrontations between Western European powers, particularly Britain and France from the 1680s to the 1890s, and Britain and Germany in the 1900s and 1910s. There was also a debate about how far air power had changed the situation at sea, both within range of land-based aircraft and with reference to aircraft carriers; and, more specifically, whether it had made the battleship less valuable, as World War Two was indeed to suggest. Naval arms limitation treaties (Washington 1922 and London 1930) governed what the leading powers could do in most categories of naval construction, at least until 1936 when the international arms limitation regime ended.

In the inter-war period, the USA and Japan made the greatest advances with naval aviation and aircraft carriers; more so than Britain, France and, in particular,

Italy and Germany, in all of which the stress remained on battleships and battle-cruisers. Improvements in aircraft, as well as more specific developments in carrier aviation, such as arrester hooks for landings, helped ensure that carriers, rather than seaplanes or airships, were seen as the way to apply air power at sea, and made it easier to envisage using carriers for operational and strategic tasks. In the 1920s, water-cooled aircraft engines were replaced by the lighter and more reliable air-cooled engine. The manoeuvrability, speed and range of carrier aircraft all improved. In 1927 the American fleet exercises included a carrier attack on Pearl Harbor, its own main Pacific Fleet base. The Japanese, meanwhile, had completed an experimental carrier in 1922. They established a separate aviation bureau and, in the 1930s, their aircraft industry produced very effective planes.

Nevertheless, battleships continued to play a central role in American and Japanese naval thinking. This left the proponents of other weaponry having to explain how their recommendations, such as carriers and submarines, would effectively combine with battleships. Under the Marusan Programme of 1937, the Japanese began to build the *Yamato* and *Musahi*, which were to be the most power-ful battleships in the world. In the USA, keels were laid for four comparable 45,000-tonne battleships in 1941.

Naval planners were very interested in the use of submarines, whose size, speed and range rapidly improved, while the range of torpedoes also increased. The American S class of 1918–21, with a range of 5,000–8,000 miles at a surface speed of ten knots, was replaced by the B class (12,000 miles at eleven knots), the P-boats of 1933–36 – the first American submarines with a totally diesel-electric propulsion, and the Gato class introduced in 1940: double-hulled, all-welded-hull submarines with a range of 11,800 miles and a surface speed of 20–25 knots. By the time of the Japanese attack on Pearl Harbor in 1941, the American navy had 111 submarines in commission and the Japanese had sixty-three ocean-going submarines.

AIR POWER

The role of air power in World War One had led to a major interest in devel-oping its potential, which accorded with a more general fascination with the transforming character of flight. Advocates of air power on land claimed that it had dramatically changed the nature of war and that bombers could be employed not merely to influence the flow of battle and campaign but also, as a strategic arm, to attack, indeed incapacitate, enemy industry and communications, and to sway an opponent's domestic opinion by bombing its cities. These arguments were pushed hard by air power theorists, especially Guilio Douhet, William Mitchell and Hugh Trenchard. An emphasis on the capacity of air power was especially conducive to those who supported a separate service organization of air power, which in Britain led to the formation of the Royal Air Force (RAF). From 1918 until 1929 Trenchard was the first chief of the air staff of the RAF. This emphasis, however, led to a downplaying of close air support as a goal.

In the USA, the stress was on heavy or strategic bombers, and this led to confidence, even complacency, that deploying B-17s in the Philippines would give a vital advantage in the event of war with Japan. American air doctrine argued that heavy bombers, protected by their own armament of machine-guns and flying in close formation in order to provide mutual support, would be able to drive off interception by fighters, a view that was to be proved wrong in daytime missions over Germany in 1943.

Under Hitler, there was a major emphasis in Germany on the development of the air force or Luftwaffe, but, in particular, on twin-engined bombers, not longer-range four-engined aircraft. A preference for sheer numbers of planes led in Germany to a lack of a balanced expenditure that would include investment in infrastructure, although the Germans were also affected by the limitations of their aero-engine industry. They were to use the Luftwaffe as mobile artillery – for tactical support at the front of the army's advance.

In the 1930s a marked improvement in the flying standards and combat characteristics of planes led to an increase in their range and armament. Improvements in fighters, which led in Britain to the development of the Spitfire and the Hurricane, began to undermine the doctrine of the primacy of the bomber, and the introduction of radar on the eve of World War Two was another blow to the latter.

BOX 6.1   THE JAPANESE IN CHINA, 1931–41

The major war in the 1930s occurred neither in Europe nor in a European colony, and also did not involve a Western power. From 1931 to 1932, Japan conquered China's northernmost region and key industrial zone, Manchuria, and in 1937 full-scale war broke out between Japan and China. In Manchuria and China, the Japanese showed that it was not necessary to introduce mass-mechanization in order to conquer large tracts of territory, the lesson that might otherwise appear to emerge from the German campaigns in Europe from 1939 to 1941. Because Japan was technologically behind the Western powers in various aspects of military innovation, such as the use of tanks, there was a greater stress on 'spirit' over *matériel*, for example with an emphasis on the use of bayonets in attack. Helped by the absence of hostile foreign intervention, and (unlike from December 1941) by the lack of other conflicts to absorb their attention, the Japanese expanded their commitment after seizing Manchuria, making further gains in China, until, in 1937, they launched what became an all-out war of conquest, although it was formally termed 'an incident'. Unlike in 1931, the Chinese government responded, ensuring that full-scale war broke out. The Japanese made major gains: the important cities of Beijing, Shanghai and Nanjing in 1937, and those of Canton and Wuhan in 1938.

However, despite expanding their army from 408,000 troops in 1937 (from when military expenditure shot up) to 2.08 million in 1941, and stationing over 1.5 million

continued

of these troops in China and Manchuria, the Japanese lacked the manpower to seize all of China and, even within occupied areas, their control outside the cities was limited. Japanese military leaders had failed to appreciate the difficulties of imposing victory. It proved far easier to destroy the Chinese navy in 1937 and to deploy overwhelming force against cities, than it was to fight in rural areas. There, the ratio of strength and space told against the Japanese, particularly when their opponents, most notably the Communists, employed guerrilla tactics and hit Japanese communications.

The political strategy, which drew heavily on racist attitudes towards the Chinese, was also inappropriate. The Japanese failed to incorporate local elites into their imperial system on any large scale: the support they did obtain was useful, but this also highlighted how limited it was. Japanese policies, such as the 'kill all, loot all, burn all' campaign launched in 1941, also showed that brutality did not work. Earlier, the massacre by Japanese forces of large numbers of civilians after the capture of Nanjing in 1937, including using people for bayonet practice, did not break Chinese morale and, instead, testified to an emerging immoral and callous attitude within the Japanese military. Imbued with racist attitudes, the Germans were to match this during World War Two, especially in Eastern Europe, and with similar consequences in terms of a failure to win over local support.

GERMAN REARMAMENT

The catalyst to a focusing of military attention on conflict between the major powers in Europe was the rise of Adolf Hitler to power in Germany in 1933 and his proclaimed determination in 1935 to ensure a wholesale overthrow of the Versailles peace settlement at the close of World War One, which had led to the loss of territory (most sensitively to Poland) as well as to serious prescribed limitations on German military strength. The resulting fears of war were accentuated by the bellicosity and aggressive policies of his allies: Fascist Italy under its dictator, Benito Mussolini, who had expansionist ambitions in the Balkans, the Mediterranean, and North and East Africa, and Japan which in the 1930s had a militaristic government. All three powers sought a new territorial order that responded to their sense of political and ethnic ranking, and they were to form the alliance known as the Axis.

The Germans made much of their commitment to military mechanization and created the first three panzer (armoured) divisions in 1935. These were designed to give effect to the doctrine of armoured warfare that was developed in Germany, in particular by Heinz Guderian. Initially drawing heavily on Britain's use of tanks in World War One, and on subsequent British thought, especially that of J.F.C. Fuller, the Germans developed their own distinctive ideas in the late 1930s. The Germans planned to use tanks in mass in order to achieve a deep breakthrough, rather than employing them, as the French did, as a form of mobile artillery in support of infantry. The panzer divisions were to seize the initiative, to move swiftly, and to be made more effective by being combined arms units incorporating artillery and infantry. Indeed, tanks were to be the cutting-edge of the successful 'lightning strike' German *blitzkrieg* operations from 1939 to 1941 at the expense of Poland (1939), the Netherlands (1940), Belgium (1940), France (1940), Yugoslavia (1941) and Greece (1941).

German ideas reflected the extent to which commanders and commentators alike sought to learn not only from World War One but also from subsequent conflicts, as the impact of new technology suggested that there was no fixed point for the learning of lessons. Thus the course of the Spanish Civil War of 1936–39 was scrutinized carefully, although all too often commentators mistakenly perceived the effectiveness that they sought.

The German emphasis on the offensive was not matched in British or French planning for war in Europe. The emphasis for the last was on defence, and, impressed by the strength of defensive fortifications revealed during World War One, France heavily fortified its German and Italian borders, while seeking to match Italy's development of its naval strength in the Mediterranean. The Soviet military made important advances in planning for large-scale offensive tank warfare, developing ideas for exploiting the potential mobility of tanks; but the army's cohesion was wrecked by the purges launched in 1937 by the Soviet dictator Joseph Stalin which led to widespread slaughter in senior military ranks. This resulted in a new caution in Soviet military leadership that entailed a rejection of the ideas for tank warfare. The purges greatly affected the performance of the Red Army against the Finns in 1939 and 1940, although the competence of General Zhukov led to victory in a major border clash with Japanese forces based in Manchuria in August 1939. The Soviet Union posed a serious complication to planners prior to the outbreak of World War Two. It appeared a wild card: neither pro-German nor pro-Western.

The second and third-rank European powers could not afford to invest heavily in mechanization and, therefore, did not pursue ambitious military strategies at the cutting-edge of capability. Instead, armies such as that of Romania, however large, remained essentially infantry forces with limited fighting power. Such forces were to play mostly only supporting roles in World War Two. Despite Mussolini's ambitions, this was also to be true of Italy.

CONCLUSIONS

It is all too easy to trace links between pre-war priorities in the 1920s and 1930s and the fate of combatants in World War Two, especially in its early campaigns, and to suggest, as a result, that these priorities were mistaken. To do so ignores the extent to which there were major changes in political goals and alliances, both before and during the war, and, as a consequence, unexpected military requirements. Thus, the need for the amphibious capability deployed by Britain and the

USA to invade Normandy on D-Day in 1944 was far from apparent until after the German conquest of France in 1940. Rather than assuming obvious demands, it is appropriate to note the variety of requirements in the inter-war years, especially colonial policing; and also to consider the range of conflict in a period that was far from inter-war for many, especially in China.

BOX 6.2   THE SPANISH CIVIL WAR, 1936–39

The major conflict in Europe between the Russian Civil War and World War Two arose as the result of an attempted coup against the left-wing government of Spain launched in July 1936, by a group of right-wing army officers (led from September 1936 by Francisco Franco) who called themselves the Nationalists. The partial success of the coup led to a long, bitter and ideological civil war which attracted both foreign intervention (Italian and German assistance to the Nationalists, Soviet to the Republicans) and attention from commentators interested in observing the changing nature of warfare. The use of air power earned particular attention. The spectacular terror bombing of civilian targets, such as Madrid (1936), Guernica (1937) and Barcelona (1938), by German and Italian planes did not actually play a significant role in the result of the conflict, but it captured the imagination of many, sowing fears, for example in Britain, that the bombing of civilian targets would be decisive in a future war as it would break civilian morale.

German and Italian assistance, especially the supply of artillery and aircraft, was important to the Nationalists, but, in the end, the divided and poorly commanded Republicans were outfought. In the important battle of Brunete in July 1937, the Republicans revealed an inexpert use of artillery and tanks, as well as poor co-ordination between the arms. Northern Spain was overrun by the Nationalists in 1937, and they drove through Aragon to the Mediterranean the following April, before capturing Barcelona on 26 January 1939 and Madrid on 28 March 1939. This led to the fall of the republic. Under Franco's dictatorship, large numbers suspected of opposition were executed.

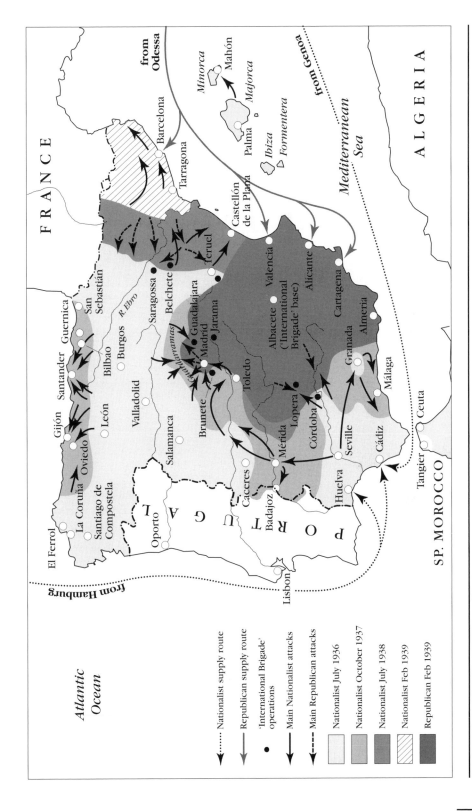

Map 6.2 The Spanish Civil War, 1936–39. After *The Times Atlas of World History* (1993), p. 264. © BCA by arrangement with Time Books.

Legend:
- ······· Nationalist supply route
- ——— Republican supply route
- • 'International Brigade' operations
- ——→ Main Nationalist attacks
- – – → Main Republican attacks
- Nationalist July 1936
- Nationalist October 1937
- Nationalist July 1938
- Nationalist Feb 1939
- Republican Feb 1939

World War Two, 1939–45

INTRODUCTION

World War Two was unique. It has been the sole war to involve all the major powers: unlike in World War One, China was a serious combatant and Japan played a major role, while the USA was directly involved for much of the conflict and in both the European and the Pacific theatres. Due to the powers involved, the geography of the war was also different, with far more of an emphasis on the Pacific and on East and South-East Asia than in World War One. Furthermore, unlike in World War One, air power was important from the outset, not only to land conflict but also to war at sea, as well as in its own strategic terms in the shape of bombing campaigns.

The scale of World War Two ensures that it is often taken to represent total war, which is understandable. Less reasonable has been a tendency to underrate the diversity of the war. Alongside the full-scale conventional conflict that engages attention, especially if mechanized, came 'lower-tech' warfare that also merits consideration, whether less intense or, at least, less technologically sophisticated conventional warfare (as for example in China), or guerrilla warfare, or 'terrorism', which, to its supporters, was resistance warfare. This range is linked to the diversity of battlefields involved, including less familiar ones in accounts of the war such as Iraq, Lebanon, Madagascar and Syria.

OPENING CAMPAIGNS

While continuous large-scale conflict began in China in 1937, World War Two is usually dated from the outbreak of conflict in Europe in 1939: Germany invaded Poland on 1 September in pursuance of Hitler's plans for territorial expansion. Britain and France entered the war on 3 September in defence of Poland, fulfilling the prediction of Marshal Foch, who, angry that the Peace of Versailles had not led to an independent Rhineland separate from Germany, had declared in 1919: 'This is not peace. It is an armistice for twenty years.'

In 1939, in a dramatic example of military effectiveness, the Germans lost fewer than 15,000 dead rapidly defeating the Poles, whose armed forces totalled over a million men. The Germans greatly outnumbered the Poles in aeroplanes, tanks and other mechanized vehicles, enjoyed the initiative, and benefited from the long and vulnerable nature of the Polish frontier and the dispersed position of the Polish army, which was strung out to defend the long frontier. The Luftwaffe having gained air superiority, the German armoured forces broke through, and isolated and enveloped Polish positions, making it difficult for them to maintain supplies or launch counter-attacks. Nevertheless, the campaign was not a walkover for the Germans and the Poles showed how a determined foe, although outclassed technologically, could make a superior conquering force pay for its conquests. Due to limited preparedness, Britain and France were unable to help the Poles by launching a strong attack on Germany's western frontier, and Hitler was, at least until he chose to attack the Soviet Union in 1941, freed from the problem Germany had faced in World War One: war on two fronts.

Indeed, in 1939, the Soviet Union came into the war in support of Germany by attacking eastern Poland in the latter stages of the Polish campaign, although war was not declared on it by Britain or France. Soviet intervention led to the partition of Poland between Germany and the Soviet Union in accordance with the Nazi–Soviet Pact of 23 August 1939. The two powers maintained an uneasy friendship until the German attack on 22 June 1941. The Soviet Union, which provided Germany with badly needed raw materials, used the opportunity to consolidate its position on its borders, seizing and annexing Estonia, Latvia and Lithuania in 1940, gaining territory from Romania, and launching an attack on Finland, the Winter War of 1939–40. The latter, however, revealed serious deficiencies in the Soviet military, especially in manoeuvrability, and led to an urgent programme of military renewal. The Germans were convinced from observing the war that the Soviet military was weak.

Conflict with Britain and France was extended on 9 April 1940 when, anxious to pre-empt the danger of British moves and keen to establish submarine bases from which to attack British shipping, the Germans invaded Norway; Denmark was rapidly taken in order to improve the German ability to operate in Norway. In this campaign, the Germans made valuable use of airborne troops, including the first parachute assault. They lost about a quarter of their surface navy in the operation, but their air power made a major impact, exacerbating the serious limitations of the Norwegian resistance and of the Anglo-French naval and land intervention.

Before Norway had finally fallen, the Germans, on 10 May, also attacked Belgium and the Netherlands, both hitherto neutral, as well as invading France. The rapid defeat of the Dutch, who surrendered on 14 May, indicated the success of German methods. Swiftly gaining and employing air superiority, the Germans advanced rapidly, using paratroopers, glider-borne forces and tanks to weaken the cohesion of the defenders. Heavy civilian casualties caused by the bombing of undefended Rotterdam speeded the surrender.

The crucial victory occurred further south: poor Allied strategy had led the Allies to move their strategic reserve into Belgium before they were aware of the main direction of the German attack. This came through the supposedly impenetrable hilly woodland of the Ardennes, bisecting the Allied line, flanking the fortifications of the Maginot Line and their defensive forces, and exposing the Allies' failure to prepare for fluid defence in depth. Supported by air superiority, the German panzer divisions proved operationally effective as formations, maximizing the weapon characteristics of the tank. When tank conflict occurred with the British or French, the Germans tended to control its pace.

Having reached the English Channel on 21 May, the Germans, nevertheless, were deprived of much of their surrounded prey by the successful evacuation of 338,000, mostly British, troops from the Dunkirk beaches (27 May to 4 June). Over another 200,000 British troops were saved in other French, mostly Channel, ports. The Germans, however, rapidly regrouped before pressing south into France. After strong initial resistance on the Somme and the Aisne, German superiority in generalship and equipment, especially tanks, prevailed. There was to be no repetition of the blocking of the German advance in 1914. Instead, rapidly advancing into central and southern France, seizing cities as far south as Bordeaux, the Germans were able to force France to accept an armistice that was far harsher than the terms imposed on France in 1871 or envisaged in 1914.

Hitler pressed on, offering peace with Britain while preparing for invasion. Negotiations were rejected by Winston Churchill, who had become prime minister on 10 May 1940 after the failure in Norway. Understandably, he did not trust Hitler. The German air assault launched in order to prepare the way for invasion by ensuring air superiority over the Channel and the invasion beaches was thwarted in the Battle of Britain: the RAF (British Royal Air Force) benefited from able command decisions, good intelligence, and a high level of fighting quality, as well as from the valuable support provided by radar. Poor German strategy, including a lack of consistency in targeting, contributed to the British success. The Germans failed to persist in their assault on the British airbases and, instead, became overly interested in attacking other targets, eventually focusing, in the 'Blitz', on Britain's cities, leading to heavy casualties, especially in London.

Meanwhile the war had spread in a new direction, as Italy came in on the German side on 10 June 1940. However, the Italian attack on France in June was thwarted, and an Italian invasion of Greece was repelled in November 1940. Furthermore, in December, the Italian forces that had invaded Egypt were driven back by the British, a term that should be taken to include Dominion and Empire forces, particularly, in this case, Australians. The British went on to conquer eastern Libya, and in early 1941 to overrun Eritrea and Italian Somaliland, finishing the conquest of Italian East Africa in northern Ethiopia later that year.

Hitler responded to Italian defeats by sending help to the Italians in Libya, which led to the British being driven back, and, on 6 April 1941, attacking Greece; on the same day Yugoslavia, which had defied German wishes, was also attacked. Virtually surrounded by its opponents, the strung-out Yugoslav defence proved vulnerable and the country fell rapidly, as Poland had done. The attack included the terror-bombing of undefended Belgrade on 6 April in order to cause heavy civilian casualties: over 17,000 people were killed. The Germans also benefited from both the international and the domestic political situation. Bulgarian, Hungarian and Italian forces joined in the invasion; each receiving part of Yugoslavia as their reward. Within Yugoslavia there was considerable disunity, and many Croats were unwilling to fight against the invaders. The British sent an expeditionary force to help the Greeks, but, with inadequate air support, it was pushed back. The tempo of the German advance, especially its rapid use of airborne troops and armour, brought a decisive advantage, as did the effective use of ground-support aircraft. This enabled the Germans to overcome successive defensive lines.

The campaign culminated with the capture of Crete by German parachute and air-transported troops. This was a risky attack, launched on 20 May, as such forces were unable to bring heavy arms with them, while the formidable British naval presence thwarted the planned maritime support for the invasion. German air attacks, however, inflicted serious damage on the British navy, while their assault force, although it took heavy casualties, was able to gain the initiative, seize airstrips, and secure resupply by air. The British evacuated their forces, those remaining surrendering on 3 June.

This success took the Germans forward into the eastern Mediterranean, but the possibility of exploiting it was lessened by British action to secure Lebanon, Syria and Iraq, and by the German focus on war with the Soviet Union which broke out on 22 June 1941. The Mediterranean was no more than a sideshow for Hitler, one where he acted in order to prevent Britain from exploiting Italian weaknesses.

SOVIET UNION ATTACKED

Hitler jeopardized the operational successes of 1939–41 by declaring war on, first, the Soviet Union and, then, the USA; but to Hitler these successes were of scant value unless they were means to his goal: he was convinced that a clash with Communism was inevitable and Germany's destiny, and that the Germans were bound to win. His policies were motivated by a crude and brutal racism in which Slavs were inferior to Germans. Hitler was also convinced that defeating the Soviet Union would lead Britain to negotiate and thus avoid the need for a hazardous invasion. Stalin refused to accept signs of imminent attack and foolishly maintained confidence in the 1939 pact.

On 22 June 1941, nearly 3.6 million German and allied troops, supported by 3,350 tanks and 1,950 planes, were launched in a surprise attack. The unprepared Red Army suffered heavy defeats at the outset and in initial counter-attacks, losing large quantities of men, tanks and aircraft, but, lulled by over-confidence in the value of a swift offensive and completely failing to appreciate Soviet strength, the Germans had not planned or prepared adequately for the conflict. Soviet doctrine, with its emphasis on defence and its stress on artillery, proved effective once the initial shock and surprise of the attack had been absorbed.

These problems were compounded by the vastness of the territory to be conquered by the Germans, and by a lack of consistency in German policy. In particular, goals shifted over the emphasis between seizing territory or defeating Soviet forces, and also over the question of which axes of advance to concentrate on. This led to a delay in the central thrust on Moscow in September, while forces were sent south to overrun Ukraine and destroy Soviet armies there: the gain of the resources of Ukraine and the crushing of Soviet forces there then appeared more important than a focus on Moscow. The delay in the advance on the latter hindered the Germans when they resumed it, not least because the Soviets proved better than the Germans at operating in the difficult winter conditions. Although the government was evacuated to Kuibyshev on the Volga, the Red Army was able to hold the assault on Moscow, their communications and command centre, and to mount a counter-attack launched on 5–6 December 1941. Once their advances had been held, the Germans lacked strong operational reserves to cope with counter-attacks, and they found it difficult to stabilize the front in the face of these attacks.

WAR IN THE PACIFIC

In December 1941, the war broadened further when Japan began hostilities against Britain, the USA and the Dutch, an assault followed by Hitler declaring war on the USA. The Axis (Germany, Italy and Japan) were now united against the Western allies. On 7 December, Japan had bombed the major American Pacific base at Pearl Harbor in the Hawaiian island of Oahu without any prior declaration of war. Keen to seize the economic resources of South-East Asia and the East Indies, especially the British colony of Malaya and the Dutch East Indies (now Indonesia), in order to support its war effort in China, Japan saw American opposition as an obstacle to its plans, and decided to cripple the American fleet in order to secure the opportunity to make rapid gains and create a powerful and far-flung defensive perimeter in the western Pacific. The seizure of the Philippines, an American colony, was seen as crucial to this process. Thanks in part to total radar silence, the Japanese carriers were undetected on their journey, but at Pearl Harbor the attacking planes found battleships, rather than the American aircraft carriers, which were not in harbour.

By the end of May 1942, having attacked American, British and Dutch colonies, Japanese forces had overrun Hong Kong, Guam, the Philippines, the Dutch East Indies, Burma, Malaya and Singapore. The last of these fell on 15 February, and its loss was a terrible blow to British prestige in Asia: not only because it had been presented as impregnable but also because of the large numbers of troops who surrendered. Japan had seized a vast area and carved out a real empire.

BOX 7.1   THE VOICE OF WAR: EXPLAINING DEFEAT: THE BRITISH FAILURE IN MALAYA AND SINGAPORE, 1941–42

Major-General Gordon Bennett of the Australian army provided a secret report immediately after the campaign that offers an instructive guide to military attitudes. It is ironic that he comments on Indian morale, as that of other Allied forces, especially the Australians, had also been a problem.

Causes of failure.

a) Prime cause. low morale Indian troops.

b) Lack of offensive spirit–retreat complex

　　1. Many commanders and senior officers imbued with retreat complex. Spirit of resignation prevailed.

　　2. Repeatedly slightest enemy opposition checked our local offensives. Many withdrawals without pressure from enemy. In short, lack of spirit in junior officers.

c) Poor quality of staff work . . . many officers inefficient . . . lack of system in obtaining and disseminating information.

d) Lack of air support . . . Adequate support could have protected navy thus obstructing coastal landings [by Japanese].

e) Wishful thinking. 2nd December Malaya Command advised no likelihood Japanese attack. Reports promulgated among formations under-estimated enemy.

f) Training neglected. Training in jungle fighting, patrols etc. neglected.

g) Lack of appreciation effect climatic conditions on stamina.

h) Poor quality 18 British Div.

Part two. Tactics.

In 1918 British method attacking position pound it heavily with artillery until opposition reduced then advance under artillery barrage. Since 1939 this method obsolete yet large conservative element officers adhered such obsolete methods. Repeatedly commanders adhered rigid methods of defence.

British defence systems provided long thin line posts along beach without depth with vulnerable flanks whereas modern perimeter system of defence on shorter flank much more effective.

Japanese tactics

1. Infiltration and outflanking.

2. Through above enemy established forces which coalesced into large groups behind our lines causing withdrawal due rigid system defence and morale.

continued

[. . .]

Part Five Equipment

[. . .]

Japanese equipment suitable. Comprised light automatic weapons, light mortars, no artillery except what was captured. Transport just sufficient to meet needs and not clutter roads and prevent movement. British too mechanically minded.

Japanese infantry clothed suitably, traveled light and used bicycles.

(Kew, National Archives, War Office Papers, 32/11749)

Despite having much of their military tied up in China, Japanese forces benefited from outfighting their opponents, who were weak and poorly prepared; from air superiority; from the operational flexibility of their plans; and from the combat quality and determination of their units. This was particularly seen in Malaya where the Japanese were outnumbered. There were also serious Allied command and operational lapses, as with the loss of most of the American planes in the Philippines on the ground on 8 December, and the British failure to provide adequate air cover to their leading warships in the region, the *Prince of Wales* and the *Repulse*, off Malaya two days later: both were sunk. British leadership did not match that of the Japanese in the Malaya and Singapore campaign.

The ability of the Japanese in the early stages of the war to mount successful attacks, to gain great swathes of territory, in the face of weak and poorly led opponents, and to establish an apparent stranglehold on the Far East, however, did not deter the Americans, as the Japanese had hoped, from the long-term effort of driving back and destroying their opponents. There was no American support for the idea of a compromise peace. As a result, the fundamentals of Japanese strategy were flawed.

AXIS ATTACKS HELD, 1942

In Russia, the Germans were able to recover from the Soviet counter-attacks of the winter of 1941–42 and to mount a major new offensive, but the Japanese failed to recover from the first defeats they encountered. Furthermore, the new German attack was to be disastrous. From the outset, the 1942 offensive – Operation 'Blue' – was jeopardized by a poorly conceived and executed plan. In this, the Germans planned the seizure of the Caucasian oilfields in order better to prepare for the lengthy struggle that American entry into the war appeared to make inevitable: most of the world's oil supplies were under Allied control or closed to the Axis by Allied maritime strength. The Allies dominated oil production in the western hemisphere (USA and Venezuela) and also in the Middle East (Iran, Iraq and Saudi Arabia), which helped to make the seizure of oilfields in Borneo and Sumatra important for Japan.

Hitler, however, underestimated Soviet strength, and also failed to make sufficient logistical preparations. Furthermore, there were serious flaws in the development of the operation, specifically in the decision to attack simultaneously towards the Volga river as well as the Caucasus, while Hitler's conviction that the city of Stalingrad, on the Volga, had to be captured, foolishly substituted a political goal for the necessary operational flexibility: German strategy was both misguided and poorly implemented. Despite a massive commitment of resources, the Germans were fought to a standstill at Stalingrad, which had been turned by their air and artillery attacks into an intractable urban wasteland. The Soviets counterattacked in November, breaking through the weak flanks to the German position. In a replay of Hannibal's victory over the Romans at Cannae (216 BCE), the Soviets held the German troops in Stalingrad, and built up massive forces on the weaker fronts held by less motivated, less well-armed Romanian and Hungarian troops, and caved them in to surround the German forces in Stalingrad. Hitler again failed to respond with the necessary flexibility and forbade a retreat from the city by the Sixth Army before it was encircled.

The key Japanese checks, in contrast, occurred at sea. The first sign of an inability to sustain early success was when the Japanese move towards Port Moresby in New Guinea, which would have increased the threat of an attack on Australia, was postponed as a result of the battle of the Coral Sea on 4–8 May 1942 with an American fleet, the first battle entirely between carrier groups.

The turning point in the Pacific was a bigger battle: the American victory on 3–7 June 1942, crucially in air attacks on 4 June, over a Japanese fleet seeking both to capture Midway Island and to defeat the Americans in a decisive battle. This was seen as a prelude to an attack on Hawaii and therefore as a crucial step in the consolidation of Japanese control in the western Pacific. The Japanese had no intention of launching a war of conquest in the continental USA, although they did establish bases in the Aleutian Islands in order to strengthen their position in the northern Pacific and block the chance of American attacks on the Kuriles and Hokkaido, the northernmost of the Japanese 'home islands'. Thus, the Japanese, after a fashion, sought limited war goals against the USA, unlike their total war objectives in China. This was a sensible response to the far greater American economic capability and to the impossibility of conquering the USA, but it underestimated American resolve.

Such a misassessment stemmed from the ideology of the Japanese regime. Like Hitler, they despised democratic and consumerist societies, thinking them essentially weak and lacking in resolve. In each case, the aggressive Axis power believed in the triumph of the will in a conflict between national spirits, and thus in the notion that commitment provided superior fighting quality and took precedence over resources. This analysis was overthrown by the ability of the USA not only to mobilize its economy for war rapidly and successfully but also to provide the necessary fighting quality.

Furthermore, Japan had violated its initial strategy of seizing the key resource area and sufficient land to provide defence in depth and waiting for the inevitable American counter-attack by building up the defence from Japan's rather limited industrial base and hoping that the USA would avoid the cost of battle. Instead,

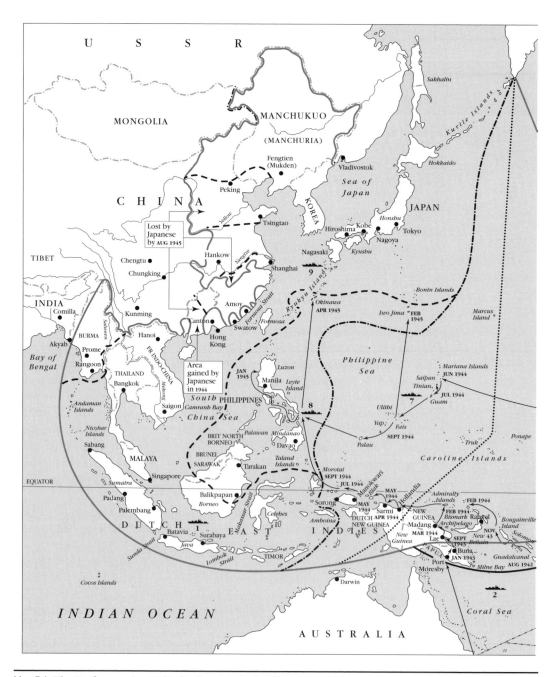

Map 7.1 The Pacific campaign, 1941–45, from *The Oxford Companion to Military History* (2003), p. 686, edited by Richard Holmes, by permission of Oxford University Press.

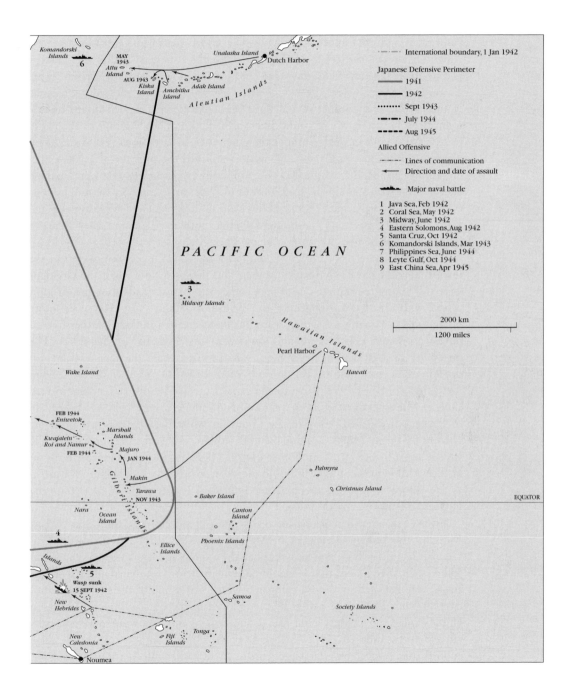

Komandorski
Islands

6

MAY
1943
Attu
Island
AUG 1943
Kiska
Island

Amchitka
Island

Adak Island

Aleutian Islands

Unalaska Island

Dutch Harbor

International boundary, 1 Jan 1942

Japanese Defensive Perimeter

——— 1941

——— 1942

········· Sept 1943

—·—·— July 1944

————— Aug 1945

Allied Offensive

—·——·— Lines of communication

◄——— Direction and date of assault

Major naval battle

1 Java Sea, Feb 1942
2 Coral Sea, May 1942
3 Midway, June 1942
4 Eastern Solomons, Aug 1942
5 Santa Cruz, Oct 1942
6 Komandorski Islands, Mar 1943
7 Philippines Sea, June 1944
8 Leyte Gulf, Oct 1944
9 East China Sea, Apr 1945

PACIFIC OCEAN

3
Midway Islands

Hawaiian Islands

Pearl Harbor

Hawaii

2000 km

1200 miles

Wake Island

FEB 1944
Eniwetok

Marshall
Islands

Kwajalein
Roi and Namur
FEB 1944

Majuro

JAN 1944

Makin

Tarawa
NOV 1943

Nara

Ocean
Island

Gilbert Islands

4

Islands

5
Wasp sunk
15 SEPT 1942

New
Hebrides

New
Caledonia

Noumea

Ellice
Islands

Phoenix Islands

Palmyra

Baker Island

Christmas Island

Canton
Island

Samoa

Society Islands

Fiji
Islands

Tonga

EQUATOR

the Japanese gave in to 'victory disease', to use their own phrase, and stayed on the offensive, weakening, if not wasting forces. In part this was a response to the American carrier-based Doolittle air raid on Tokyo and other cities on 18 April 1942 which helped lead the Japanese to the failed, flawed attack on Midway.

The Japanese were hit in the Midway operation by flawed preparation which contrasted with the more effective repair effort that had returned damaged American aircraft carriers to service, and with the American ability to intercept and decipher Japanese radio messages. The sinking of four Japanese carriers in the air battle at Midway, and the loss of many aircraft and pilots, shifted the balance in the Pacific, as the initiative and the arithmetic of carrier power moved rapidly against the Japanese, whose confidence was badly hit. Their attempt in the battle to lure the American carriers under the guns of their battleships was thwarted by American prudence. As a result, Midway established the primacy of carriers.

Having gained the advantage, the Americans were now safe from Japanese carrier offensives, and also in a position to provide carrier support for amphibious operations in the Pacific. The Japanese were to stage renewed offensives on the Burma/India frontier and in southern China, both in 1944, but they were no longer in a position to mount one in the Pacific.

There was also a more profound failure for the Axis. In geopolitical terms, the loss of Japanese naval offensive capability, and that at a time when the Germans were still taking the initiative in Russia and North Africa, made thoughts of joint action with the Germans against the British in South-West Asia even more implausible. Germany and Japan were unable to create a military partnership, or obtain economic assistance that to any extent matched that of the Allies. The possibility of joint action, never high, was thwarted when the Japanese did not develop their conquest of Burma and their successful naval raid on Ceylon (Sri Lanka) in April 1942. Most of the carriers involved in the latter were instead sunk at Midway. German advances towards South Asia were held by the British in Egypt and the Red Army in the Caucasus, while Britain benefited from the rallying of much Indian opinion behind Britain, especially the increase of the Indian army to become a million strong in 1942, the largest volunteer army in history. Although this army was not in shape yet to drive the Japanese from Burma, as the failure of the Arakan operation indicated, it was a major barrier to any Japanese attempt to invade India.

British offensives had also ensured that the Allies dominated both South-West Asia and the Indian Ocean. From May to July 1941 they overthrew the pro-German regime in Iraq, and also conquered Lebanon and Syria from Vichy forces (the French government that recognized German victory was based at Vichy). The Iraqis were defeated in a rapid campaign which was a mix of the flying columns, river steamers and use of native allies employed in the wars of imperial conquest of the nineteenth century, and the application of modern weaponry, especially aircraft and armoured cars. This enabled the British both to overrun a large country and to overcome far larger forces. As in earlier interventions around the Indian Ocean and in Iraq in the nineteenth and early twentieth centuries, Britain benefited not only from clear naval superiority but also from the availability of Indian troops.

BOX 7.2 THE BATTLE OF THE ATLANTIC, 1939–45

Taking the battle to the Axis required naval mastery in both the Atlantic and the Pacific. At sea, as in World War One, the Germans were more effective in submarine than surface warfare. Surface ships made some damaging attacks on Allied merchant shipping, in pursuit of a strategy of disrupting the British commercial system and diverting British warships from home waters, but they were all hunted down, the *Bismarck* in 1941 being the most prominent German loss. The Germans failed to use their warships as a concentrated force. The sinking of the *Scharnhorst* at the close of 1943 greatly lessened the surface threat, and thus accentuated the tendency to use the British Home Fleet for operations in distant waters, and this was further secured when the *Tirpitz* was destroyed by bombing in its Norwegian anchorage in November 1944.

Once Norway and, even more, France had been conquered in 1940, however, German submarines (and surface ships) were better able than in World War One to attack Allied shipping. This was especially so in Atlantic waters, across which again ran the vital supply routes for Britain, and therefore for any army to be built up to invade France. Yet, because it was not until 1943 that the Germans devoted enough emphasis to submarine construction, they had insufficient submarines to achieve their objectives. The submarines also lacked adequate air support. Nevertheless, the development of 'wolf pack' tactics for attacks on convoys, and improvements in submarine specifications, particularly the 'snorkel', which allowed the underwater starting of diesel engines (reducing their vulnerability to air attack), increased their military effectiveness.

The Allies, in turn, were helped by the rapid adoption of convoys (unlike in World War One), the extension of air cover, especially due to long-range land-based aircraft, and the improvement of radar, as well as by their ability to intercept and decipher German naval codes. The building of far more merchant shipping from 1942, particularly by the Americans, was very important to Allied victory, as was the availability of more escort vessels and their improved armaments, including sonar and fire-ahead depth charges. The battle of the Atlantic was won by the Allies in the spring of 1943, although it continued to be a struggle until the end of the war. In May 1943, when forty-one submarines were lost, the Germans withdrew their submarines to areas where there was less Allied air power. In the battle of the Atlantic there were heavy casualties on both sides: 28,000 of the 42,000 men who served in the German submarine service, a centre of Nazi fervour, were killed.

Thanks to the weakness of Japanese air power and anti-submarine doctrine and preparation, the American submarine assault on Japanese shipping was to be far more successful than that of the Germans. This badly affected the articulation of the Japanese war economy and lessened the value of Japan's conquests in South-East Asia.

In August 1941 British and Soviet troops entered Persia (Iran). They rapidly gained control, forcing the pro-Axis shah to abdicate in favour of his son. This was of great benefit to the successful Allied determination to control the major sources of oil production, and to provide routes by which military supplies could be shipped to the Soviet Union. The provision of these supplies both helped to compensate for earlier Soviet losses to German attack and was also a way to hit at Germany at a time when British and American main forces were not yet in conflict with her in Western Europe. The other principal supply routes to the Soviet Union were from the USA via Alaska to Siberia and from Britain by sea to northern Russia, a hazardous route that was exposed to German air and naval forces based in Norway. The seizure of Persia also increased British strategic depth, providing another zone of defence for India in the event of the Germans over-running the Caucasus and/or Egypt. Strategic depth was also secured in the Indian Ocean: concern about possible Japanese submarine bases in Vichy-run Madagascar led, in 1942, to its conquest by the British who enjoyed the benefit there of carrier-borne air superiority.

The Allies also successfully attacked in North Africa in 1942. Having checked the Germans advancing towards Cairo and Alexandria to the west of the Nile in July, the British counter-attacked that October–November at El Alamein. The availability of larger British forces was important, but so also was air superiority and superior operational planning and execution. The British proved particularly adroit at the use of artillery in a systematic fashion, and in some respects the battle was a replay of their fighting methods in 1918. Furthermore, in Operation Torch that November, Anglo-American forces invaded Vichy-held Morocco and Algeria, rapidly seizing both. In response, the Germans overran Vichy France and moved troops into Tunisia in order to retain a presence in North Africa. The Allies were beginning to mount not a series of counter-attacks but a planned attempt first to undo Axis conquests and then to take the war to the Axis states themselves.

BEATING GERMANY, 1943–45

Although the Americans and British made an important contribution by their successes in the Mediterranean and, from 1944, in Western Europe, the Red Army absorbed the bulk of the German forces, especially on land: over two-thirds of the German army was always engaged on this Front. After Stalingrad, the Eastern Front was largely a prolonged struggle of attrition; although there was usually much more obvious movement than on that Front in World War One. Formidable foes on the defensive, the Germans succeeded in stabilizing the Front in early 1943 after the loss of Stalingrad, in part thanks to Field Marshal Manstein's skilled employment of counter-attacks and due to the difficulties the Red Army encountered in sustaining the offensive.

Thereafter, however, the Germans were outfought. Their attempt to regain the initiative with the Kursk offensive of July 1943, Operation Citadel, was defeated. The Germans launched formidable tank assaults on the northern and southern sides of a large Soviet bulge on the front line, but the Soviets were well prepared.

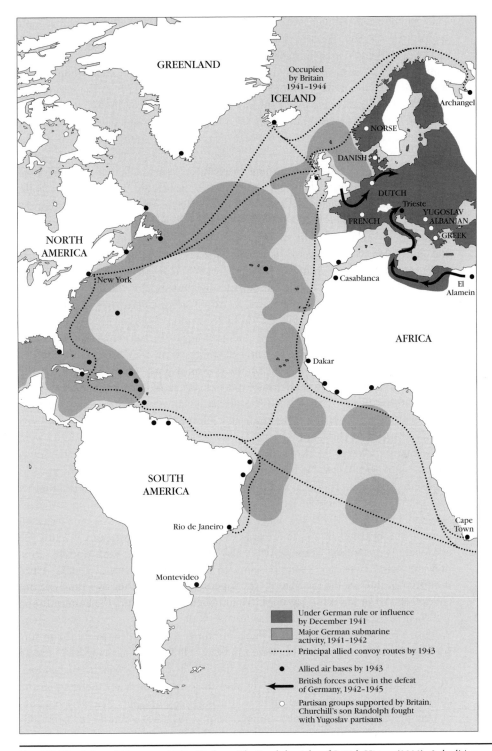

GREENLAND

Occupied
by Britain
1941–1944

ICELAND

Archangel

NORSE

DANISH

DUTCH

Trieste

YUGOSLAV

ALBANIAN

FRENCH

GREEK

NORTH
AMERICA

New York

Casablanca

El
Alamein

AFRICA

Dakar

SOUTH
AMERICA

Rio de Janeiro

Cape
Town

Montevideo

Under German rule or influence
by December 1941

Major German submarine
activity, 1941–1942

Principal allied convoy routes by 1943

Allied air bases by 1943

British forces active in the defeat
of Germany, 1942–1945

Partisan groups supported by Britain.
Churchill's son Randolph fought
with Yugoslav partisans

Map 7.2 The defeat of Germany, 1942–45, from *The Routledge Atlas of British History* (2003), 3rd edition, by Martin Gilbert, p. 110. © Routledge/Taylor & Francis Informa.

They had constructed concentric lines of defences, and these weakened and finally stopped the German assaults. The Germans suffered especially badly at the hands of Soviet artillery, yet again demonstrating that artillery was the most underrated arm in the war; anti-tank guns indeed were the most underrated weapons. The availability of large Soviet armour reserves was also important to the flow of the battle. Once the offensive had been blocked, the Soviets rapidly switched over to the offensive, making far more gains than the Germans had done in the battle. For the remainder of the war the Germans stood on the strategic defensive on the Eastern Front.

The Red Army proved increasingly successful in attack, adept at developing co-operation between armour, artillery and infantry, at making the latter two mobile, and at developing logistical support so as to maintain the impetus of attack, the last a key element. The Red Army indeed achieved what has been seen as its own blitzkrieg. This was especially so in the breakthrough attacks in Ukraine in March and April 1944 which drove the Germans back across the Bug, Dniester and Pruth rivers, and those from June to September 1944 (Operation Bagration), which overran Belarus (White Russia) and took the Soviets close to Warsaw, in the process destroying much of the German Army Group Centre and causing over a half a million casualties.

The Germans were outgeneralled and outfought. In less than two and a half years' fighting the Red Army drove the Germans from the Volga to the Elbe, a distance greater than that achieved by any European force for over a century, and one that showed that a war of fronts did not preclude one of a frequent move-ment of those fronts. This was not simply an advance on one axis but one from the Black Sea to the Baltic across much of Eastern Europe, and an advance that destroyed much of the German army.

Germany's allies were also defeated and knocked out of the war. The Soviet advance into the Balkans led in 1944 to the overthrow of pro-German govern-ments in Romania, Bulgaria and Hungary, and to the German evacuation of Greece, Albania and Yugoslavia. Finland responded to the shift of fortune by aban-doning Germany in 1944. The Finns subsequently joined the Soviets in attacking German forces based in Arctic Norway. Soviet operational methods towards the end of the war stressed firepower, but also employed mobile tank warfare: attri-tion and manoeuvre were combined in a co-ordinated sequence of attacks. Once broken through, mobility allowed the Soviets to prevent their opponents from falling back in order, while strong German defensive 'hedgehogs' were enveloped and then bypassed.

Meanwhile the Germans and Italians in North Africa had been forced to sur-render by American and British forces in May 1943. The Germans had initially made good use of their interior lines in Tunisia in order to fight the advancing American and British forces separately, and their attack on the Americans in the battle of the Kasserine Pass had inflicted much damage on units that were not ade-quately prepared for high-tempo conflict. In part, this was a matter of the blood-ing or experience that the Germans had gained through earlier conflict. American combat effectiveness rapidly improved, however, while the Axis forces in Tunisia suffered from the impact of Allied air superiority, especially on their supply links from Italy, and, once the Allies had gained the initiative, they were able to win a speedy victory.

The Allies pressed on to invade Sicily that July and mainland Italy that September. Amphibious power and air support allowed the Allies to seize the initiative. While the overthrow of Mussolini by his own ministers temporarily wrecked Axis cohesion, a rapid German response gave them control of central and northern Italy. The mountainous terrain and the east–west river lines made this excellent defensive terrain. Much of the fighting in Italy proved to be conventional infantry combat, with artillery playing a major role: the terrain was not well suited to armour. The Allied attempt to circumvent this with the Anzio landing in 1944 proved very risky, as the exploitation of the landing to create and secure a strong defensive perimeter proved difficult. A series of hard-fought Allied offensives were required to surmount successive defensive lines – Milan only fell in April 1945. The German units sent to Italy, however, were not available to fight the Soviets, nor to resist the Allies in France.

D-DAY

On 6 June 1944, in Operation Overlord, Anglo-American forces landed in Normandy. J.F.C. Fuller, the leading British military thinker of the period, was to claim in the *Sunday Pictorial* on 1 October 1944 that:

> Had our sea power remained what it had been, solely a weapon to command the sea, the garrison Germany established in France almost certainly would have proved sufficient. It was a change in the conception of naval power which sealed the fate of that great fortress. Hitherto in all overseas invasions the invading forces had been fitted to ships. Now ships were fitted to the invading forces . . . how to land the invading forces in battle order . . . this difficulty has been overcome by building various types of special landing boats and pre-fabricated landing stages.

To Fuller, these boats and landing stages matched the tank in putting the defence at a discount. He argued that Operation Overlord marked a major advance in amphibious operations, not only because of its unprecedented scale but also because Allied capability transformed the nature of the task in taking the war to the Germans in France. There was now no need to capture a port in order to land, reinforce and support the invasion force. The unsuccessful Dieppe operation, an attack across the English Channel in 1942, had shown that attacking a port destroyed it, which indicated that such a goal was inappropriate; but, in 1944, the Germans still, mistakenly, anticipated that the Allies would focus on seizing ports.

The invasion of Normandy benefited from the experience gained by the British and Americans in North African and Italian landings in 1942 and 1943, although the scale of the operation and the severity of the resistance, both anticipated and actual, were both more acute in Normandy. The latter ensures that, although the overlooked significance of Soviet offensives in Eastern Europe in 1944 need due attention, nevertheless, it is still necessary to underline the importance of Overlord.

Overlord was a triumph for combined operations, but also a product of the success of the Allied military over the previous two years. In part, this success was a matter of victory in conflict. The British, Canadian and American navies had won the Battle of the Atlantic, without which it would not have been viable to sustain the major preparations necessary in Britain prior to the launch of any invasion. In order to confront the German forces in France it would be necessary to land and support far more troops than had been the case with Operation Torch in North Africa in 1942. The ability to arm and support these numbers was an aspect of the Allied success in mobilizing the productive resources of much of the world's economy, but especially that of the USA. The Allied ability to mount amphibious operations rested ultimately on American shipbuilding capacity, and most of the 42 million tons of shipping built by the Allies during the war was constructed by the Americans.

The USA also produced 297,000 aeroplanes during the war. Numbers alone, however, did not suffice. It was also necessary to take the war to the Axis and to outfight them. By the summer of 1944 absolute air superiority over northern France had been obtained. The effectiveness of Allied ground-support air power there owed much to the long-term process of gaining air superiority over the Luftwaffe. As important as success in conflict was the process of training and other preparations that contributed to an increase in confidence in the overall fighting quality of land forces. Uneasiness over this factor remained, however; unsurprisingly so, because, as in World War One, the use of large numbers of men with little or no combat experience posed major problems for prediction.

Prediction was an issue for both sides. Anticipating an attack, which Hitler was confident could be repelled, the Germans, nevertheless, could not prioritize it because of the Soviet pressure in Eastern Europe; Soviet successes forced a reallocation of German units intended for the West.

In France, although they had developed the Atlantic Wall system of fortifications, the Germans lacked adequate naval and air strength to contest an invasion, and indeed were in a far worse state for both than the British had been when threatened with invasion in 1940. Furthermore, much (although by no means all) of the German army in France was of indifferent quality, as well as short of transport and training and, in many cases, equipment.

These problems made the quality of German command decisions particularly important; but these proved inadequate. In the past, such failings during the war, for example during Operation Barbarossa in 1941, have generally been blamed on Hitler's untutored and maladroit interventions, but, more recently, alongside this there has come a stress on drawbacks in German planning as a frequent aspect of more widespread deficiencies in German war-making. In the particular case of D-Day, the German failing related both to their assessment of where the attack was likely to fall and about how best to respond to it. The Germans were surprised by the Normandy landing. In part due to Allied attempts, including the apparent build-up of units in South-East England, they had concentrated more of their defences and forces in the Calais region, which offered a shorter sea crossing from

Britain and a shorter route to Germany. Normandy, though, was easier to reach from the invasion ports on the south coast of England, particularly Plymouth, Portland and Portsmouth. Even after D-Day, Hitler remained anxious about a subsequent additional landing near Calais. As another instance of German intelligence failures, the Germans anticipated a Soviet assault in Ukraine instead of White Russia where it actually came.

The German commanders in the West were also divided about how best to respond to any landing, particularly over whether to move their ten panzer (tank) divisions in France close to the coast, so that the Allies could be attacked before they could consolidate their position, or whether to mass them as a strategic reserve. The eventual decision was that the panzer divisions, whose impact greatly worried Allied planners, should remain inland, but their ability to act as a strategic reserve was lessened both by the decision not to mass them and by Allied air power. This decision reflected the tensions and uncertainties of the German command structure.

The German response was also affected by Allied operations. Air power helped ensure that the Allies were able to secure the flanks of their landing by the use of parachutists and glider-borne troops. These landings were particularly important to the landing on the right flank of the Normandy operation, at Utah Beach on the eastern base of the Cotentin peninsula, as the Germans were unable to bring up reserves to support their coastal defences there. The disorganized nature of the American airdrop, which matched that of the Sicily operation the previous year, further handicapped the defence as there were no co-ordinated targets to counter-attack. The Americans took very few casualties on Utah, in large part because the crucial fighting had already taken place inland.

On the next beach, Omaha, the situation was less happy. The Americans were badly prepared in the face of a good defence, not least because of poor planning and of confusion in the landing, including the launching of assault craft and Duplex Drive (amphibious) Sherman tanks too far offshore, as well as a refusal to use the specialized tanks developed by the British to attack coastal defences (for example, Crabflail tanks for use against minefields). The Americans sustained about 3,000 casualties, both in landing and on the beach, from positions on the cliffs that had not been suppressed by air attack or naval bombardment. The experience of Mediterranean and Pacific landings had not been taken on board. Air power could not deliver the promised quantities of ordnance on target on time. Eventually the Americans on Omaha were able to move inland, but, at the end of D-Day, the bridgehead was shallow and the troops in the sector were fortunate that the Germans had no armour to mount a response. This owed much to a failure in German command that reflected rigidities in part stemming from Hitler's interventions.

The Canadian and British forces that landed on Gold, Juno and Sword beaches further east (the Canadians on Juno) benefited from careful planning and preparation, from the seizure of crucial covering positions by airborne troops, who landed within their planned drop zones, from the effective use of specialized troops, and from German hesitation about how best to respond, although there was particularly hard fighting on Gold. The sole German armoured division in the area, 21st Panzer Division, did not counter-attack until the early afternoon. German armour approached the Channel between Juno and Sword beaches, but was blocked. At the cost of 2,500 troops killed that day, the Allies were back in France: 132,000 troops had been landed, while the airborne force was 23,000 strong.

The over 11,000 sorties flown by Allied air forces that day had a major impact: the Luftwaffe was kept away, while, although air support could not always suppress defensive fire, it made a valuable contribution. The largely British naval armada both provided heavy supporting fire – heavier fire than from air attack – and also prevented disruption by German warships. There was no equivalent to the challenge posed later that year by the Japanese fleet to the American landings in the Philippines, but attacks by destroyers, torpedo boats, and submarines based in French Atlantic ports were still a threat to the landing fleet.

This brief summary of what occurred also helps indicate what was distinctive about Overlord. In Operation Dragoon, the Allied landing in the south of France on 15 August, for example, the weakness of the defending force ensured that there was no major battle comparable to that in Normandy: resistance both on the beaches and inland, where an Anglo-American parachute force landed, was light, and casualties were few. An assault on a fortified coastline on the scale of Overlord was unique. Had the projected invasion of Japan gone ahead as planned, the Allies would have confronted an even more formidable challenge. Indeed in April 1945 Douglas MacArthur, the American commander in the Philippines, told a British visitor, Major-General William Penney, that his troops had not yet met the Japanese army properly, and that when they did they were going to take heavy casualties. General George Marshall, the American chief of staff, considered using atom bombs in tactical support of a landing on Kyushu: this was seen as the site for the first landings in Japan, and it was there that the Japanese had concentrated most of their forces.

Such an invasion appeared absolutely crucial to the defeat of Japan. Due to the importance of the Eastern Front, that was not the case with Germany and the Normandy landings, but, if the Western Allies were to play a major role in the defeat of Germany on land, then they had to invade France. However valuable, operations in Italy could not engage the major German forces in Western France, and, once the Germans had responded speedily and successfully in 1943 to the fall of Mussolini, the possibility of an effective rapid Allied exploitation of successes there was limited.

Even with the success of Overlord, it proved difficult for the Allies to break out of Normandy, and they both faced a hard battle and fell behind the anticipated phase lines for their advance. Despite air attacks, especially on bridges, the Germans were able to reinforce their units in Normandy, although the delays forced on them both ensured that the Allies gained time to deepen their bridgehead and obliged the Germans to respond in an *ad hoc* fashion to Allied advances, using their tanks as a defence force, rather than driving in the bridgehead.

The Italy campaign had not been a strategic irrelevance as far as the goal of the defeat of the Germans in France was concerned. Allied amphibious operations in the Mediterranean in 1943 provided valuable experience in planning and execution, not least in air support, airborne attacks, and the use of landing craft. The landings of 1943, especially that at Salerno, also provided warnings about the difficulty of invading France, not least in terms of the German response. In 1943, the latter would have been a more serious problem in France than it was to be in 1944 as, although the Germans had not proceeded so far with their defensive preparations as they were to have done by D-Day, the Allies did not yet have sufficient air dominance to seek to isolate the area of operations.

If Overlord was unique in scale, it also indicated the unpredictable nature of force requirements. There had been inter-war interest in enhancing amphibious capability, but it had been a low priority. For both the British and the Americans it was highly unlikely that there would be the need to invade a hostile French coastline. Were Germany to attack in the West again the more likely scenario was, as in World War One, of France resisting and receiving assistance from Britain, and maybe the Americans, through the Channel and Atlantic ports.

BOX 7.3   AMPHIBIOUS WARFARE

The essential typology of amphibious invasions remained the same in 1944 with the position from the outset of such operations; and indeed is still the case today. In essence, the question focuses on issues of depth, exploitation and counter-attack. If the target is a restricted one, then the situation is very different from when the landing is but a prelude to a major need for exploitation. Thus, for example, in the eighteenth century, the task in attacking French positions was very different to that presented in the American War of Independence. In the former case it was necessary to capture Louisbourg or Guadeloupe, Martinique or Pondicherry, and so on, and not to consider subsequent exploitation. All (in the case of islands) or the bulk of the opposing force was fixed by the process of invasion, and there was only a limited need to consider the possibility of a counter-attack.

This, however, was not the case in the American War of Independence, as the seizure of major port positions, such as New York in 1776, Philadelphia in 1777, and Charleston in 1780, was only a prelude to a need to engage American forces. The latter was even more clearly seen when the British tried to mount amphibious attacks on the European coastline during conflicts with France and her allies in the seventeenth, eighteenth and early nineteenth centuries. These were different in intention to Overlord, but they indicated the hazard of trying to mount an operation in the face of the greater speed with which defending forces on land could move. The very process of amphibious landings in the age of sail and rowing boats provided a crucial constraint in terms of time, as indeed did the difficulties of moving horses by sea in poorly stabilized boats. As a consequence, amphibious forces were vulnerable when launched against the land mass. The technological context of the situation altered during the twentieth century, in part because the very process of

continued

landing was speeded up, but also because, thanks to air power, it became possible to land troops by parachute or glider, and to try both to suppress defensive fire and to limit the possibility of counter-attack when invading a land mass.

This, therefore, looked towards the modern concept of littoral attack, rather than simply a landing. Such a concept reflects the power projection of modern forces and weaponry, and also the reduction of mass in modern warfare. In comparison to the large numbers of men and machines involved in campaigns in World War Two, the numbers now involved are relatively low, although the invasion of Iraq in 2003 served as a reminder that it could still prove necessary to transport and support over 150,000 men. The smaller the invasion force, the more it is possible to think of aerial assault and airborne supplies as major components, with a reduced need therefore to focus on the actual landing.

That could not be the case in 1944. Despite the major development of airborne capacity during the war, a development seen in particular in 1944, there was no way in which the vast numbers of men and supplies required to contest control of France could be moved in any way other than over the beaches. Normandy was a far more formidable target than Crete had been for the Germans in 1941. Furthermore, despite the advances in bombing, ground-attack, and airborne assault, it was not possible to overcome the defences prior to the landing.

The range of possible amphibious taskings in modern military planning remains large. It includes both small-scale power projection and also such possible large-scale objectives as a Communist Chinese invasion of Taiwan or American intervention in Cuba in the event of disorder after the death of Castro. The former possibility cannot be abstracted from its political context, as the nature of the American response would be crucial. In particular, the prospect of an American naval response would challenge any sea and air dominance the Communist Chinese were able to achieve. The need for co-operation between the particular arms is the point that emerges most clearly from a consideration of D-Day and other past amphibious operations. That situation is unlikely to change.

Instead, France had fallen. The unexpected nature of the challenge facing the Allies in 1944 was a problem, as, very obviously, it had earlier been for the Germans when they had planned an invasion of Britain in 1940, and, as the latter showed, improvisation was not an option. It could not be a substitute for the necessary capability and preparations. In contrast, the Allies benefited from a purposed process of planning that applied resources to tasks clearly defined in the light of experience. This sounds easier than was the case, not least because each invasion posed unique issues and problems. Furthermore, by 1944 the combined experience of such invasions, which included American amphibious operations in the Pacific, ensured that very different lessons could be drawn – for example, concerning the desirability of surrendering surprise by mounting a lengthy prior bombardment which was, in particular, to be an issue in discussions over how best to prepare for the landing on Omaha Beach.

DEFEATING GERMANY, 1944–45

The Germans were eventually outfought in Normandy and the Allied breakout was followed by a deep exploitation, much of it by American mechanized forces, that drove the Germans out of France and Belgium. Hopes of ending the war in Europe that year, however, proved abortive. Strengthening German resistance, and the logistical strains stemming from the rapid Allied advance, led to the Allies being held near the German frontier that autumn, especially in the Vosges and at Arnhem. They were then put under considerable pressure by a German counter-attack in the battle of the Bulge. This surprise attack in the Ardennes, launched on 16 December 1944, was, however, different to that in 1940. Allied air superiority ensured that the Germans now attacked only when heavy cloud restricted the affects of this superiority. The Germans planned, as in 1918, to break through a weak section of the Allied front and to drive towards the sea, but, aside from the fact that, even if successful, this would only have delayed Allied victory in World War Two (in 1918 there was no Soviet advance), they lacked the strength to exploit early gains.

Having checked the Germans, the Allies resumed the advance. They fought their way to, and across, the Rhine. There was then a rapid advance as German resistance collapsed. Further east Soviet forces fought their way into Berlin, destroying the Nazi regime: Hitler committed suicide on 30 April 1945. The Americans and British joined the Red Army in forcing unconditional surrender on the Germans, a war goal announced at the Casablanca summit conference in January 1943, with a pledge to destroy 'philosophies . . . based on conquest and the subjugation of other people'. While Germany was being overrun and, subsequently, once it had surrendered, there was scant popular resistance to the Allies.

Allied attacks simultaneously from a number of directions had made it difficult, although not impossible, for the Germans to shift reserves between theatres. In late 1942 Operation Torch coincided with the Soviet counter-attack at Stalingrad; in 1943, Operation Husky, the Allied invasion of Sicily, helped lead Hitler to call off the Kursk offensive; and in 1944, Operation Bagration was launched soon after D-Day.

DEFEATING JAPAN, 1943–45

The destruction of Japanese power posed an unprecedented problem of scale, as no other Axis state had such an extensive perimeter. The Allies, particularly the Americans in the Pacific, also had to co-ordinate air, sea and land forces, and to defeat their opponents in all three spheres. To do so required a synergy or successful interdependence in operations: gaining and using air superiority, in particular, made Japanese land and sea units vulnerable, while the capture of islands ensured that new forward air bases could be established from which further advances could be supported – airbases could take heavier planes than carriers, and these could fly further and carry heavier payloads.

In the winter of 1942–43, the Americans successfully applied their strength in breaching the Japanese defensive perimeter by capturing the island of Guadalcanal. The island itself was of limited importance, but its capture or retention became a symbol of military capability and determination. American naval successes weakened the ability of the Japanese to support their forces on the island, while heavy Japanese losses of aircraft and crew in the struggle helped the Americans to seize the initiative in 1943 as they began a process of island hopping in the Solomon Islands: the Americans could decide where to attack and could neutralize bases, such as Rabaul, that they chose to leapfrog. This lessened the extent of hard, slogging conflict and thus compromised the strategic depth represented by the Japanese defensive perimeter and also helped the Americans maintain the pace of their advance.

Aircraft carriers played a major role in the island hopping, and the ability to deploy them both in the south-west and the central Pacific reflected the extent to which superior American resources permitted the simultaneous pursuit of more than one offensive strategy. As with the Red Army in Eastern Europe, the Americans were able to advance on more than one axis. This not only resulted in serious resource pressures on the defender, with the availability of sufficient reserves a particular issue, but also placed great strain on command skills, especially with the allocation of reserves.

As a result of their carriers, air power could be applied from the sea as never before. The Japanese also continued building warships, but they could not match the Americans and were now particularly short of trained pilots. A major organizational defect in the Japanese naval air arm was that an air group was integral to its carrier, with no reserve air groups to replace the strike element of carrier task forces once they were shot down. It also proved near impossible for Japan to train pilots fast enough to replace losses. Problems with training also affected the German air force, ensuring that fighting quality deteriorated.

The vast extent of the Pacific created unprecedented problems of war-making and infrastructure for both sides. Substantial fleets had to operate over great distances, and needed mobile support and maintenance. Logistics was a particular strain, not least the provision of oil for both ships and their planes, and America's control of much of the world's oil proved especially valuable to the struggle in the Pacific. The scale of planning was also substantial: in August 1943 the Combined Staff Planners outlined a schedule culminating in an invasion or siege of Japan in 1947.

President Roosevelt had rejected the Japan First policy in order to concentrate on fighting Germany. He was a keen advocate of the 'Second Front' in Europe: an invasion of France in order to engage with the main German forces in Western Europe, while the first major American invasion, Operation Torch, was launched in 1942 in the European theatre, and much of America's air power was devoted to the Combined (with Britain) Air Offensive against Germany. The need to resist

Japanese advances, however, committed large American forces to the Pacific, and once there they were employed in offensive operations.

The Americans advanced both in the south-west and the central Pacific, while Australian and American forces drove the Japanese back in New Guinea in difficult jungle fighting. To seize Pacific bases, especially airfields, the Americans attacked key islands. These involved difficult assaults on well-prepared and highly motivated defenders, but, having captured their goals in the Gilbert Islands in November 1943, they pressed on to do the same in the Marshall Islands from January to April 1944. Few Japanese surrendered, and their willingness to fight to the death created an alien fighting environment for the Americans, compounding the difficulty of operating in hostile terrain, thick cover, and a harsh climate. This provided a dimension of total war, as did the high casualties suffered over what were relatively small islands. Before the island assaults, American air and sea power provided a massive techno-logical advantage but, once landed, the Americans found that the capability gap was far narrower, and, instead, that fighting was a matter of closing with the enemy in circumstances that favoured the defence.

Naval capability was the key, and this was not only a matter of carriers. Covering a landing on Bougainville in the Solomons in November 1943, a force of American cruisers and destroyers beat off an attack by a Japanese counterpart with losses to the latter in the first battle fought entirely by radar.

Superiority in the air gave the Americans the crucial advantage. In June 1944, the American Task Force 58, with over 900 planes, covered an amphibious attack on the Mariana Islands – Saipan, Tinian and Guam – leading to a struggle with the Japanese First Mobile Fleet and its 400 planes. Japanese attacks, launched on 19 June, were shot down by American fighters with no damage to the American carriers, in what the Americans termed the Mariana Turkey Shoot: the associa-tion of war with hunting was a long one. The Japanese also lost two carriers to American submarines. The Americans were even more successful next day, sinking or damaging Japanese carriers with a long-range air attack in the failing light. Aside from providing a forward logistical base, the Marianas gave the Americans the opportunity to bomb Japan with B-29 heavy bombers. In the last major naval battle, that of Leyte Gulf that October, the Japanese fleet was also comprehensively defeated.

Meanwhile, although very successful in their offensive in southern China in 1944 and gaining much territory, the Japanese had failed to knock China out of the war. Nevertheless, controlling, for the first time, a continuous ground route from Manchuria to Vietnam gave Japan a land axis that was independent of American maritime intervention, and thus provided Japan with strategic depth. Furthermore, overrunning Chinese airfields from which American planes could bomb Japan obliged the Americans to focus on seizing islands that could provide bases, such as Saipan. This campaign also gravely weakened the idea of a land-based invasion of Japan.

In Burma, in contrast, the Japanese were outfought on the ground. The simplicity of their determined offensive tactics were no longer adequate against British troops who, thanks to improved training, were better able to operate in the jungle, not least to patrol and fight there. The British also benefited from superior logistics, medical support, air power and artillery. In March to July 1944 they heavily defeated a poorly planned and executed Japanese invasion of north-eastern India, designed to provoke a rising by Indian nationalists, followed by a Japanese advance on Delhi. Instead, British forces held onto their positions at Imphal and Kohima in Assam. The British invaded Burma that December, defeating the Japanese at Meiktila in March 1945 and reconquering the country.

In the Pacific, the Americans could choose where to land, but the fighting and logistical problems of operations on shore both remained formidable. Having successfully invaded the Philippines in 1944, the Americans found that operations on land involved them in heavy casualties. The invasion served as a reminder that Japanese forces could tie down large numbers of Americans, and thus underlined the need to select targets carefully. Indeed, the invasion seemed to some critics a cul-de-sac on the route to Japan. In the background were service rivalries and the views of individual commanders, especially Douglas MacArthur, who pressed for the operation. This was not a unique episode nor a characteristic only of American war-making. Instead, for all militaries, abstractions such as national policy or strategic culture have to be understood in terms of support from particular interests, as well as pressure for specific views. At the same time, the American navy

Plate 7.1 *Iwo Jima Landing*, watercolour by Harry Reeks. On 19 February 1945 American forces invaded the Pacific Island of Iwo Jima. It took thirty-six days to conquer the island and more than one third of the American marines employed were killed (5,391) or wounded (17,372); 23,000 Japanese troops were killed. Anne S.K. Brown Collection.

knew that it needed Subic Bay and other ports for an invasion of Japan, and American politicians saw the Philippines as American: they therefore had to be retaken by force of American arms as soon as possible.

Early in 1945, the Americans seized the islands of Iwo Jima and Okinawa in order to provide airbases for an attack on Japan. The overcoming of the well-positioned and determined Japanese forces was slow and involved heavy casualties. The Japanese fought to the end, a sacrificial policy perhaps emerging out of the earlier stress on 'spirit' that matched the use of *kamikaze* (suicide) planes against American warships. These policies affected American tactics and armaments. For example, the number of anti-aircraft guns on American warships was dramatically increased, which resulted in a need for larger crews in order to man them.

Such Japanese tactics led to fears about the Allied casualties that an invasion of Japan would entail. Instead, the two deliverable atomic bombs the Americans had manufactured were dropped by American aircraft on the Japanese cities of Hiroshima and Nagasaki in August 1945. The consequences were devastating. About 120,000 people were killed outright by the bombs, with a further 160,000 eventually dying through radiation poisoning.

The Japanese surrendered unconditionally: the atom bombs had exposed the inability of their armed forces to protect the nation, although the earlier fire-bombing of Japanese cities, the destruction of their merchant shipping, and the declaration of war on Japan in August 1945 by the Soviet Union, all contributed to the surrender. Soviet operational effectiveness led to the rapid conquest of Manchuria.

The use of the atomic bomb prevented not only the heavy cost to both sides of an invasion, but also, probably, a resort by both sides to chemical and biological weapons. Furthermore, the Japanese Empire remained a formidable force at the time of the surrender – still in occupation of much of China, South-East Asia and the East Indies. To secure the surrender of these armies without engaging them in battle was an important goal. Much of the current criticism of the use of the atom bomb fails to place it in terms of the particular pressures of 1945.

BOX 7.4   AIR POWER, 1939–45

It had been widely predicted before the war that air power would be the war-winning arm. This was not in fact to be the case in Europe, although against Japan air power was far more effective, both in the naval war in the Pacific and in the dropping of the atomic bombs.

Air attack was important to the German offensives of the early stages of the war. Ground-support dive-bombing was valuable, especially in Poland (1939), France (1940) and Greece (1941), while the terror bombing of cities, for example Warsaw in 1939, Rotterdam in 1940 and Belgrade in 1941, was seen as a way to break the will of opponents. However, the inadequately prepared Germans were outfought in the sky when they attacked Britain in 1940, and their bombing that winter of cities,

continued

especially London, in the Blitz caused heavy casualties and inflicted much damage but failed to wreck morale. Against Britain, German air power failed as both strategic arm and operational tool. Aside from the deficiencies arising from the lack of a strategic bombing arm, the Germans also suffered from the integrated British air defence system, not least the use of radar. Focusing on ground support, German air power was of tactical value on the Eastern Front, but lacked the capability to achieve strategic goals.

Similarly, Axis air power had serious deficiencies in affecting the war at sea. In the Mediterranean, where British shipping was exposed to attack from nearby land bases, for example on Sicily, it was possible for German (and Italian) aircraft to inflict serious damage, but the air assault on the British bases in Malta failed to neutralize the island's capacity to act as a base for the challenge of Axis air and sea communications between Italy and North Africa. German air power made only limited contribution to the campaign against Britain in the Atlantic. The Germans lacked carriers, and the Luftwaffe did not concentrate on long-range anti-shipping aircraft.

In contrast, despite initial opposition from the advocates of a focus on bombing Germany, the Allies were able to use air power to make a major contribution to the war against German submarines. Subsequently, the Germans were battered by air offensives of hitherto unprecedented scale. Ground-support operations were very important to the advancing Allied armies, particularly to Anglo-American forces, for example in Normandy in 1944. There, aircraft proved effective against tanks.

Despite heavy losses among British and American aircrew in the Combined Bomber Offensive, strategic bombing also had an impact, not least by leading the Germans to devote resources, especially aircraft and anti-aircraft guns, to resisting it. German interception proved especially effective against daytime bombing, the American preference, and encouraged the British to rely on night-time bombing. This, however, compromised accuracy, which encouraged an emphasis on area bombing. Despite the limited precision of free-fall bombs dropped from high-flying planes, such bombardment disrupted Axis industrial production and communications. Industrial economies rely on the integration of components from different sources, and bombing communications hindered this integration, affecting the efficiency of the entire German war economy. More specifically, oil production in 1944 and 1945 was hit by bombing, while the air assault also delayed the construction of a new faster class of German submarine, so that this did not become operational until too late to challenge Allied command of the sea. Furthermore, strategic bombing seemed a necessary demonstration of Anglo-American commitment and resolve, and thus an important contribution to keeping the Soviet Union in the war, in the absence of the Second Front invasion of France that Stalin pressed for, and which the Western Allies were not ready to mount until June 1944. As such, it matched the pressure on the Western Allies to mount attacks in 1915 and 1916 in order to reduce pressure on Russia, pressure that led both to the Gallipoli operation of 1915 and to offensives on the Western Front.

The impact and morality of the Allied bombing of cities, causing heavy civilian casualties, have, however, been more controversial, and the destruction of much of the German city of Dresden towards the close of the war, in February 1945, with 130,000 civilian casualties, is a cause of particular controversy. At the time, though, when contemporaries could recall the terror of German bombing attacks, and of German unpiloted missile (V1 and V2) attacks on London in 1944 and 1945, there was less concern about the ethics of the policy.

The American air assault on Japan lasted less time than the Combined Bomber Offensive, but was devastating. Low-altitude night-time area bombing of cities from February 1945 killed large numbers due to high population density in the cities and the flammable character of Japanese buildings made of timber and paper. The weakness of the Japanese resistance enabled the Americans to fly lower than when bombing Germany and to carry less defensive armament, thus increasing the payload of bombs. On 10 March 1945, in the first major low-level raid on Tokyo, in which 334 B-29s were used (only fourteen were lost), more people (over 83,000) were killed than in the atomic bomb attack on Nagasaki on 9 August. Aside from individual loss and pain, the combined effect of the raids was to spread devastation and economic ruin, to wreck communications, and to weaken seriously the Japanese people, state and war economy.

BOX 7.5   THE VOICE OF WAR: THE DECISION TO DROP 'THE BOMB'

Statement issued on behalf of President Truman shortly after the first atomic bomb was dropped on Hiroshima:

[H]ardly less marvelous has been the capacity of industry to design, and of labor to operate, the machines and methods to do things never done before, so that the brain child of many minds came forth in physical shape and performed as it was supposed to do . . . It was to spare the Japanese people from utter destruction that the ultimatum was issued at Potsdam. Their leaders promptly rejected that ultimatum. If they do not now accept our terms they may expect a rain of ruin from the air . . . We are now prepared to obliterate more rapidly and completely every productive enterprise the Japanese have above ground in any city. We shall destroy their docks, their factories, and their communications. Let there be no mistake; we shall completely destroy Japan's power to make war.

(President Truman, *Year of Decisions, 1945*

(London, 1955), pp. 352–3)

WAR AND SOCIETY

The scale of the war and the nature of operations, especially bombing and submarine attacks on trade, put unprecedented pressure on societies. Bombing, evacuation, rationing and single parenting brought much hardship on the home fronts of the combatants. Family arrangements and social assumptions were also challenged and changed by the large number of women who played a role in the war economy. The coming of a war more global in its scope than World War One gave a renewed boost to the role of states and the control of societies, and the mobilization of national resources led to state direction of much of the economy. It was necessary to produce formidable amounts of equipment, to raise, train, clothe and equip large numbers of men, to fill their places in the workforce, especially with women, and to increase the scale and flexibility of the economy. In the non-totalitarian societies, particularly Britain and the USA, but also Australia, Canada, New Zealand and other allies, free trade and largely unregulated industrial production were both brought under state direction. Economic regulation and conscription were introduced more rapidly and comprehensively than in World War One.

In Germany, in contrast, the pre-war years had already seen an active moulding of society to further the goals of conflict: for Hitler, peace and war were part of the same process. Once the Soviet Union had been invaded in 1941, the conflict was more stridently presented within Germany as a people's struggle, and one that was seen in millenarian terms as a fight for racial mastery and a contest of wills. This helped ensure that Nazi ideology was at the centre of the military struggle, and also influenced the way in which the war was waged, particularly the brutality shown to Russians and in occupied areas in Eastern Europe. Hitler was committed to a total reordering of the Soviet Union, including a demographic revolution of slaughter and widespread resettlement. The genocidal treatment of the Jews was the culmination of a totalizing ideological militarism.

The Germans were not alone in this strategy of warfare against a people. They found active support, especially in Croatia and Ukraine. German allies and protégés, and then Soviet occupiers and their allies and protégés, also followed their own agenda of slaughter and 'ethnic cleansing'. Thus, the pro-German Ukrainian Insurgent Army killed large numbers of Poles in what is now western Ukraine in 1943 and 1944. In turn, the Soviet authorities brutalized peoples within the Soviet Union who Stalin distrusted as pro-German, especially Crimean Tartars and Chechens. The occupation of the Baltic republics was followed by renewed deportations and slaughter.

The German and Japanese treatment of occupied areas was an aspect of the character of this total war. In part as a result, the slaughter of the war was particularly acute for the Soviet Union and China. These occupation practices undermined the possibility of winning local support and also encouraged large-scale resistance, especially in the Soviet Union and China. Aside from its military role, which could be considerable, by forcing the occupation power to protect communication routes, resistance achieved the vital political goal of weakening collaboration and undermining co-existence, isolating the German and Japanese (and other Axis) militaries. In New Guinea, natives, many of whom had treated Japanese forces as liberators in 1942, were repelled by Japanese conduct and instead co-operated with Allied reconquest, not least by providing crucial carriers for supplies.

More generally, the Germans and Japanese mistook force for efficiency. In practice, there were multiple inefficiencies in the German war economy, in part reflecting the natural inefficiencies of a totalitarian regime that lacks the efficiencies of market discipline, but also due to the particular idiocies of the Hitlerian regime. In particular, the duplication of agencies (state, party, army, SS, air force in particular) led to confusion in policy implementation and focused decision-making on Hitler who was unable to provide clear, coherent, and systematized direction. Many of the preferences of the war economy, however, reflected more than poor leadership by Hitler. For example, the focus on quality rather than quantity in weaponry proved a mistake, as did the division of production among a large number of types, rather than the mass production of a smaller number of durable models pursued by the Allies.

Plate 7.2 *Let's Give Him Enough and On Time*, Norman Rockwell, oil on canvas. During World War Two Norman Rockwell was one of the many artists enlisted to help by producing posters used to assist the military and persuade all Americans to help the war effort. Posters were used for recruitment, to boost production, to motivate, to assist rationing and conservation, and linked the home front to the military front. Courtesy of the National Museum of the US Army, Army Art Collection, Washington D.C.

BOX 7.6   THE VOICE OF WAR: THE ETHICS OF KILLING

Discussion arose on rights or wrongs of shooting men who had baled out of aircraft and are on their way to earth or sea. Spaatz had heard that his boys had started it the day before in the Straits[1] chiefly owing to a report that they had received that the Boche[2] thought them soft and squeamish. Mary C's[3] views were that the Boche did it regularly, ethics did not arise and we should do it if the pilots etc. were going to fall into their own lines or into the sea ie anywhere where they were not going to be eliminated as far as further flying was concerned. Spaatz and Kueter not so sure, again not on ethical ground but on danger of diverting aircraft from their proper mission in order to protect their own pals who had taken to their parachutes. I always thought that there was some understanding that once in a parachute drop you were immune. Entirely illogical and inconsistent with total war. Same applied to American slaughter of Jap. [sic] soldiers in the sea after sinking the big convoy in the Solomons area.[4]

(Major-General William Penney, recording lunch on 14 April 1943
with Lieutenant-General Carl Spaatz, the American commander
of the Allied North Africa Air Forces)

1 Between Sicily and Tunisia.
2 Germans.
3 Air Vice-Marshal 'Maori' Coningham, commander of the Desert Air Force.
4 London, King's College, Liddell Hart Centre for Military History, Penney papers 3/2, Penney diary.

The Soviet system was similarly brutal and totalitarian and in conquered areas could be particularly ruthless. In 1939 and 1940, 1.17 million people were deported from Soviet-occupied Poland to Soviet labour camps, and in 1940 about 127,000 more were deported from the Baltic states. Many others were slaughtered. The Soviet Union proved better able to cope with the demands of mobilizing resources than its German rival, which also had to support war with the Western allies and to cope with bombing. The Soviets were particularly successful in moving large quantities of industrial plant and many millions of workers to the east, far beyond the range of likely German advance or air attack. Once relocated, these industries turned out vast quantities of military *matériel*, out-producing the Germans for example in numbers of tanks. The Soviet economic system was well suited to the particular requirements of state-directed mobilization. A symptom was the production of large quantities of *matériel* by the inmates of Soviet gulags: forced labour camps. Like the Western allies, the Soviets expected women to work for the war economy. The strain of the war on Soviet society was immense: probably 25–27 million people died as a consequence of the war.

WHY THE AXIS LOST

Allied victory is frequently discussed in light of their ability to out-produce the Axis, an approach that can make the result of the struggle seem inevitable. Resources were indeed important. The USA produced formidable quantities of munitions – $186 billion worth – and an infrastructure to move them. This production was essential. The Americans used over one million tonnes of 105 mm ammunition in the battle for Okinawa alone. The production-line nature of American manufacturing was harnessed for the war economy: by March 1944 the USA was producing one aircraft every 194 seconds. The American military was also the most mechanized, which was especially important in the movement of troops and supplies and to the maintenance of the tempo of the advance. In turn, mechanization accentuated the logistical demands of war, especially for oil. In contrast, the German army was a less than modern force with a small heavily mechanized component.

Allied resource superiority affected the conduct of the war at the strategic, operational and tactical levels, not least by providing the basis for successful combined-arms operations. Durable weapons were produced in large quantities: the American Sherman tank was the first truly universal fighting vehicle, able to fight in such different environments as Europe, the south-west Pacific and the North African desert.

In contrast, German attempts to improve their war economy faced the structural weaknesses of the Nazi state. Will was no substitute, and violence was part of a process of hasty improvisation that could not act as a substitute for the rational crisis management required by the Germans. Hitler, however, was aware of the role of resources and this affected his military planning; while the German military was more operationally than strategically oriented. In 1940 Hitler invaded Norway to control Swedish iron ore exports through the Norwegian port of Narvik. Subsequently, he kept large numbers of men in northern Finland in order to hold Petsamo and its nickel reserves, sought to secure the manganese at Kivri Rog in Ukraine, wished to seize the Caucasus oilfields, and sought to hold onto the Crimea in order to prevent Soviet planes from being able to bomb the Ploesti oilfields.

More than resources, however, were involved in the result of the war. Both political factors – which determined the identity of the two sides – and fighting quality was important. The former were especially important in the first two years of the war. Thereafter, the war became less fluid than it had been in its first two years, because Hitler's mindset and the Japanese assault on Pearl Harbor and the Allies' response to both helped ensure that the conflict ended through unconditional surrender, rather than the unilateral negotiations that might otherwise have been a response to his failure to defeat the Soviet Union in 1941 and 1942. The Germans were unable to translate their central position into lasting political or military success, because, due to Hitler's attitudes, peace was not an option. There was to be no second Nazi–Soviet pact, while Hitler's declaration of war on the USA on 8 December 1941 was a major strategic mistake that transformed the complexion of the conflict: he changed an undeclared naval war in the Atlantic into a major American effort that matched that directed against Japan.

These factors helped to give an attritional character to the later years of the war, which creates problems in its analysis: it is too easy to focus on just one part of the war and to treat it as characteristic of the entire conflict. This is a mistake, for individual rivalries such as the Soviet Union and Germany or USA and Japan, however important, provide an insufficient guide to the wide-ranging nature of the struggle. For example, to assess Japanese war-making it is necessary to understand the very different requirements of operations in Burma, China and the Pacific, and also to appreciate the important differences between the parts of the Japanese military, most obviously the army and the navy.

Planning and command skills, and the ability to articulate and integrate different arms, a long-established aspect of effectiveness, became more important with the greater range of available technology. Command and fighting skills played a major role in the defeat of the Axis, for example in the outfighting of the Germans on the Eastern Front and of the Japanese in Burma. On the German side, there is still a tendency to regard their defeat as due to being beaten in resource production by the Allies, and to minimize or ignore the extent to which they were outfought. All-too-much of the work on the German side is based on post-war analyses of their own campaigns by German commanders and staff officers. These place the responsibility for defeat on resource issues, the size and climate of the Soviet Union, and, above all, Hitler's interventions, ignoring archival evidence that highlights battlefield mistakes by German commanders. Separately, there is also a failure to appreciate the extent to which the German army was involved in atrocities, and, indeed, that military violence against unarmed civilians was integral to its conduct during the war.

Clearly both resources and fighting were crucial. For example, the extent of the American shipbuilding capability, and the consequent ability to do far more than just replace losses, was central to the ability to secure and then exploit naval superiority in the Pacific. Yet, in addition, the Japanese navy had to be both beaten in battle by the Americans and weakened by their air and submarine assault on the Japanese war economy. Japanese defeats in part reflected the balance of fighting quality, command skills and luck in particular battles, as well as flawed Japanese doctrine, seen for example in the less successful use of submarines compared to that by the Americans.

CONCLUSIONS

For the political and military leaders of all the combatants it became clear that a rapid victory in a major war was unlikely, and that sustaining such a conflict would indeed have serious social implications. Confidence in popular responses varied, but was less pronounced than might be suggested by a focus on the wartime propaganda of togetherness. This propaganda itself reflected the sense, even among the totalitarian powers, that popular support had to be wooed. Concern about the populace also led to a social politics that put a greater emphasis than hitherto on social welfare.

Social and cultural shifts and tensions were also seen within the military. For example, the implications of mechanized warfare included the cult of the technocrat and the decline of the aristocratic cavalry horseman and officer.

The war also brought far-reaching changes in Western colonies, particularly when these colonies were conquered. In India there was a major shift in military culture, with a determined attempt by the British to promote Indians, as well as recruitment from races hitherto seen as lacking in martial quality. More generally, the strains of the conflict helped undermine the Western colonial empires, especially in South-East Asia and the Near East, and this was to prove a crucial background to post-war military events around much of the world.

CHAPTER 8

Wars of Decolonization, 1945–94

INTRODUCTION

The most important shift in global power after World War Two was the fall of the Western empires (with the exception of that of the USA which still remains in its Pacific territories). This was a shift that involved a large amount of conflict, although much decolonization, especially in Oceania, the West Indies, and French sub-Saharan Africa, was accomplished without warfare. Decolonization, however, fuelled both the Cold War, providing it with a series of battlefields and areas for competition, and provided the context, and often cause, for struggles within newly independent states.

THE LATE 1940s

Initially, there were major attempts to reintroduce Western imperial control in colonies where it had been disrupted during World War Two. This was peaceful in some territories, such as the British colonies of Hong Kong, Malaya and Singapore, but led to conflict in the Dutch East Indies, French Indo-China (now Vietnam, Laos and Cambodia), and the French colonies of Madagascar and Syria. Syria had been promised independence by the French in 1944, but French policy during the continued Anglo-French occupation led to fighting, which began in

1945 and escalated with the French shelling Damascus. French and British troops were finally withdrawn in April 1946. The following year there was an anti-French rising in Madagascar, but this was firmly repressed, as the Sétif rebellion in the French colony of Algeria (then part of metropolitan France) had been in 1945.

The Dutch were less successful in the Netherlands East Indies (now Indonesia). Returning after the end of the war, they were unable to suppress the resistance of nationalists, who had been encouraged during the Japanese occupation and who had declared independence in 1945. Nor did the Dutch prove able to cope with the political challenge of nationalism. In November 1946 they negotiated the Linggajati agreement, recognizing the position of the nationalist government on Java and Sumatra, and undertaking to co-operate in the creation of a democratic federation; but the Dutch commitment to the agreement was limited and, when it lapsed in June 1947, following divisions within the nationalist movement, the Dutch made a major attempt to secure their position, not least because there were about 300,000 Dutch citizens in the East Indies.

Thanks to a large-scale deployment of troops, about 150,000 men, and the support of local allies, especially on the outer islands where there was hostility to the nationalists who were mostly based in Java, the Dutch in two police actions (they did not present the struggle as a war) – in late 1947 and December 1948 – did limit the extent of Java and Sumatra controlled by the nationalists, and, by the end of 1948, the Dutch were in a strong position on Java. However, a combination of American anti-colonial pressure, post-World War Two Dutch weakness, the strains of resisting guerrilla warfare, and the intractability posed by nationalist determination, forced the Dutch to back down. The Americans were willing to press the Dutch to withdraw, a very different position to that adopted towards the French in Indo-China, because their opponents were viewed as nationalists ready to stand up against Communists: the Americans took a very different view of Communist nationalists. The Dutch accepted, first, an armistice on 1 August 1949 and then Indonesian independence on 2 November 1949.

The Indonesians then moved into Dutch Borneo, the Celebes, the Moluccas, the Lesser Sunda Islands and West Timor; although western New Guinea (still then held by the Dutch) and East Timor (still then held by Portugal) did not follow until later. Far from being inconsequential, the conflict in the Dutch East Indies transferred control over a very populous area: the second most populated colony after British India. It was also important that the conflict led to the maintenance of territorial cohesion, rather than to a return to the pre-Dutch pattern of numerous states.

The British were also involved in a process of imperial withdrawal in the late 1940s. The most important departure was from British India. There, World War Two had helped undermine British rule, and post-war volatility made it impossible to provide a level of stability sufficient to serve as the basis for a restoration of the processes of accommodation that ensured widespread consent. The rise of the nationalist Congress Party had challenged the British position, not least by hitting the effectiveness, business and morale of government. In addition, the increased sectarianism of Indian politics, with the rise of the Muslim League and its distrust of the Hindu-dominated Congress Party, made imperial crisis management, let alone control, impossible. The British hope for a quasi-federation of Muslim and Hindu India fell victim to their inability to reach compromises, leading to a reluctant agreement to partition. The British decision to withdraw in August 1947 was marked by large-scale violence, which was inter-communal (with much of what would subsequently be termed ethnic cleansing), rather than directed at the British. India was divided between the new states of India and Pakistan. The following year, independence followed for Burma and Ceylon (now Sri Lanka), although, at least initially, without the large-scale violence seen in British India.

Inter-communal violence, in this case Arabs versus Jews, was also central in Palestine. There, the British mandate ended on 14 May 1948, with the government keen to get an embarrassing problem off its hands. It had found it impossible to maintain order, and had also faced major difficulties at sea, trying to prevent illegal immigration by Holocaust survivors. The British departure was followed by war (see pp. 217–18), just as that from India led to conflict between India and Pakistan over Kashmir.

THE MALAYAN EMERGENCY

Elsewhere, however, the British made a major attempt to maintain their imperial position. The surrender of Japan was followed by the reimposition of control in occupied areas, including Malaya, Singapore and Hong Kong, and, from 1948, a serious effort was made to resist a Communist insurrection in the economically crucial colony of Malaya. In what was termed the Malayan Emergency, the British initially failed to devise an effective strategy, but this changed with the development of successful, and intertwined, military and political plans: 'hearts and minds' policies restricted the appeal of the Malayan Communist Party, which was largely based in the minority Chinese population, although these policies also rested on the ability to coerce if necessary, while local economic growth, which benefited greatly from demand stemming from the Korean War, also helped. There was also an appropriate military policy: British effectiveness owed much to the use of helicopters and transport aircraft which greatly enhanced mobility, to improvements in their intelligence system, and to the use of counter-insurgency forces skilled in jungle craft and able to understand the local situation. Rather than requiring protection, a problem with force deployment in many counter-insurgency struggles, such forces could take the war to the guerrillas. This was complemented by steps to control the population that entailed the careful supervision of food supplies and the resettlement of much of the rural population, a crucial move. The context was totally different, but it is instructive to contrast the British army in Malaya then and in the conflict with the Japanese from 1941 to 1942. In the Emergency, the British knew the military environment and, in particular, understood the jungle to an extent that was absent in 1941 and 1942. Morale was also higher, in part because the British were not only in a stronger position but also able to take the initiative.

Partly due to Malaya's geographical isolation, and certainly to the absence of a neighbouring Communist state, the Communists lacked adequate Chinese and Soviet support, and they also failed to create a parallel system of government;

while the British did not allow the Emergency to deter them from their political course: moves towards self-government (1955) and independence (1957), which the British correctly saw as the best way to win popularity and thus defeat the Communists. On the local level there was a parallel move toward normality, with pacified areas benefiting from an easing of the emergency regulations.

Having largely beaten the insurgents by 1954, the British maintained the pressure over the following years, in particular by the effective use of the now well-developed intelligence apparatus, further weakening the Communists, and were rewarded with mass surrenders in December 1957. In the 1960s, British success in Malaya was to be contrasted with American failure in Vietnam. The contrast frequently focused on greater British commitment to, and skill in, 'hearts and minds' policies, and on the deficiencies of the American stress on firepower. While this was correct, the problem facing the Americans in Vietnam, in terms both of the political situation there and of the international context, was far more difficult.

FRANCE IN INDO-CHINA

France was less successful in Indo-China from 1946 to 1954, in part because, unlike the British in Malaya, the French faced an opponent that had a safe neighbouring base after the Communists won the Chinese Civil War in 1949. Important differences of interest between the Viet Minh and the Chinese Communists that in part reflected long-standing tensions between China and Vietnam affected the degree of support that was provided, but assistance from 1950 helped ensure that the Communist and nationalist Viet Minh pushed the French back from their border posts in the Le Hong Phong II offensive in late 1950. In addition, the French reliance on the road system to link their positions led to a vulnerability that the Americans later were better able to avoid in Vietnam thanks to their vastly greater air transport capability, while the French also lacked any recent experience in counter-insurgency operations. The Viet Minh were defeated, however, when they switched to mass attacks on French *hérissons*, fortified hedgehog positions, in the open areas of the Red River delta in North Vietnam in 1951 and 1952, for example at Vinh Yen and Mao Khé, and in the Day River campaign. In these campaigns, the French benefited from a vigorous command and from being able to employ their conventional forces and air power, which used napalm among other weapons. The Maoist doctrine of moving from guerrilla operations to conventional warfare did not work in 1951 and 1952, just as it was later to fail in Vietnam in 1968 and 1972.

Nevertheless, the Viet Minh were helped by the extent to which, in contrast to the British in Malaya, French forces were spread out over a large area of operations, while the French also faced more numerous opposition and enjoyed less local support, which affected their capacity to use existing local administrative systems to win backing. The French strategy of creating a puppet independent state under Bao Dai, the former emperor, which led in December 1950 to the Convention of Saigon, did not win much popular support. Furthermore, in 1952 the vigorous command of Jean de Lattre de Tassigny, commander from December 1950 until late 1951, was replaced by the less adroit generalship of General Raoul Salan. The cumbersome advances he ordered were vulnerable to Viet Minh attacks on their lines of communication: in the absence of secure aerial resupply, the latter always proved a problem for counter-insurgency forces.

From 1952 the Viet Minh, who were receiving more Chinese help than hitherto, were increasingly successful in taking over the north-west of Vietnam, threatening both neighbouring Laos (part of Indo-China) and the French-allied tribes on the Laos–Vietnam border that produced opium, its profits a valuable support to the French, not least by financing local allies. The opium crop was captured by the Viet Minh in 1952, but by the French the following year, hitting Viet Minh finances and affecting their operations.

In 1954 the struggle climaxed when the Viet Minh succeeded in defeating the French in position warfare at Dien Bien Phu, a forward base about 200 miles by air from Hanoi near the border with Laos. This position had been developed from November 1953 by French parachutists, in Operation Castor, in order to protect both native allies and the opium crop, to threaten an invasion route into northern Laos, and to lure the Viet Minh into a major battle which it was hoped would enable the French to negotiate a settlement from a position of strength.

The French parachutists who arrived on 20 November 1953 rapidly overcame the small garrison at the airstrip in Dien Bien Phu, and, by March 1954, the French had a force of close to 11,000 men in the valley, dug in in a series of strongpoints. General Henri Navarre, the French commander in Indo-China, had assumed that if the Viet Minh attacked they would only choose to use one division, but in the event, Vo Nguyen Giap, the Viet Minh commander, deployed four divisions. During the battle the French were to add from the air another 4,000 men to the garrison, but Giap was able to commit and supply even more reinforcements, a crucial margin of advantage in enabling him to outfight the French.

Viet Minh attacks began on 13 March 1954, and were helped by the French failure to occupy the high ground from which their bunkers could be bombarded, by the folly of the French assumption that their artillery could overcome Viet Minh guns, and by the weakness of French air power. The Viet Minh had American 105 mm cannon, captured by the Chinese Communists in the Chinese Civil War, and also Chinese anti-aircraft weapons and Soviet Katyusha rockets. During the siege, the Viet Minh fired 350,000 shells. Artillery bombardment of the airstrip prevented the French from landing planes after 27 March, and, instead, they were dependent on reinforcements dropped by parachute. The outgunned and poorly-chosen French strong points were successively stormed, although, thanks to their mass infantry attacks, the Viet Minh suffered far more casualties in combat. The cost of these human-wave attacks indeed led Giap to shift to the use of advancing trench positions. The last assault was launched on 6 May. By then, the net had been drawn so tight that air-supply drops were able to bring scant relief to the garrison; indeed, most fell into Viet Minh hands. The remains of the isolated French force finally surrendered on 7 May, their bases overrun. A total of 6,500 troops were captured.

The poorly led French had finally proved unable to defeat their opponents in either guerrilla or conventional warfare. The French army had shown an ability to learn during the war, and had developed counter-insurgency tactics, but in 1954 it could not respond adequately to the Viet Minh's dynamic synergy of guerrilla and conventional warfare, a synergy that reflected their organizational and doctrinal flexibility, and their successful logistics. After Chinese participation in the Korean War in November 1950 led to greater American concern about Communist expansionism and Chinese policy in East Asia, the Americans, who had begun to supply assistance in May 1950, provided massive quantities of military equipment to the French. In 1952 the USA pressed France not to make peace with the Viet Minh, and by 1954 was paying over three-quarters of French costs in the conflict; but this could not sway the struggle. American policy was both an aspect of the new strategy of the containment of Communism and an effort to support France that owed much to concern about the implications for the defence of Western Europe of developments in Indo-China.

After Dien Bien Phu, the French, who suffered from growing domestic criticism of the war, abandoned Indo-China; although fighting continued into the summer and, until they left, the French were still in control of the major centres of population such as Hanoi and Saigon. France's will had been broken by defeat – Dien Bien Phu having taken on a major symbolic importance – and the Americans were unwilling to help with a wide-ranging military intervention. Instead, under a new government led by Pierre Mendès-France, a critic of the war, 1954 saw a ceasefire and the Geneva Conference which led to a provisional military demarcation line in Vietnam along the seventeenth parallel, with the hope of reunification once elections had been held and the guarantee of the independence of Cambodia and Laos. This was not to be a lasting settlement: neither North Vietnam nor the government of South Vietnam were happy to accept partition, but it provided a political exit strategy, a solution that enabled the French to leave.

FRANCE IN ALGERIA

The French were also unsuccessful in Algeria, despite committing considerable resources to its retention. In order to concentrate on Algeria, which had been declared an integral part of France (and thus not a colony) in 1848, the French granted its neighbouring protectorate of Tunisia independence in 1956, although nationalist guerrilla activity there since 1952 had made only limited impact in the towns. The French protectorate in Morocco, where guerrilla activity had become widespread in 1955, also ended in 1956. Algeria was different. It was dominated by a settler population (*colons*) of over a million, and the 8.5 million native Moslems had no real power and suffered discrimination. Attempts to improve their position, for example the Loi-Cadre of 1947, were limited and not pressed home by the government. An insurrection by the Front de Libération Nationale (FLN) began in October 1954, much encouraged by French failure in Vietnam, but at first it was restricted to small-scale terror operations. Terror, however, had a major political impact and posed a serious military problem. Terrorist acts destabilized the French relationship with the indigenous Moslems: thousands of loyalists were killed by the terrorists, while the French army found it difficult to identify their opponents and alienated Moslems by ruthless search and destroy operations; relations between *colons* and Moslems also deteriorated.

In 1955 the scale of FLN operations increased, and the war hotted up with massacres, reprisals, and a commitment by the French to a more rigorous approach, which led to more effective French tactics: static garrisons were complemented by pursuit groups, often moved by helicopter. A switch to a more mobile force structure indeed had been important to overcoming Algerian resistance to French conquest in the 1840s. These helicopter assault forces were stepped up in 1959, in large part in response to the arrival of significant numbers of large helicopters: Boeing Vertol H-21 helicopters, called *bananes*, which could fly entire units as well as light artillery. Eventually, the French deployed 175 helicopters, as well as 940 aircraft. The designation of large free-fire zones, cleared by forced resettlement, in which aircraft could bomb and strafe freely, increased the effectiveness of the aircraft. Unlike later insurgent forces under air attack, the FLN lacked anti-aircraft missiles, which were particularly effective against slower-moving helicopters, while the arid terrain was far more exposed to strafing and to the deployment of troops than the forested lands of Indo-China. The indiscriminate character of the French use of strafing and bombing was, however, all too characteristic of a failure to distinguish foes from the bulk of the population.

The combination of air reconnaissance, air attack and helicopter-borne units in a series of sweeps in north Algeria in 1959 led to the killing of a large number of insurgents, while *harkis* – locally raised auxiliaries – served to consolidate control in swept areas: the use of the latter built on the divide and recruitment policies that the French had always employed in their colonies and that had been more generally characteristic of Western imperial control. These sweeps gravely damaged the FLN within Algeria, although other FLN units remained outside, attacking French positions from the Tunisian frontier, across the Morice Line which the French had built.

In some respects, the Algerian War prefigured that of the Americans in Vietnam, although, because of their long involvement in Algeria the French were more determined than the Americans were to be and, by now, thanks to their war in Vietnam, also had more experience of counter-insurgency warfare. Learning from their experience in Indo-China, the French had developed a 'theory of parallel hierarchies' which they applied to Algeria, putting significant resources into intelligence and civilian organizational efforts. The FLN was badly damaged in 1959 (the year in which it established a provisional government), just as the Viet Cong was to be in 1968, but the continued existence of both, and their intractability, made the military option appear a dead-end, not only to critics but also to some within government, and, in each case, created pressure for a political solution. French forces in Algeria rose from about 65,000 in late 1954 to 390,000 in 1956, after, first, reservists and, then, conscripts were sent. The dispatch of both these groups was unpopular in France, and greatly increased political opposition to the conflict.

In France, the pressures of the war helped to bring down the constitutional system of the Fourth Republic in 1958 and also to set General de Gaulle, who had formed a government in 1958 and become president at the close of the year, against the *colons* and much of the military leadership in Algeria, who were opposed to negotiations with the FLN. In January 1960 the *colons* tried to seize power in Algiers, but were faced down by de Gaulle who wished to retain control of Algeria (as well as influence over Morocco and Tunisia) but who, albeit hesitantly, was more concerned about France's other political and strategic interests and, in the last resort, was willing to abandon Algeria.

The granting of independence to most of France's other territories in Africa in 1960 made her position in Algeria appear anachronistic, and the French faced both serious financial problems and mounting international pressure to negotiate. In particular, as part of a determined effort to sway international opinion, the FLN sought to accentuate American concerns about French policy in order to prevent the French from using the issue of the Cold War to win valuable international support. Convinced that France would fail and worried that backing France would alienate Arab opinion, not least by encouraging support for radical pan-Arabianism as advocated by the pro-Soviet president of Egypt, Gamal Abdel Nasser, the Americans indeed were increasingly unwilling to support the French. In early 1961, de Gaulle ordered a truce, and in April, in the Generals' Putsch, some of the army, angry with negotiations with the FLN, attempted to seize power in Algeria; the putsch was unsuccessful because most of the army in Algeria refused to back it. The Organisation Armée Secrète (OAS), an illegal terrorist movement that wanted to keep Algeria French, waged a terror campaign against Gaullists and Moslems alike, both in Algeria and in France where it unsuccessfully sought to assassinate de Gaulle. The resulting three-part struggle of the government, the OAS and the FLN led to extensive slaughter in 1962 as independence neared. The government's agreement with the FLN provided for security for the *colons*, but most (nearly a million) fled to France, as did the *harkis*.

A summary of this conflict illustrates the general difficulty of mounting effective counter-insurgency operations. Tough anti-insurrectionary measures, including widespread torture, which was seen as a justified response to FLN atrocities, gave the French control of Algiers, the capital, in 1957. However, although undefeated in battle, and making effective use of helicopter-borne units, the French were unable to end guerrilla action in what was a very costly struggle. And French moves were often counter-productive in winning the loyalty of the bulk of the population. There were also operational problems: aside from the difficulty of operating active counter-insurgency policies there was also a need to tie up large numbers of troops in protecting settlers and in trying to close the frontiers to the movement of guerrilla reinforcements, so that much of the army was not available for offensive purposes, a situation that helped the insurgents.

It is easy to see the failure of the French as a failure of European imperialism, but the Egyptians militarily were to be less successful in Yemen from 1962 to 1967 (see pp. 215–17). Furthermore, Algeria returned to civil conflict in 1992, as the FLN state proved unable to meet expectations, was perceived as corrupt and Westernized, and proved unwilling to respond to the popular will: the army cancelled the election in 1991 that the FIS (Islamic Salvation Front) was about to win. The FIS in turn destabilized the state by widespread brutal terror, while, in response, the government adopted the earlier techniques of the French, including helicopter-borne pursuit groups, large-scale sweep and search operations, and the use of terror as a reprisal; all with only partial success. About 150,000 people died before the government amnesty of 1999 defused tension and led to a return to peaceful politics.

BRITAIN AND DECOLONIZATION

The nature of the conflict in Algeria in the 1990s, which led to major casualties, especially civilians slaughtered by the FIS and, allegedly, by the government, suggests that it is misleading to see Western military and political structures and methods as necessarily at fault in the failures of counter-insurgency operations in the 1950s and 1960s, a point that was also to be borne out by Vietnamese problems when they intervened in Cambodia in 1978 and 1979. It is also appropriate to note Western colonial successes, such as the Malayan Emergency (see pp. 156–7) and the British suppression of the Mau Mau uprising in Kenya from 1952 to 1956 (see Box 8.1). It proved difficult to control Cyprus during the Greek Cypriot insurgency of 1954–59, although regaining the military initiative in 1956, again by applying the Malayan lessons, helped contain the crisis, while the use of sympathetic Cypriots was also important.

The major British failure was not a counter-insurgency struggle but a poorly conceived war with an independent state that had formerly been a key military

BOX 8.1   THE MAU MAU UPRISING, 1952–56

In tackling insurrection in their leading East African colony, Kenya, from 1952, the British benefited from a wide-ranging social reform policy, including land reform, in which the government distanced itself from the minority white colonists and sought to win African 'hearts and minds'. The move from the initial defensive stage, in which the British suffered from not learning the lessons from Malaya, to a recapture of the initiative, in which these lessons were applied, was crucial. This move entailed the development of an integrated system of command and control encompassing army, police and administration, and the implementation of appropriate military tactics. In 1954, in Operation Anvil, the British isolated and combed the capital, Nairobi, a move that denied the Mau Mau urban support. The successful use of loyal Africans, including former insurgents, was also important, as were (until 1955) larger-scale sweep operations and, later, air-supported forest patrols. From 1955, success led to the withdrawal of British troops, and this accelerated after the capture of Dedan Kimathi, the leading Mau Mau commander, in October 1956. The following month the police were able to take over responsibility for operations.

asset of the Empire. In 1956, Britain and France attacked Egypt in an intervention publicly justified as a way of safeguarding the Suez Canal, which had been nationalized by the aggressive Egyptian leader, Gamal Abdel Nasser, that July and that appeared threatened by an Israeli attack on Egypt with which Britain and France had secretly colluded. Nasser's Arab nationalism was seen as a threat to Britain's Arab allies, especially Jordan and Iraq, and to the French position in Algeria, and the British prime minister Anthony Eden saw Nasser as another dictator. Employing the argument that the appeasement of Hitler in the late 1930s had been a serious mistake, decision-makers felt that it was important to stop a dictator in his tracks and to shore up the prestige of Britain and France as imperial powers.

Although poorly planned and affected by shortages of equipment, both reflections of the limited amphibious capability of British forces, the invasion still saw a major display of military power, with a large force sent to the eastern Mediterranean and the extensive use of warships and air attack, including helicopter-borne troops and parachutists. Much of the Egyptian air force was destroyed as a result of air attacks on its bases, and the amphibious assault was a success. Nevertheless, the attack was rapidly abandoned, in large part because of American opposition, although the Soviet threat to fire missiles against Anglo-French forces also helped raise tension. Concerned about the impact of the invasion on attitudes in the Third World, the Americans, who were ambivalent about many aspects of British policy, refused to extend any credits to support sterling, blocked British access to the International Monetary Fund until she withdrew her troops from Suez, and refused to provide oil to compensate for interrupted supplies from the Middle East. American opposition was crucial in weakening British resolve and led to a humiliating withdrawal, although, had the British and French persisted, it is unclear how readily they could have translated battlefield success into an acceptable outcome, a point that was to be recalled before the attack on Iraq in 2003. In 1958, both the USA (in Lebanon) and Britain (in Jordan) were to deploy forces in the region as Syria's espousal of left-wing Arab nationalism threatened friendly regimes, but these deployments were easy to contain as they were in support of friendly governments.

The Suez crisis revealed the limitations of British strength, encouraging a new attitude towards empire in Britain, which led to rapid decolonization, especially in Africa, but also in the West Indies and Malaysia. Decolonization was also hastened by a strong upsurge in colonial nationalist movements. The combination of nationalism and the mass mobilization of people and resources that had characterized industrializing nations in the nineteenth century spread to the non-European world and helped to undermine the logic and practice of colonial control: it was no longer practical to rely on local consent. The Western 'right to rule' colonial peoples could not be sustained in the political climate of the later twentieth century. There were examples of successful military counter-insurgency, but the political contest was lost as imperialism came to seem ideologically and politically bankrupt, and this factor indeed was to be more important in the collapse of Western control over most of the world than changes in military capability and effectiveness. In the British Empire, particularly in West Africa, nationalist movements caused problems, which policy-makers did not know how to confront, as they sought to rest imperial rule on consent, not force.

Decolonization proceeded on the assumption that Britain would withdraw from those areas that it could no longer control, or, equally importantly, from those areas where the cost of maintaining a presence was prohibitive. Colonies also appeared less necessary in defence terms, not least because, in 1957, Britain had added the hydrogen bomb to the atom bomb, while the American government encouraged decolonization and also sought to manage it as a means of increasing informal American control. American imperial power and influence did not rest on territorial control to the degree seen with the European empires.

The military dimension of decolonization included not only the containment of independence movements but also a process of changing the character of locally-raised forces. Prior to independence, these were developed in the hope that imperial influence, or at least an order beneficial to Western interests, would continue, and this helped disseminate Western military practice in what was to become the Third World. The policy represented a continuation of the former one of using colonial auxiliaries, but also a development of it as functions hitherto discharged by Europeans were handed over.

Belgium had abandoned the Belgian Congo in 1960, leading to a situation of great chaos. France also gave most of its sub-Saharan colonies independence in 1960, although without comparable disorder, and it maintained considerable political, economic and military influence in them. The British and, even more, Portuguese and Spaniards were still ready to fight to retain colonies, although the major British conflict in the early 1960s was not in a colony but, from 1963 to 1965, on behalf of a state comprised of former colonies, Malaysia, that was attacked by neighbouring Indonesia. The crisis began in 1962 with the Indonesian-supported Brunei revolt (Brunei was a British protectorate), which was suppressed by British forces from the Singapore garrison. President Sukarno of Indonesia then turned on Sabah and Sarawak, colonies in Borneo, which the British had transferred to Malaysia.

The Indonesians had good weapons, especially anti-personnel mines and rocket launchers, but the British and Commonwealth forces, who numbered up to 17,000 men (more than the Americans had in Vietnam in 1963), were well led, had well-trained, versatile troops, and benefited from complete command of air and sea. The British also made effective use of helicopters, and had a good nearby base at Singapore, and excellent intelligence, and were helped by an absence of significant domestic opposition in Britain to the commitment. As with the earlier Malayan Emergency, the British proved adept at fighting in the jungle and taking the war to their opponent. The British used a flexible response system to counter Indonesian incursions, and, eventually, followed up with cross-border operations of their own, putting the Indonesians onto the defensive. Indonesian attempts to exploit tensions within Malaya by landing forces by sea and sending parachutists there failed. Anglo-Malaysian firmness prevented the situation deteriorating, until a change of government in Indonesia in the winter of 1965–66 led to negotiations.

There was also tension in the Middle East, where the British acted to protect allies and their surviving colony. In 1958, there was an intervention to support Jordan, while in 1961 British and Saudi Arabian troops were moved to Kuwait to thwart a threatened Iraqi attack. Claiming Kuwait as part of Iraq, the Iraqi government had deployed troops towards the frontier.

More seriously, in Britain's colony of Aden, nationalist agitation, which had been increasingly strident since 1956, turned into revolt in 1963. The resulting war, which continued until independence was granted in November 1967, involved hostilities both in the city of Aden and in the mountainous hinterland of what is now part of Yemen. The British deployed 19,000 troops, as well as using tanks and helicopters, but their position was undermined by their failure to sustain local support. This extended to a crucial erosion of support among local auxiliaries: the British-officered Federal Reserve Army proved unreliable, and, in June 1967, the South Arabian Police and the Aden Armed Police rebelled in the city of Aden. Furthermore, the British were unable to support allied sheikhs in the interior against the guerrilla attacks of the National Liberation Front (NLF). The British used the scorched earth tactics and the resettlement policies seen in Malaya, but the NLF's inroads led them to abandon the interior in the early summer of 1967. In tactical terms, the NLF made effective use of snipers. Reduced to holding on to Aden, a base area that had to be defended from internal disaffection, and where the garrison itself had to be protected, which largely nullified its value, the only initiative left to the British was to abandon the position, which they did in November 1967. Once the British were clearly on the way out they found it hard to get intelligence, and this made it difficult to mount operations.

PORTUGAL AND DECOLONIZATION

There was no large-scale independence conflict in Spanish Sahara and the death, in 1975, of Franco, the long-standing Spanish dictator, was followed in 1976 by Spanish withdrawal. The situation was very different in Portugal's African colonies, and the major effort to retain a colonial empire after the French withdrawal from Algeria was made by Portugal whose conservative government saw Portugal's imperial position as its national destiny and Christian duty. Guerrilla movements in Portugal's colonies began in Angola in 1961, Guinea-Bissau in 1963, and Mozambique in 1964. The Portuguese benefited from divisions among their opponents, especially between the MPLA and UNITA in Angola, and from weaponry that included helicopters and tactical air support. Napalm and aggressive herbicides were also used. The support of South Africa was also important: then a white-ruled state opposed to black liberation movements, it viewed Angola and Mozambique as its forward defences. The Portuguese were able to retain control of the towns, for example crushing a rising in Angola's capital, Luanda, in 1961, but found it impossible to suppress rural opposition. Their opponents could also operate from neighbouring states that were hostile to Portugal, such as Tanzania to the north of Mozambique, and Angola's neighbours, Zaire and

Zambia. Guerrilla forces moved from attacks on border villages to a more extensive guerrilla war, which sought to win popular support and to develop liberated rural areas.

Native opposition to imperial rule in Africa looked back to earlier resistance to conquest, but post-1945 mass nationalism was also affected by political movements current in the period, not least Socialism. Indeed, it is possible to trace a development in post-war decolonization struggles with a growing politicization in terms of more 'modern' political ideologies, as well as their location in the Cold War. This was particularly the case in Africa from the mid-1960s. Some earlier uprisings, such as the Mau Mau in Kenya and that among the Bakongo in northern Angola, displayed many facets of old-style peasant uprisings or militant tribal identity. Although these elements still played a part, the uprisings from the mid-1960s were more explicitly located in a different ideological context – that of revolutionary Socialism. There was direct reference to the revolutionary war principles of the Chinese leader Mao Zedong, training by foreign advisers, especially from the Soviet Union, China and Cuba, and a provision of more advanced weapons, although many did not arrive in any quantity until the early 1970s. Anti-personnel and anti-vehicle mines restricted the mobility of counter-insurgency forces on land, and Soviet surface-to-air SAM-7 missiles hit their low-flying aircraft and helicopters, which threatened a key aspect of counter-insurgency warfare. In addition, the guerrillas benefited from Soviet rocket-propelled grenade launchers, and from the durable Kalashnikov AK-47 self-loading rifle, which became the guerrilla weapon of preference.

The impact of these shifts was seen in the struggles in Portuguese Africa. In Angola, the MPLA's military wing, the EPLA, received weaponry and training from Communist powers, including Cuba, and sought to follow Maoist principles, although the Portuguese were able to inflict heavy casualties on it. The sense of a wider struggle was captured in the name of two forward bases: Hanoi I and II, Hanoi being the capital of Vietnam. Also in Angola, the FNLA, a rival guerrilla movement, received Chinese weaponry. In Mozambique, FRELIMO, formed in 1962, was steadily able to widen its sphere of operations, not least because the Portuguese forces did not receive adequate reinforcements: the Portuguese government focused on retaining control of Angola, where most Portuguese settlers lived. A wider economic strategy was seen in FRELIMO operations from 1968 against the Cabora Bassa dam project on the Zambezi, a project that linked South Africa, which was to receive electricity from the dam, to Portugal, while by 1972 FRELIMO was operating further south near Beira. Militarily, Soviet and Chinese rocket launchers and, from 1974, SAM-7 anti-aircraft missiles shifted the balance of military advantage, and it was clear that Portugal could not win. In Guinea-Bissau, PALEC had SAM-7 missiles from 1973 and Cuban instructors. The missiles challenged Portuguese air superiority and powerfully contributed to the sense that the Portuguese had lost the initiative.

Although the Portuguese were reasonably successful in Angola, failure elsewhere sapped support for the war in the army and in Portugal. Nevertheless, making a formidable effort that cost up to 40 per cent of the annual budget, the Portuguese were still able to control many key rural areas, especially the central highlands of Angola. Until 1974 the 70,000-strong army in Angola, supported by secret police, paramilitary forces, settler vigilantes, African units and informers, effectively restricted guerrilla operations there and, more generally, protected the 350,000 white settlers in the colony, many of whom were recent immigrants encouraged to settle in the 1950s as the Portuguese government sought to develop its colony. A left-wing revolution in Portugal in April 1974, however, proved the catalyst to independence, demonstrating the crucial role of events in the metropole. In turn, these events were greatly affected by the war, for the revolution owed much to military dissatisfaction with the intractable nature of the conflict, as well as to civilian hostility to military service: in response to long tours of service in Africa there was desertion and large-scale emigration by young men. The change of government led to the granting of independence to the colonies the following year, and most of the settlers returned to Portugal.

ELSEWHERE IN AFRICA

The end of the Portuguese Empire was the last of the 'classic' wars of decolonization. The dissolution of the European colonial empires continued as remnants were given independence or surrendered. In 1977, when Djibouti became an independent state, France withdrew from its last African territory, although it retained rights to maintain forces and use bases in former colonies such as Djibouti. Defence and military co-operation agreements were also the basis for a system of French military advisers, local military commanders were trained by the French, and the French maintained their influence in Africa through fiscal support and military intervention, for example in Chad and the Ivory Coast. In June 2003, when the French sent troops to eastern Congo as part of a multinational peacekeeping force, they were supported by French planes from French bases at Ndjamena in Chad and Libreville in Gabon. This military presence was seen as an important aspect of France's great-power status.

In southern Africa, anti-Western decolonization struggles continued after the end of the Portuguese Empire. In order to maintain control by its minority white settler population, Southern Rhodesia (now Zimbabwe) had unilaterally declared independence from Britain in 1965. Initial African guerrilla opposition, which began in 1966, suffered from the extent to which the Zambezi valley offered a difficult approach route, in terms of both support for the guerrillas and terrain. From late 1972, however, it proved possible to operate through Mozambique as Portuguese control there was slackening. Full-scale guerrilla warfare was waged from then until 1979. As in other decolonization struggles, the African opponents of the government were largely divided on tribal lines, and this was also linked to contrasts in foreign bases and support, and in military strategy. The Ndebele-based ZAPU sought to apply Maoist concepts of guerrilla operations, while the Shona-based ZANU under Robert Mugabe preferred more conventional operations. The Rhodesian military proved better at attacking infiltrating guerrillas than its government was successful in winning 'hearts and minds', while the burden of the war was accentuated when South African military support was withdrawn in 1975. Increasingly isolated, the Rhodesian government conceded majority (African) rule, and Southern Rhodesia briefly returned to British control before, in 1980, becoming an independent state as Zimbabwe.

In South African-ruled South-West Africa (now Namibia), SWAPO (the South West Africa People's Organization) had begun guerrilla attacks in 1966. SWAPO received Soviet assistance, and Soviet and Chinese assistance was also sent to the guerrilla organizations that sought to overthrow the minority white governments of Southern Rhodesia and South Africa. The Communist powers believed that the overthrow of Western colonies and pro-Western states would weaken the capitalist economies by depriving them of raw materials and markets, and would also challenge their geopolitical position and strategic advantages. In the event, with the exception of Zimbabwe under Robert Mugabe, the successor governments found it economically necessary to trade with the West, and actively sought Western investment.

Opposition to minority white rule had become more vigorous in South Africa, with the Soweto rising of 1976 spreading to major cities. The government responded with a mixture of firmness and concessions. The former involved policing, the recruitment of local auxiliaries, intelligence, subversion, and military strikes against foreign guerrilla bases. As part of an agreement to limit the conflict in Angola, South Africa withdrew from South-West Africa in 1990. As with the British in India, however, political factors, not military failures, led to the major shift in control in South Africa. The minority white government chose to pursue a policy of peaceful change, in part because the end of the Cold War had robbed the government of the ideological justification (key to its relationship with conservatives in the USA) underpinning its racist policies. The first majority-franchise election followed in 1994, and led to the African National Congress peacefully gaining power. As with Indonesia and most states that experienced decolonization, there was no return to pre-colonial political units.

CONCLUSIONS

The conventional list of wars of decolonization is not a full one. There are two other categories to be considered. The first is decolonization struggles against non-Western states. These reflect the extent to which, whatever their political structure, whether democratic (India, post-Communist Russia), or autocratic (China, Burma, Ethiopia, Iraq), or both (Israel, a democracy which acts in an autocratic fashion in occupied territory), many states, both large and small, were, or indeed still are, at least as far as part of their population is concerned, imperial and colonial. This is the case, for example, with India in Kashmir, China in Tibet and Xinkiang, Indonesia in West Irian, and Ethiopia in Eritrea. Thus what, in one perspective, were, or are, regional separatist struggles can also be seen as wars of decolonization or of nationalism.

Secondly, there were decolonization issues involving Western powers after 1975. These took, and take, two forms, the first, regional separatist struggles that employ the language of decolonization and anti-imperialism, for example by

Catholic Nationalists in Northern Ireland rejecting the link with Britain, and by Corsican separatists angry with being part of France; and, the second, attempts to claim the colonies of Western powers even if colonial rule is supported by the local population. The Spanish refusal to accept the views of the population of Gibraltar is a good instance of this, although the subsequent blockade, when applied, could best be described in terms of police and customs harassment rather than as a military operation: it was truly war by other means, a low-intensity operation that precluded conflict. The Argentinian invasion of the Falkland Islands in the South Atlantic in 1982 was a different matter (see Box 8.2).

BOX 8.2 THE FALKLANDS WAR, 1982

That Britain was to fight a last imperial war in 1982 was totally unexpected. The Falklands, a group of islands in the South Atlantic, had been under British control from 1833, but were claimed, as the Malvinas, by the Argentinians. The military junta that seized power in Argentina in December 1981 was convinced that, because the British government was uncertain of the desirability of holding onto the colony, it would accept its capture by the Argentinians. The junta's naval member, Admiral Jorge Anaya, insisted that the navy's plan for seizing Britain's territories be implemented. The decision, in 1981, to withdraw the Antarctic patrol ship *Endurance* was seen as a sign of British lack of interest in the South Atlantic, and, on 2 April 1982, in Operation Rosario, the virtually undefended islands were successfully invaded.

The British prime minister, Margaret Thatcher, assured that the navy, whose leadership saw this as an opportunity to show its role, could fulfil the task, and determined to act firmly in what was seen as a make-or-break moment for the government, decided to respond with Operation Corporate. This depended on an expeditionary force, dispatched from 5 April, that included most of the navy: fifty-one warships were to take part in the operation. As another sign of British maritime strength, sixty-eight ships were contracted and requisitioned, including the cruise ships *Queen Elizabeth II* and *Canberra*, which were used to transport troops, and the container ship *Atlantic Conveyor*, which was sunk by an Exocet missile, taking a large amount of stores to the bottom. The speed with which the operation was mounted contrasted markedly with the time taken for the Suez expedition in 1956.

The British lacked a large aircraft carrier, and therefore airborne early warning of attacks, but they did have two smaller anti-submarine carriers equipped with ski-jump launch pads and Sea Harrier vertical/short take-off and landing (V/STOL) fighter-bombers. These planes were able both to contest Argentinian air assaults on the task force and to attack the Argentinians on the Falklands. The twenty Sea Harriers were armed with Sidewinder A1M-L missiles which offered an important edge in aerial combat. On 25 and 26 April, the British recaptured the subsidiary territory of South Georgia, and, on 1 May, large-scale hostilities began when Port

continued

Stanley, the capital of the Falklands, was bombed, with an attempt made to disable its runway. The following day, HMS *Conqueror*, a nuclear-powered submarine, sank the Argentine cruiser *General Belgrano* with the loss of over three hundred Argentinians. This was crucial to the struggle for command of the sea as it discouraged subsequent action by the Argentinian navy against the task force.

French-supplied Exocet missiles fired by the Argentinians and bombs led to the loss of a number of British warships, including HMS *Sheffield* on 4 May and HMS *Coventry* on 25 May, showing that anti-aircraft missile systems – in this case Sea Darts and Sea Wolfs – were not necessarily a match for manned aircraft, and revealing a lack of adequate preparedness on the part of the British navy, which had had to rely on missile systems not hitherto tested in war. However, the Argentinians could not sink the two carriers which provided vital air support (but not superiority) for both sea and land operations.

The Argentinians on the Falklands outnumbered the British force, and also had both aircraft and helicopters, while the British were short of ammunition because they had underestimated requirements and were operating at the end of a very long supply line. Nevertheless, landing from 21 May at San Carlos, British troops advanced

Plate 8.1 Sinking of the *General Belgrano*. Lifeboats move away with survivors as the Argentine cruiser sinks in the south Atlantic, victim in the Falklands War of a torpedo from the submarine HMS *Conqueror*. Photo taken by Argentinian soldier from a life raft, 2 May 1982, © Associated Press.

continued

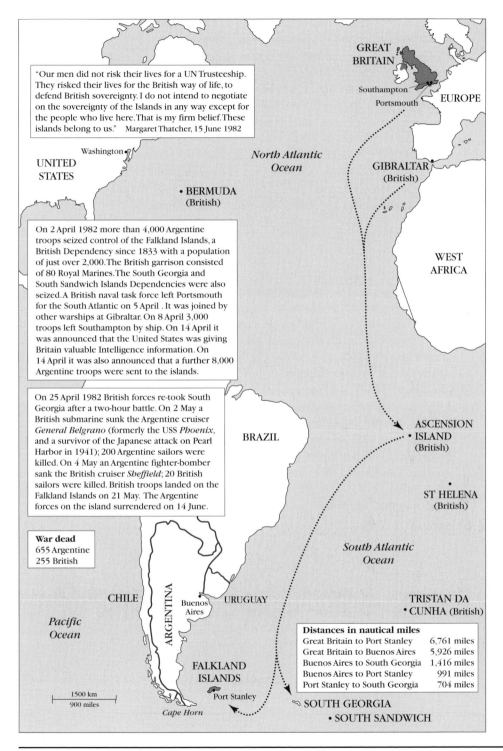

"Our men did not risk their lives for a UN Trusteeship. They risked their lives for the British way of life, to defend British sovereignty. I do not intend to negotiate on the sovereignty of the Islands in any way except for the people who live here. That is my firm belief. These islands belong to us."   Margaret Thatcher, 15 June 1982

GREAT BRITAIN

Southampton
Portsmouth

EUROPE

UNITED STATES

Washington

North Atlantic Ocean

GIBRALTAR (British)

• BERMUDA (British)

WEST AFRICA

On 2 April 1982 more than 4,000 Argentine troops seized control of the Falkland Islands, a British Dependency since 1833 with a population of just over 2,000. The British garrison consisted of 80 Royal Marines. The South Georgia and South Sandwich Islands Dependencies were also seized. A British naval task force left Portsmouth for the South Atlantic on 5 April . It was joined by other warships at Gibraltar. On 8 April 3,000 troops left Southampton by ship. On 14 April it was announced that the United States was giving Britain valuable Intelligence information. On 14 April it was also announced that a further 8,000 Argentine troops were sent to the islands.

On 25 April 1982 British forces re-took South Georgia after a two-hour battle. On 2 May a British submarine sunk the Argentine cruiser *General Belgrano* (formerly the USS *Phoenix*, and a survivor of the Japanese attack on Pearl Harbor in 1941); 200 Argentine sailors were killed. On 4 May an Argentine fighter-bomber sank the British cruiser *Sheffield*; 20 British sailors were killed. British troops landed on the Falkland Islands on 21 May. The Argentine forces on the island surrendered on 14 June.

BRAZIL

ASCENSION
• ISLAND
(British)

•
ST HELENA
(British)

War dead
655 Argentine
255 British

South Atlantic Ocean

CHILE

Pacific Ocean

ARGENTINA

Buenos Aires

URUGUAY

TRISTAN DA
• CUNHA (British)

Distances in nautical miles
Great Britain to Port Stanley   6,761 miles
Great Britain to Buenos Aires   5,926 miles
Buenos Aires to South Georgia   1,416 miles
Buenos Aires to Port Stanley   991 miles
Port Stanley to South Georgia   704 miles

1500 km
900 miles

FALKLAND ISLANDS

Port Stanley

Cape Horn

SOUTH GEORGIA
• SOUTH SANDWICH

Map 8.1 The Falklands War, 1982, from *The Routledge Atlas of British History* (2003), 3rd edition, p. 130, by Martin Gilbert. © Routledge/Taylor & Francis Informa.

on Port Stanley, fighting some bitter engagements on the nearby hills, and forcing 11,400 isolated, demoralized and beaten Argentinians to surrender on 14 June. American logistical and intelligence support aided the British, particularly 12.5 million gallons of highly refined aviation fuel. Nevertheless, in the end, it was a matter of bravely executed attacks, the careful integration of infantry with artillery support, and the ability to continue without air control. Fighting quality and tactical flexibility permitted operational execution. The Argentinian will to fight on had been destroyed, and this was crucial as the Argentinians still had plentiful troops, artillery and supplies. By landing, the British had not ensured success, as the Argentinian plan rested on fighting on from fixed positions in order to wear down British numbers and supplies, and to take advantage of the forthcoming grim South Atlantic winter. The onset of the latter obliged the British to act.

Decolonization was an important aspect of Western Europe's relative decline, and this was linked to American hegemony in the non-Communist world. The relationship was not simple, as the diminished range of global political interests that stemmed from decolonization was matched by a period of rapid economic growth in the 1950s and 1960s, particularly in Germany and Italy (neither of which needed to defend empires), but also in France. However, as this growth, like that of Japan, was not applied to military force-projection, it did not challenge the impression of American dominance of the West. Decolonization also indicates the general difficulty of separating military from other aspects of history, and this was true of the causes, course and consequences of decolonization. As far as the military aspect was concerned, the defeat of colonial powers in some struggles contributed to a more general sense of imperial military weakness and vulnerability, but it is also important to note the commitments stemming from other interests, which are covered in the next chapter.

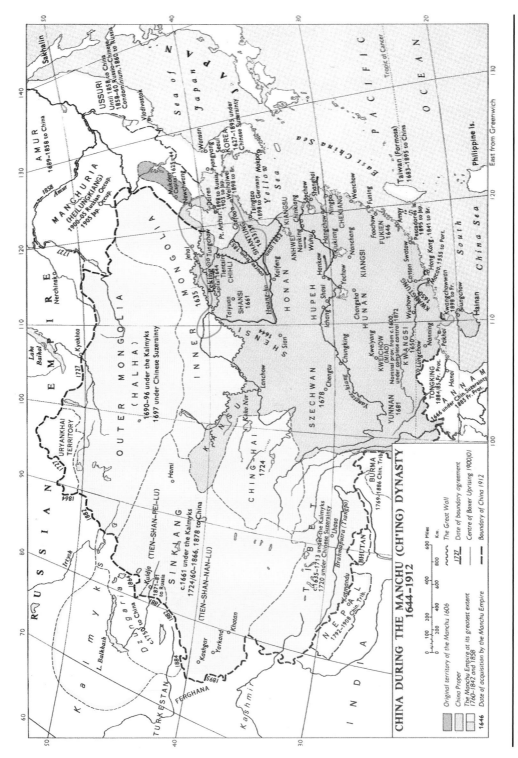

Colour map 1 China during the Manchu Dynasty, 1644–1912. © George Philip & Son Ltd.

Spanish Possessions   Portuguese Possessions   British Possessions   French Possessions

1815 *Date of acquisition*

Colour map 2 The world in 1830: European possessions and states of European origin. © George Philip & Son Ltd.

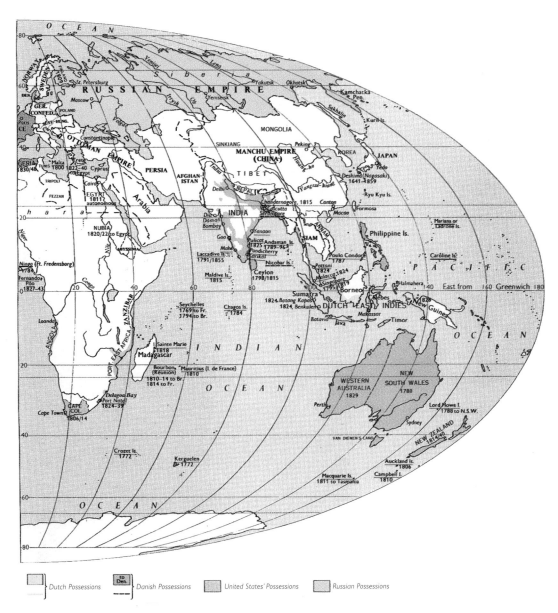

Dutch Possessions	Danish Possessions	United States' Possessions	Russian Possessions

or period of possession

Colour map 3 The world in 1878: European possessions and states of European origin. © George Philip & Son Ltd.

O C E A N
Spitsbergen
Claimed by Norway, Sweden and Russia from c.1850

RUSSIAN EMPIRE
St. Petersburg
Moscow
NORWAY SWEDEN
DEN.
GER. EMPIRE
POLAND
Paris
AUSTRIA-HUNGARY
ITALY
GREECE
OTTOMAN EMPIRE
Constantinople
Malta
Cyprus 1878
TRIPOLI
FEZZAN
NIGERIA Tunis
EGYPT 1866 Vice-Royalty
Cairo
Arabia
PERSIA
AFGHAN-ISTAN
Siberia
Yenisei
Ob
Irtish
Volga
Tashkent
KULDJA 1871-83
Yakutsk
Okhotsk
Kamchatka Pen.
Sakhalin 1853/75
1858
Kuril Is. 1875 to Jap. 1869
MONGOLIA
SINKIANG
MANCHU EMPIRE
(CHINA)
TIBET
Peking
Hwang-ho
KOREA
Yangtze-kiang
Shanghai
JAPAN
Tokyo
Ryu Kyu Is. 1874/79 to Jap.
Canton
Formosa
Hong Kong 1841
EGYPTIAN SUDAN
DARFUR 1874 to Egypt
ABYSSINIA
HERRAR 1874 to Egypt
EQUATORIA 1871 to Egypt
Bahrein 1867
Delhi
NEPAL
INDIA
Diu
Daman
Bombay
Goa
Calcutta 1833
Chandernagore
Pondicherry
Karikal
Mahé
Laccadive Is.
Kuria Muria Is. 1854
Rangoon
Andaman Is. 1857
Nicobar Is. 1869
Ceylon
SIAM
CAMBODIA
ANAM
COCHIN CHINA 1863/67
Macao
Pattani
Manila
Philippine Is.
Mariana or Ladrone Is.
Caroline Is.
P A C I F I C
FULANI EMPIRE
Lagos 1861
Fernando Poo 1843
RIO MUNI 1843
GABON 1844
Loanda
ANGOLA
Congo
CAMEROON
Maldive Is.
Sumatra
Labuan 1846
Molucca
Singapore
DUTCH EAST INDIES
Borneo
Celebes
Makassar
Batavia
Java
Sulu Arch. 1876/99
Halmahera
Timor Ambeno 1859/1906
140 East from 160 Greenwich 180
New Guinea
O C E A N
Fiji Is. 1874
Amirantes 1841
Seychelles
Comoro Is. 1841/86
ZANZIBAR
Madagascar
Chagos Is.
Réunion
Mauritius
I N D I A N
O C E A N
Northern Territory
WESTERN AUSTRALIA
AUSTRALIA
SOUTH AUSTRALIA
QUEENSLAND
New Caledonia 1853
Loyalty Is. 1853
Walvis Bay 1878
SOUTH AFRICAN REP. (TRANSVAAL) 1876-81
KALAHARI DESERT
O.F.S.
Port Natal
CAPE COL.
Cape Town
Amsterdam I. 1843 St. Paul I.
Crozet Is.
Kerguelen
Perth
NEW SOUTH WALES
VICTORIA
Melbourne
Sydney
Lord Howe I.
TASMANIA
NEW ZEALAND
Auckland Is. 1842 to N.Z.
Macquarie Is. to Tasmania
Campbell I. 1842 to N.Z.
O C E A N

Danish Possessions   United States' Possessions   Dutch Possessions   Russian Possessions

G. Guatemala,   H. Honduras,   N. Netherlands,   NIC. Nicaragua,   O. F. S. Orange Free State,   S. Salvador

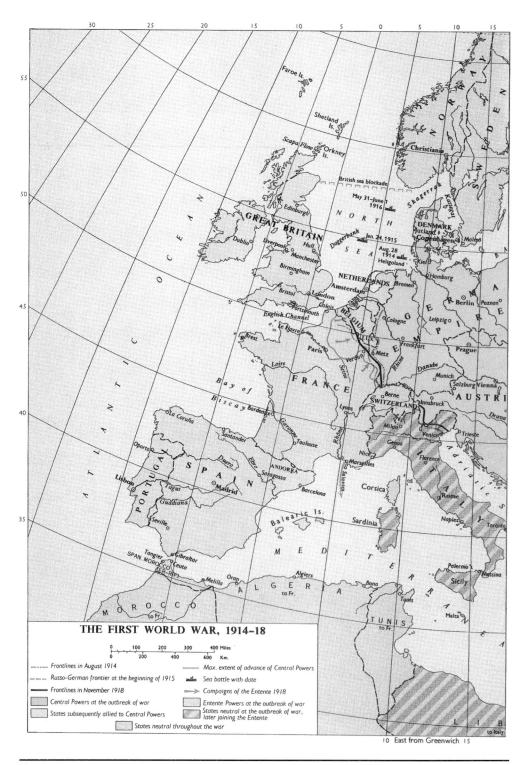

THE FIRST WORLD WAR, 1914–18

0	100	200	300	400 Miles
0	200	400		600 Km.

----- Frontlines in August 1914

— — — Russo-German frontier at the beginning of 1915

——— Frontlines in November 1918

Central Powers at the outbreak of war

States subsequently allied to Central Powers

States neutral throughout the war

——— Max. extent of advance of Central Powers

▬▬ Sea battle with date

- - -> Campaigns of the Entente 1918

Entente Powers at the outbreak of war

States neutral at the outbreak of war, later joining the Entente

10   East from Greenwich   15

Colour map 4 World War One, 1914–18. © George Philip & Son Ltd.

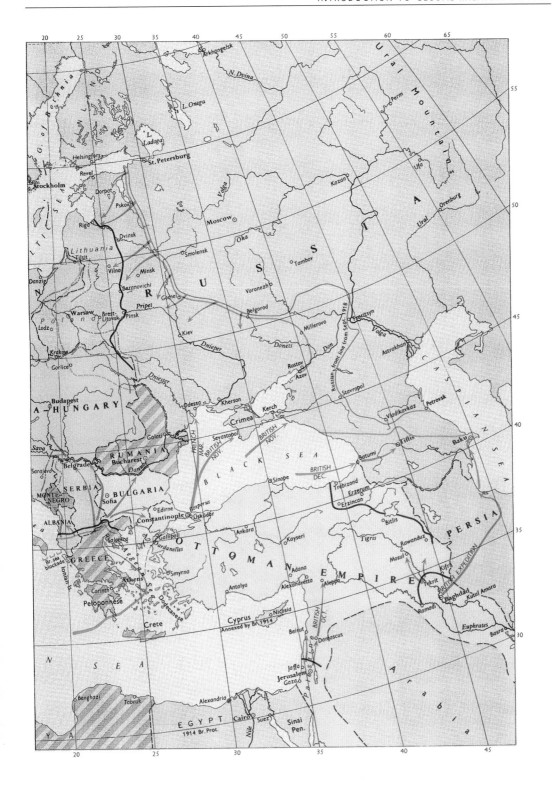

All states which attained independence after 1954 are coloured,

1946 *Date of independence after 1945*

A. *Albania,* B. *Belgium,* BU. *Burundi,* C. *Costa Rica,* CAM. *Cambodia,* CZ. *Czechoslovakia,* D.R. *Dominican Rep.,* G. *Guatemala*

W.I. *West Indies, Associated States*

Colour map 5 Decolonization, 1945–68. © George Philip & Son Ltd.

names of small islands which became independent are underlined in red

▬▬▬ Demarcation Lines (in Germany, Korea, Vietnam) and Cease Fire Line in Kashmir 1949

H. Honduras,   I. Israel,   J. Jordan,   L. Lebanon,   M. Malawi,   N. Netherlands,   NIC. Nicaragua,   P. Panama,   R. Rwanda,   S. Salvador,   Sikkim (Indian Prot.)

with United Kingdom from 1967

Independent and dependent member state
of the British Commonwealth

Independent and dependent member states
of the French Union

United States' Possessions

1949 Date of independence

A. *Albania*, B. *Belgium*, C. *Costa Rica*, CAM. *Cambodia*, CZ. *Czechoslovakia*, D.R. *Dominican Rep.*, G. *Guatemala*,

Colour map 6 The world in 1950. © George Philip & Son Ltd.

Spanish Possessions   Portuguese Possessions   Netherlands and Overseas Territories   Territories placed by U.N. under Trusteeship in 1946

Demarcation Lines (in Germany, Korea, Vietnam) and Cease Fire Line in Kashmir 1949

H. *Honduras*, I. *Israel*, J. *Jordan*, L. *Lebanon*, N. *Netherlands*, NIC. *Nicaragua*, P. *Panama*, S. *Salvador*, *Sikkim (1947 independent, 1950 Indian Prot.)*

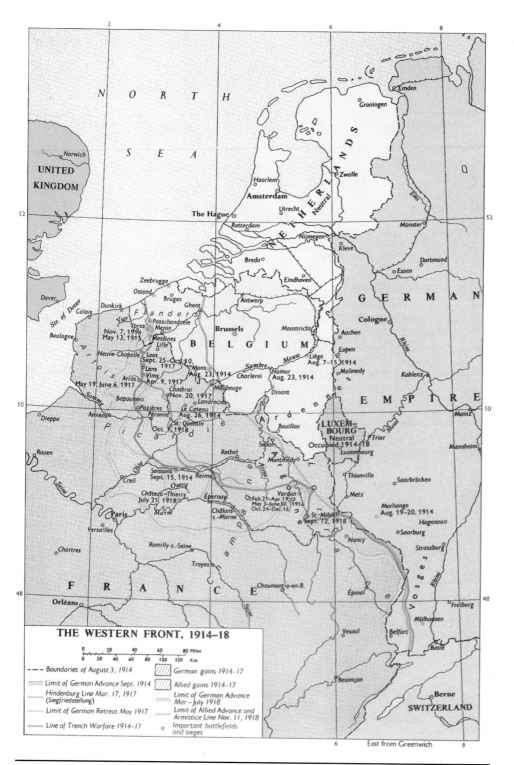

Colour map 7 The Western Front, 1914–18. © George Philip & Son Ltd.

The Cold War, 1945–90

INTRODUCTION

The Cold War, the great superpower standoff between the USA and the Soviet Union, the confrontation between Communism and Western values, was not a formal or frontal conflict between the superpowers but a period of sustained hostility involving a protracted arms race, as well as numerous proxy conflicts in which the major powers intervened in other struggles. These conflicts in turn sustained attitudes of animosity in the USA, the Soviet Union and elsewhere, exacerbated fears, and contributed to a high level of military preparedness, including the most serious arms race in history, one indeed that led to the prospect of the devastation of much of the world through the use of atomic weaponry.

The Cold War is usually approached through a consideration of the partition of Europe between Communism and the West in the aftermath of World War Two, with subsequent discussion of the serious confrontation along this front line between the two systems: the Iron Curtain erected by the Communists to control access to and exit from Eastern Europe. This was indeed important, but it is appropriate to begin not there but rather in East Asia, where control or hegemony over a large portion of the world's population was actively contested, not least in three bitter wars, and where the legacy of the Cold War remains very important to current rivalries and alignments.

The end of World War Two in 1945 was followed by peace in some areas, especially the occupied Axis states, but, elsewhere, saw the continuation, or fresh outbreak, of warfare, which reflected the degree to which World War Two was an umbrella conflict that encompassed many struggles, some of which had preceded the war and continued after it. Furthermore, the end of the war itself left issues unresolved that were to be clarified by the use of force.

The militarized character of the late 1940s and early 1950s also, in part, reflected the difficulty of moving to a peacetime situation. This was particularly apparent in the occupied Axis territories, as, in place of peace treaties and rapid disengagement, there was an attempt to organize large-scale reconstructions of civil society that ultimately rested on military strength. Thus in Eastern Europe, North Korea, Sakhalin and the Kuriles, Communism and state ownership were enforced in the shadow of Soviet forces, while in what became West Germany there was a process of disarmament and de-Nazification, and in Japan, where the occupation lasted until 1952, the process was anchored by socio-political changes including land reform; in both Germany and Japan, however, wartime industrial companies continued intact into the post-war period. The numbers of troops involved in support of these occupations were considerable, and represented important military commitments that affected the ability to demobilize, not least because the reconstructions of civil society were an aspect of the confrontation with the rival ideological-political bloc. Furthermore, the troops used for these occupation duties were available for force projection, so that when the Korean War broke out in 1950 American and Australian units in Japan could be sent to reinforce South Korea.

As after World War One, the establishment of the new territorial order involved the use of force as well as much violence. This was especially the case with enforced population movements in order to create more homogeneous states, for example of Germans from Eastern Europe, especially Czechoslovakia and Poland, to Germany. In places, there was large-scale resistance. In south-eastern Poland, many Ukrainians resisted first expulsion into the Soviet Union and then, from 1947, deportation into the areas of Poland cleared of Germans, with the Ukrainian Insurgent Army defying the Poles, and the Poles killing large numbers of Ukrainian civilians. In the Baltic republics, then forcibly joined to the Soviet Union, opposition by 'Forest Brothers' continued until 1956.

THE CHINESE CIVIL WAR, 1946–49

The Chinese Civil War has hitherto proved the largest conflict in terms of number of combatants and area fought over since World War Two. As an episode in military history, the Chinese Civil War proves an instructive counterpoint to the latter, indicating the difficulty of drawing clear lessons from the conflicts of the 1940s, although it ought to be stressed that there has been far less scholarship on the Chinese Civil War, and that much of the work published on it has reflected ideological bias, being designed to cast a favourable light on one of the combatants. In opposition to the Nationalist government the Communists, under Mao Zedong, had developed a three-stage revolutionary war model, and during World War Two were able to use a combination of clandestine political-social organization (Stage 1) and guerrilla warfare (Stage 2) in order to advance the Communist position, but were unable to move successfully into the conventional realm (Stage 3) until after the Japanese withdrawal from China.

The Nationalist government was gravely weakened by the long war with Japan, being particularly hard hit by Japanese advances in 1944 and 1945, and, despite American support, was totally defeated on the Chinese mainland by the Soviet-backed Communists after World War Two. This defeat would have been less likely bar for the war: prior to the Japanese attack on China, the Chinese Communists had been in a vulnerable position in their conflict with the Nationalists, but following that attack the Communists benefited from having become, during the 1930s and early 1940s, the dominant anti-Japanese force in northern China.

In the Chinese Civil War, technology and the quantity of *matériel* did not triumph, as the Communists were inferior in weaponry and, in particular, lacked air and sea power. Their strategic conceptions, operational planning and execution, army morale, and political leadership, however, proved superior, and they were able to make the transfer from guerrilla warfare to large-scale conventional operations; from denying their opponents control over territory, to seizing and securing it. The Nationalist cause was weakened by poor leadership, inept strategy, and, as the war went badly, poor morale, while corruption and inflation affected civilian support. Nevertheless, the classic treatment of the war, as a Communist victory of 'hearts and minds' that indicated the superior virtues of Communism over the Nationalists as well as the strength of the People's Liberation Army and its brave peasant fighters, has been qualified by a greater emphasis on the importance of what actually happened in the fighting.

Until 1948, the Nationalists largely held their own. When the American use of atomic bombs led to Japan's sudden surrender in August 1945, the Communists liberated much of the north of China from Japanese forces, capturing large quantities of weaponry. Negotiations with the Nationalists actively sponsored by the USA, which sought a unity government for China, broke down, as the Communists were determined to retain control of the north. In 1946, the Nationalist troops transported north by the American navy occupied the major cities in Manchuria, China's industrial heartland; most of the rest of the region, though, was held by the Communists. The following year Communist guerrilla tactics had an increasing impact in isolating Nationalist garrisons in the north. Despite pressure in the USA to intervene militarily on the Nationalist side, particularly from the Republican opposition which raised the charge of weakness toward Communism, the Truman government wisely decided not to do so. The American military had little regard for the Nationalist army and little faith that it could win anything no matter how much help the US provided.

In 1948, as the Communists switched to conventional, but mobile, operations, the Nationalist forces in Manchuria were isolated and then destroyed, and the Communists conquered much of China north of the Yellow river. Communist victory in Manchuria led to a crucial shift in advantage, and was followed by the rapid collapse of the Nationalists the following year. The Communists made major gains of *matériel* in Manchuria, and it also served as a base for raising supplies for operations elsewhere.

After overrunning Manchuria the Communists focused on the large Nationalist concentration in the Suchow–Kaifeng region. In the Huai Hai campaign, beginning on 6 November 1948, each side committed about 600,000 men. The Nationalists suffered from maladroit generalship, including inadequate co-ordination of units and poor use of air support, and were also hit by defections, an important factor in many civil wars. Much of the Nationalist force was encircled thanks to effective Communist envelopment methods, and, in December 1948 and January 1949, it collapsed due to defections and combat losses.

Communist victories that winter opened the way to advances further south, not least by enabling them to build up resources. The Communists crossed the Yangzi river on 20 April 1949, and the rapid overrunning of much of southern China over the following six months testified not only to the potential speed of operations but also to the impact of military success in winning over support. The weakness of the Nationalist regime was also shown by the rapid way in which it unravelled. Nanjing fell on 22 April, and Shanghai on 27 May, and the Communists pressed on to overrun rapidly the other major centres. Jiang Jieshi took refuge on the island of Formosa (Taiwan), which was all he retained control over. It was protected by the extent to which limited aerial and naval capability of the Communists made it difficult for them to mount an invasion and, eventually, by American naval power. Meanwhile, in 1950 and 1951, Tibet were conquered by the Communists, their larger and battle-hardened forces overcoming resistance in the frontier region before negotiating a peaceful advance to the capital of Tibet, Lhasa, which was occupied in October 1950.

The new strategic order in Asia was underlined in January 1950 when China and the Soviet Union signed a mutual security agreement, although this masked serious ideological and strategic disagreements which became overt in the Sino-Soviet split a decade later. Communism was far from monolithic.

THE KOREAN WAR, 1950–53

The Communists had won in the Chinese Civil War, but the Americans were determined that they should not be allowed further gains in East Asia. At the close of World War Two, in a partition of Korea, a hitherto united territory that had been conquered by Japan, northern Korea had been occupied by Soviet forces and southern Korea by the Americans. In the context of the difficulties posed by Korean political divisions and growing American–Soviet distrust, both of which sapped attempts to create a united Korea, they each, in 1948, established authoritarian regimes: under Syngman Rhee in South Korea and Kim Il-sung in North Korea. There was no historical foundation for this division, while each regime had supporters across Korea and both wished to govern the entire peninsula. The regime in North Korea, whose military buildup was helped by the Soviet Union, was convinced that its counterpart in the South was weak and could be overthrown, and was likely to be denied American support. The South Korean army, indeed, lacked military experience and adequate equipment, while American military assistance was limited.

The bitter rivalry between the two states, as each sought to destabilize the other, which, from 1948, included guerrilla operations in South Korea supported by the Communist North, led eventually to full-scale conflict. On 25 June 1950 the North launched a surprise invasion of South Korea, attacking with about 135,000 troops and using T34 tanks and Yak aeroplanes provided by the Soviets that gave them an advantage over their lightly armed opponents. The South Koreans were pushed back, but enough units fought sufficiently well in their delaying actions during their retreat south to give time for the arrival of American troops. As with the South Vietnamese during the Vietnam War, the role of the South Koreans has been underrated in most accounts due to a focus on American operations.

The North Korean invasion led to intervention by an American-led United Nations (UN) coalition, which was determined to maintain policies of collective security and containment, and was concerned that a successful invasion of South Korea would be followed by Communist pressure elsewhere, possibly on Berlin or on Taiwan. Unlike later UN operations this involved major combat roles. The leading UN contingent was American, and the second largest was British. The Americans also provided most of the air and naval power, as well as the

Plate 9.1 *Adjusting Rockets*, by Ivor Hele, Korea, 1952. Two Australian ground crew load rockets onto a Meteor jet on a runway in Korea. Study in pen and brush and sepia ink, pencil, white gouache crayon on paper. Australian War Memorial, ART 40352.

commander, General Douglas MacArthur, their commander-in-chief Far East. The UN forces benefited from the backing of a stable South Korean civilian government and from a unified command: MacArthur's control over all military forces, including the South Korean army, provided a coherence that was to be lacking in the Vietnam War. American capability was enhanced by the presence of their occupation forces in nearby Japan, and by the logistical infrastructure and support services provided by Japanese facilities and resources.

Thanks to their major role in World War Two, the Americans were better able than they would have been in the 1930s to fight in Korea. Nevertheless, since 1945, due to large-scale post-war demobilization as the 'peace dividend' was taken, there had been a dramatic decline of available manpower and *matériel*. American fighting effectiveness had also declined, as was shown by the experience of some American units in the first year of the Korean War. Reservists, for example, proved to be poorly trained.

After almost being driven into the sea at the end of the peninsula in the first North Korean onslaught, the Americans and South Koreans, who successfully retained the Pusan perimeter there against attack, managed to rescue the situation by Operation Chromite. This daring and unrehearsed landing on the Korean west coast at Inchon on 15 September 1950 applied American force at a decisive point. Carried out far behind the front, about 83,000 troops were successfully landed in difficult, heavily tidal waters and pressed on to capture nearby Seoul, wrecking the coherence of North Korean forces and their supply system, which had been put under great strain by the advance towards Pusan; this achieved a major psychological victory. The capture of Seoul enabled the UN forces in the Pusan area in the south to advance. The North Koreans were driven back into their own half of the peninsula and north toward the Chinese frontier, the UN forces advancing across a broad front against only limited resistance.

The UN advance was not welcome to the Chinese, who suddenly intervened in October 1950, exploiting American overconfidence. MacArthur had been confident that the Chinese would not act. Mao Zedong, however, felt that UN support for Korean unification was a threat, while success in the Chinese Civil War had encouraged him to believe that American technological advantages, especially in airpower, could be countered, not least by determination. As with the Japanese in World War Two, however, American resilience, resources and fighting quality were underestimated in this the sole war between any of the world's leading military powers since 1945.

Attacking in force from 20 November against the over-extended and, because of an advance on different axes, poorly co-ordinated coalition forces, the Chinese drove them out of North Korea in late 1950, capturing Seoul in January 1951. The Chinese, nominally Chinese People's Volunteers, not regulars, proved better able to take advantage of the terrain and outmanoeuvred the coalition forces, which were more closely tied to their road links. The fighting quality and heroism of some retreating units limited the scale of the defeat, but nevertheless it was a serious one.

In response, MacArthur requested an expansion of the war to include a blockade of China, which the American navy was able to mount, as well as permission

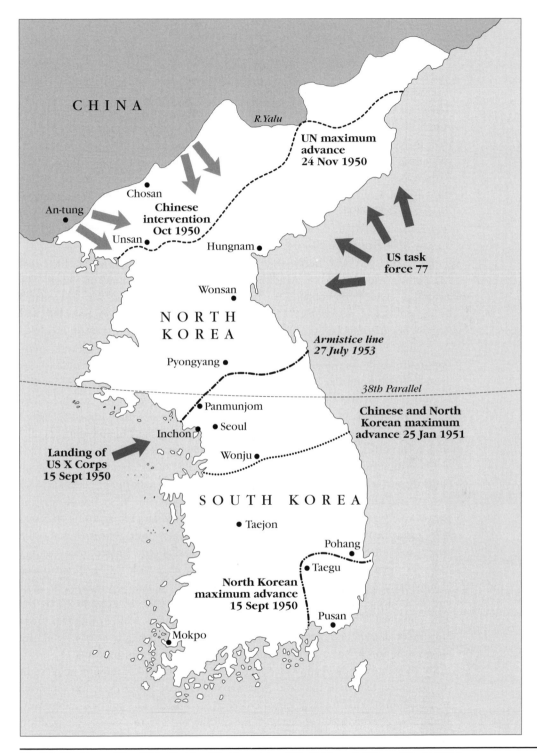

Map 9.1 The Korean War, 1950–53. After *The Times Atlas of World History* (1993), p. 274. © BCA by arrangement with Time Books.

to pursue opposing aircraft into Manchuria and to attack their bases, and to employ Nationalist Chinese troops against the Chinese coast (as a second front) or in Korea. These proposals were rejected by the joint chiefs of staff as likely to lead to an escalation of the war, with the possibility of direct Soviet entry. American restraint therefore helped ensure that the conflict did not become World War Three, or a nuclear war, and the war served as an important introduction for American politicians to the complexities of limited warfare. In turn, Stalin did not wish to take the risk of formal Soviet entry into the war.

During the war, the Chinese made a full transition to a conventional army, with tanks, heavy artillery and aircraft continuing the process started during the Chinese Civil War. The UN forces, however, were now a more formidable opponent than when the war started. The Chinese were fought to a standstill in mid-February and late May 1951, as UN supply lines shortened and as Chinese human-wave frontal attacks fell victim to American firepower.

Thereafter the war became far more static. The attritional conflict that MacArthur had sought to avoid by Operation Chromite now prevailed. The advantage given to the defence by Korea's mountainous terrain was accentuated by the politics of the conflict. Operational intensity and casualties both fell, and lengthy negotiations became more important, with offensives tied to their course. As trench replaced manoeuvre warfare, the role of artillery became more important, while, as the defences on both sides became stronger, the tendency for a more fixed front line was accentuated. With the Americans seeking an exit strategy from the war in the shape of the territorial *status quo* and a ceasefire, there was no attempt to move forward from stalemate. The eventual armistice, signed on 27 July 1953, left a military demarcation line along the Thirty-Eighth Parallel with an unfortified demilitarized zone two kilometres deep on either side.

Over three million had died in the war: 33,741 were classified as American battle deaths, with 2,827 non-battle deaths, but the vast majority of casualties were Korean; the same was true for Vietnamese in the Vietnam War. For Korea, the war was very far from limited, the South Korean military alone losing 415,000 killed, and the war closed with the partition of the peninsula between two hostile states well-entrenched and with this hostility unlanced. Indeed, the conflict had seen many of the symptoms of civil war, not least with the harsh treatment of opponents by advancing Korean forces, both North and South Korean. 1953 saw an armistice agreement, not a peace treaty, and tensions, exacerbated by the war, remained high in Korea. Although Chinese forces were withdrawn from North Korea, a process completed in 1958, the USA still retains a strong military presence in South Korea in order to deter North Korea from invading.

By the time the Korean War ended the pattern of the Communist–Western confrontation known as the Cold War was set. Outside Korea there was a process of radicalization that further helped entrench ideological and political differences. Thus, Mao Zedong used conflict with the USA in order to consolidate the position of the Communist Party within China, and to push through land seizure, killing large numbers from social groups such as landowners judged hostile to Communism in the process. Furthermore, the war led to a process of militarization and a major increase in military expenditure, especially in the West; in the Communist bloc both were already the case. For example, in the USA military expenditure rose, as a percentage of total government expenditure, from 30.4 per cent in 1950 to 65.7 per cent in 1954, and a military-industrial complex came to play a greater role in the American economy and governmental structure. Unlike after World War Two, the USA did not disarm. Conscription was revived, and the size of the armed forces greatly expanded, with the army being increased to 3.5 million men. The Americans also put pressure on their allies to build-up their military, and they duly complied. For example, military expenditure by both Britain and Canada rose greatly. Indeed the Korean War helped ensure that NATO was transformed into an effective alliance.

The Korean War also greatly increased American sensitivity to developments and threats in East Asia, leading to an extension of the containment policy towards the Communist powers, including pressure for German rearmament, the maintenance of American army, navy and air power in Japan (where bases were preserved after the occupation was ended), and a growing commitment to the Nationalist Chinese in Taiwan.

THE VIETNAM WAR

More generally, a sense that the situation might slip out of control through a 'domino effect', as the fall of one country to Communism led to that of others, encouraged the American government to take a greater interest in the course and consequences of the Western retreat from empire, especially in Indo-China where the French were under great pressure.

Although nationalism was crucial to the 'liberation struggles' there and elsewhere, they were also characterized by Communist exploitation as the Soviet Union and China sought to challenge the USA indirectly by encouraging supporters to attack US allies. These attacks brought together notions of popular warfare, nationalism, and revolutionary Communism, in a programme of revolutionary struggle in which success was believed to be inevitable. Conversely, Western governments feared that Third World anti-colonial movements and nationalism would be exploited by the Communist powers, and this encouraged a view that the West's front line ran round the world and that Communism had to be contained.

The USA was determined to keep the front line not only away from the Western hemisphere but also as close to the Communist bloc as possible. This entailed a variety of strategies, including membership of, and support for, NATO in Western Europe, the most important of a number of regional defence agreements; an American hegemony in the Pacific that rested on naval power and on bases, including those obtained under the peace treaty with Japan; military assistance to allied countries; proactive covert operations, some of which can scarcely be defined in terms of containment; and an active engagement to resist the Communist advance in the Third World, particularly the use of liberation struggles. The last brought the Americans to Vietnam.

Map 9.2 The Vietnam War, 1959–75, from *The Oxford Companion to Military History* (2003), p. 955, edited by Richard Holmes, by permission of Oxford University Press.

Vietnam had been partitioned after the defeat and withdrawal of the French in 1954. The Communist Viet Minh were left in control of North Vietnam, and an American-supported government was established in South Vietnam, where, from 1957, it faced a Communist rebellion by the Viet Cong, which led to more overt and widespread American intervention. The South Vietnamese government was corrupt and unpopular. It had won the 1955 election using fraud, and it represented best the landowning elite that composed it. The Catholic identity of the regime further compromised its popularity in what was a largely Buddhist country. The Viet Cong, in contrast, offered an apparently attractive programme of socio-economic transformation, including land reform, and won considerable support, providing a basis for military action.

From 1959, forces from North Vietnam were infiltrated into South Vietnam in support of the Viet Cong. The Americans were concerned that a failure to support South Vietnam would lead to the further spread of Communism in South-East Asia. In response, the commitment of American 'advisers' to South Vietnam, including the foundation in February 1962 of Military Assistance Command, Vietnam, encouraged pressure for increased support, and by 1963 there were 16,000 American advisers. American intervention helped limit Viet Cong advances in 1962, but the combination of the lack of fighting quality of much (but by no means all) of the South Vietnamese army (which grew in size from 150,000 men in 1960 to 250,000 in 1964) and flawed advice from the Americans, in particular an emphasis on firepower, failed to win victory. Meanwhile, invalidating notions, supported by France in particular, that South Vietnam could have been neutralized through negotiation, the North Vietnamese were determined to maintain the struggle. Meeting in December 1963, the ninth plenary session of their Communist Party's Central Committee criticized the Soviet notion of 'peaceful existence' with the West, decided to step up the war in South Vietnam, and pushed forward more militant politicians.

Apparent attacks on American warships (possibly provoked by American support for South Vietnamese commando raids) by the North Vietnamese in the Gulf of Tonkin off Vietnam in August 1964 led Congress to pass a resolution permitting President Johnson 'to take all necessary measures to repel any armed attack against the forces of the United States and to prevent further aggression'; in short, to wage war without proclaiming it. This was the preferred American option because Johnson wanted to avoid an explicit choice between war and disengagement, as well as to apply more easily the strategic concept of graduated pressure. In a general sense, the credibility of American power seemed at issue, and there was a belief in Washington that the line against further Communist expansion had to be drawn somewhere, and that this was it. The Americans were concerned about the impact of developments in South Vietnam for those elsewhere in Indo-China, especially Laos, where Communist moves greatly perturbed its neighbour Thailand, an American ally; they were also concerned about their more general implications throughout South Asia and the West Pacific. The Vietnam struggle could be put alongside China's successful 1962 war with India and Indonesian attacks on Malaysia, apparently to indicate a widespread threat as part of a crisis that America could and should respond to and affect by acting in

South Vietnam. In late 1964 regular units of the North Vietnamese army were sent south in strength, and by 1965 the South Vietnamese army was on the verge of collapse.

The American response was delayed by Johnson's wish to avoid anything that might compromise his chance of re-election in November 1964, but by the end of 1964 American forces in South Vietnam had reached 23,000; they shot up to 181,000 in 1965, 385,000 in 1966, and peaked at 541,000 in January 1969. Aside from the important contribution by the South Vietnamese, massive American involvement was supplemented by troops from South Korea, the second largest international contingent with 48,000 troops, Australia, New Zealand, Thailand and the Philippines. Although the war effort was less international than the Americans had wished, and than had been the case in the Korean War, it reflected a widespread concern about the strategic position in South-East Asia and the Communist advance, as well as a need to support the USA. Thus Australia, which had troops in Vietnam from 1962 until 1972, was anxious to secure American support in the event of confrontation with Indonesia.

The Communists were well led and organized, and their political system and culture enabled them to mobilize and direct resources and to maintain a persistent effort. American involvement permitted the North to promote the war as a national crusade against Western imperialism. Military struggle and political indoctrination were seen to act in symbiosis, and the North Vietnamese and Viet Cong were more willing to suffer losses than the Americans; their coercive political system anyway gave individuals scant choice. Limited War theory was a concept that was not shared by the Vietnamese, and American strategy was wrongly based on the assumption that unacceptable losses could be inflicted on the North Vietnamese in the way that they could on the Americans. In fact, in the face of North Vietnamese and Viet Cong determination and morale the Americans cracked first, after an inability to secure victory had resulted in an attrition that led to apparent stalemate. Viet Cong morale, which owed much to coercion and indoctrination, was apparently sustained despite heavy casualties. In contrast, American morale suffered once success proved elusive, and serious drug use and indiscipline grew, affecting unit cohesion and operations.

Looked at differently, the Americans came to appreciate the consequences of Limited War: that it could lead to failure, and did so rapidly once their initial hopes for success had been thwarted. Subsequent debate as to whether total war, which with the technology of the period might have encompassed nuclear weapons, would have led to American victory can only go so far, as the intention was not to fight such a war. Concern that China might intervene, as in the Korean War, discouraged any American invasion of North Vietnam, and thus dramatically reduced the options available to the Americans. The Chinese also provided North Vietnam with large quantities of *matériel* and substantial numbers of support troops.

When the Americans intervened in force in 1965 their opponents were already operating in sizeable units, and this led, from 1965 to 1968, to battles that were won by the Americans. Initially, the Americans focused on defending coastal areas that were the centres of South Vietnamese power and the areas of American deployment, but they then moved into the interior. They were able to advance into parts of South Vietnam which had been outside the control of Saigon and to inflict serious blows on the Viet Cong in the Mekong delta. In addition, direct mass Viet Cong attacks on American positions were generally repulsed with heavy casualties, for example at the siege of Plei Me in the Central Highlands in 1965. Under General William Westmoreland, commander of the US Military Assistance Command, Vietnam, the Americans sought to attack throughout South Vietnam, establishing firebases from which operations would be mounted in order to inflict casualties on their opponents and wear down their strength. The helicopter played a major role in this extension of activity, particularly with the use of the new 1st Cavalry Division (Airmobile). Westmoreland's strategy of attrition involved killing, capturing, wounding and causing to desert more enemy forces than they could reasonably replace.

Yet the activity only brought so much advantage, and in part it conceded the initiative to the enemy. Although heavy casualties were inflicted, opposing numbers rose as North Vietnam responded to the American build-up by sending troops down the Ho Chi Minh Trail: the supply route from North Vietnam via Laos. Furthermore, there was no concentration of opposing power that could be rapidly fixed and readily destroyed, and no front line comparable to that in Korea. Indeed, the Korean War provided scant experience for the nature of the conflict in Vietnam. American advances concealed the extent to which they shared the initiative with their opponents, while the need to devote so much strength to building up forces, logistics and security limited American combat strength. More generally, the strategy of attrition indicated the difficulty of devising a limited war strategy that had the potential for victory.

By the end of 1967 the situation nevertheless appeared promising, and Westmoreland felt that he was winning. This was inaccurate, and the Tet offensive of 1968, which involved Viet Cong and North Vietnamese attacks on cities and military bases across South Vietnam, indicated the resilience of the opposition. These assaults, mounted under cover of the Lunar New Year celebrations of Tet, were launched in accordance with Maoist ideas in the belief that they would engender a popular uprising; but none followed, and the attacks were beaten off with heavy losses, hitting Viet Cong morale. The US benefited from a pre-Tet decision to move some combat units back from near the border, where they had been concentrated. This decision, taken on 10 January, was in response to indications that Viet Cong and North Vietnamese forces were being built up near the cities. However, the Americans failed to anticipate the timing and, more particularly, scale and character of the attack: over-optimistic assumptions about enemy casualties in the border battles of late 1967 were matched by an inability to believe that a full-scale attack on the cities would be mounted.

About 85,000 Viet Cong and North Vietnamese forces attacked from 30 January 1968, with thirty-six of the forty-four provincial capitals and five of the six autonomous cities being among the targets. Attacks on twenty-three airfields were also a testimony to the role of air power. Over two divisions were used for the attacks in and close to Saigon, but these attacks were largely contained and overcome within several days. The most serious and longest battle was waged

Plate 9.2 Portrait of a shell-shocked US marine during the Tet offensive, Hué, Vietnam, 1968. The city was not regained until after difficult house-to-house struggles. The Americans lost 216 dead, the Vietnamese 384 and their opponents over 5,000. Photo by Don McCullin, © Contact Press Images.

for control of the city of Hué, the former imperial capital, much of which fell on 31 January. The city was not regained until 25 February, after both difficult house-to-house struggles within its walls and an eventually successful cutting off of supply routes into the city. The Americans lost 216 dead, the South Vietnamese forces 384 dead, and their opponents over 5,000.

Part of the nature of the conflict, as well as its brutality, were shown by the slaughter or 'disappearance' of about 5,000 South Vietnamese civilians by the Viet Cong during their occupation: their crime was that they came from social categories judged unacceptable in the Maoist society that the Communists were trying to create. To the Communists, class war was not simply a concept but an integral aspect of operations, linking political and military strategies. The American equivalent – 'hearts and minds' – proved less effective, and was harder to link to American military strategy. The massive use of American air and artillery power during the recapture of Hué destroyed about half of the city, making over 100,000 people homeless. By the end of February 1968 it was clear that the North Vietnamese/Viet Cong offensive had failed to achieve its goals. There was no popular uprising, and the Americans and South Vietnamese had not been defeated, although their losses were heavier than in earlier battles.

While the Americans could repel mass attacks on their strong points and drop thousands of bombs from a great height without much opposition, their will for the war was worn down by its continuation, while they could not deny control of the countryside to their opponents. American units suffered from a lack of accurate intelligence, and this helped to lead them into ambushes. General Vo Nguyen Giap, the North Vietnamese commander, was an effective leader who developed logistical capability to give effect to his strategy of denying his opponents (first France from 1946 to 1954, and then South Vietnam and the USA) control over territory while maintaining operational pressure on them. Giap was less successful, as in 1951 against the French, and in 1968 and 1972 against the South Vietnamese and Americans, when he turned to positional warfare and to mass attacks against opposing forces in reasonable positions (not Dien Bien Phu); but his military strategy and, crucially, the political determination of the North Vietnamese government did not depend on continual success.

The jungle nature of the Vietnamese terrain limited the options for American air power, which was applied for strategic, operational and tactical goals and, in the last case, played an important role in helping army and marine units under attack, as at Khe Sanh in 1968, complementing artillery support in this valuable role. Over half the $200 billion the USA spent on the war, a sum far greater than that expended by other Western powers on decolonization struggles, went on air operations, and nearly eight million tons of bombs were dropped on Vietnam, Laos and Cambodia; South Vietnam indeed became the most heavily bombed country in the history of warfare. There were also major American bombing offensives against North Vietnam, which were designed to fulfil both operational and strategic goals: to limit Northern support for the war in the South and to affect policy in the North by driving the North Vietnamese to negotiate. These attacks, however, faced serious opposition from Soviet surface-to-air missiles, supplied from April 1965, as well as from Soviet MiG-17 and MiG-21 aircraft.

Air power also played a major role in the unsuccessful attempt to block Viet Cong supply routes, as well as the more successful endeavour to provide tactical and supply support for American troops on the ground. Tactical support led to the use of slow-flying gunships able to apply massive firepower, although the Viet Cong were proficient in entrenching in order to minimize their losses. Helicopters were extensively used, not least in supplying positions and in applying the doctrine of airmobility: airlifted troops brought mobility and helped take the war to the enemy.

The Americans had to adapt to fight in a variety of unfamiliar terrains, including dense jungle and rice paddies. The jungle nature of much of the terrain gave the Viet Cong ideal cover, and ensured that superior American technology had little to aim at. Partly as a result, both Westmoreland's quest for battle, in which American firepower could be applied in order to ensure successful attrition, and the search-and-destroy operations pursued until 1968 in order to build up a 'body count' of dead Viet Cong, were each of limited effectiveness, not least because it was difficult to 'fix' the Viet Cong. The Americans lacked adequate intelligence of their opponents' moves, and, instead, the Viet Cong tended to control the tempo of much of the fighting, mounting ambushes that caused heavy casualties, and then ambushing relief units in their turn.

As with the air offensive against supply lines, the Americans displayed a preference for seeing the Viet Cong as a regular force that could be beaten by conventional means, rather than an understanding of their doctrine and operational methods, although in practice this was part of a sequence of asymmetrical conflicts in which the Americans had engaged, most obviously with the war against the Native Americans. Yet these were in the distant past, and whereas the marines had had experience in the 1920s and 1930s of such operations in Central America and the West Indies, they were not part of the recent experience of the other services.

Furthermore, the creation of a political organization by the Viet Cong ensured that thinking of the task in terms of battle rather than war (the misleading tendency of much simple military history) was mistaken, as more than the defeat of the guerrillas was required. The American army, however, bereft of an adequate counter-insurgency doctrine and lacking a reliable political base in South Vietnam, preferred to seek largely an exclusively military solution, and, as in the Korean War, to emphasize big-unit operations not pacification. Without the latter, however, its operations were of limited value and, instead, alienated civilian support. Many Americans found it difficult to try to understand the nature of the war they were engaged in, and to appreciate the extent to which their opponents, by refusing to fight on American terms, nullified American advantages and thus multiplied the difficulties that the terrain posed for the Americans. The Americans failed to appreciate that although they had more firepower and mobility than the French had done they were faced with the same problems of Communist determination, and that, even if it was achieved, victory in battle would not change this.

Doctrine and tactics altered once Westmoreland had gone. Creighton Abrams, who became American commander (of Military Assistance Command Vietnam) in June 1968, preferred, instead, to rely on small-scale patrols and ambushes, which, he argued, provided less of a target for his opponents than large-scale sweeps. Abrams set out to contest the village-level support the Viet Cong enjoyed and to counter the impact of Tet, which had led to a regrouping of American and South Vietnamese troops as units were pulled back to defend the cities. In 1969 the Americans inflicted serious blows on the Viet Cong, whose capability had already been badly compromised by the failure of the Tet Offensive in which the Viet Cong and the North Vietnamese had lost close to half the troops used.

The pacification programme entailed a 'battle for hearts and minds', involving American-backed economic and political reforms. 'Hearts and minds' policies are rarely easy, especially for a military not trained for these tasks, but they were particularly difficult to implement, not only due to Viet Cong opposition and intimidation, and the effectiveness of their guerrilla and small-unit operations, but also because the South Vietnamese government was half-hearted, corrupt and weak, and thus unable to take advantage of military success. The Americans could not find or create a popular alternative to the Viet Cong. As the Americans also brought much disruption, including high inflation, and devastation through the use of firepower, pacification faced serious additional problems, while the culture clash between the Americans and their South Vietnamese allies hindered co-operation.

Domestic financial and economic problems, as well as political opposition and his own disillusionment at continued signs of North Vietnamese vitality, had led

Johnson – his views confirmed by a policy review by a group of senior outside advisers, the 'Wise Men' – to reject, in March 1968, Westmoreland's request for an additional 206,000 men in Vietnam; instead, he authorized only 13,500 more troops. Military difficulties, combined with political pressures within the USA, resulted in an attempt to shift more of the burden back on the South Vietnamese army by improving its capability, and some success was achieved. Indeed, Vietnamese units fought better in response to the Tet Offensive than had been anticipated.

Domestic opposition in America to involvement in Vietnam rose because of the duration of the conflict and because the goals seemed ill defined. By denying the Americans victory in the field, and instead continuing to inflict casualties, the North Vietnamese and Viet Cong helped to create political pressures within America and to sap the will to fight, although, in so far as the sources permit a conclusion, their objectives were focused on success in South Vietnam: affecting American public opinion was only a side issue. In the USA the absence of victory led many to see the continuing casualties as futile, especially when the Tet Offensive led to questioning of Pentagon pronouncements about the course of the conflict.

As with the French in Algeria and the Portuguese in Africa, the conscription necessary to sustain a large-scale American presence in an increasingly unpopular war played a major role in the growth of disenchantment. A majority of the Americans who went to Vietnam were volunteers, not draftees, but from 1965 to 1973 about two million Americans were drafted, and draftees accounted for a third of American deaths in Vietnam by 1969. The draft led to a massive increase in anti-war sentiment. Opposition was widely voiced and 'draft dodging' common, with many Americans taking refuge in Canada. Johnson abandoned his re-election bid on 31 March 1968 because he had failed to end the war, and, once elected, his successor Richard Nixon, who had promised peace with honour, pressed ahead with substituting Vietnamese for American troops, so that he could bring the men back home and end the draft.

American disengagement under Nixon was not to be an easy process, however. In 1969, knowledge that withdrawal was beginning and a sense that the conflict was pointless, led to a marked, cumulative, and escalating decline in morale and discipline among the troops, with repercussions on fighting quality and sense of purpose that not only affected the wartime military but also made it face a major task of post-war rebuilding.

Nixon also had only limited success in Indo-China. Although he planned to move the burden of the ground war onto the South Vietnamese army, which was over a million strong at the close of 1971, there were to be more American casualties after 1968 than earlier in the conflict, and 1972 was to see a North Vietnamese offensive greater in scale than that in 1968. Although seen as realists, beginning negotiations with the North Vietnamese in Paris in January 1969, Nixon and his secretary of state, Dr Henry Kissinger, had stuck with Vietnam, indeed extending the war. They feared that a precipitant withdrawal would affect American interests around the world. Instead, in April 1970, Nixon widened the scope of the war by launching an American–South Vietnamese ground invasion of neutral, neighbouring Cambodia to destroy Communist bases there after bombing had failed to do so. This 'incursion' succeeded in the short term, helping to strengthen the Allied position in South Vietnam, while, in Cambodia, the USA provided military aid and air support for the government of General Lon Nol which had seized power in March 1970. In turn, the North Vietnamese provided help to the Khmer Rouge, the Cambodian Communist movement led by Pol Pot, which seized power in Cambodia in 1975; the 'incursion', which was of dubious legality, further lessened support in America for the war.

In South Vietnam, the Communists, following Maoist principles, came to rely in the 1970s more heavily on conventional operations mounted by the North Vietnamese. This was a consequence not only of the casualties and damage that Tet had inflicted on the Viet Cong but also of the failure of Rolling Thunder, the American bombing of North Vietnam launched in March 1965, to destroy the war-supporting capability of North Vietnam, and also of the failure of the air offensives launched against the Ho Chi Minh trail. The latter was crucial to North Vietnamese logistics, and the failure to cut it on the ground was a major limitation in American war-making. In March 1972, the North Vietnamese launched the Nguyen Hue campaign (to the Americans the Easter Offensive), a conventional invasion of South Vietnam across the Demilitarized Zone. This led to a heavy American air response in the Linebacker I air campaign of May to October 1972, which hit the North Vietnamese supply system, cutting the movement of supplies to their forces. The conventional nature of the force that had invaded the South – fourteen divisions, including tanks and trucks that required fuel – made the air attacks more devastating than those directed against the Viet Cong had been, and this had a major impact on the conflict on the ground.

The enhanced effectiveness of American air power by 1972 was due not only to North Vietnamese operational goals and methods but also to a marked improvement in American air capability that reflected both the displacement of earlier doctrine, stemming from adjustment to the varied needs of the Vietnam war, and the use of laser-guided bombs which compensated for an earlier failure of bomb accuracy from high altitudes above anti-aircraft fire. These precision weapons hit North Vietnamese logistics by destroying bridges, and were also very useful in close air support (for example against tanks). Furthermore, advances in ground-based radar technology helped in the direction of B-52 strikes.

America meanwhile strengthened its diplomatic position by a *rapprochement* with China in 1972, a step that made it less serious to abandon South Vietnam. This transformation in the geopolitical situation had far-reaching consequences. Using the pressure of further heavy air attacks on North Vietnam, the B-52 raids in the Linebacker II campaign of December 1972, Nixon was able to negotiate a peace settlement, the Paris Peace Agreements, which were signed on 27 January 1973. That month he announced the end of all hostile acts by American forces in Vietnam.

The American withdrawal, completed in March 1973, left South Vietnam vulnerable however. The war continued, with heavy Vietnamese casualties, and in April 1975 South Vietnam was overrun, in the Ho Chi Minh Campaign, by a renewed invasion from the North. Conventional North Vietnamese divisions achieved what the Viet Cong fighting in more adverse conditions in 1968, and the earlier conventional attack in 1972, had failed to do. Some of the South Vietnamese units fought well, but the strategy was poor and the regime weak.

The Vietnamese War demonstrated that being the foremost world power did not mean that a state could beat, say, the 15th. This was because power existed in particular spheres and was conditioned by wider political circumstances. In this case, these included the danger of a confrontation with other Communist powers and growing opposition to the war in the USA. The Americans themselves suffered more than 58,000 killed, while large numbers were wounded physically or mentally, the last leading to a considerable number of suicides. In addition, a sense of defeat and division had a major impact on American society.

Aside from the personal traumas, which, collectively, were also a major social issue, indeed crisis (although of course far, far less than the casualties and damage suffered by the Vietnamese), the Vietnam War also led in the USA to a major rethinking of the political context of force projection. The War Powers resolution, passed by a Democratic-dominated Congress in November 1973 over Nixon's veto, stipulated consultation with Congress before American forces were sent into conflict and a system of regular presidential report and congressional authorization thereafter. This law was to be evaded by successive presidents and was not to be enforced by Congress, but it symbolized a post-Vietnam restraint that discouraged military interventionism in the 1970s – for example against the Cubans in Angola and the Somalia–Ethiopia conflict – and helped ensure that, in the 1980s, the more bellicose Reagan government did not commit ground forces in El Salvador or Nicaragua, let alone Angola. In March 1991, in the aftermath of the first defeat of Iraq, President George H.W. Bush stated 'By God, we've kicked the Vietnam syndrome once and for all', but the legacy of the conflict continued to influence not only civilian views but also attitudes among military leaders, leading to a reluctance to get involved in counter-insurgency operations, and an emphasis on a clear mission, a containable conflict and an obvious exit strategy.

CONFRONTATION IN EUROPE

To turn from East Asia, where conflict occurred, to Europe, where it did not, is nevertheless to focus on a key front line in the Cold War. In the late 1940s the wartime alliance between the Soviet Union and the Western allies against Hitler had collapsed quickly. The breakdown of co-operation over occupied Germany, culminating in the Soviet blockade of West Berlin in 1948 and 1949, and the imposition of Communist governments in Eastern Europe, especially Czecho-slovakia in 1948, led to pressure for a Western response. In 1949, the foundation of the North Atlantic Treaty Organization (NATO) created a security framework for Western Europe: the original members – the USA, Canada, Norway, Denmark, the UK, Netherlands, Belgium, France, Luxembourg, Iceland, Italy and Portugal – were joined by Greece and Turkey in 1952. This was followed by the creation of a military structure, including a central command, and by the stationing of substantial American forces in Europe. The threat of Soviet attack led to pressure for West German rearmament, and in 1955 West Germany was admitted to NATO.

The two sides prepared for war, and tension was accentuated by the Soviet willingness to use force to maintain its interests within its own bloc, most prominently by invading Hungary in 1956 and Czechoslovakia in 1968, in each case with large forces and suppressing liberal dissent. While these episodes showed that conventional weaponry could be used to suppress internal opposition, competition between the USA and the Soviet Union led to pressure for more sophisticated weapons to provide an edge in the event of any conflict. As electronics became

---

■ BOX 9.1   THE VOICE OF CONFRONTATION: REPORTS FROM THE AUSTRALIAN HIGH COMMISSION IN LONDON

1   27 August 1953

Yesterday the Head of the Central Department, Foreign Office, commented . . . he believed that the 'struggle for Germany' would go on for years, that West Germany would be integrated with the Western defence system, and that the Russians would retain their hold over East Germany unless and until the Communist regimes in Eastern Europe had become so weakened (and there was little evidence of this at present) as to make their position in East Germany untenable . . . he concluded that the Russians were no more prepared to permit the re-unification of Germany based on a freely elected all-German government than were the Western powers willing to sacrifice West Germany for the prospect of a Germany united under Communist control.

(Australian National Archives, LH 1953/015)

2   11 December 1953

Mr. Dulles [secretary of state] said the United States accepted the concept of the 'long haul'. The task now was to set a pace which could be sustained over a considerable period; if not we might be so exhausted that we should collapse before our objective was achieved. This did not mean our effort should be static; we should take account of:

a) the varying and (he hoped) improving economic strength of NATO countries and

b) variations in the risk which would have to be periodically re-assessed.

. . . the forward strategy could not be achieved without a German contribution.

Lord Ismay [secretary-general of NATO]. In his opinion the stated military requirements could never be met under a peace time economy.

(Report of NATO foreign ministers discussions on Bermuda on 6 December 1953) more important, technological superiority, rather than mass production, became the key factor in weaponry and force structure, and this helped give the USA a vital advantage: its economy was better suited to the new military requirements.

The change in weaponry also had a major impact on the requirements for soldiers. Weaponry in which machinery played a major role ensured that skill, rather than physical strength, became more important, and this was accentuated as the machinery became more complex. This led to greater military concern about the quality of both troops and training, and encouraged military support for a professional volunteer force rather than conscripts. The burden of training the latter was heavy and the military skills of most of them were limited. A greater proportion of the civilian population was not suitable for military service, and certainly not for skilled service. Furthermore, the heavy logistical and financial burden of maintaining conscript forces in the context of rising Western living standards and expectations became an unacceptable burden, leading to an end or lessening of conscription: Britain phased it out from 1957 to 1963, and the USA from 1969 to 1973. The shift towards skill not only lessened the logic of conscription but also led to the inclusion of women in many militaries.

The dissemination of advanced weaponry to ordinary units led to a change in the character of infantry as armies became fully motorized and mechanized. In place of advances on foot, or essentially static position warfare, planning for infantry focused on rapid mobility. This was seen as necessary as it was assumed, by both sides, that any war touched off by a Soviet invasion of Western Europe would be rapid.

Although the defence of West Germany led to NATO forces preparing fixed defences, a flexible defence was called for by Western strategists, not least with counter-attacks to take advantage of the use of nuclear weaponry. Furthermore, only a flexible defence would allow the Western forces to regain, and exploit, the initiative. From 1959 to 1963, in a process termed ROAD (Reorganization of the Army Division), there was a reorganization and re-equipment of the American army, focused on a heightened flexibility that benefited from the provision of new tanks, helicopters, self-propelled artillery and armoured personnel carriers.

In addition, the victory of the Israelis against Egyptian and Syrian defensive positions in the Six-Day War of 1967 and, eventually, after initial Egyptian and Syrian successes, in the Yom Kippur War of 1973 (see pp. 221–2), showed the value of mobility and the vulnerability of forces with a low rate of activity; and the Americans devoted considerable attention to lessons to be learned from the Yom Kippur War, not least as the Egyptians and Syrians were armed by the Soviets. The Israelis themselves sought to develop more integrated command structures, establishing Israel Ground Forces Command as a first move.

Also putting an emphasis on mobility and tempo, the Soviets planned a rapid advance into NATO rear areas in Western Europe, which would compromise the use of Western nuclear weaponry. The Soviet emphasis on the offensive led to a stress on combined arms operations with a large contribution from armour. In Soviet conventional operational methods, lead divisions were to attack until they were fought out, and were then to be replaced by second and third echelon forces, taking full advantage of their numerical superiority over their NATO foes and

BOX 9.2 HUNGARY AND CZECHOSLOVAKIA

The high costs of the Cold War placed a crippling burden on the Soviet Union, and helped limit the appeal of Communism to its citizens, although economic problems stemming from the dominant role of state planning were more important, as was the inability to develop the consumer spending that was so important to economic growth and public satisfaction in the USA and Western Europe. This lack of popularity made it difficult for the Soviet government and those of their Communist allies to view change and reform with much confidence, and the maintenance of powerful armed forces by the Soviet Union was, in part, designed to prevent internal disaffection. Soviet willingness to use force to maintain its interests within its own bloc was displayed, most prominently, by invading Hungary in 1956 and Czechoslovakia in 1968. In both cases, and again with the Polish Solidarity movement in 1981, the KGB presented nationalist opposition as ideological sabotage actively sponsored by Western intelligence agencies, and this sabotage was seen as a threat to the continuation of Communism.

In Hungary in 1956, after initial hesitation, the determined use of armour, supported by air attacks and helicopters, in Operation Whirlwind, crushed opposition, ending attempts to replace a Soviet client regime and create an independent Socialist state, which, it was feared, would be seen as an American triumph. In response, the Hungarians attacked tanks with Molotov cocktails (petrol bombs) and sniped at Soviet troops. Heavily outnumbered, the resistance was brutally crushed, with about 20,000 people killed and 200,000 going into exile, whereas Soviet forces lost 2,250 dead, missing and wounded. Affected by UN reluctance to act, the simultaneous Suez Crisis, the absence, due to Austrian neutrality, of direct land access to Hungary, the fear of touching off a general war, the posture of NATO, and a lack of reliable information about options, the Americans, for all their talk of 'rollback', were unwilling to intervene, while, to deter American intervention, the Soviet army deployed troops along the Austrian frontier. Earlier that year, strikers in the streets of Poznan had been crushed by the Polish army, with fifty-six killed.

In 1968, about 250,000 Soviet troops, backed by Polish, Hungarian and Bulgarian forces, suppressed a liberalizing Communist regime in Czechoslovakia, although there was less fighting than in Hungary in 1956, because the Czech government decided not to offer armed resistance as it feared the consequences for the civilian population and knew that there was no prospect of Western support. Demonstrators relied on non-violent protest, for example throwing paint against tanks. Even so, ninety-six Soviet soldiers were killed, as well as about 200 Czechs and Slovaks. The protests had a major impact on international opinion but failed to dislodge the Soviets, and Czechoslovakia remained under firm Communist control until the fall of the Soviet bloc. Under the Brezhnev doctrine, the Soviet Union claimed the right to intervene with force when Communist governments were under threat. The invasion of Czechoslovakia, nevertheless, probably undermined the capabilities and readiness of Warsaw Pact forces, as a lack of certainty about the loyalty of national contingents weakened the alliance, while the need to consider how best to respond to possible risings affected military planning. As another sign of tension, the police were used to break student protests in Poland in 1968.

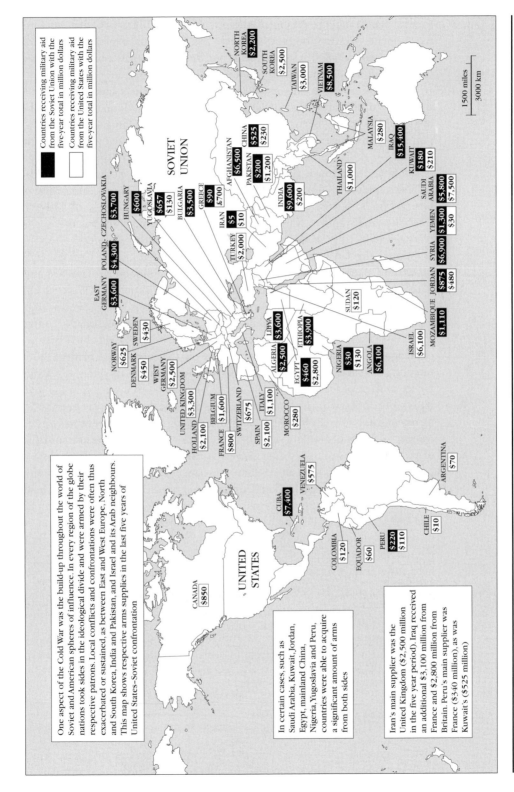

Countries receiving military aid from the Soviet Union with the five-year total in million dollars

Countries receiving military aid from the United States with the five-year total in million dollars

One aspect of the Cold War was the build-up throughout the world of Soviet and American spheres of influence. In every region of the globe nations took sides in the ideological divide and were armed by their respective patrons. Local conflicts and confrontations were often thus exacerbated or sustained, as between East and West Europe, North and South Korea, India and Pakistan, and Israel and its Arab neighbours. This map shows respective arms supplies in the last five years of United States–Soviet confrontation

In certain cases, such as Saudi Arabia, Kuwait, Jordan, Egypt, mainland China, Nigeria, Yugoslavia and Peru, countries were able to acquire a significant amount of arms from both sides

Iran's main supplier was the United Kingdom ($2,500 million in the five year period). Iraq received an additional $3,100 million from France and $2,800 million from Britain. Peru's main supplier was France ($340 million), as was Kuwait's ($525 million)

SOVIET UNION

UNITED STATES

NORTH KOREA $2,200
SOUTH KOREA $2,500
TAIWAN $3,000
VIETNAM $8,500
MALAYSIA $280
IRAQ $15,400
KUWAIT $180 $210
SAUDI ARABIA $5,800 $7,500
YEMEN $30
SYRIA $1,300
JORDAN $875
MOZAMBIQUE $1,110
THAILAND $1,000
CHINA $525 $230
AFGHANISTAN $6,500
PAKISTAN $200 $1,200
INDIA $9,600 $200
IRAN $5 $10
GREECE $90 $700
TURKEY $2,000
BULGARIA $3,500
YUGOSLAVIA $130
HUNGARY $600
CZECHOSLOVAKIA $3,700
POLAND $4,300
EAST GERMANY $3,600
NORWAY $625
SWEDEN $430
DENMARK $450
WEST GERMANY $2,500
UNITED KINGDOM $3,300
HOLLAND $800
BELGIUM $1,600
FRANCE $2,100
SWITZERLAND $675
SPAIN $2,100
ITALY $1,100
MOROCCO $280
ALGERIA $2,500
LIBYA $3,600
EGYPT $460 $2,800
ETHIOPIA $3,900
SUDAN $120
NIGERIA $30 $130
ANGOLA $6,100
ISRAEL $6,100
CANADA $850
CUBA $7,400
VENEZUELA $575
COLOMBIA $120
ECUADOR $60
PERU $220 $110
CHILE $10
ARGENTINA $70

1500 miles
3000 km

Map 9.3 The Cold War and arms supplies, 1984–88, from *The Routledge Atlas of Russian History* (2004), 3rd edition, p. 147. © Routledge/Taylor & Francis Informa.

thereby sustaining the tempo of the offensive. In contrast to this emphasis on replacement, Western forces, which were less numerous, depended on reconstitution, with individual unit replacements and battlefield repair and recovery, in order to sustain units in contact with the enemy indefinitely.

Essentially building on the operational policy of their successes in the latter stage of World War Two, with its penetration between German defensive hedgehogs and the speedy overcoming of Japanese forces in Manchuria, the Red Army put a premium on a rapid advance. Thus, Plan Granite, which they helped produce for the Egyptians, included, in its last phase, the reconquest of the whole of the Sinai from Israel, although, in the event, in 1973 the Egyptians settled for far more limited goals. Under Marshal N.V. Ogarkov, who became chief of the General Staff in 1977, the Soviets developed earlier concepts of Deep Battle (mobility and rapid advance), which had been enhanced by the spread of mechanization in their army and by the growth of airborne forces.

In turn, the Americans advanced the doctrine of, first, Active Defence and then of AirLand Battle as their military reformulated its thinking and practice after the Vietnam War. They placed a renewed emphasis on protecting Western Europe, rather than planning for counter-insurgency operations elsewhere, an emphasis that responded to Soviet capability but that was also doctrinally convenient for both the army and the air force, each of which had found the Vietnam War challenging. AirLand Battle led to a stress on the integration of firepower with mobility, maximizing the potential of American forces, in order to thwart the Soviet concept of Deep Battle. AirLand Battle also led to investing in the modernization of conventional weaponry to achieve these goals, and it matched the Soviets in recognizing a level of conflict (and thus planning) in war between tactics and strategy – the operational level. The last led to an important reconceptualization of warfare, as it was argued that success at this level was crucial to victory.

Although not tried out in conflict in Germany, AirLand influenced notions of effective synergy between land and air, and suggested that NATO would be better placed than had been argued to repel a Soviet conventional attack in Europe. The AirLand strategy was designed to permit the engagement and destruction of the second and third echelon Warsaw Pact forces at the same time that the main ground battle was taking place along the front. This strategy also met the USAF's need for a clear role after the damage done by the Vietnam War to the doctrine of strategic airpower. Some of America's allies moved in a similar direction, the French creating a *Force d'Action Rapide* with five divisions designed to resist the Soviets in southern Germany.

As a result of the changes in the American army that followed the 1973 Yom Kippur War it became very different in doctrine, strategy, tactics, organization and weaponry. The AirLand strategy was first to be used against Iraq in 1991.

PLANNING FOR ARMAGEDDON

Overhanging all else during the Cold War was the nuclear deterrent. America's nuclear monopoly, which appeared to offer a means to deter, if not coerce, the

Soviet Union, had lasted only until 1949, when, thanks to successful spying on Western nuclear technology, the Soviet Union completed its development of an effective bomb that was very similar to the American one. This development had required a formidable effort, as the Soviet Union was devastated by the impact of World War Two, and it was pursued because Stalin believed that only a position of nuclear equivalence with the USA would permit the Soviet Union to protect and advance its interests. However, such a policy was ruinous financially; seriously harmful to the Soviet economy, as it led to the distortion of research and investment choices; and militarily questionable, as resources were used that might otherwise have developed conventional capability. Although the Communist governments that followed Stalin, after he died in 1953, introduced changes in some aspects of policy, they did not break free from his legacy of nuclear competition.

Even when America alone had had the bomb, the value of the weapon was limited as it was insufficiently flexible (in terms of military and political application or acceptance of its use) to meet challenges other than that of full-scale war. Thus the Americans did not use the atom bomb (of which they then indeed had very few) to help their Nationalist Chinese allies in the Chinese Civil War. Similarly, American possession of the bomb did not deter the Soviets from intimidating the West during the Berlin Crisis of 1948–49. Nevertheless, the availability of the bomb encouraged American political and military reliance on a nuclear deterrent, which made it possible to hasten the demobilization of their forces. This had the unintended consequence of leaving the USA more vulnerable when the Korean War broke out in 1950 as their conventional forces were weaker than they would otherwise have been.

The American–Soviet nuclear duopoly that began in 1949 did not last long. Britain, France, China, India and Pakistan followed with their own atomic weapons in 1952, 1960, 1964, 1974 and 1988 respectively, while Israel and South Africa also developed a nuclear capability. Conversely, neither West Germany nor Japan developed such technology. This reflected the absence of any policy of *revanche* on the part of the post-war leaderships that gained control after Western occupation ceased, which spoke well of the post-war Allied rebuilding effort. It also accorded with American-directed Western security policies.

The destructive power of nuclear weapons increased when the atomic bomb was followed by the hydrogen bomb. This employed a nuclear explosion to heat hydrogen isotopes sufficiently to fuse them into helium atoms, a transformation that released an enormous amount of destructive energy. The USA first tested a hydrogen bomb in 1952, destroying the Pacific island of Elugelab with the explosion. The development of the hydrogen bomb was seen as a way to reconfirm American nuclear superiority, but it again was rapidly thwarted, as the USA was followed by the Soviet Union in 1954, Britain in 1957, China in 1967 and France in 1969.

Delivery systems for nuclear weapons had, in the meantime, changed radically. In the late 1940s and early 1950s, the Soviet Union had been within range of American bombers based in Britain (with bases in northern Iraq seen as the best way to threaten southern Russia), but the USA itself had been out of range of

Soviet nuclear attack. American doctrine focused on massive nuclear retaliation in response to any Soviet use of their larger non-nuclear forces in Europe or elsewhere, and the use of the atom bomb in 1945 ensured that there was a new thrust to air power, one provided by the apparent ability of a small number of bombs to make a decisive difference. The major role of this in American strategy was linked to the creation, in 1947, of an independent air service in the USA – the United States Air Force (USAF).

In order to fulfil its independent role, and to take the leading part in the Cold War, American air force thinking was dominated by strategic nuclear bombing: the ability to strike at Soviet centres was seen as an effective deterrent, indeed as the sole counter to Soviet conventional strength and the vulnerability of America's allies and interests, as well as a war-winning capability, and therefore as the essential purpose of American air power. This emphasis was given added force by the role of officers from Strategic Air Command in the senior ranks of the Air Staff, by a fascination with aerial self-sufficiency and big bombers, and by the absence of a powerful drive for integrated warfare, which would have encouraged the development of doctrines for co-operation by the USAF with the army and navy. Strategic nuclear bombing also played a major role in British air planning.

In both countries the legacy of inter-war air doctrine and of the World War Two 'strategic' (i.e. war-winning) bombing campaigns played a major role. In contrast, the value of close air support shown by Allied air operations in 1944 and 1945 was neglected, and, in the USA, the Tactical Air Command that was founded in 1948 as an equal to Strategic Air Command was rapidly downgraded and swiftly lost most of its aircraft. This emphasis was to have a detrimental effect both on the use of air power during the Vietnam War and on the more general understanding of air power capability.

During the Cold War, the crucial strategic zone was defined as the North European Plain, and the Soviet Union had a great superiority in conventional forces there, which was enhanced as Soviet forces were modernized and as the military effectiveness of their Eastern European allies was enhanced. This led to a series of responses in NATO planning (which was very much dominated by the USA), each of which focused on the degree to which nuclear weaponry would be involved, and when. The essential stages were: an immediate nuclear response to a conventional Soviet assault; the massive nuclear retaliation outlined in 1954 by John Foster Dulles, the American secretary of state; the flexible response theory which was capable of many interpretations, outlined under the Kennedy administration (1961–63); and, eventually, American stress on an enhanced conventional response, albeit with the potential backing of strategic and tactical nuclear weaponry.

In the early 1950s it was feared that the Korean War might be the first stage of World War Three, and/or that Western Europe might receive similar treatment to South Korea. In response to the threat of attack, NATO developed as a defensive system, supporting its plans with the creation of airfields, radar stations, telecommunications and an oil pipeline system, as well as with the preparation of resistance networks able to operate if the Soviets occupied territory. This built on the view that resistance had played a role in undermining the German position during World War Two. There was also a major effort to develop opposition in the Soviet bloc in order to lessen the military value of Eastern Europe in the event of war. Aside from support for resistance groups, for example in Albania and the Baltic States, the development of émigré forces, and a major propaganda offensive, there was a growing interest in trying to exploit divisions between the Soviet Union and its satellite regimes. Meanwhile, in military terms, as NATO countries were unable to match the build-up of conventional strength their military planners called for, there was a growing stress, especially from 1952, on the possibilities of nuclear weaponry both as a deterrent and, in the event of war, as a counterweight to Soviet conventional superiority. Nuclear strength was seen as a condition of conventional warfare in defence of West Germany.

Atomic weaponry meanwhile was not employed during the Korean War, despite plans to do so and also pressure from General MacArthur for its use to counteract Chinese numerical superiority. Instead, the war was fought with a strengthened conventional military, although in 1953 the use of the atom bomb was threatened by the Americans in order to secure an end to the conflict. This encouraged the view that nuclear strategy had a major role to play in future confrontations, as indeed did the heavy cost of fighting the Korean War and the extent to which it had revealed deficiencies in the American military; however, the war also caused a revival in the American army and led to its growing concern with 'readiness'.

The need to respond to Soviet conventional superiority on land and in the air, at least in terms of numbers, also encouraged an interest both in tactical nuclear weaponry and in the atom bomb as a weapon of first resort. The tactical nuclear weapons that were developed, such as bazookas firing atomic warheads with a range of one mile, were treated as a form of field artillery. The use of the atom bomb as a weapon of first resort was pushed by Dwight Eisenhower, NATO's first supreme allied commander from 1950 until 1952 and US president from 1953 until 1961. Aware of NATO's vulnerability, he felt that strength must underpin diplomacy for it to be credible. In December 1955 the NATO Council authorized the employment of atomic weaponry against the Warsaw Pact, even if the latter did not use such weaponry.

The cost of increasing conventional capability was a factor in encouraging a reliance on nuclear strength, as were the manpower implications in a period of very low unemployment of trying to raise larger armies, and, more specifically, the particular vulnerability of Western forces to Soviet attack in Western Europe. Thus, nuclear weaponry appeared less expensive and politically more acceptable, as well as militarily more effective, either as a deterrent or, in the event of deterrence failing, as a decisive combat weapon. Building up nuclear strength seemed the best way to increase the capability in both respects.

This policy led to what was termed the 'New Look' strategy and, more particularly, to the enhancement of the American Strategic Air Command, which resulted in the USAF receiving much more money in defence allocations than either the army or the navy. The deployment of B-52 heavy bombers in 1955 upgraded American delivery capability, and a small number of aircraft appeared able, and rapidly, to achieve more than the far larger Allied bomber force had done against Germany from 1942 to 1945. Thus, Western deterrence appeared both realistic and affordable, and it was hoped that nuclear bombers would serve to deter both conventional and atomic attack, although doubts were expressed about the former.

Already, however, in 1949, the American navy had found its programme rejected and its major construction projects cancelled – not least for super carriers capable of carrying heavier bombers – in favour of the USAF's plans for strategic bombing. With the 'New Look' the number of divisions in the army fell from eighteen in June 1956 to fourteen by that December, and the number of naval vessels from 973 to 812. The decline in conventional capability, which was resisted within the military, both harmed the ability to respond to the demands of the Vietnam War and further ensured a reliance in planning on nuclear weaponry.

America's allies were also faced with difficult policy choices. Both in Western Europe and in the Far East they relied on the American nuclear umbrella, but this made them heavily dependent on American policy choices. Part of the rationale behind the development of independent nuclear deterrents by Britain and France was the doubt that the USA would not necessarily use its atomic weaponry if Europe alone was attacked; and there was also concern that the 'New Look' strategy might lead to a diminished commitment to Europe. Only an air force capable of dropping nuclear bombs seemed to offer a deterrent, but, as with the USA, the emphasis on this development affected conventional capability. The determination of Britain and France to develop a nuclear capability represented a significant shift from their earlier emphasis on colonial defence.

American focus on strategic air power encouraged concern about the Soviet counterpart, and in 1954 and 1955 there was fear in the USA of a 'bomber gap', with Soviet inter-continental bombers able to drop atomic weapons on North America. This encouraged both a stepping up of the American bomber programme and the construction of early-warning radar systems in Canada designed to warn of Soviet attacks along the shortest axis over the North Pole: the Pinetree Network (in 1954), and the Distant Early Warning and Mid-Canada Lines (both in 1957). The North American Air Defence Command, established in 1958, was important to the development of joint air-defence systems involving the USA and Canada.

ROCKETS

The situation changed in 1957 when the Soviet Union launched Sputnik I, the first satellite, into orbit. The launch revealed a capability for inter-continental rockets that brought the entire world within striking range, and thus made the USA vulnerable to Soviet attack, both from first strike and from counter-strike. In strategic terms, rockets threatened to give effect to the doctrine of air power as a strategic tool capable of devastating opponents advanced in the 1920s and 1930s, at the same time as they rendered obsolescent the nuclear capability of the American Strategic Air Command, which were already challenged by Soviet air defences. The strategic possibilities offered by nuclear-tipped long-range ballistic missiles made investment in expensive rocket technology seem an essential course of action, since they could go so much faster than planes and, unlike them, could not be shot down. This altered the character of both anti-nuclear defence and nuclear deterrence, as the latter now apparently required an enhanced level of military readiness. The development of inter-continental missiles also altered the parameters of vulnerability, and ensured that space was seen even more in terms of straight lines between launching site and target. As the major targets were in the USA and the Soviet Union, this led to concern with axes via the North Pole.

The wider significance of Sputnik was not restricted to military strategy. It also appeared to prove Soviet claims, trumpeted at the time of the Twenty-Second Party Congress in 1961, that it was overtaking the USA and Western Europe, not simply in military hardware but also in technological capability as well as in standards of living. This public relations coup was totally misleading, in part because statistics were manipulated, but also because of a systemic Soviet failure to ensure that accurate figures were obtained and that proper balance sheets were produced. Nevertheless, Western concern about Soviet growth lent added point to anxiety about its apparent expansionism and military capability.

In fact, aside from high Western growth rates, the American army and air force (somewhat separately) had been developing long-range ballistic missiles after World War Two, using captured German V-2 scientists, and the so-called 'missile gap' of 1959–60 reflected more on domestic American politics, being used as a way by Kennedy and others to criticize the Eisenhower administration than on reality. From 1957 there was a twofold Western response to the enhanced Soviet capability and to the crucial uncertainty about further developments. Notions of graduated nuclear retaliation, through the use of 'tactical' (short-range) nuclear weapons in association with conventional forces based in Western Europe, were complemented by a policy of developing an effective inter-continental retaliatory second-strike capability in order to make it dangerous to risk attack on the USA. This attempt to give force to the notion of massive nuclear retaliation entailed replacing vulnerable manned bombers that had to overfly the target in order to bomb it with less vulnerable submarines equipped with Polaris missiles and also with land rockets based in reinforced silos. The invulnerability of American nuclear weaponry was thus enhanced.

The Americans fired their first inter-continental ballistic missile in 1958, and, in July 1960, off Cape Canaveral, the submarine USS *George Washington* was responsible for the first successful underwater firing of a Polaris missile. The following year, the Americans commissioned the USS *Ethan Allen*, the first true fleet missile submarine. Submarines could be based near the coast of target states, but were highly mobile and hard to detect. They represented a major shift in force structure, away from the American air force and towards the navy, which argued that its invulnerable submarines could launch carefully controlled strikes, permitting a more sophisticated management of deterrence and retaliation. Other states followed. The first British Polaris test missile was fired from a submarine in 1968, while the French commissioned their first ballistic missile submarine in 1969.

The inhibiting effect of the destructive potential of inter-continental nuclear weaponry served as much to enhance the possibility of a nuclear war, by increasing interest in defining a sphere for tactical nuclear weapons and in planning an effective strategic nuclear first strike, as it did to lessen the chance of a great power war, or to increase the probability that such a conflict would be essentially conventional. The risk of nuclear destructiveness, nevertheless, made it important to prevent escalation to full-scale war, and thus encouraged interest in defining forms of warfare that could exist short of such escalation.

In the early 1960s, American concern about the nuclear balance increased. John F. Kennedy, US president from 1961 to 1963, had fought the 1960 presidential election in part on the platform that the Republican administration under Eisenhower had failed to maintain America's defences. Kennedy aimed for a strategic superiority over the Soviet Union and increased defence spending. The Soviet leader from 1957 until 1964, Nikita Khrushchev, however, deployed missiles in Cuba, a newly Communist state from which the USA was in close range and which, in turn, was being threatened by the USA. The ballistic missiles in Cuba had a range of 1,040 nautical miles, which made Washington a potential target. This deployment brought the world close to nuclear war in 1962, although that very prospect may have helped prevent conventional military operations which would have begun, as was planned, with an American air attack on the Soviet bases on Cuba.

In the event, the USA imposed an air and naval quarantine to prevent the shipping of further Soviet supplies, considered an attack on Cuba, and threatened a full retaliatory nuclear strike. Cuba was successfully isolated, the Americans deploying a total of 183 warships, and the Soviet Union agreed to remove the missiles in return for the Americans both withdrawing their Jupiter missiles (which carried nuclear warheads) from Turkey and agreeing not to invade Cuba. The previous year, during the Berlin Crisis, Kennedy had reaffirmed the willingness to use atomic weaponry even if the Soviets did not. This was because West Berlin was particularly vulnerable to Soviet conventional attack.

Kennedy, nevertheless, sought to move from the idea of 'massive retaliation' with nuclear weaponry to a policy that did not automatically assume escalation to nuclear war. This was an aspect of a more general strategy of 'Flexible Response' adopted in 1962 as an answer to the prospect of Communist 'wars of national liberation' around the world. Flexible Response presented a spectrum of conflict, from nuclear deterrence and conventional warfare at one end, to guerrilla combat and non-military applications of national power at the other. Whatever the language, as it was unlikely that any conventional conflict between the two blocs would be anything less than devastating, and would rapidly become nuclear, the deterrent helped prevent the devastation of high-tech conventional warfare between well-resourced alliances.

The increase in American defence spending in the early 1960s, the rise of their number of nuclear warheads, the prominence of the Soviet climbdown during the Cuban crisis, and the prospect of massive American nuclear retaliation, lessened the Soviet threat in Europe, although American preparations encouraged the KGB, the Soviet secret service, to report, inaccurately, that the USA was planning a nuclear first strike, which increased tension. In 1965, Robert McNamara, the American secretary of defense, felt able to state that the USA could rely on the threat of 'assured destruction' to deter a Soviet assault. Submarine-launched missiles provided the Americans with a secure second nuclear strike against the Soviet Union as part of a triad that included bombers, ground-based missiles and sea-launched launches.

Such strength did not, however, prevent further attempts by the nuclear powers to enhance their nuclear attack and defence capabilities, for the logic of deterrence required matching any advance in the techniques of nuclear weaponry. For example, having decided in 1967 to proceed with the development of multiple independently targeted re-entry vehicles (MIRVs), first tested in 1968, in 1970 the Americans deployed Minuteman III missiles equipped with MIRVs, thus ensuring that the strike capacity of an individual rocket was greatly enhanced. As a consequence, warhead numbers, and thus the potential destructiveness of a nuclear exchange, rose greatly, while the Americans cut the response time of their land-based inter-continental missiles by developing the Titan II, which had storable liquid propellants, enabling in-silo launches and reducing the launch time, thus improving the reaction time of the missiles in a nuclear conflict.

The American position in the 1970s was challenged by the Soviet response, part of the action–reaction cycle that was so important to the missile race, and, more generally, to military developments: the ability of powers to understand such cycles and to judge how best to respond to them is crucial to their effectiveness. After 1962, the Soviets, their government from 1964 until 1982 presided over by Leonid Brezhnev, had made major advances in comparative nuclear potency, especially in the development of land-based, inter-continental missiles, producing a situation in which war was seen as likely to lead to MAD (mutually assured destruction), as both sides appeared to have a secure second-strike capability, ensuring that a surprise attack would not wipe out the opposition's ability to strike back. As a consequence, MAD-based strategies of deterrence and of graduated response were developed on the Western side, although it was never clear whether the Soviets agreed with the 'nuclear calculus' as it was called. At the same time, the *rapprochement* between China and the USA lessened the relative strength of the Soviet Union, and discouraged it from risking war, as any conflict was likely now to be one waged on two fronts.

In the 1970s, enhanced capability on both sides was matched by attempts to lessen the possibility of nuclear war. The American–Soviet Anti-Ballistic Missile Treaty of 1972 (SALT I), which President Nixon felt able to conclude thanks to the MIRV programme, limited the construction of defensive shields against missile attack to two anti-ballistic missile complexes, one around a concentration of inter-continental ballistic missiles and the other around the capital. By leaving the USA and the Soviet Union vulnerable, the treaty was designed to discourage a first strike, as there would be no effective defence against a counter-strike. Thus, atomic weaponry was to be used to prevent, not to further, war. At the time of the Yom Kippur War (see pp. 221–2), however, the Americans put their forces on nuclear alert in response to the threat of Soviet intervention. The SALT I treaty, which limited the two powers' nuclear arsenals, also served as the basis for further negotiations which led to the SALT II treaty in 1979. In 1975, the Helsinki Agreement ratified Europe's frontiers and territorial divisions between West and East.

BOX 9.3   THE COLD WAR AT SEA

The decline of the battleship ensured that carriers were the big ships. America dominated carrier capability, and planned the use of its carrier strength for a variety of purposes. In the 1950s and early 1960s American carriers were assigned strategic bombing duties, not least the use of a nuclear strike capability, but in the Korean and Vietnam Wars they were used extensively to provide ground support. The most extensive use of carriers was during the Vietnam War when they provided a nearby safe base for air operations over both North and South Vietnam. Improvements in supply methods since World War Two, especially resupply from other ships, ensured that carriers were able to stay at sea for longer. During most of 1972, no fewer than six American carriers were on station off Vietnam, a formidable presence, and that summer an average of 4,000 sorties were flown monthly. The absence of hostile submarine attacks provided a mistaken impression of the general invulnerability of carriers.

The USA was not alone in the use of carriers. Three French carriers had operated off Vietnam against the Viet Minh in the 1946–54 war, and two were used in the Suez Crisis. The British deployed carriers during the Korean War, and also used three in the Suez Crisis; they increased the capability of their carriers with the introduction of the angled flight deck, the steam catapult, and, in 1960, the first vertical/short takeoff and landing (V/STOL) aircraft based on carriers. These planes did not require fleet carriers, and financial problems in 1966 led Britain to the cancellation of the CVA-01, a planned fleet carrier, and instead to a reliance on smaller carriers with their shorter range V/STOL fighters.

The development of the Soviet fleet designed to support Soviet interests across the world, to challenge the deployment of American and allied forces, and, more specifically, to threaten American carriers with their nuclear-strike aircraft, led to changes in American naval doctrine and force structure. Traditional Soviet naval doctrine had emphasized support for land forces in the Baltic and Black seas, and the quest for naval superiority in these areas, but Soviet forces based in these seas could only gain access to the oceans through straits and shallow waters where they were vulnerable, and a similar problem affected the naval base of Vladivostok on the Sea of Japan. As a result, the Soviet navy developed their ability to enter the Atlantic without such restrictions, building up their Northern Fleet based at Murmansk so that it became the largest Soviet fleet, with a particularly important submarine component about 400 strong by 1956. The subsequent introduction of submarines capable of firing ballistic missiles (see p. 201) made submarine and anti-submarine capability particularly important.

The development of the Northern fleet obliged NATO powers to develop nearby patrol areas for submarines, as well as underwater listening devices so that they could follow Soviet moves, and also to create a similar capability in the waters through which Soviet submarines would have to travel *en route* to the Atlantic, both in the Denmark Strait between Iceland and Greenland and between Iceland and Britain. The Americans feared that Soviet submarines would attack their trade routes, or launch missiles from near the American coast.

The Soviet navy also developed an important surface fleet, especially from the 1960s, including missile cruisers whose anti-ship missiles posed a major threat to Western warships. In 1967 and 1973, the Soviet navy was able to make substantial deployments in the eastern Mediterranean, and from the late 1960s the Americans focused on planning for naval conflict with the Soviets rather than using the fleet to attack the Soviet mainland.

THE AFGHAN WAR

Under the shadow of nuclear confrontation, the proxy conflicts that were an aspect of the Cold War continued. In the 1980s, the Soviet Union was involved in an unsuccessful counter-insurgency campaign that became part of this conflict. A major contrast with the Vietnam War was that Afghanistan bordered the Soviet Union, helping to increase Soviet concern and to ensure that the Soviet government did not feel that it had an easy exit strategy. The Soviets had been major aid donors to Afghanistan from the 1950s, taking its side in a frontier dispute with American-backed Pakistan. In 1973 the monarchy was overthrown in a coup, and an authoritarian strongman, Mohammed Daoud Khan, took power. In turn, in the Saur Revolution on 28 April 1978, Daoud was overthrown and killed in a coup mounted by the Soviet-backed People's Democratic Party of Afghanistan.

Bitterly divided, the new government responded with repression to opposition, and its attempts to reform society (not least with equality for women, which was unacceptable to the bulk of the Islamic society, and land reform) led to rebellions from late 1978, including a serious rising in the city of Herat in May 1979. The government met these with considerable brutality, not least with the colonial-era remedy of 'pacification' by bombing, which, despite the improved specifications of aircraft, was little more effective than it had been in the first half of the century.

After a coup from within the regime on 16 September 1979 did nothing to stem the tide of chaos, the Soviets intervened from 27 December 1979, overthrowing the government and installing Babrak Karmal as president. The Soviet intervention appears to have resulted from concern about the stability of their position in Central Asia, then part of the Soviet Union, and from their unwillingness to see a client state collapse. Contemporary suggestions that the Soviet Union was seeking to advance to the Indian Ocean, reviving the old fears about the North-West Frontier of India, appear overstated, although also show a degree of geopolitical continuity that should not be underrated.

The Soviets were able to overthrow the Afghan government in 1979, in part by the use of airborne troops, and to seize the cities. Thereafter, however, they found it impossible to crush guerrilla resistance in a conflict that lasted far longer than anticipated, and finally withdrew from Afghanistan in 1989. The bellicose nature of its society, and the fragmented nature of its politics, made Afghanistan difficult to control, and the Soviets and their Afghan allies held little more than the cities.

The Soviet forces were poorly trained for the conflict, especially in counter-insurgency warfare for which they lacked experience; their doctrine and tactics were designed for high-tech conflict with NATO in Europe, and they had inadequate air support. Without that, the infantry was vulnerable. The Soviets also had to confront an intractable military environment: they faced obdurate opponents, harsh terrain, disease, and, crucially, the difficulty of translating operational success into lasting advantage. In addition, relations between the Soviet and Afghan armies were poor, while the initial inclusion in the invasion force of a large percentage of Uzbeks, Tajiks and Turkmen led to tension with the Pushtuns in southern Afghanistan. In turn, the opposing guerrillas were seriously divided, largely on ethnic grounds.

The Soviets failed to understand both their opponents and the nature of Afghan politics and society, and their belief that insurgency movements were the characteristic of progressive forces, as they saw themselves, and, in contrast, that conservative systems lacked popularity, ensured that they lacked both the necessary military doctrine and an understanding of the relationship between military moves and political outcomes. The Soviet contempt for religion was also a serious issue in a society that took Islam seriously. As in the Vietnam War, 'hearts and mind' did not work, and the Soviets suffered from the lack of effective counter-insurgency doctrine, strategy and tactics. The block and sweep was a new operation for the Soviet military, but it further alienated Afghan opinion. Driving the population off land that could not be controlled was the strategy followed from 1983, but this did not win support and was further compromised by indiscipline and atrocities which entrenched divisions. Soviet sweeps or operations, such as the relief of Khost in late 1987, were followed by a return to base that brought no permanent benefit. The Soviets were unable to force large-scale battle on their opponents, who generally proved able to avoid Soviet advances; and, although the airborne special forces were able to carry the fight to opposing Afghans, they were not employed with sufficient frequency.

The Soviets also deployed too few forces, 120,000 troops at the peak, in large part for political and logistical reasons, in a country much bigger than South Vietnam, and therefore lacked the numbers required for the consecutive operations that Soviet war-fighting envisioned; to maintain the operational dynamic, the Soviet commanders conducted operations with smaller forces than they were trained for. In addition, convoy escort tied down a large portion of the Soviet combat forces, necessarily so because the Soviets were totally dependent on supplies from the Soviet Union. The pro-Soviet Afghan army contributed little to operational effectiveness.

As part of the Cold War, the guerrillas benefited from ample foreign support, including, from 1986, American ground-to-air Stinger missiles and their British counterpart, the Blowpipe, which brought down Soviet helicopter gunships, forcing them and aircraft to fly higher, which cut the effectiveness both of their ground support and of their bombing. As was always the case, Cold War alignments overlapped with others, in this case Islamicist anger at the occupation of an Islamic state, which led to Saudi, Iranian and Pakistan support for the guerrillas, although rivalries within the Islamic world ensured that competing assistance was channelled to rival factions. This matched, for example, the Soviet–Chinese rivalry in support for resistance movements in Angola, Zimbabwe, and elsewhere. The Afghan guerrillas also made extensive use of captured Soviet RG6–7 anti-tank grenade launchers, which proved effective against all Soviet vehicles. The supply of the guerrillas by the USA, Britain and Saudi Arabia through Pakistan helped make it more important strategically to the West, and also increased American interest in its stability. Ironically, some of the guerrillas were subsequently to become part of the al-Qaeda network, whose terrorism was directed against the USA, Britain and Saudi Arabia.

Technology was useful to the Soviets, particularly with aerial resupply, but it could not bring victory. Although, thanks to the size of their military and the control of the state over domestic opinion, the Soviets could afford their manpower losses in Afghanistan, Mikhail Gorbachev, who became general secretary of the Soviet Communist Party in 1985, decided to end the commitment. He saw it as an intractable struggle that was detrimental to the Soviet Union's international position, particularly his wish to improve relations with the West, as well as domestically unpopular. The Geneva Accords of 14 April 1988 led to a Soviet withdrawal, completed by February 1989, although Soviet military and financial aid to the Afghan government continued. It held out against the guerrillas, who were weakened by serious divisions, while their murderous treatment of prisoners did not encourage defections. As in South Vietnam, the departure of the supporting outsiders did not lead to the fall of the regime at once, but in 1992 it was eventually followed by it; this and subsequent events are discussed on pp. 251–3.

Failure in Afghanistan hit the morale of the Soviet military, and had an impact on its response to the crisis of the collapse of Soviet dominance in Eastern Europe and of the Soviet Union itself. In turn, these crises led to the demoralized character of the Russian military in the 1990s.

THE LAST STAGES OF THE COLD WAR

The early 1980s saw a marked heating up of the Cold War. The overthrow of the Shah in Iran in January 1979 had already led to greater American concern with the Persian Gulf. Manifested in the Carter Doctrine in January 1980, this led to the establishment, two months later, of the Rapid Deployment Task Force, which was to become the basis of Central Command, the Tampa-based Area Command (responsible for policy in the Gulf Wars) which was co-equal with other regional commands. This task force was presented as a body able to provide a rapid response across the world. As it contained both army and marine units, this was also an important initiative in joint structures, which looked towards the present organization of Western forces.

The Soviet invasion of Afghanistan in December 1979 was seen by Western governments not as a frontier policing operation designed to ensure a pliant government but as an act of aggression that needed to be countered, an approach that drew on a tendency to exaggerate Soviet economic resources and military capability. Under Ronald Reagan, American president from 1981 to 1989, and Margaret Thatcher, British prime minister from 1979 to 1990, this determination was matched by action. Reagan sought to build up American military and moral strength so as to be able to negotiate with the Soviets from a position of strength. He was also anxious to halt the spread of Soviet influence around the world, especially, but not only, in Central America. His presidency witnessed a development of covert operations outside formal military structures, and American support for anti-Communist insurgents in Afghanistan, Nicaragua and Angola – the last thanks to a repeal of the Congressional ban on involvement. There was also a marked build up in the American military. This focused on the deployment of tactical nuclear weapons, carried on Cruise and Patriot intermediate-range missiles, and on the development of new nuclear and space-mounted weaponry, but also included expansion in all the services. The 'Star Wars' programme, outlined by Reagan in a speech in 1983, was designed to enable the Americans to dominate space, using space-mounted weapons to destroy Soviet satellites and missiles.

Tensions rose to a height in 1983, with the Soviets fearing attack during a NATO exercise; the shooting down, over Soviet airspace, of a Korean airliner suspected of espionage; and the deployment of Cruise and Pershing missiles in Western Europe. With the KGB providing inaccurate reports of American plans for a surprise nuclear first strike, the Soviets also deployed more weaponry, although they could not match American use of information technology. Nevertheless, six Typhoons, the largest ballistic missile submarines built, entered Soviet service from 1980, as did their most impressive surface warships, including the *Kuznetsov*, their only big aircraft carrier. Brezhnev's successor as leader from 1982 to 1984, Yuri Andropov, was an ex-KGB head.

Advanced technology contributed enormously to greater American effectiveness, and American planning benefited from major developments in the capability of air power. This included advances stemming from more powerful air-to-air radars, the enhancement of air combat resulting from heat-seeking short-range missiles and their radar-guided, long-range counterparts, and the use of AWACS (Airborne Warning and Control System) aircraft. In the event of conflict with the Soviet Union, the Americans planned to employ stealthy attack aircraft and 'smart' laser-guided weapons fired from stand-off platforms. Laser-guided projectiles and programmed cruise missiles would inflict heavy damage on Soviet armour, while advanced aircraft, such as the F-15 and F-16, would win air superiority and also attack Soviet ground forces. Stealth technology would permit the penetration of Soviet air defences, obliging the Soviets to retain more aircraft at home, and would also threaten their nuclear deterrent. Co-ordination would be made possible by computer networking, a new generation of spy satellites capable of providing greater detail on the situation on the earth, as well as AWACS aircraft and the Global Positioning System.

Behind the front line in Eastern Europe and the Soviet Union, the Soviet order sat increasingly uneasily on societies where individualism, consumerism and demands for change and freedom could not be accommodated by inherently inefficient command economies and by Communist ideology. The rise to power in the Soviet Union in 1985 of Mikhail Gorbachev, a leader committed to reform at home and good relations abroad, greatly defused Cold War tension, not least by leading to Soviet disengagement from Afghanistan and Angola. Gorbachev was also willing to challenge the confrontational world-view outlined in KGB reports. For example, he was convinced that American policy on arms control was not motivated by a hidden agenda of weakening the Soviet Union, and this encouraged him to negotiate. Thatcher proved particularly keen to do so. She saw Gorbachev as a man with whom she could 'do business'. Reagan was also far readier to negotiate than his rhetoric about a Soviet 'evil empire' might suggest. In 1987, the Soviet government accepted the Intermediate Nuclear Forces Treaty, which, in ending land-based missiles with ranges between 500 and 5,000 kilometres, forced heavier cuts on the Soviets, while also setting up a system of verification through on-site inspection. In 1990, NATO and the Warsaw Pact were able to agree a limitation of conventional forces in Europe, while in July 1991 START I led to a major fall in the number of American and Soviet strategic nuclear warheads.

Aside from reducing international tension, Gorbachev unintentionally ended the Cold War, because his reform policy, which sought to modernize Soviet Communism, instead unravelled its precarious domestic basis and at the same time failed to provide sufficient food, let alone reasonable economic growth. Furthermore, his pressure on Soviet satellite states in Eastern Europe for reform led to their fall, as Gorbachev was unwilling to use the Soviet military to maintain their governments in power when they faced pent-up popular pressure for change. These governments themselves had totally failed. East Germany, apparently the most successful, but its economy in fact wrecked by ideological direction, was on the edge of bankruptcy in the autumn of 1989: it had only been able to continue that long thanks to large loans from the West, especially West Germany. The fall of the Communist regimes in Eastern Europe led to the dissolution of the Warsaw Pact in 1990 and the withdrawal of Soviet forces.

The end of the Soviet Union, when it came from 1989 to 1991, was rapid and accompanied by little fighting. Issues of classification are also raised, as the fall of the Soviet Union was at once a stage of the Cold War and also an important stage in decolonization for, however much the Soviet Union was in theory a federation, it also rested on a powerful degree of Russian, as well as ideological (Communist), imperialism. Counter-reform attempts by the Soviet military, keen to preserve the integrity of the Soviet Union, led to action against nationalists in Georgia (1989), Azerbaijan (1990), Lithuania (1991), Latvia (1991), and Moldova (1992), and there was an attempted coup in Moscow by hardline Communists in August 1991, but they were unable to prevail. Gorbachev also wanted to preserve the Soviet Union, if necessary as a loose confederation, and, when the Baltic republics (Estonia, Latvia and Lithuania) declared their independence, he supported the attempt to maintain the authority of the Soviet Union by sending troops into the republics in January 1991, leading to clashes in Vilnius and Riga.

BOX 9.4   THE VOICE OF THE COLD WAR

Nikita Khrushchev, the Soviet leader, declared in August 1961: 'We placed Gagarin and Titov in space, and we can replace them with bombs which can be diverted to any place on Earth.'

However, the growing weakness of the Soviet state, and the division and confusion of the government's response, was accentuated by the strength of nationalist sentiment, especially in the Baltic republics, the Caucasus and western Ukraine. As with much of decolonization, it was the war that did not happen that is worthy of consideration. Instead of such a conflict, nationalism in the republics, in December 1991, led to their peaceful independence and thus to the collapse of the Soviet Union, while Gorbachev resigned to be replaced by Boris Yeltsin. With Soviet Communism in ruins and Chinese Communism increasingly market-orientated and looking in particular to the American market, the Cold War was over.

CONCLUSIONS

From the late 1940s to the late 1980s, the Cold War marked the apparent culmination of military history, being the latest as well as the current stage both of total war and of an approach to confrontation and conflict in terms of symmetrical warfare. Now, its significance appears less obvious. Indeed, in so far as the Cold War has direct relevance to present-day conflicts it is largely in terms of the extent to which superpower confrontation interacted with struggles in the Third World, not least the anti-colonial insurrections discussed in the previous chapter and the wars between non-Western states considered in the next. American predominance helped ensure that the Western European states eventually abandoned their colonies, both because of a lack of more than occasional American support for their empires and because this predominance guaranteed their position in Europe. Arms and other support from the USA and the Soviet Union massively sustained the conflicts discussed in the next chapter.

CHAPTER 10

Wars Between Non-Western Powers, 1945–90

INTRODUCTION

Conflict between non-Western powers was no mere postscript to the history of war in this period, or indeed in any other. Nor is it helpful to treat such conflicts as in some way simply adjuncts of the Cold War. That element was indeed important, not least due to the provision of weapons, munitions, finance, training and advice by protagonists in the Cold War, but the conflicts also had an autonomy in cause, course and consequence. This is particularly so if the range of conflict is considered, as it included not only struggles between sovereign states but also large-scale insurgencies and other instances of civil conflict. In many cases, both owed their origins to the after-effect of rapid decolonization as groups that had succeeded in ousting imperial powers, or benefited from their departure, found it less easy to govern successfully or to manage relations with neighbours. These struggles drew, in part, on pre-existing tensions – for example between regions with different ethnicities, religions and/or economic interests held together within the artificial boundaries of many states – and helped shape competing nationalisms; but there was also a powerful element of novelty stemming from the ideological struggles of the Cold War and their interaction with indigenous identities. In Indonesia, for example, the mid-1960s witnessed a very bloody civil war in which Communists were killed in large numbers by Islamic nationalists who were powerful in the army. Similarly, in Iraq the Communists were kept from power by Ba'ath nationalists.

Wars in the Middle East tend to dominate attention under the heading of conflict between non-Western powers. They were, indeed, important both in their own right and because their course, especially those of the Arab–Israeli wars of 1967 and 1973, was scrutinized carefully by analysts seeking insights on tactical and operational effectiveness. For example, Egyptian success with anti-tank weaponry against Israeli tank attacks in 1973 encouraged commentators to stress its importance. The use of advanced weaponry by the combatants, particularly of American planes and tanks by the Israelis in 1973, and Soviet counterparts by their opponents, made it possible to view these conflicts as testing grounds for a clash between the two powers; but although that element was important the course of Arab–Israeli struggle involved far more than this factor, while most conflicts between non-Western powers did not take this form of full-scale conflict between conventional forces.

BORDER WARS

The causes of warfare were varied. Decolonization had led to a far greater number of independent states in Africa and Asia, and many of these became involved in conflict. Border disputes arising from the departure of colonial powers were responsible for numerous struggles, for example between India and Pakistan (1947–48 and 1965), and, at a far smaller scale, Morocco and Algeria (1962–63), and, despite the 1964 Cairo Declaration confirming Africa's frontiers, Mali and Burkina Faso (1995); as well as for China's border war with India in 1962. Border disputes were also important in leading to the Iraqi attack on Iran in 1980.

Border clashes were sometimes intertwined with insurrectionary movements. This was the case with the India–Pakistan war over Kashmir in 1947 and 1948, when Pakistan tried to exploit Islamic opposition to Indian rule in Kashmir, leading the Indians to fly in troops. The results of the successive India–Pakistan wars indicated the value of the far larger Indian military, but other factors also played a role in Indian success, underlining the point that far more than resources were responsible for success in war. In 1965, for example, the Indians chose to advance not in Kashmir, as the Pakistanis had anticipated, but, instead, in the Punjab, using tanks to drive on Lahore and Sialkot. The Pakistanis had been encouraged by India's defeat by China in 1962, but the Indians, with their Soviet T55 tanks, fought better than had been anticipated. Indeed victory over Pakistan led to a recovery of Indian confidence after defeat by China. In 1965, unlike in 1947 and 1948, there was large-scale conventional conflict, including the use of large quantities of tanks and artillery.

Other border conflicts were more small-scale and obscure and tend to be ignored in military history, although, for the forces concerned, they were important, not least in setting goals. For example, in 1969 the army and police in Guyana stopped a Venezuelan-backed secessionist rising in the Rupununi region.

INTERVENTION WARS

In Africa, border clashes frequently interacted with rebellions. Libya intervened in neighbouring Chad in the 1980s, both in order to pursue a territorial claim to a northern strip of the country and in order to support protégés seeking to control the entire country. Overt Libyan intervention in 1983 with about 6,000 troops led to a military response by France, formerly the colonial power in Chad, and Zaire (Congo), which enjoyed the benefit of intelligence provided by American aerial surveillance: in part this conflict was an aspect of the Cold War as Libya had been armed by the Soviets. The Libyan advance was also reliant on Soviet doctrine and training, but this was not going to be a conflict decided by armoured vehicles and related tactics. Instead, the Chad forces opposed to Libya benefited from light vehicles and a raiders' search for mobility, and used mortars and anti-tank rockets in order to inflict heavy casualties on the Libyans.

These tactics were employed again in the 'Toyota War' of March 1987, with the Libyans losing over 3,000 troops and much of their armour as they were driven from most of the north of Chad. French aircraft were used against Libyan ground forces on a number of occasions, but the French did not act at the close of 1990 when a new faction invaded Chad from Sudan and overthrew the government. Attempted coups, rebellions and ethnic clashes continued there for years. Libyan claims were seen as a challenge by other neighbours as well. In 1977, Egypt mounted a successful surprise attack on Libyan frontier positions in order to indicate its anger with Libyan pretensions and policies.

More generally, foreign military intervention could lead to the overthrow of governments, as with the Vietnamese conquest of Cambodia from 1978 to 1979, and the Tanzanian overthrow of Idi Amin, the megalomaniac military dictator of Uganda in 1979. Amin had seized power in a coup in 1971, then had ruled by terror, slaughtering opponents; had greatly increased the size of the army; and had attacked neighbouring Tanzania, alleging that its government supported military operations by Ugandan exiles. This served as an excuse for Ugandan attacks in 1971, 1972, and, more seriously, on three occasions in the winter of 1978–79.

After the last, the Tanzanians, citing self-defence, invaded and overthrew Amin. The latter campaign was typical of many in Africa. The fighting quality of the Ugandan army varied greatly, with elite units mounting a resistance that most of the demoralized army was unwilling to offer. Infantry played a significant role in the conflict, slowing the rate of the Tanzanian advance on Entebbe, the Ugandan capital, to around ten miles a day. Tactical mobility was crucial in clashes, helping ensure that light anti-tank weapons were used to destroy armoured personnel carriers, which were largely road-bound. Libyan military intervention on behalf of Amin could not sway the struggle, but, again, helped to locate it, at least in part, in terms of Cold War rivalries.

SOUTH ASIA

More generally, the removal of the constraints of Western control or hegemony led states to pursue regional territorial and political interests, often using force to that end. Thus, India sent troops into Kashmir in 1947, overran the princely state of Hyderabad in 1948, occupied the Portuguese possessions of Diu and Goa in 1961, conquered East Pakistan in 1971 (helping to create the state of Bangladesh), annexed neighbouring Sikkim in 1975, sent 100,000 troops to help Sri Lanka against Tamil insurgents in 1987 (withdrawing in 1990), and intimidated neighbouring Nepal in 1995.

Indian operations revealed the growing capability of 'Third World' military systems: in 1947, India sent troops by air to Kashmir, while in 1961 it used 71,000 troops to overrun Goa, which only had a garrison of 4,000 men, in one day. Although allied to Portugal in NATO, the Americans refused appeals for help (Goa indeed was outside the geographical scope of NATO). A total of 160,000 Indian troops were sent into East Pakistan in 1971, while at the same time other Indian units fought Pakistani forces in West Pakistan.

The Indian military, one of the largest in the world, also played a major role in maintaining the cohesion of the country. In 1984 the Indian army stormed the Golden Temple of Amritsar, the leading Sikh shrine, which had become a major terrorist base for Sikh separatists, although this action led to Sikh mutinies in the Indian military. From 1987 there was also the need to confront Muslim insurgency in Kashmir. In 1998, India, which had exploded a nuclear device in 1974, demonstrated its ability to launch a rocket with a nuclear warhead. India's military build-up was directed not only against internal problems and Pakistan but also against China, which was seen as a threat both on their common border and because of its support for India's neighbours Pakistan and Burma. The geostrategic tension between the two powers was an important aspect of the struggle for regional dominance in South Asia that was seen during the Cold War and that became more important thereafter.

China was successful in 1962 against India, whose forces were poorly prepared for high-altitude operations, but to a much lesser extent in 1979 against Vietnam. In 1962 the Chinese heavily outnumbered the Indians, and as a result of road-building benefited from superior logistics, at least in the zone of conflict. The struggle arose from a long-standing dispute over the mountainous frontier, which dated back to colonial days, and that was exacerbated by a regional struggle for predominance. The Indians began the war, on 10 October, with an unsuccessful attempt to seize the Thag La Ridge, and the Chinese then responded with an offensive launched on 20 October, defeating and driving back the Indians. An Indian counter-offensive on 14 November was defeated and, on the next day, the Chinese outmanoeuvred the Indian defensive positions near Se La, inflicting heavy casualties. Having revealed that the Indians would be unable to defend the frontier province of Assam, the Chinese declared a unilateral ceasefire on 21 November and withdrew their troops. Theirs was a limited operation in which prospects for exploitation were gravely restricted by logistical factors. In total, the Indians had lost 6,100 men dead, wounded or taken prisoner.

In 1979 the Chinese eventually sent about 120,000 troops across a frontier where it was far easier to operate to confront an equal number of Vietnamese, in response to Vietnam's attack on China's ally, Cambodia, the previous year. This attack had accentuated the long-term, indeed pre-colonial, tension between China and Vietnam, a tension then exacerbated by China's *rapprochement* with the USA. The Chinese captured three provincial capitals, but were knocked off balance by the Vietnamese decision to turn to guerrilla tactics. The Vietnamese benefited from their extensive recent experience of conflict with the USA and South Vietnamese, while the Chinese military lacked such experience and suffered from a dated army and flawed doctrine. Affected by poor logistics, inadequate equipment and failures in command and control, the Chinese withdrew, with maybe 63,000 casualties, and without forcing Vietnamese forces to leave Cambodia. Vietnam did not withdraw its forces from Cambodia until 1990. Nevertheless, the Chinese had shown that they would not be deterred by Soviet–Vietnamese links, and their invasion testified to growing Soviet diplomatic weakness.

THE MIDDLE EAST

Other would-be regional powers also built up their forces, as Iran did with its enormous oil wealth in the 1970s, and mounted attacks. In an instructive episode that showed much about military capability in the second half of the century and also demonstrated many of the characteristics of Third World conflict, President Nasser of Egypt sent troops to Yemen in an attempt to support the new revolutionary regime established in September 1962 by a military coup against the conservative rule of Iman Muhammed al-Badr. The Royalist opposition to the new regime was backed by Saudi Arabia, which provided money, weapons and bases, while Jordan sent military advisers. The Egyptians had anticipated a commitment of only three months, but found themselves in an intractable situation that offered a parallel to other counter-insurgency operations of the period. Aside from the inherent difficulty of the task, which owed much to the bellicose and fissiparous character of Yemeni society, and to the harsh nature of the arid terrain, the Egyptian army was not prepared for operations in Yemen. It lacked adequate planning for operations there, was critically short of information about both Yemeni political alignments and the terrain, was short of adequate communications equipment, and was not prepared, by training or doctrine, for counter-insurgency conflict. Instead, their experience was in conventional operations against Israel, most recently in 1956.

In the initial operations in October and November 1962, the Egyptians found their attempts to control the entire country thwarted by opposition that made more effective use of the terrain in Yemen, not least by ambushing road-bound Egyptian columns: the mobility that mechanized vehicles brought was often inflexible. The Egyptians responded at the close of November by focusing on a defensive triangle of key cities where they intended to build up the Republican army, but it failed to realize their hopes, performing worse than the South Vietnamese military, and only becoming an important element from 1966. Royalist successes, instead, led the Egyptians to build up its forces and to return to the offensive in February 1963, regaining, in Operation Ramadan, control over most major towns and much territory. To secure these gains from Royalist counter-attacks, the number of Egyptian troops rose from 15,000 in the winter of 1962–63 to 36,000.

In many respects there were parallels with the Vietnam War. The Royalists had bases in neighbouring Saudi Arabia (the equivalent of North Vietnam), and supplies from there, and made good use of the terrain, not least in mounting ambushes. The Egyptians, in contrast, like the Americans in the Vietnam War, had control of the air, which they used for bombing, ground attack and air-mobility, the last, for example, seen with the seizure of the town of Sadah in February 1962 after paratroopers had established a runway on which troops could be landed. The Egyptian ability to take the initiative was, however, not matched by success in achieving results. As with so many counter-insurgency struggles, unless occupied, territory could not be retained; but the occupation of territory itself did not produce benefits. Furthermore, the difficulty of achieving results, combined with the absence of an exit strategy, hit the morale of the Egyptian forces. To them, Yemen appeared a hostile environment, both physically and culturally, and, as in the Vietnam War, difficulties in identifying the enemy contributed to this sense of alienation. Discipline was weakened, corruption developed in the officer corps, and military and domestic support for the war fell. The inflexibility of the Egyptian military made it difficult to adapt doctrine and tactics to engage the guerrillas, although there were some improvements in tactics, not least with the use of helicopter-borne aerial resupply.

In 1964 the Egyptian forces in Yemen were increased to 50,000 men, but they still faced problems in using the roads, and, indeed, early in the year, the capital, Sana, was besieged by the Royalists. The Egyptian attempt that summer to kill the Iman led to the capture, successively, of two of his headquarters, but he was able to escape into Saudi Arabia, and the campaign did not lead to the end of the war. Once the Egyptians withdrew, the areas they had captured in the north-west were reoccupied by the Royalists. The following year, despite deploying 70,000 troops, the Egyptians again faced problems in responding to ambushes that cut supply routes and left their positions isolated and vulnerable. Much of the east of the country was overrun by the Royalists, and Egyptian frustration led to plans for an attack on Royalist bases in Saudi Arabia, which had already been repeatedly bombed.

At the same time – and the parallel with the Vietnam War is instructive – the Egyptians tried to negotiate. In August 1965, Nasser and King Faysal of Saudi Arabia signed the Jeddah Agreement in which they undertook to stop helping their protégés, and, by the summer of 1966, there were only 20,000 Egyptian troops in Yemen. However, the hopeful signs of the previous autumn were wrecked by the failure of peace talks between the Republicans and the Royalists, and by Nasser's interest in using Yemen as a base for seizing control of Aden after the British withdrew (see p. 165). This reflected a revival of the expansionist interests seen under Mehmet Ali in the early nineteenth century (see pp. 47–8). As a result, the Egyptians reoccupied parts of Yemen they had abandoned, although it was the increasingly effective Republican troops that played the major role in operations against the Royalists in 1966 and 1967.

Israel's total victory over the Egyptian forces in Sinai in June 1967 led to pressure for an evacuation of Yemen so that forces could be concentrated in preparation for a future conflict with Israel, and the fig-leaf of an agreement with Saudi Arabia (which, despite its promises, continued to supply the Royalists) allowed them to do so, mostly in October, although not finally until December 1967. Once the Egyptians had left, the Republicans, ironically, proved more resilient than had been anticipated, successfully defending Sana against siege in the winter of 1967–68. Saudi support for peace finally led to the end of the war, and the formation of a coalition government for Yemen in 1970. Thus, the latter stages of the war were very different to the situation in South Vietnam.

In contrast to Egypt's lengthy commitment to Yemen, Syria's unsuccessful invasion of Jordan in 1970 in support of a rebellion by Palestinian guerrilla forces was a struggle between conventional forces: the Jordanians fought well and benefited from effective air support against Syrian ground forces which, in turn, lacked air assistance. The Jordanians, who enjoyed important American diplomatic support, succeeded in expelling the Palestinian guerrillas. In 1976, however, Syria successfully sent troops into Lebanon in response to an appeal from the president for support of the Maronite-dominated Lebanese Front against the Druze–PLO (Palestinian Liberation Organization) alliance. The Syrians then turned against the Maronites (Christians) and occupied much of the country. After Greek Cypriots keen on union with Greece had staged a coup, another regional power, Turkey, successfully invaded Cyprus in 1974, partitioning the island between the Greek and Turkish Cypriots and creating a situation that has lasted until today.

ARAB–ISRAELI WARS

In the Middle East there was a series of wars between Israel and Arab neighbours (1948–49, 1956, 1967, 1973 and 1982). The Arabs proved unwilling to accept the culmination of the Zionist movement in the form of an independent Israel. Rejecting the UN partition resolution of 29 November 1947, they sought to drive the Jews from Palestine as the colonial power, Britain, withdrew. Fighting broke out throughout Palestine in December 1947 and became full scale when the British mandate ended on 14 May 1948. From 1948 to 1949 Israel was able to establish its independence and gain more territory than in the abortive partition plan, in the face of poorly co-ordinated and badly-prepared moves by the regular forces of Egypt, Iraq, Jordan and Syria, and the irregular forces of the Palestinians and the Arab Liberation Army. The Arabs benefited from more weaponry and firepower as well as from taking the initiative, but the Israelis had more troops by the last stage of the war, and also the determination born of a conviction that their opponents intended genocide; they certainly at least intended what was later to be termed 'ethnic cleansing'. More mundanely, the Israelis had interior lines of communication, while the supply of Czech small arms, and to a lesser extent aeroplanes, was crucial to their ability to do well. It is, however, important to note that the Israelis were less successful in their fighting with Iraqi, Jordanian and Syrian forces than in conflict with the Egyptians, the Palestinians and the Arab Liberation Army. This contrast was responsible for the post-war shape of Israel. Lacking a unified command, the rival Arab forces suffered from serious problems with logistics, but the Israelis found the regulars formidable opponents.

The war ended with the partition of Palestine between Israel, which, determined to make the Palestinian home a Jewish homeland, gained, as a result of relative success in the war, far more than had been envisaged in the UN partition resolution in 1947, and Egypt and Jordan, each of which also gained part of the proposed Arab state. The latter was not established. Indeed, Jordan's army, the Arab Legion, was more concerned to seize the west bank of the Jordan than to destroy Israel, and its forces only operated in the territories allocated to the Palestinians. Although Jordan, which annexed the west bank in 1950, was able to reconcile itself to the existence of Israel, Egypt and Syria were far less willing to do so, and this ensured a high level of tension, as did the presence of Palestinian refugees, many of whom had been driven from their land by Israeli action.

In 1956, as part of the Suez Crisis, Israel attacked Egypt on 29 October in concert with Britain and France, overrunning the Sinai Peninsula, but withdrew in the face of American and Soviet pressure. The weak resistance put up by the Egyptians reflected Israeli success in gaining the initiative, as well as the poorly trained nature of the Egyptian army and its inability effectively to use the Soviet and other weapons it had received. In particular, the Egyptians, who fought well in prepared positions, suffered from inadequate combined-arms training and from the rigid tactics of their armour, while Israeli success indicated that the reserve system, which provided the bulk of their army, worked. The Israelis also benefited from having numerical superiority in Sinai, in part because Nasser, Egypt's leader, correctly anticipated an Anglo-French invasion of the Suez Canal zone to the west. When Britain and France attacked, Nasser indeed ordered his already embattled troops in Sinai to retreat. The whole of the Sinai Peninsula was conquered in under a hundred hours at the cost of 172 Israeli fatalities. After the campaign, Israel, let down by the failure of Britain and France to sustain their invasion, agreed to withdraw in return for the deployment of United Nations peacekeeping troops along the frontier.

After the 1956 war, both Israel and, even more, her Arab neighbours increased their military expenditure, while Egypt's unification with Syria in 1958 created, in the United Arab Republic, the prospect of more united Arab action, especially in 1960. However, pan-Arabism was always weaker in pretension than rhetoric: the union was overthrown by a group of Syrian officers in 1961, while the United Arab Command, created in 1964 by a meeting of Arab leaders in order to prepare for war with Israel, faced acute national divisions. Nevertheless, a serious Israeli–Syrian border clash in 1964 was followed by an upsurge of Palestinian guerrilla attacks on Israel in 1965 and 1966, with Israeli reprisal attacks on Palestinian bases in Jordan. In November 1966 an Egyptian–Syrian defence treaty seemed to move Egypt closer to Syria's desire for war. Meanwhile, Israel developed a military able to underwrite a doctrine that called for a rapid advance in the event of war. Wanting any conflict to be swift, the Israelis built up their air power and their tank force.

In 1967, rising regional tension, particularly Egyptian sabre-rattling, led to a pre-emptive Israeli attack on Egypt. Nasser was encouraged in his blustering by his desire to retain the leadership of the Arab cause: the aggressive attitude of the new Syrian government towards Israel challenged his prestige. Nasser also felt under pressure from economic problems arising from his misguided attempt to force-start the economy through state planning. His expulsion of the UN peace-keeping force from the Sinai frontier and the closure of the Gulf of Aqaba to Israeli shipping provoked Israel and reflected a failure to appreciate the limitations of the Egyptian military, which, in turn, was overly concerned about Yemen, where several of its leading units were deployed. The Israeli attack began on 5 June 1967 with a surprise attack on the Egyptian airbases launched by planes coming in over the Mediterranean from the west: not the direct route of attack. The Egyptians, who had failed to take the most basic defensive precautions, lost 286 planes in just one morning, and, in addition, their runways were heavily bombed.

As the war spread it led to the Israeli conquest not only of the Gaza Strip and Sinai from Egypt but also of the West Bank section of Jordan and the Golan Heights from Syria. Gaining the initiative was crucial to the execution of the Israeli's well-prepared plans, as were training and morale that were better than those of their disunited opponents. In Sinai, the Egyptians suffered from a failure to appreciate the calibre of the Israeli military and the nature of Israeli operations, and from an absence of adequate, effective reserves: the large number of poorly trained reservists in the Sinai were no substitute, and, more generally, Arab forces suffered from a lack of adequately-trained troops. The war in Sinai was also a large-scale tank conflict. Soviet T54 and T55 tanks used by the Egyptians were beaten by American Patton and British Centurion tanks used by the Israelis, who showed greater operational and tactical flexibility, not least in successfully searching for vulnerable flanks and thus overcoming the strength of prepared Egyptian positions. The Egyptian command system, weakened by cronyism and complacency, proved totally inadequate to the challenge. Having broken into the Egyptian rear, the Israelis ably exploited the situation, and they also benefited greatly from the destruction of the Egyptian air force at the outset of the war: Egyptian ground forces were badly affected by Israeli ground-support air attacks, for which operations in Yemen had given them no experience. When Field Marshal Amer instructed the army to retreat from Sinai to the Suez Canal on 6 June, the unplanned withdrawal was chaotic, the cohesion of the army collapsed, and resistance to the Israelis disintegrated. The Egyptians lost about 10,000 dead and 5,000 captured, as well as much of their equipment: about $2 billion worth was destroyed while Israel captured 320 tanks.

The conflict in Sinai also underlined the key role of field maintenance and repair in mobile warfare, the Israelis proving more effective than the Egyptians in every case. As always, overnight repair of equipment and its return to the battle line proved a key element in the war-making ability of a modern army. Non-battle losses through mechanical failure are apt to be more costly than battle losses.

Given misleading assurances by Nasser, Jordan joined in on the Egyptian side on 5 June, only to have its air force destroyed and the West Bank overrun. The Israelis had not anticipated a ground war with Jordan, but Jordanian support for Egypt led the Israelis to attack once they were certain that the Egyptians had been defeated. Syria refused to provide assistance to Egypt, but it shelled Israeli positions, and, on 9 June, the Israelis, keen to take advantage of an opportunity to occupy the Golan Heights, attacked. As Egyptian and Jordanian forces had already been wrecked, with the Jordanians accepting a ceasefire late on 7 June and Egypt early on 9 June, the Israelis were able to focus on the Syrians, reflecting the importance of sequential warfare and their ability to respond rapidly to problems.

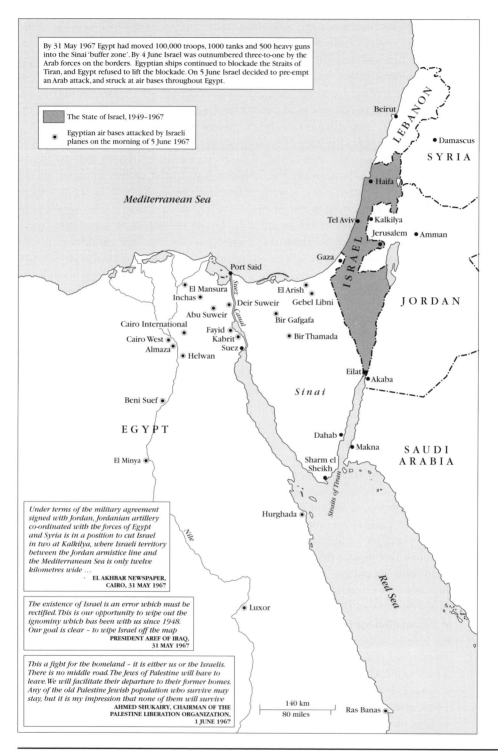

By 31 May 1967 Egypt had moved 100,000 troops, 1000 tanks and 500 heavy guns into the Sinai 'buffer zone'. By 4 June Israel was outnumbered three-to-one by the Arab forces on the borders. Egyptian ships continued to blockade the Straits of Tiran, and Egypt refused to lift the blockade. On 5 June Israel decided to pre-empt an Arab attack, and struck at air bases throughout Egypt.

The State of Israel, 1949–1967

Egyptian air bases attacked by Israeli planes on the morning of 5 June 1967

Mediterranean Sea

LEBANON

Beirut

Damascus

SYRIA

Haifa

Tel Aviv • Kalkilya

Jerusalem • Amman

Gaza

Port Said

El Mansura

Inchas

El Arish

Deir Suweir

Gebel Libni

Abu Suweir

Cairo International

Bir Gafgafa

Fayid

Cairo West

Kabrit

Bir Thamada

Almaza

Suez

Helwan

JORDAN

ISRAEL

Beni Suef

Sinai

Eilat

Akaba

Dahab

Makna

El Minya

Sharm el Sheikh

SAUDI ARABIA

EGYPT

Nile

Straits of Tiran

Hurghada

Under terms of the military agreement signed with Jordan, Jordanian artillery co-ordinated with the forces of Egypt and Syria is in a position to cut Israel in two at Kalkilya, where Israeli territory between the Jordan armistice line and the Mediterranean Sea is only twelve kilometres wide …
EL AKHBAR NEWSPAPER, CAIRO, 31 MAY 1967

The existence of Israel is an error which must be rectified. This is our opportunity to wipe out the ignominy which has been with us since 1948. Our goal is clear – to wipe Israel off the map
PRESIDENT AREF OF IRAQ, 31 MAY 1967

Luxor

Red Sea

This a fight for the homeland – it is either us or the Israelis. There is no middle road. The Jews of Palestine will have to leave. We will facilitate their departure to their former homes. Any of the old Palestine Jewish population who survive may stay, but it is my impression that none of them will survive
AHMED SHUKAIRY, CHAIRMAN OF THE PALESTINE LIBERATION ORGANIZATION, 1 JUNE 1967

140 km
80 miles

Ras Banas

Map 10.1 The Middle East crisis, 31 May to 5 June 1967, from *The Routledge Atlas of the Arab-Israeli Conflict* (2002), 7th edition, p. 67. © Routledge/Taylor & Francis Informa.

Gaining the initiative, and using their aerial superiority for ground attack, the Israelis benefited from a collapse in Syrian morale. The failure of the Soviet Union, Syria's patron, to intervene was also important, not least because the Soviets had stirred up Syria against Israel and had made some preparations to intervene. At the end of the war, having lost about a thousand men, Israeli forces were fewer than 60 kilometres from Damascus and less than 110 kilometres from Cairo.

Israel remained in occupation of the regions conquered in 1967, ensuring that it now controlled a large Arab population. In the long term, the presence of a large Arab population within Israel – and, even more, in Israeli-occupied territories – was to challenge the security of Israel, while the consequences of the occupation helped destabilize its politics. Furthermore, the failure of the Arab regular armies encouraged some of the Palestinians to resort to terrorism, not only in the Middle East but also further afield. Attacks on Israelis included those at the Munich Olympics in 1972 and the hijacking of planes to Entebbe in Uganda in 1976. In addition, over 600,000 Arab refugees, many of whom had fled Palestine in 1948 and 1949, were based in neighbouring Arab states, where they challenged the stability of Jordan and helped overthrow that of an already divided Lebanon, which moved into full-scale civil war from 1975.

Meanwhile, Egypt and Syria, totally unwilling to accept Israel's gains in 1967 and to negotiate peace, had been rearmed by the Soviet Union and, from 1968 to 1970, Egypt launched major artillery bombardments of Israeli positions. Nasser was determined to show that the Six-Day War of June 1967 was only a stage in a longer conflict. In turn, the Israelis mounted their own bombardments and, from 1969, the conflict spread to the air until, in August 1970, the USA arranged a ceasefire.

In 1973, however, conflict resumed in the Yom Kippur War, in which Egypt and Syria ultimately failed in their plan to inflict defeats in a surprise attack and then to establish strong defensive positions that would lead to superpower mediation. Suffering from an over-confidence similar to that which had affected the Arabs in 1967, and from a failure to appreciate intelligence of Arab preparations, the Israelis were unprepared for the surprise attack, Operation Badr, launched on 6 October against the weakly defended Israeli Bar Lev line on the east bank of the Suez Canal. This position rapidly fell, while the Syrians, attacking simultaneously, broke the Israeli line on the Golan Heights. This simultaneous assault divided the Israeli response.

The fall of the Bar Lev line was a serious blow to Israeli prestige in the shape of a reputation for invincibility. Furthermore, in responding to the Egyptian attack the Israelis found it difficult to penetrate the integrated air-defence missile system that the Egyptians had received from the Soviets, while, in their newly-established positions east of the Suez Canal, the Egyptians repelled a series of Israeli counter-attacks, inflicting serious damage on Israeli armour. The Israelis suffered from a doctrine that, based on the experience of 1967, exaggerated the effectiveness of tank attack and failed to provide adequate combined-arms capability, especially sufficient artillery support and mobile infantry, a lesson learned from tank conflict in World War Two. Israeli aeroplanes and tanks proved vulnerable to mobile ground-to-air and air-to-ground missiles, and to Sagger anti-tank guided missiles.

The Israelis, nevertheless, were able to drive the Syrians back, advancing into Syria and repelling counter-attacks. In response to Syrian pressure for help, the Egyptians changed their strategy and moved their armoured reserve forward, attacking on 14 October. This was a mistake, because, no longer taken by surprise, the Israelis were strong in defence, not least as the Egyptians advanced beyond their anti-aircraft cover. In an attack that highlighted the deficiencies of Egyptian tactics, the Egyptians lost heavily. The Israelis' American-made M48 and M60 tanks had double the rate and range of fire of the Soviet T55 and T62 tanks.

In turn, benefiting from this destruction of the Egyptian reserve, the Israelis attacked, exploiting the Egyptian failure to cover their entire front, and, more generally, their limitations in manoeuvrist warfare, and crossing the Suez Canal at a point where the Egyptians were weakest from the night of 15–16 October. The Israelis then defeated Egyptian counter-attacks, and encircled Egyptian forces before a ceasefire ended the war on 24 October: a first ceasefire on the 22nd had been breached by Israeli advances on the 23rd and 24th.

As in 1967, the failure of Arab armies in 1973 demonstrated the vulnerability of forces with a lower rate of activity, the problems arising from losing the initiative, and the need for a flexible defence. Arab militaries lacked effective practice, especially information acquisition and management, unit cohesion and command skills, while Israeli forces were more effective in using the initiative. In the 1973 war, command skills were particularly tested by the need to adapt to large-scale use of tanks: attacks such as the Syrian advance with 800 tanks through the Israeli lines, and one by Egypt on 14 October in which the Egyptians lost about 260 tanks, were clashes for which there was planning but scant experience. Egypt and Syria lost about 2,250 tanks in the war, the Israelis 840.

The 1973 war was mostly waged on land and in the air, but at sea both sides deployed missile boats, the Israelis sinking at least nine Egyptian and Syrian ships and driving their navies back to harbour. As with aircraft carriers in World War Two, the emphasis was on an accurate first strike, but, compared to then, all ships now depended in part on the use of electronic counter-measures to block missile attacks.

The USA tried to ease regional pressures, which threatened the world economy because of the concentration in the Middle East of oil production and reserves and because the Arab oil-producing countries followed the Yom Kippur War with a major hike in prices designed to put pressure on the West. The Carter administration helped arrange a peace settlement between Egypt and Israel, with the Camp David Accords of September 1978 followed by the Egypt–Israel treaty of March 1979 under which all Israeli settlers and troops were to have left the Sinai within three years. However, with one front secure, Israel was able to focus on Lebanon: its determination to act as a regional power, its anxiety about Syria and its concern about terrorism all centred there. The instability in the country served as the basis for terrorism, and led, in Operation Litani, to Israeli's invasion of southern Lebanon in 1978 and the destruction of the Palestine Liberation Organization's infrastructure before it withdrew its forces. Israel was now backing the militia of the Maronite Christians. The Israeli advance benefited from close air support. Syria already had occupied much of Lebanon in 1976 in order to prevent the civil war between Maronite Christians and Palestinian refugees from producing a result that was unwelcome to Syrian dominance. Israel's determination to take the initiative was further demonstrated in 1981 when Iraq's nuclear reactor was destroyed in an air-raid, blocking Iraq's attempt to develop an atom bomb.

In June 1982, still helped by the peaceful nature of their relations with Egypt, the Israelis, in what they termed Operation Peace for Galilee, again invaded southern Lebanon, hitting the Syrians hard and this time advancing as far as Beirut, which they besieged in July and August and occupied in September. The Israelis relied on helicopter support for their integrated advancing units of armour/ infantry/artillery/engineers, and the Palestinian refugee forces in Lebanon were heavily outgunned. The Israeli Cabinet had not wanted an advance to Beirut or conflict with the Syrians, but were pushed into both by the defence minister, Ariel Sharon, who was a determined advocate of aggressive policies. The Syrians initially fought well, but once their missile batteries in Lebanon had been knocked out, and their air force badly pummelled by Israeli planes armed with Sidewinder missiles and supported by electronic counter-measures, they proved vulnerable to Israeli attack, now supported by clear superiority in the air.

It proved impossible however to 'stabilize' the local situation in Israel's interests. In August 1982 the Israeli candidate, Bashir Gemayel, was elected president of Lebanon, but he was assassinated the following month, destroying the basis of a settlement between Israel and Lebanon. Israel now found itself with an onerous commitment and with local allies that required support. The slaughter, in September 1982, of Palestinians in the Sabra and Shatila refugee camps in Beirut by Israel's Lebanese allies, the Maronite Phalange militia, and the Israeli bombardment of the city, badly compromised Israel's reputation and did not achieve its long-term military or political goals.

More generally, conflict in Lebanon demonstrated the limitations of advanced weapons. In 1982, a multinational Western force was sent to Lebanon to try and bolster its stability, but the forces soon became targets as the British had in Aden in the 1960s. In September 1983, the American Sixth Fleet bombarded Druze militia positions on the hills near Beirut in support of the Lebanese army, firing shells the size of small cars; yet the following month neither the Americans nor the French could prevent the destruction of their headquarters in Beirut by lorries full of high explosives driven by suicidal guerrillas; the British, more attuned to terrorist moves, thanks to their experience in Northern Ireland, blocked a comparable move. As a result of their losses, and of a more general sense of political impotence, the American marines sent to Lebanon in 1982 were withdrawn in 1984.

Subsequently, unable to cope with the cost of the occupation, the Israelis had to withdraw from the bulk of Lebanon (1985). Eventually, Israel abandoned the Security Zone within Lebanon established along the frontier: they faced a guerrilla force, the Hizbullah, willing to take casualties, enjoying foreign support, especially from Iran, and able to respond tactically (for example with surface-to-air missiles) to such Israeli advantages as air power, while still maintaining pressure on Israel. The Israelis armed local allies, which reduced the pressure on the Israeli army, but these allies had only limited success. The collapse of Israeli influence in Lebanon was matched by Syrian success, and, in 1990, the Syrians played an important role in bringing the Lebanese civil war to an end.

In December 1987, the *intifada*, a rebellion against Israeli rule in occupied Arab territories, and specifically against the pace of Israeli settlement on the West Bank, began with stone-throwing crowds challenging Israeli authority. Initially spontaneous though soon organized, the *intifada* was to underline the weakness of imposed political settlements in the Middle East where the bulk of any population felt alienated, and also to expose the limitation of regular troops in the face of popular resistance. Unable to cow opposition with violence, the Israeli High Command found it difficult to deal with what was to them a novel form of warfare, not least because the conflict was waged in the glare of the world's media. There was no concentrated target for the Israeli military, such as that which faced the Saudi Arabians in November 1979 when the Grand Mosque in Mecca was seized by Shia militants: it was stormed. The Oslo Agreement of 1993 led in 1994 to the creation of a Palestinian autonomous territory under Yasser Arafat and to a peace treaty between Israel and Jordan. Conflict, however, resumed between Israel and the Palestinians from 2000.

BOX 10.1   THE IRAN–IRAQ WAR, 1980–88

Seeking to exploit the chaos following the overthrow of the shah, and to gain both a favourable settlement of border disputes and regional hegemony, Saddam Hussein, the dictator of Iraq, who had used oil money to build up its military, invaded Iran in September 1980, launching a struggle that lasted until 1988 and that involved more combatants (probably over 2.5 million by 1988) and casualties (reportedly up to one million) than other conflicts of the period. The Iraqis planned to use the same methods as those employed by Israel against Egypt in 1967: a surprise air attack to destroy the opponent's air force, followed by a tank offensive. However well-conceived the operational plan, the Iraqis proved incapable of executing it. The surprise Iraqi attack on ten air bases on the night of 22 September failed because of a lack of adequate expertise and targeting equipment, a failure that ensured that the Iranian air force survived and was, in turn, able to attack Iraqi oil facilities successfully on 25 September, hitting the financial underpinnings of the Iraqi war effort.

On the ground, the Iraqis lacked the mobility and tactical flexibility shown by the Israelis. Instead, their advance was slower and their tanks were frequently employed as artillery, downplaying their capacity for manoeuvre warfare. Iraqi forces also lacked adequate logistics and sufficiently flexible command systems. More seriously, their war aims were misconceived, and there was no clear exit strategy, in part because the nature of Iranian politics had been misread, for, far from collapsing, the Iranian forces fought back, helped by an upsurge in patriotism. To take Khorramshahr on 24 October to 10 November, the Iraqis had to resort to hand-to-hand combat. The following May the city was recaptured by Iranian forces making skilful use of night attacks. The Iranians also benefited from the use of helicopters, not least firing heat-seeking missiles against Iraqi tanks, and from the employment of SAM 7 surface-to-air missiles. The Iranians outnumbered the Iraqis, but international isolation made it difficult to keep their equipment maintained (always a major problem with foreign sources of supply), and the Iraqis benefited from assistance from most other Arab states as well as from powers fearful of Iran and its espousal of Islamic fundamentalism, including the USA. This help was variously financial, particularly from Kuwait and Saudi Arabia, and the sale of weapons, especially by France and the Soviet Union.

The Iraqis used chemical weapons against Iranian attacks, and both sides employed missiles, targeting opposing capitals. The war also saw the first modern 'martyrdom operation' by an Islamic group when an Iranian-backed Shia movement was responsible, in 1981, for the suicide bombing of the Iraqi embassy in Beirut. The war also spread to involve attacks on shipping in the Persian Gulf, which led to Western naval commitments there. Having driven the Iraqis back the Iranians finally accepted international pressure for peace in 1988 because they could not sustain the costs of the offensive. By the end of the war, the Iraqis had lost maybe 105,000 dead, and the Iranians maybe 262,000.

Plate 10.1 Ramadan prayers. An Iraqi soldier who has left the safety of the trenches prays towards Mecca during Ramadan, June 1984, on Iraq's southern front in the Majnoon Island area. Photo by Don Mell, © Associated Press.

REBELLIONS

Aside from wars between states there was also conflict as governments faced rebellions. These overlapped with other categories of conflict. Thus, in Angola, the long-standing rebellion against the MPLA government by UNITA carried forward their rivalry in the war of independence against Portuguese control (see p. 165), a rivalry that included a tribal and regional dimension, with UNITA based in the Ovimbundu tribe of southern Angola. The Portuguese tried in early 1975 to transfer power to a coalition government willing to oversee free elections, but conflict began on 1 February when the MPLA and FLNA clashed in Luanda. Within six months, the MPLA had defeated its opponents and seized power.

The clash between UNITA and the MPLA was also closely intertwined both with the Cold War, as the MPLA government looked to the Soviet Union and Cuba while UNITA received American backing, and also with the continuing struggle against 'white' rule in Southern Africa, which, in turn, was related to the Cold War. South Africa provided money, weaponry and advisers to UNITA, as well as bases in neighbouring South West Africa, and more direct intervention, including air cover for UNITA in southern Angola. In 1975, South Africa sent a large force into Angola in order to weaken the MPLA. Further attacks followed in 1978 and 1979 as the South Africans attacked SWAPO bases in Angola, such as Lubango, from which their position in South-West Africa was under attack. Angolan forces were attacked anew by South Africa in 1981 and 1982, and, after the failure of the Lusaka Accord of 1984, a ceasefire was not agreed until 1988.

The war had become too costly for the Soviet Union, Cuba and South Africa, and the failure of the UNITA/South African siege of the city of Cuito Cuanavale in the winter of 1987–88 encouraged negotiations, not least because it indicated the limitations of South African air power in the face of surface-to-air missiles. Ironically, American aid for UNITA was matched by the purchase of oil by American oil companies, especially Gulf Oil, that helped enable the Angolan government to buy arms to fight UNITA. As a result of the ceasefire, the South Africans withdrew at once, while the Cubans finally left in 1991. However, the MPLA and UNITA ceasefire, only signed in 1989, speedily collapsed, leading to an upsurge in conflict, a fresh bout of diplomacy, and a peace in 1991 that lasted until UNITA rejected the results of the 1992 election. There was a similar struggle in Mozambique, where, after the end of Portuguese rule in 1975, South Africa had also supported the RENAMO rebels against the FRELIMO government. The government was backed by troops from Zimbabwe and Tanzania and received Soviet arms.

Ethnic tensions played a role not only in Angola and Mozambique but also in a host of conflicts in sub-Saharan Africa. Some of the most bloody occurred in the former Belgian colonies of Burundi and Rwanda where the Hutu and Tutsi were the major groups. In 1959, the Tutsi rulers of Rwanda were overthrown by the Hutu majority, with about 10,000 killed, and subsequent attempts by Tutsi émigrés to regain power by guerrilla action failed and led to the killing of maybe another 30,000 Tutsi. This was to be the background to serious conflict in the early 1990s (see pp. 248–9).

Across the world, many rebellions were separatist in origin and occurred with increasing regularity after 1945: one people's nationalism was often treasonable separatism to the state in question. In 1946, the shah led the Iranian army into Tabriz, producing a bloodbath that cowed Azerbaijani separatism. The rebellious Karens in Burma were supported by Chinese Nationalist forces that had taken refuge at the close of the Chinese Civil War. A rebellion in Kham in 1956, begun by Khampa nomads, was followed in neighbouring Tibet in 1959 by an uprising that had started as a massive demonstration in the capital Lhasa. The Chinese responded with artillery, although the course of events remained controversial while the extent of earlier guerrilla action is unclear. In 1959 the Moroccan army crushed a revolt by the Berbers in the Rif mountains, while in the 1960s Congo suppressed Kataganese separatism.

The Indonesian army suppressed Communist and Islamic opposition, including the Darul Islam (*House of Islam*) in west Java in the 1950s, as well as the Republic of the South Moluccas in 1952 and military-supported separatist rebellions in Sumatra and Sulawesi in 1957 and 1958. The latter was backed by CIA aircraft. The Indonesians also unsuccessfully sought to overthrow Brunei in 1962 by fomenting a rebellion, and to conquer northern Borneo from British-supported Malaysia from 1963 to 1965 (see p. 164). The Indonesians annexed western New Guinea (as West Irian) in 1963, successfully invaded East Timor in 1975, and brutally resisted demands for independence by the Free Papua Movement in Irian and the Fretilin movement in East Timor.

The reliance on force in East Timor proved seriously counter-productive, as it failed to assuage local separatism and also led to international condemnation, especially after the shooting of unarmed demonstrators at a cemetery in Dili on 12 November 1991 led to hundreds of deaths or injuries and was filmed by Western journalists. In 1999, the Indonesians responded to continued separatism and to international pressure by giving East Timor the choice of independence or regional autonomy. The people overwhelmingly chose independence, despite serious pressure from militias supported by the army. After the election, the coercion was stepped up, but international attention and anger mounted and finally led the Indonesians to accept the popular verdict. Australian forces under UN auspices secured the new situation, while in Indonesia failure helped discredit the government.

In the Middle East, the Kurds had mounted separatist efforts against Iraq and Turkey since the inter-war period, leading to a response by both that was frequently intertwined with regional- and great-power politics. Thus, in Iraq, where conflict with Kurdish insurgents had been intense from 1961 to 1966 and in 1969 and 1970, the Kurdish rising of 1974–75 was supported by neighbouring and hostile Iran with artillery and anti-aircraft cover, as well as by the provision of American and Israeli arms: Iraq was an ally of the Soviet Union and an opponent of Israel. In Syria, the Alawite-dominated regime and army brutally crushed a rising by Sunni Muslims at Hama in 1982, causing heavy casualties. Religious risings were most common in the Islamic world but were generally unsuccessful, that in Sudan in 1970 being crushed by forces supported by tanks and planes.

In South Asia, attempts by the Pakistani army, which was dominated by troops from the Punjab in West Pakistan, to suppress the Bengali nationalism of East Pakistan provoked a rebellion in 1970 that was supported by India, leading to the creation of the state of Bangladesh. The Pakistani army was more successful in quelling a tribal uprising in Baluchistan from 1972 to 1976 that arose from attempts to limit autonomy and tribal power. In 1983, Tamil separatism began a long-standing war in northern Sri Lanka, while India faced rebellion in Kashmir and from Sikh radicals.

Rebellions led to a variety of military situations. Conflict in the Congo in the 1960s was wide-ranging and bloody, but lacked the large-scale use of troops and front lines seen in the Nigerian Civil War of 1967–70. The slaughter of large numbers of Ibos – possibly 30,000 – in the massacres that followed the second coup of 1966 in Nigeria had led to a collapse of Ibo support for the notion of a federal, multi-racial Nigeria. The new Nigerian government, composed of officers, and the product of the coup, was unsympathetic to the Ibo demand for a looser confederation, while the Ibo leadership challenged the legality of the federal government. After the Ibo republic of Biafra was proclaimed in the south-east of Nigeria, the federal government launched a 'police operation' in July 1967 that became a civil war. The federal forces benefited from overwhelming numerical superiority, including an army of 120,000 troops, and from the availability of British and Soviet weaponry, while France sought to support Biafra. The Nigerian navy was crucial, both in imposing a debilitating blockade of Biafra and in enabling the Nigerians to seize ports and coastal positions, and thus increase the number of fronts on which the Biafrans were under attack.

Although there were some able commanders and some brave troops on both sides, operations and fighting in the war showed the problems, for both sides, of rapidly expanding armies with untrained men. The application of force proved difficult: air attacks were frequently ineffective and artillery was often poorly aimed. Infantry weaponry was more important in the fighting, while the Nigerian army also made good use of armoured personnel carriers. The role of ethnic and factional considerations, however, weakened the federal army's fighting competence. Logistical support in the difficult terrain was not improved by chaotic command and organizational systems characterized by corruption.

The Biafrans, who fought a conventional war with front lines, had no answer to the air power of their opponents, and little response to their armoured vehicles. After the initial stages of the conflict they were also heavily outnumbered. Unlike the Viet Minh and the Viet Cong, the Biafrans were swiftly cut off from foreign land links, and this exacerbated their lack of food and military supplies. The Nigerian government felt no hesitation in using starvation to help destroy the Ibos. The hard-pressed Biafrans finally collapsed after their airstrip at Uli was overrun in 1970, severing their remaining supply link. This was the first major war in sub-Saharan Africa fought to a resolution with modern weapons in which all the commanders were African.

Further east, Ethiopia eventually conceded independence to Eritrea in 1993 after a long secessionist movement in which the Ethiopian position had finally collapsed in April and May 1991, in part because of the fall of the Mengistu regime in Ethiopia in the face of successful opposition by the Ethiopian People's Revolutionary Democratic Front and the Tigré People's Liberation Front.

Sudan, however, continued to be devastated by a civil war which had been waged from 1963 until 1972, and then again from 1983. Successive governments based in the Arabic-speaking Islamic north thwarted southern separatism, beginning with the suppression of a military revolt in the south in 1956 soon after independence, but were unable to subjugate the vast region. The southern separatists of the Anya-Nya movement had initially lacked modern weapons, many relying on spears, but their use of guerrilla tactics gravely weakened the army's position in the south. The size of Sudan also told against the army. It was more successful in its policy of turning for support to the Nuer tribe, rivals of the Dinka tribe that was prominent in the resistance. The latter, however, benefited from support from, or at least bases in, the neighbouring states of Ethiopia, Uganda and Zaire (Congo), as well as from the Israeli provision of military equipment, so that the struggle became an aspect of the Arab–Israeli confrontation. The internationalization of the conflict appears less intense than those in Indo-China because of the absence of American intervention, but it was important in fuelling the war. The Sudanese government received Soviet weapons and advisers, and also support from Egypt. The importance of international support was shown in 1971 when agreements between Sudan and both Ethiopia and Uganda (which led to the end of Israeli aid via Uganda) cut support for the rebels and encouraged them to negotiate.

The 1972 Addis Ababa agreement included southern autonomy as well as the incorporation of southern troops into the army, but in 1983 government pressure, including an attempt to introduce Islamic *sharia* law, led to a revival of guerrilla warfare, soon under the leadership of the Sudan People's Liberation Army. Civilians became a target for both sides, with food aid and famine used as weapons. The ground-to-air missiles of the Sudan People's Liberation Army made the aerial resupply of government garrisons, such as Juba, hazardous. Although a truce was agreed in the autumn of 2002, lasting peace seems unlikely, not least because of the strength of uncompromising militant Islam on the government side, and in 2004 this led to brutal policies in the Darfur region of the country that resulted in slaughter and the large-scale flight of refugees.

Many other rebellions were small scale, for example the unsuccessful attempts in 1966 by the former kingdom of Buganda to secede from Uganda; the Shifta war of 1963–67, when Somalis in north-east Kenya unsuccessfully sought to break away to join Somalia; and the separatist movement in the Senegalese province of Casamance that began in the early 1980s. Such struggles, nevertheless, were important to the history of individual states, and in aggregate terms made up much of the military history of the world. They also ensured that insurgency and counter-insurgency capability, operations and doctrine played a major role in this history. In such struggles effectiveness was often intertwined with political will. For example, in Cuba in 1958, when Batista's divided, demoralized and incompetent army attacked Castro's guerrillas, the offensive was poorly co-ordinated and lacked both adequate air power and foreign support. Once the campaign had failed, the government suffered a crucial loss of nerve and lost the initiative, with fatal consequences.

The political context was also crucial in other insurrections. Governments that were flexible and able to devise effective and interrelated political and military strategies enjoyed more success. Thus, in the defeat of the Hukbalahap rebellion, the peasant-backed Communist guerrilla movement on Luzon in the Philippines from 1946–1954, the government benefited from American arms, but counter-insurgency operations were supplemented by land reform to win over the peasantry. Oman suppressed Yemeni-backed rebellious tribesmen in the extensive Dhofar region from 1965 to 1975, in part thanks to foreign, particularly British and Iranian, assistance, but also because Sultan Qaboos, who deposed his father in 1970, was a more adept politician. The limitations of insurgency warfare spurred recourse to terrorism from the 1970s (for example, in Northern Ireland), with its more restricted requirements for popular and military support.

COUPS

Conversely, governments faced with insurgency challenges also had to confront the risk that elements in the military might themselves seize power, and this often helped determine the relationship between military capability and organization. Thus, in the mid-1950s the field forces of the Iraqi army, with the exception of the Royal Guards Brigade, were, for security reasons, not usually provided with ammunition. Coups were an important part of the military history of the period. In July 1958 the Iraqi monarchy was overthrown in a coup that involved the seizure of the usual targets of such uprisings, including the broadcasting headquarters and the airport. In Africa and elsewhere, coups followed decolonization, although any listing has to note the very different levels of violence seen in coups, which, in large part, reflected their contrasting causes. Many coups arose from the rejection of the civilian governments established at independence and their attempt to control the military, for example the coup in Sudan in 1958 and that in Cambodia which deposed Prince Sihanouk in 1970; but the politicization of the military by civilian governments keen to use its strength to help achieve its goals also helped encourage the military to overcome inhibitions to the use of force. Other coups were the product of inter-military divisions. Coups in Africa included those in Egypt (1952 and 1954), Sudan (1958, 1985, 1989), Togo (1963, 2005), Zanzibar (1964), Zaire (1965), Nigeria (1966, 1985), Ghana (1966, 1972, 1978, 1979), Sierra Leone (1967 and 1997), Mali (1968), Libya (1969), Uganda (1971, 1980, 1985, 1986), Madagascar (1972), Rwanda (1973), Ethiopia (1974), the Central African Republic (1979, 1981, 2003), Equatorial Guinea (1979), Liberia (1980), Upper Volta (1982), Mauritania (1984, 2003), Lesotho (1986), Ivory Coast (1999) and Niger (1999). In Pakistan, military regimes were created in 1958, 1969, 1977 and 1999.

The frequency of coups in Latin America indicated, however, that coups were not only linked to decolonization. Coups there included those in Peru in 1948, 1962 and 1967, Venezuela in 1948 and 1958, Bolivia in 1951, Colombia in 1953 and 1957, Guatemala in 1954, 1978, 1982 and 1983, Argentina in 1955, 1962, 1966, 1970, 1976 and 1981, the Dominican Republic in 1963, Brazil in 1964,

Chile in 1973, Paraguay in 1989, Grenada in 1983, Haiti in 1991 and 2004, and Ecuador in 2000. The use of force both played a role in changes in civilian government, such as those in Peru and Colombia in the 1980s and 1990s, and also led to the creation of military governments, reflecting the widespread conviction among Latin American militaries that their function included the suppression of internal enemies (i.e. what were judged left-wing tendencies).

Although some military regimes, such as that created in Niger in 1999 when the president was shot dead by the head of his bodyguard, who then seized power, were short term, others were long-lasting – for example in Brazil from 1964 until 1985, and in Chile from 1973 until 1990. In the short term, authoritarian regimes reliant on force were less powerful or rigid in practice than they appeared, and they operated by accepting the circumvention of their nostrums and structures by their own members, as well as by vested interests and by the public itself. In the long term, these regimes found it difficult to contain political problems and to satisfy popular demands. Thus in Thailand the military lost power in 1992, while in Indonesia, General Suharto, the army chief of staff, who had benefited from the coup of 1965 to take over power in 1967 and become president in 1968, was forced to surrender power in 1998. However, in Myanmar (Burma), where the military ruled as the State Peace and Development Council, the elections held in 1990 were annulled when a pro-democracy movement won, and the military has held onto power since.

Unsuccessful coups, such as those in Gabon in 1964, Sudan in 1971 (and, allegedly, 2004), Iran in 1980, Spain and Gambia in 1981, Nigeria in 1990, Equatorial Guinea in 1997 and 2004, and Congo in 2004, and plans for coups, as in Egypt in August 1967 and April 1971, were also an important aspect of military history and helped ensure that governments had to see coup avoidance as one of the most important tasks of their military policy.

FORCE AND THE STATE

More generally, the use of force as the arm of the state, whether military or civilian, was another important aspect of military history. This could involve peaceful operations, but was often brutal. Thus, in 1977, 1979 and 1991, the Iraqi army suppressed Shia agitation, in the latter two cases with heavy casualties. The militarized nature of many regimes was readily apparent. Under General Qassem, who ruled Iraq from 1958 to 1963, the heavily fortified Ministry of Defence compound was the centre of government, protected by about 2,000 troops. When Qassem was overthrown, the compound was attacked from the air before being besieged. Having surrendered, Qassem was killed. Earlier, in 1958, the Iraqi monarchy had been overthrown in a coup.

The continuum between coups and civil wars was not easily segmented for the purposes of definition. Nor was that between ethnic tension and civil war, as was shown from 1987 to 1990 in Natal, then part of white-ruled South Africa, when the Zulu Inkatha movement fought the United Democratic Front, which was linked to the then-banned African National Congress. This struggle for dominance involved control over land and employment, and the ability to negotiate with the apartheid government. Police involvement further complicated the struggle, which was at once a conflict between groups within a state where the government could still deploy considerable force, and a disorganized upsurge of ethnic violence and lawlessness.

Civilian governments also used force to intimidate the population. In China, having, in the Great Proletarian Cultural Revolution, used Red Guards to terrorize alleged reactionaries, Mao Zedong, from late 1968, accepted the use of the army to restore order. In 1989, under his less authoritarian successor Deng Xiaoping, the army was still used to suppress brutally the Democracy Movement in Beijing. In 1992, the Peruvian president, Alberto Fujimori, used the army to shut down the Congress and the courts. In Zimbabwe in the early 2000s, Robert Mugabe, who in the 1980s had consolidated his control at the expense of his rival Joshua Nkomo by employing large-scale force, used troops to try to break a national strike and to crush demonstrations. Troops were also used for policing, as in Jamaica in 1999 when there were joint patrols with the police. The military was also employed as the arm of the state in First World countries. In Britain, 19,000 servicemen were deployed in the winter of 2002–3 in Operation Fresco in order to provide emergency fire cover during a fire service union strike.

LATIN AMERICA

Latin America saw little intra-state conflict. A would-be regional power, Argentina, engaged in an arms race and naval confrontation with Chile, with which it had a territorial dispute, and, in 1982, provoked war with Britain over the Falklands, an island group in the South Atlantic (see Chapter 8). Argentina had come close to war with Chile in 1978 when it rejected a mediation settlement in a border dispute over three small islands in the Beagle Channel, but the fall of its military government after failure in the Falklands war finally led it to accept this verdict. There was also a border dispute between Peru and Ecuador. The Football War of 1969, in which the army of El Salvador invaded neighbouring Honduras after a visiting Honduran football team had been attacked in San Salvador, and the football victory of El Salvador had been followed by anti-Salvadorean riots in Honduras, appeared ridiculous, and was certainly short, although the root causes were more complex. They owed much to long-standing difficulties exacerbated by large-scale Salvadorean migration into Honduras.

Conflict across much of Latin America involved both local rivalries and the intervention of the major powers. The seizure of power in Cuba by Fidel Castro had initially been acceptable to the Americans, but his leftward move led to support for an émigré attempt to seize power which miscarried in the Bay of Pigs invasion in 1961, in part because the absence of American air support left the invaders vulnerable, although their assessment of the political situation inside Cuba was also over-optimistic. Cuba then became more prominent when the stationing of Soviet missiles there in 1962 led to an American blockade that threatened to lead to conflict between the USA and the Soviet Union (see p. 202).

After the Soviets had backed down, the Americans demonstrated their strength in the Caribbean by successfully intervening in the Dominican Republic in 1965, sending in nearly 23,000 troops to prevent it from becoming a second Cuba, a misreading of the risks in fact posed by a rebellion against the conservative regime there. The Americans enforced peace and oversaw an election in 1966 that produced another conservative government, that under Joaquin Videla Balaguer, before withdrawing, while leaving a Military Advisory and Assistance Group that helped the American government to oversee developments by maintaining close links with the army. The USA also became concerned about Cuban support for Latin American radical movements, although attempts to repeat Castro's success were unsuccessful: Che Guevara dismally failed when he tried to mount a revolution in Bolivia in 1967. In the 1970s, however, the commitment of Cuban forces to conflicts in Africa (see p. 226) became an important aspect of the Cold War.

The Americans, who like the Soviets were major trainers of foreign military personnel, devoted particular effort to training the Latin American military. Combined with higher morale and greater determination than was shown by the Cuban army from 1956 to 1959, this helped lead to the defeat of radical insurrections. From the mid-1950s, and particularly after Castro's success in Cuba, Latin American military establishments were restructured in accordance with American views, the first Latin American counter-insurgency school being founded, with American aid, in Colombia, and an American-trained unit helped crush Guevara's revolution in Bolivia. As a result, military help was seen as part of a programme that included economic aid and political support for the development of democratic regimes that were seen as necessary in order to secure pro-American societies. The emphasis on these respective goals varied, with a particular ambivalence when political developments did not match geo-strategic aspirations. This ambivalence had existed from the outset of the Cold War, with American aid to Greece and Turkey from 1947 being primarily military and with scant emphasis on the democratic reforms that were proclaimed.

The Communist challenge in Latin America was seen by the USA as more insidious than that of the Germans during World War Two, because Communism was seen both as a geo-strategic threat to the USA itself, directed by the Soviet Union, and as a diffuse social challenge to the coherence and stability of Latin American regimes. Following the 1951 Military Security Act, the USA signed bilateral agreements with twelve Latin American states, the latter agreeing to focus their production of strategic materials on the USA and not to trade with hostile states in return for American military assistance. Concern about radicalism encouraged the CIA to oppose the government of President Jacobo Arbenz Guzman in Guatemala and, finally, in 1954, to instigate a successful coup. The American government also supported the Chilean armed forces under General Pinochet when they overthrew the Marxist Allende government in 1973.

Nicaragua was seen as a threat after 1979 when the Sandinista National Liberation Front overthrew the dictatorship of Anastasio Somoza Debayle. The left-wing Sandinistas drew inspiration and support from Cuba, and also provided backing for left-wing rebels in El Salvador. Concerned about the risk of instability throughout Central America, and determined to mount a robust response, the

Reagan government that came to power in 1981 applied economic, political and military pressure on the Sandinistas, providing funds to train and equip the Contras, a counter-revolutionary force that was based in neighbouring Honduras. Although the Contras helped to destabilize Nicaragua, they could not overthrow the Sandinistas. Instead, diplomatic pressure from the international community resulted in free elections in 1989 that led to the replacement of the Sandinista government.

In El Salvador, the Reagan government provided advisers, arms (including helicopter gunships) and massive funds to help the right-wing junta resist the Farabundo Marti National Liberation Front (FMLN); however, the commitment of numerous advisers was not followed by ground troops. This enabled the Americans to define the struggle as low-intensity conflict, although it did not appear so to the population of El Salvador as they were caught between guerrillas and brutal counter-insurgency action, which frequently took the form of terror. The war revealed the classic weaknesses of guerrilla operations, not least the difficulty of moving from rural power and harrassing attacks to dominance of the countryside, control of the towns and an ability to achieve victory. The war also showed the weaknesses of counter-insurgency strategies, including the problems of using military strength to ensure civil peace, especially the weaknesses of air attack. While the Cold War was fading in Europe it continued in El Salvador, with a large-scale FMLN offensive in November 1989. This took over part of the capital, San Salvador, for a week, but could not touch off a popular uprising. Equally, the failure of the government to prevent the offensive led its American sponsors to press for negotiations which eventually, in 1992, bore fruit with a settlement under which the FMLN translated its activism to civilian politics.

CONCLUSIONS

The internal use of force was central to the military history of much of the world, although it both militarized society and compromised military professionalism. This aspect of military history has been underrated in part because it plays no important role as far as the USA, the world's leading military power, is concerned. By providing opportunities for able individuals and strengthening the sense of national identity, the American military took a role in the long-term reintegration of the American South after the Civil War and was also the last resort in the event of apparent challenges to internal stability, but the constraints on the use of force were far greater than in most Third World states, while the availability of the National Guard kept the regular military at a remove from the issue. In contrast, militarized states, such as those in Latin America, owed their character not so much to conflict with each other as to the domestic use of force, and this was accentuated by radical insurrectionary challenges such as those of the Tupamaros guerrillas in Uruguay and from the Shining Path in Peru. This situation continued after the end of the Cold War and helps define much of modern military history.

CHAPTER 11

War in the 1990s

▌ INTRODUCTION

The end of the Cold War with the collapse of the Soviet Union (dissolved in 1991) as a result of domestic pressures did not lead to the 'end of history', or the 'peace dividend', foretold by some of the more superficial commentators who believed all too readily that it represented a triumph for American-led democratic capitalism and that there would be no future clash of ideologies to destabilize the world. However, in what was a revolution in strategic affairs, the Western powers, led by the USA, were now able to intervene more frequently against states that earlier would otherwise have looked for Soviet support, not least because UN resolutions were not vetoed in the Security Council. In addition, the established parameters within which peacekeeping was generally expected to take place, particularly that conflict had already ended and that the government of the state in question accepted the deployment of peacekeepers, were interpreted increasingly generously, as seen with the use of terms such as 'peace support', 'peace-making' and 'peace-enforcement'.

American force projection was not challenged by a revived Russia because the collapse of the Soviet Union was not followed by a stronger Russia. Instead, it faced serious economic difficulties as the dismantling of the old command economy exposed the uncompetitive nature of much Soviet-era industry, while it proved difficult to establish effective monetary and fiscal mechanisms. Western loans were necessary in order to prevent a total collapse of Russia in the 1990s and, even so, debt payments caused a severe crisis in 1998, leading to default and devaluation. Former Russian allies joined NATO: Poland, the Czech Republic and Hungary being the first to do so in 1997.

With Russian weakness, the arithmetic of deterrence, underlined as it was by the risk of mutually assured destruction, no longer discouraged overt Western intervention in the Third World. Indeed, in January 1994 the American and Russian leaders agreed not to target each other's states with their strategic nuclear weapons. The end of the Cold War also increased the number of potential allies for the West, and thus deepened its logistical capability and strengthened its capacity for force projection. At the same time, this capacity was put at the service of a mixture of regional goals, and a universalist aspiration to secure a more benign world order, that posed serious challenges not only to Western military capability but also to related political goals. In particular, there were acute issues of prioritization between alternative commitments, and also of how best to devise sensible political missions that matched military capability, and how best to organize and enhance the latter in order to secure missions. A variety of military devices and doctrines such as American preparation for confronting two major regional crises simultaneously, and American (from 1992) and British reconceptualization of naval warfare towards littoral power projection, were important, but did not address the issues of the sensible assessment of objectives and the political management of conflict.

THE GULF WAR, 1990–91

The 1990s opened with a second Iraqi invasion, this time of neighbouring Kuwait. A far smaller and weaker target than Iran, oil-rich Kuwait rapidly fell on 2 August 1990, and six days later Saddam Hussein declared Kuwait Iraq's nineteenth province. The response defined high-spectrum warfare for the decade. Concerned about the impact of Iraqi expansion in the centre of the world's oil production, George H.W. Bush, the American president, rapidly began diplomatic and military preparations for conflict, and Iraq's failure to press on to attack Saudi Arabia ensured that the initiative thereafter rested with its opponents. On 3 August two American carrier groups were ordered towards the region, and on 8 August, in response to a Saudi request for ground troops two days earlier, the first American troops arrived. The build-up of coalition forces in neighbouring Saudi Arabia benefited from the availability of Saudi oil and bases, and was matched by a blockade intended to hit Iraqi trade, especially oil exports.

Iraq's refusal to meet a UN deadline for withdrawal, led, on 17 January 1991, to the start of a major air offensive. Although aircraft from twelve countries were involved, the Americans were central to the offensive, which worked because of the rapid success in overcoming the sophisticated Iraqi anti-aircraft system: Saddam had used French and Soviet technology to produce an integrated system in which computers linked radars and missiles. Iraq's heavily-outnumbered air force did not intervene in force; instead the MiG-29s flew to Iran where they were added to the air force. The air offensive benefited from state-of-the-art American weaponry: B-2 Stealth bombers able to minimize radar detection bombed Baghdad

– one of the most heavily defended cities in the world – and did so with impunity, while the Americans made effective use of guided bombs. Thermal-imaging laser-designation systems were employed to guide the bombs to their target, and pilots launched bombs into the 'cone' of the laser beam in order to score a direct hit. The use of stealth and precision meant that it was possible to employ a direct air assault aimed at overcoming the entire Iraqi air system, rather than an incremental roll-back campaign. The destruction of the air-defence system, with only one aircraft lost (to an Iraqi MiG-29) on the first night, was a triumph not only for weaponry but also for planning that made full use of the opportunities presented by the weapons, while also out-thinking the Iraqis – for example by getting them to bring their radars to full power and thus exposing them to attack. As a result of the air assault Iraqi forces were to be short of supplies, their command and control system was heavily disrupted so that they could not 'understand' the battle, and their morale was low.

Air power was crucial to the first three phases of the operation: destroying Iraqi command and control, isolating the battlefield, and weakening Iraqi forces in the Kuwaiti theatre of operations. In phase four – the ground campaign – the initial plan for a one-corps operation was superseded, due to a recognition of the need for heavy forces, by a two-corps plan relying on American and British armoured divisions.

In February 1991, Iraqi forces were driven from Kuwait in a swift land campaign in which the Iraqis were out-generalled and out-fought by coalition forces that benefited not only from superior technology but also from their ability to maintain a high-tempo offensive in executing a well-conceived plan that combined air and land strength. Allied fighting quality, unit cohesion, leadership and planning, and Iraqi deficiencies in each, all played a major role in ensuring victory. The Americans employed satellite surveillance, Patriot anti-missile missiles against Iraqi attacks, Cruise missiles, and guided bombs to provide precise bombardment. In the ground war, which began at 4 a.m. on 24 February, the Iraqis were defeated with heavy casualties, while their opponents lost few men: the Americans suffered 143 battle fatalities, 33 of them from 'friendly fire'.

The poorly-led Iraqis had surrendered mobility by entrenching themselves to protect their conquest of Kuwait. Predictions that the entrenchments would be difficult to take, and that the Iraqis would force attritional warfare on the coalition, causing heavy casualties, proved mistaken. While the Iraqis were attacked on the direct route to Kuwait City, their right flank was outmanoeuvred by a rapid American advance to the west which put tremendous pressure on the Iraqis as the outflanking American forces turned to attack them on 27 February and destroyed much of the Iraqi army. The following morning, President George H.W. Bush ordered a ceasefire, with the Iraqis having lost over 50,000 dead, as well as 81,000 prisoners and nearly 4,000 tanks, in a hundred hours of non-stop combat.

Despite the rapid victory the American doctrine of AirLand Battle (see p. 196) proved, like other military concepts, more difficult to execute in practice than to advance in theory and to train for, not least due to the problems of synchronizing air and land forces under fast-moving combat conditions. However, compared to earlier conflicts, such as the Linebacker II air offensive on North Vietnam in

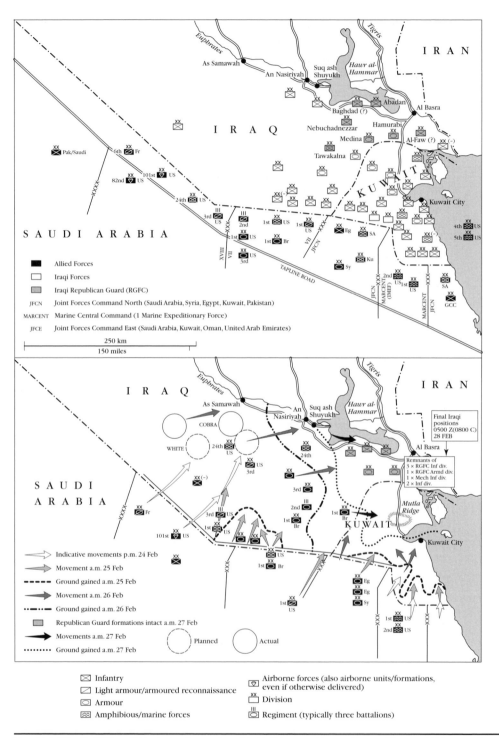

Map 11.1 The Gulf War, 1991: the land campaign, 24–28 February. *Top:* positions of forces 24 February; *bottom:* Allied envelopment of Iraqi forces. From *The Oxford Companion to Military History* (2003), p. 389, edited by Richard Holmes, by permission of Oxford University Press.

December 1972, there was unified control over air operations – a single air manager (the joint force air component commander), target acquisition and accuracy were effective, and the pace of the air attack was maintained even if some of the high-tech weaponry, such as the Patriot missile and British runway-cratering bombs, did less well than was claimed at the time. In addition, important parts of the Allied military did not employ weaponry that was available. For example, the Americans used 9,300 precision-guided munitions, but most of their aircraft were not equipped nor their pilots trained for their use and instead employed unguided munitions, which made up 90 per cent of the aerial munitions used. This was despite the extensive and effective use of precision-guided munitions in the Linebacker I and II campaigns in Vietnam in 1972. Similarly, although the Americans had developed stealth aircraft, most of their planes lacked the expensive capability. Cruise missiles, however, successfully provided a new capability for surface warships.

The conflict also saw Iraqi Scud missile attacks on Israel, and, although they did not achieve their desired aim of bringing Israel into the war and thus jeopardizing Arab support for the USA (especially from Saudi Arabia and Syria), they underlined Israeli vulnerability. Concerned that their deterrence had been lessened as a result of its inaction, the Israeli government wished to take reprisals, but aside from discouraging weather conditions they were affected by American opposition to such action. The USA did, however, provide Israel with satellite information and Patriot batteries. The need to counter the military and, even more, political threat from Scud missiles, dramatized the implications of the spread of weaponry. American anti-missile doctrine had long focused on Soviet inter-continental ballistic missiles, but the Scuds indicated that short-range anti-missile defences and doctrine were also necessary, and drew attention to the problems of relying on the Patriot missiles for that purpose.

For the American and British navies, the war marked the major change that followed the end of the Cold War. In place of a doctrine focused on defeating Soviet naval forces in a struggle for maritime routes came littoral force projection and amphibious capability, at the expense of a state with no real naval power.

The failure to keep military objectives and political goals in harmony, however, helped ensure that the Gulf War did not lead to the hoped-for overthrow of Saddam Hussein. The American decision to end the offensive was taken in haste, in a war that was very high tempo, without an adequate consideration of how to translate the outcome of the campaign into a durable post-war settlement. This was linked to military factors, specifically the persistence of 'friction' and 'fog': a failure to distinguish victory from operational success helped ensure that the wrong decisions were taken. The civilian leadership permitted the decision to end the war to be governed by military considerations, specifically the expulsion of Iraqi forces from Kuwait; but the major goal, in fact, was political: the need to create a stable post-war situation in the Gulf, the military preconditions for such stability being ultimately a political judgement.

Instead, after the coalition ceased its advance, Hussein was able to use his forces, particularly the Revolutionary Guard and its artillery and tanks, to smash a rebellion by the country's Shia majority, causing heavy casualties and destroying Shia shrines in Karbala and Najaf. In contrast, in Operation Provide Comfort, a multi-service, multinational task force protected the Kurds in northern Iraq from action by Hussein's forces. The war was followed by the long-term use of Allied air power in order to try to prevent Iraq from rebuilding its military, an expensive commitment that had only limited success – not least because policing Iraqi 'no-fly zones' was easier than influencing developments on the ground.

The understandable focus on the American contribution to the war, which included over half a million military personnel, has led to an underestimation of its impact on other states. For all those militaries that took part, the war raised issues of force projection, logistics and inter-operability, although the last was eased by the experience of many in co-operation through NATO. The contribution of those that did not send forces into the combat zone, but did provide financial support and/or indirect military help by freeing coalition units for operations (principally Germany and Japan), was also important.

AMERICAN OPERATIONS

Although it was far more small-scale, and was to be overshadowed by the Gulf War, the Americans had already shown on 20–24 December 1989, in Operation Just Cause, that airborne forces could play a major role in overthrowing the government of General Noriega in Panama, which had played a prominent part in drug-smuggling into the USA. Overwhelming force brought the Americans rapid success with limited casualties, although, in part, that reflected the limited nature of the resistance. The unpopular Noriega regime was not in a position to inspire and concert the latter.

The operation was far more successful than the attempt to rescue the American hostages in Iran in 1980, or Operation Urgent Fury against Grenada in 1983. Urgent Fury had been motivated by concern about Grenada's leftward move, and the possibility that this would lead to a Soviet military presence. As such, it was really part of the Cold War. The Caribbean island was seized by American forces, but the operation saw inadequate inter-service co-ordination, which led to delay and to most American losses being to 'friendly' fire. These problems had been remedied by 1989, so that in Panama joint operations worked, as they had not done on Grenada, and objectives had been more clearly defined, while new weapons, including the AC-130 Gunship, performed successfully.

The improvement in joint operations was an important aspect of a more profound period of change in the American military following the end of both conscription and the Vietnam War. Morale, cohesion and effectiveness in the army had been particularly poor in the early 1970s due to the legacy of Vietnam, and it proved necessary to rebuild military capability. This was done. Operationally effective, the move away from mass conscript forces potentially lessened the domestic political sensitivity of military commitments, but failure in Beirut from 1982 to 1984, a poorly conceived and managed intervention, and the more lasting impact of the Vietnam War, encouraged the formulation of what became known as the Weinberger doctrine, after Casper Weinberger, secretary of defense, which pressed for commitments only in the event of predictable success and a clear exit strategy, and called for the use of overwhelming force. This helped ensure that the protection of the military took precedence over diplomatic goals and became the strategic object.

SOMALIA AND HAITI

American intervention in the 1990s ensured that Somalia generally rates a mention in global military history, but this intervention was in fact tangential to a bitter and lengthy period of conflict in that country. Following Somalia's failure in the Ogaden war with Ethiopia in 1977 and 1978, a weaker President Barré had faced growing opposition from clans which, increasingly, obtained heavier arms. In addition, the Somali National Movement mounted a serious challenge from 1978, although in 1988 the government was able to drive them from the northern towns they had seized, albeit causing heavy civilian casualties in the process. In 1989 and 1990, other resistance movements further eroded Barré's position, full-scale civil war broke out, and Barré fled into exile in January 1991, mounting unsuccessful attempts to return that April, as well as in April and September 1992. Somalia was split into areas controlled by clan factions, each of which deployed artillery and armoured vehicles, as well as the light lorries carrying heavy machine-guns which were a distinctive feature of Somali warfare. Several of the clans made use of child fighters.

The United Nations intervened in 1992 in order to bring humanitarian relief, although also, if necessary, to disarm the factions. The UN forces, however, were inadequate to the latter task, and the ambiguity of the mission helped to lead to chaos. The Americans, who in Operation Restore Hope initially provided 28,000 men of the 37,000-strong UN force, were determined to remove Mohamed Farah Aidid, whose faction dominated the capital Mogadishu. Aidid opposed the UN intervention, and on 5 June 1993 his men ambushed a Pakistani unit, killing twenty-five men. This led the UN, supported by the US, to move against Aidid. On 3 October 1993, the American Task Force Ranger captured several Aidid supporters (but not Aidid) in a raid, but then met opposition, with two helicopters shot down. In the clash that continued until the force was relieved by American, Pakistani and Malaysian troops early next day, the Rangers lost sixteen dead and eighty-three wounded, while about 300 Somalis were killed.

In reaction to their losses the Americans abandoned aggressive operations in Somalia, a decision that was seized on by Osama bin Laden, leader of the Islamic terrorist movement al-Qaeda, to argue that the Americans could be forced to retreat. This helped inspire bin Laden's 'Declaration of War against the Americans Occupying the Land of the Two Holy Places', issued in August 1996, that called for the expulsion of American forces from Saudi Arabia (a legacy of the Gulf War of 1990–91) and for the overthrow of what was seen as the pro-American Saudi government.

The UN forces withdrew from Somalia in March 1994. Faction fighting continued and the number of factions increased, as did civilian casualties. By 2003, the country was divided into about twenty-five warring fiefdoms and clashes continued in 2004. After 1994, no American combat troops were sent on peace-keeping missions to Africa, and in 2003, when pressure built up for UN intervention in the mounting crisis in Congo, the American government made it clear that it would not send troops, while in Liberia the Americans essentially provided logistical support for Nigerian peacekeepers. American interests in sub-Saharan Africa had been directly attacked when al-Qaeda mounted truck bomb attacks on American embassies in Nairobi and Dar es Salaam, but American engagement with the continent remained limited.

Earlier and nearer home, in Operation Uphold Democracy in 1994, the USA had sent 20,000 troops to Haiti in pursuit of a UN mandate to restore Jean-Bertrand Aristide, the president deposed by a military coup in 1991, and as a way to stop the flight of Haitian refugees to the USA. This restoration was achieved by negotiation rather than force, although it proved difficult to make Haitian society conform to the goals of the subsequent US-dominated UN peacekeeping

BOX 11.1   NORTHERN IRELAND

The British failed to suppress IRA (Irish Republican Army) terrorism in Northern Ireland, but they contained the situation sufficiently to allow negotiations that produced a peace settlement in 1998. British troops had been deployed on local streets from 1969 in order to maintain control in the face of serious rioting, but, despite the confidence of the Unionists and of some of the army that a military solution was possible, IRA terrorism proved impossible to suppress. Given the difficulties of their task, the British army maintained a high level of professionalism, but that did not protect them from criticism from many who seemed less willing to condemn the deliberate terrorist policy of murder of civilians and military employed by the IRA. In 1972 alone there were 1,853 bomb incidents, although that year the army also successfully regained control of 'no-go areas' of Londonderry and Belfast hitherto controlled by the IRA. This led the IRA to follow the course of terrorism, rather than that of waging guerrilla warfare. They drew on nationalist support in the Catholic community and benefited from international support from Catholic Irish nationalists in the USA and from Libya, whose leader saw the struggle as a war of national liberation, one that enabled him to strike at Britain.

The British made heavy use of helicopters to supply fortified posts, as roads were vulnerable to mines, and used intensive intelligence gathering in order to strike at terrorists and their arms supplies; but there was a limit to what could be achieved. At the same time, the terrorists were unable to drive the army out of Northern Ireland, while by the 1990s the IRA was running low on supporters willing to lose their lives. More generally, large social welfare payments, funded from the British Exchequer, helped lessen nationalist support. Of all modern forms of warfare, that of terrorism seems most likely to lead to an impasse.

mission, and the later history of Haiti was far from benign. Corruption and violence associated with the Aristide regime culminated with his overthrow in 2004. This was due to a domestic rising, but was linked to American pressure that led to the deployment of American and French troops.

The peacekeeping and humanitarian support goals of the interventions in Haiti and Somalia were correctly described as low-intensity conflict, as any comparison to the wars with Iraq would demonstrate, but they were difficult and dangerous for the troops involved, and the mission culture that stemmed from the nature of peacekeeping added to the difficulty. It proved hard to secure adequate and timely intelligence, both military and political, and to bring the two into line, while the unpreparedness of the American military for operating in urban environments was revealed. The relative ease of Operation Just Cause in Panama was no real preparation for the problems, both military and political, of Mogadishu. The fate of the latter intervention ensured that Operation Uphold Democracy was supported by adequate force, and it was no accident that American defence expenditure rose markedly in the mid-1990s. Yet the adequacy of force depends largely on the political context and the skill with which the mission is crafted. The American preference for being prepared for war-fighting led to a practice of overwhelming force that worked in Panama and Haiti, but that differed from the British preference for minimum necessary force, as well as from the necessity for long-term commitment focused on nation-building.

CHECHNYA

Meanwhile, the Russians, who were even worse prepared for such tasks, had encountered serious problems in the Caucasus, where Islamic independence movements were able to rely on considerable popular support, in part because of a tradition of ethnic strife, as well as on the mountainous terrain. They tried to extend the break up of the Soviet Union to Russia. Boris Yeltsin, the Russian leader, unwilling to accept such separatism, not least because of the oil in the area, responded by invading the rebellious region of Chechnya in December 1994, capturing the capital, Grozny, in January 1995 after a lengthy siege in which they employed devastating firepower, particularly intensive artillery barrages and bombing. Russian brutality and intransigence, however, encouraged resistance which the Russians were unable to crush. In 1996 they withdrew under a peace agreement in order to strengthen Yeltsin's position during the 1990 presidential campaign.

The 1994–96 campaigns revealed the deficiencies of the badly led, badly equipped, badly trained, badly motivated and under-strength Russian forces. Not least among these deficiencies was the lack of appropriate training and doctrine for counter-insurgency warfare, although it is also necessary to emphasize large Chechen numbers and the extent to which the Chechens were well-armed and determined; many had also been trained through conscription in the Soviet army. The rebels were also able to receive support across the region's borders.

The Russian preference for firepower reflected the dominance in their doctrine and practice of preparations for war with the West, while, more seriously, the Russians appeared to have no response other than force and could not use that effectively, nor really afford it. The Russians added to the usual problems affecting counter-insurgency policies the difficulty of transforming these into peacekeeping; they failed at both.

The renewed Russian attack on Chechnya in 1999 and 2000 was provoked by Chechen moves into neighbouring Daghestan, and by explosions blamed on Chechen terrorists that may have been the work of the Russian secret police. It reflected the determination of Boris Yeltsin's prime minister and eventual successor as president, Vladimir Putin, to assert control. The campaign led to the fall of Grozny in January 2000, but indicated similar military deficiencies. As with other forces battling insurgency, the Russians suffered from the problem of inadequate intelligence, which reflected the limitations of surveillance in such contexts. In such a situation there was an over-reliance on firepower responses, often poorly directed. Guerrilla opposition in Chechnya, including suicide bombings there and elsewhere in Russia, continued, and in response the Russians mounted raids on guerrilla areas and seized suspected Chechens. Opposition was firmest in the mountainous south.

THE FORMER SOVIET UNION

Russian intervention across the area, in turn, created problems for the newly independent republics in the Caucasus. Thus, the Georgian army used force from 1992 to resist separatism by the Muslim province of Abkhazia, but the latter received Russian military assistance. In addition, following the collapse of the Soviet Union, the newly-independent republics of Armenia and Azerbaijan fought, until 1993, over control of the region of Nagorno-Karabakh, a struggle won by Armenia. There was also a bitter clan-based civil war in Tajikistan. A 25,000-strong, Russian-dominated, peacekeeping force helped ensure the defeat of the southern groups, including Islamic fundamentalists, that had contested the dominance of northerners, although the resolution was not peace but rather a guerrilla struggle. At a smaller scale, Uzbeks and Meskhetian Turks fought in the Fergana region of Uzbekistan. Further west, the 'Trans Dniester Republic', supported by former Soviet forces in the 14th Army, sought to break away from the newly independent republic of Moldova.

The USA and other Western powers benefited from the collapse of the Soviet Union to establish a degree of military co-operation with some of the successor states. This was an important instance of the relationship between military assistance programmes and political, ideological and economic change, if not transformation. For example, from 1994, Ukraine's military was given US money under military co-operation programmes, and some of their officers were trained in the USA. The deficiencies of the Soviet military were cruelly demonstrated in the accidental sinking of the nuclear submarine *Kursk* in 2000.

YUGOSLAVIA

While the fall of the Soviet Union led to conflict in the Caucasus, the disintegration of Yugoslavia in 1991 had the same effect in the Balkans. A federal state held together earlier by its Communist dictator Tito, Yugoslavia was divided between ethnic groups, most prominently Serbs and Croats, that sought independence for the areas they dominated and pursued the widest possible definition of the latter. Franjo Tudjman, the authoritarian president of Croatia from 1991 to 1999, used nationalism to provide both identity and rationale for his power, and the same was true of Serbia under Slobodan Milosĕvić. In 1991, in the far north of the country, about 70,000 men out of a population of only two million Slovenes mobilized in order to resist attempts to prevent Slovene independence, and the Serb-dominated Yugoslav army did not push the issue to widespread conflict. It made a far greater effort in Croatia, which, unlike Slovenia, had a border with Serbia and also contained a large Serb minority. This war spilled over into Bosnia, a part of Yugoslavia that was ethnically mixed, with large Croat, Serb and Bosnian Muslim populations, and which suffered from both Croat and Serbian expansion. Each of the communities in Bosnia formed an army, and the Bosnian Serbian and Bosnian Croat forces co-operated with the armies of Serbia

Plate 11.1 Mass grave on collective farm in Pilice, near Srebrenica, 1996. The previous year the Bosnian Serbs murdered about 7,000 unarmed Muslim males. Black and white photo by Gilles Peress © Magnum Photos.

and Croatia, pursuing both their own and joint objectives. The conflicts in Yugoslavia were brutal, but also limited. War involved demonstration and negotiation, a politics by military means that was intensely political, a mixture of sudden and brief brutality with truces, and convoluted strategies of diplomacy.

Western intervention to end the conflict was weakened by a combination of American reluctance, not least from the military leadership, and European weakness. Despite this, settlements were eventually imposed in Bosnia in 1995 and in Kosovo in 1999, at the expense of the expansionism and ethnic aggression of a Serbian regime that unsuccessfully looked for Russian sponsorship. Although the West played a major role, with 3,515 sorties flown (and 100 Cruise missiles fired) in Operation Deliberate Force in 1995 (the first NATO combat mission), the ability of Serbia's opponents, especially the Croats, to organize military forces capable of opposing the Serbs in the field was important in preventing Serb victory. This ability was seen in the autumn of 1995 when the Croats and the Bosnian Muslims, who had been brought together in large part by American pressure, were able to mount successful offensives against the Bosnian Serbs, the Croats overrunning first western Slavonia and then the Krajina. The attacking forces may have numbered 200,000 men. Combined with NATO air attack and diplomatic pressure, this pushed the Serbs into accepting the Dayton peace agreement that November.

The brutal slaughter of civilians by the Serbs (and, to a lesser extent, by their opponents) was an all-too-familiar feature of conflict in much of the modern world, and reflected the extent to which ethnic groups were seen as the units of political strength, and thus as targets. In July 1995, the Bosnian Serbs murdered about 7,000 unarmed Muslim males in Srebrenica, which had been designated a safe zone by United Nations representatives whose peacekeeping force was too weak and too focused on self-preservation to prevent the massacre. What was termed 'ethnic cleansing' – the expulsion of members of an ethnic group – was more common. It was generally associated with the Serbs, but was also used by the Croats, for example in the Krajina, and although that does not excuse Serb actions it helps explain the paranoia that characterized their policy-makers. In turn, such action against civilians led to pressure on outside powers to adapt existing views on peacekeeping in order to adopt a proactive policy of peace enforcement focused on humanitarian goals. This overcame earlier hesitations about action.

In order to suppress separatist demands and to destroy support for the Kosovo Liberation Army, later in the decade the Serbs also used the tactics of ethnic cleansing in Kosovo, part of Serbia with a majority ethnic-Albanian and Muslim population. The Western response over Kosovo was coercive diplomacy, which in 1999 became a forceful humanitarian mission: Operation Allied Force. The resulting seventy-eight-day bombing, and Cruise-missile assault by American, British and French forces in 1999, was less effective than Operation Deliberate Force had been in 1995, and caused far less damage to the Serb military than was claimed, although it did help lead in 1999 to the Serb withdrawal and the Serb acceptance of a ceasefire, followed by the establishment by Britain, France, Germany, Italy and the USA of a NATO peacekeeping force. Thereafter, the continuing isolation of Serbia, in a form of economic and financial warfare, contributed to an erosion of support for Milosĕvić and his fall in the face of Serbian popular action in 2000.

In 1999 George Robertson, the British secretary of state for defence, publicly scorned commentators who warned about the difficulty of winning the Kosovo conflict by air power alone, and also about the contrast between output (bomb and missile damage) and outcome, although the use of air power in Bosnia had already amply demonstrated the problems of managing an air assault when the alliance responsible was divided about its application. The air attack in 1999 suffered the loss of only two aircraft, but the subsequent Serbian withdrawal from Kosovo revealed that NATO estimates of the damage inflicted by air attack, for example to Serb tanks, had been considerably exaggerated. Benefiting from the limitations of Allied intelligence information and its serious consequences for Allied targeting, and from the severe impact of the weather on air operations (a large number cancelled or affected), the Serbs, employing simple and inexpensive camouflage techniques that took advantage of terrain and wooded cover, preserved most of their equipment, despite 10,000 NATO strike sorties. Furthermore, the air offensive had not prevented the large-scale expulsion of Kosovars from their homes, and this badly compromised the success of the operation. Indeed, Operation Horseshoe, the ethnic-cleansing campaign, increased as the air attack mounted.

The Serb withdrawal in 1999 may have owed more to a conviction, based in part on Russian information, that a NATO land attack was imminent, as well as to the withdrawal of Russian support, than to the air offensive, although French, German and eventually American rejection of British pressure for such an invasion indicated their doubts of its feasibility. Indeed a land attack on Kosovo faced a serious logistical challenge, and was dependent on the willingness of neighbouring countries to provide access and bases. This contributed to the mistake of not preparing adequate options in the event of the air offensive failing.

The crisis suggested that air power would be most effective as part of a joint strategy, and, indeed, ground and air threats were not totally separate. The eventual threat to the Serbs on the ground from a NATO invasion made their forces vulnerable to air attack, as it made dispersal, rather than concentration, a less viable proposition. Although the damage to the Serbian army from air attack was limited, the devastation of Serbia's infrastructure, in the shape of bridges, factories and electrical power plants, was important, not least because it affected the financial interests of the elite as well as their morale, and the functioning of the economy. Thus, there was a marked contrast between the limited tactical, but possibly more effective strategic, impact of air power. The majority of the Kosovars expelled returned to their homes in the wake of the Serbian withdrawal. Their return was key to the claims of 'success' for the NATO operation.

THIRD WORLD CONFLICT

As with the situation prior to 1990, it would be misleading to ignore the number of conflicts between 'Third World' forces, some of which, as in Afghanistan and

Somalia, provided the background for Western intervention. More generally, the process by which the Taliban seized power in Afghanistan is rather indicative of post-1990 conflict than the American intervention in that country from 2001. Conflict between 'Third World' forces took a number of forms, ranging from regular warfare across front lines, to insurrections, ethnic conflict, terrorism and coups. Most of this conflict occurred in Africa, but there were also important instances in Latin America, Asia and Oceania. The numbers involved could be considerable: in 1999 it was estimated that Indian security forces resisting insurgency in Kashmir, which included not only the army but also the Central Reserve Police Force and the Border Security Force, numbered 400,000. As an instance of conventional conflict in the 'Third World', in 2000 Ethiopia invaded Eritrea in a frontier struggle that was also a conflict over hegemony. As with many 'Third World' wars, it is difficult to be precise about events, but the Ethiopians benefited from superior air power, better armour (Russian T-72 tanks) and greater numbers, only to find that the Eritreans fought well, taking advantage of the terrain.

In contrast, in Liberia from 1989 and Sierra Leone from 1991, the chaos that accompanied what was referred to as 'failed states' saw conflict that lacked much central direction. In both, drugged teenagers (many of them orphans) and outright looters had little, if any, idea of the cause they were fighting for, except for their own personal gains. Political objectives beyond the capture of power were hazy, and 'wars' benefited from the large-scale availability of small arms and were financed primarily by criminal operations and forced extortions. There were no chains of command or (often) even uniforms that distinguished 'troops' from each other or from other fighters, and, politically, this was an instance of a more widespread process in which warlords moved from being rebels to presidents or vice versa, while ethnicity helped exacerbate conflict.

The Nigerian army played a role in peacekeeping in Sierra Leone and Liberia that reflected its own regional agenda. Poorly trained for the task, the Nigerians tended to use firepower as a substitute for policing, although in both cases the situation was very difficult: drug-taking adolescent fighters operating on behalf of factions had reduced both countries to a form of gangland chaos, and this made it difficult for regulars to identify opponents who could be defeated. In Sierra Leone the civil war was declared over in January 2002, and an international peacekeeping force began to disarm combatants. However, in Liberia, a coup in 1980 was followed by a rebellion by Charles Taylor started in 1989, and, after he became president in 1997, by a rebellion against him that began in 1999 and that led to his opponents advancing into the capital, Monrovia, in 2003. He resigned in the subsequent chaos, and Nigerian peacekeepers took over Monrovia.

In Rwanda in central Africa, civil war was neither so disorganized nor so sustained, but was extremely bloody when it occurred. In 1990, the Tutsi émigrés of the Rwanda Patriot Front invaded Rwanda from Uganda, beginning a civil war that lasted until peace agreements in 1993 that were monitored by a small, largely Belgian UN peacekeeping force. That year, however, a Tutsi coup in neighbouring Burundi against the Hutu government led to the killing of over 100,000 Hutus, increasing tension. In April the following year, an extremist group of Hutus seized power in Rwanda, touching off the slaughter of about 800,000 Tutsi. The failure of the international community to prevent genocide raised a question mark against both the UN's ability to enforce norms and the willingness of the world's leading power, the USA, to act.

CONCLUSIONS

This chapter flows naturally into the next, and the conclusions to both can be summarized there. As far as the 1990s specifically were concerned, the sense of opportunity for power projection provided at the outset by the combination of the collapse of the Soviet Union, the rapid defeat of Iraq, and belief in a revolution in military affairs had already started to slacken, especially with the setback in Somalia and the delay in Kosovo. The problems of securing victory in Iraq in 2003 and 2004 were to underline the difficulties affecting power projection.

CHAPTER 12

War in the 2000s

INTRODUCTION

Writing about a period that is in progress poses many problems, not least those of significance and sympathy. The future becomes present and can readily upset the analysis. Will the American-led clash with radical Islamic fundamentalism, for example, be no more than an interlude before great power confrontation revives with China challenging American interests over Taiwan? This chapter invites readers to speculate and to advance their own priorities for discussion as they consider the evidence of the continued variety and prominence of conflict.

THE WAR ON TERRORISM

The attacks launched by Osama bin Laden's al-Qaeda (The Base) terrorist movement on New York and Washington on 11 September 2001 helped ensure that the American government took a more determined position in warfare in the early 2000s than had been the case in the Balkans in the late 1990s. The replacement of Bill Clinton by George W. Bush as president in early 2001 was also significant, while, at least initially after September 11, the Americans benefited from widespread international support in their self-proclaimed 'War on Terrorism'. The American government felt it necessary in resisting terrorism to strike back against it, and this led to attacks, overt and covert, on what were identified as terrorist bases and supporters, which represented another stage in the movement towards action that had followed the end of the Cold War.

In 2001, Russia lent diplomatic support to the American air offensive against the Taliban regime in Afghanistan, which had provided sanctuary for al-Qaeda, despite the fact that this campaign, launched on 7 October, entailed the establishment of American bases in Central Asian republics that had until 1991 been part of the Soviet Union, such as Uzbekistan.

The Taliban had emerged from the chaos that was Afghanistan in the early 1990s. The Afghan regime of President Najibullah, who had been put in power by the Soviets in 1986, finally fell in April 1992 when the guerrillas entered Kabul: the government had been greatly weakened by the defection of its strongman, Abdul Rashid Dostum. Victory was followed by an upsurge in already strong ethnic-regional tensions within Afghanistan; in particular, the Northerners who had seized the capital in 1992 were opposed by Gulbuddin Hekmatyar, a Pushtun and the leader of the Afghanistan Islamic Party, who attacked Kabul. As the country was divided by warlords and the economy collapsed, looting became the best way to supply warring forces.

This situation was challenged by the Kandahar-based and Pakistan-backed Taliban movement, which sought stability and religious orthodoxy. Benefiting from Pushtun support, and the profits of opium-dealing, the Taliban overran

Plate 12.1 War damage in Karte Char district of Kabul, 2001. Civil war in Afghanistan after the departure of Soviet forces in 1989 inflicted serious damage, with the capital, Kabul, bombarded. Photo © Simon Norfolk.

much of the country in 1996, seizing Kabul that year. Bribes helped dissolve much of the opposition. However, in the non-Pushtun areas, particularly in the north, the Taliban encountered serious resistance, and this helped provide the Americans with allies when they attacked the Taliban regime in 2001.

The fall of the Taliban regime, which had refused to hand over Osama bin Laden and other al-Qaeda members, was seen as a success for American air power, which included long-range B-52 and B-1 'stealth' bombers, extensive aerial refuelling enabling planes to fly very long missions, aircraft and Tomahawk Cruise missiles from carrier groups and warships in the Arabian Sea, AC-130 gunships, unpiloted drones providing reconnaissance of firing missiles, and CBU-130 'Combined-Effects Munitions' which spread cluster bombs. The availability of dual mode, laser and GPS (Global Positioning Systems) guidance for bombs increased the range of precision available, while the air assault benefited from the effective and, crucially, rapid management of information from a number of sources, including forward air controllers and ground-based GPS devices; in addition, the absence of hostile air power and of effective ground-fire was also important.

The Taliban, however, ultimately had to be overcome on the ground by rival Afghan forces, particularly the United Front, the so-called Northern Alliance, while the lack of coherence of the Taliban regime and the porosity and changeable nature of alignments in Afghanistan were also both important to the war's outcome. Warlords switched allegiance, in large part as a result of bribes, and the Taliban position collapsed on 9–13 November 2001 with the fall of the cities of Mazar-e Sharif, Herat and Kabul. The Taliban was unable to regroup after the fall of Mazar-e Sharif: defections that stemmed from its divisions accentuated a failure of command and control. American air power and Afghan ground attack combined to ensure the fall of more firmly defeated Kunduz on 26 November. Taliban forces tried to regroup at Kandahar, but, as their regime unravelled, abandoned it on 7 December.

The Taliban position had been broken by the combination of American air attack and Afghan ground assault, the latter an instance of the proxy warfare seen throughout the Cold War, while the willingness of President Musharraf of neighbouring Pakistan to cut links with the Taliban and provide assistance, including permitting American overflying and moving troops into border areas, was important. The air attack helped switch the local political balance within Afghanistan, but the victorious campaign did not lead to the clear-cut pro-American triumph that had been hoped for. Instead, it became readily apparent that the war had provoked a regrouping and realignment of factions, uneasily presided over by the weak, new pro-Western president, Hamid Ka'rzai, whose power extended little further than the capital Kabul. Far better than nothing, but not forcing opponents to accept the will of the victor. Furthermore, analysis of the impact of the air attack revealed that while it had been considerable in the initial attacks in northern Afghanistan it subsequently became less so in the ground operations launched by American and allied forces against Taliban and al-Qaeda survivors near Tora Bora (December 2001), and in Operation Anaconda, east of

Gardez (March 2002). This was attributed to the Taliban ability to respond by taking advantage of terrain features, for camouflage and cover.

Operations by the International Security Assistance Force against al-Qaeda supporters in Afghanistan were the most prominent aspect of the American and American-allied 'War on Terrorism' that followed September 11, 2001, but they were far from the only moves. Instead, American special operations units were deployed against Islamic terrorist movements linked to al-Qaeda, particularly on and near the Philippine island of Mindanao where, from 2003, the Americans provided military support to the army against the Abu Sayyaf group. The same year, the republic of Georgia was provided with help against an al-Qaeda force in the region of the Pankisi Gorge, which was also a base for Chechen rebels.

Terrorism linked to al-Qaeda also affected other countries, with, for example, suicide bombings in Turkey in 2003. Links with al-Qaeda were also attributed to other movements, possibly with less cause. The suicide bombers who struck Tashkent, the capital of Uzbekistan, an ally of the USA, in March 2004 may have been linked to al-Qaeda via the Islamic Movement of Uzbekistan.

Counter-terrorist operations posed serious difficulties for military responses, not least the identification of opponents and the brevity of the period in which it was possible to fix opponents and engage with them. There are also conceptual problems in such conflict: the terminology used towards opponents delegitimates them – instead of 'freedom fighters' and 'war', we have 'terrorists' and 'terrorism', but this can make it more difficult to conceive of a strategy that matches political with military methods and goals, and may make it more difficult to probe the possibilities for an exit strategy; the extreme anti-Western position of al-Qaeda and its allies, however, do not make negotiations an option.

BOX 12.1   AMERICAN STRATEGY, 2002

The National Security Strategy issued in September 2002 was both strategically and operationally ambitious. Pressing the need for pre-emptive strikes in response to what were seen as the dual threats of terrorist regimes and 'rogue states' possessing or developing weapons of mass destruction, the strategy sought to transform the global political order to lessen the chance of these threats developing. To that end, its first paragraph proposed a universalist message that linked the end of the Cold War to the new challenge:

> The great struggles of the twentieth century between liberty and totalitarianism ended with a decisive victory for the forces of freedom ... These values of freedom are right and true for every person, in every society – and the duty of protecting these values against their enemies is the common calling of freedom-loving people across the globe and across the ages ... We will extend the peace by encouraging free and open societies on every continent.

THE REVOLUTION IN MILITARY AFFAIRS

Striking against terrorist bases, as in Afghanistan, became part of an American doctrine of pre-emptive attack against hostile states. As a result, conflict returned to the Persian Gulf in early 2003 when Iraq was attacked by a preponderantly American force, with the participation of a large section of the British military and of small Australian, Polish, Czech and Slovak contingents. The campaign, and the preparations for it, was conducted in the glare of media attention and pundit discussion, and there was considerable speculation as to how far it corresponded with current notions about a revolution in military affairs (RMA), as well as related debates about the character of modern Western military capability and development.

The RMA linked developments in weapon systems with a doctrine that meshed with theories of modernization that rest on the adoption of technological systems. Furthermore, the RMA justified the cut in the American army: from eighteen divisions in 1990 to ten in 2003, part of a reduction of about a third in the active-duty force in the 1990s that was a response to the rising real cost of personnel. The RMA also met the need to believe in the possibility of high intensity conflict and of total victory, appeared to counter the threats posed by the spread among rivals of earlier technologies and their development of new ones, and seemed to give substance to the possibility of reordering the world by overthrowing or intimidating 'rogue states' and spreading liberty.

Integral to the RMA are a number of concepts, each rich in acronyms and jargon. The common focus is on 'smart' doctrine: operational planning and practice in order to take advantage of a new generation of weapons and the possibilities posed by advances in information technology. The emphasis on precise information as a means, as well as a tool, of conflict relates to its use in order to locate forces accurately, thus overcoming the friction of war, as well as to destroy enemy units with semi-automated weapons. Accurate targeting is required if precision weaponry is to be effective. Cruise missiles, a prime example of such weaponry, are no longer possessed solely by the USA, and their spread continues. In August 2004, Australia announced it would spend up to A$450 million on buying air-launched cruise missiles with a range of at least 250 kilometres. This, in turn, leads to the goal of 'information dominance' in order to deny the capability for accurate targeting to opponents. The RMA also calls for 'network-centric warfare': a highly integrated and digitally linked information system stemming from a realization of the new capability of information systems, rather than the traditional practices and structures of command and control known as platform-centric.

In one respect, information dominance is a continuation and application of the intelligence warfare that had characterized the Cold War, particularly the development of satellite surveillance of the entire world capable of providing reliable 'real time' information. By the end of the twentieth century, the USA, Britain, Australia, Canada and New Zealand were joined in Echelon, an electronic eavesdropping service, Britain significantly not being linked to European Union (EU) partners, while France and Germany also co-operated in such covert monitoring. Access to satellite information became a major issue in military planning. The

USA, which dominates the field, is unhappy about European Union attempts to acquire capability, seeing this as misplaced duplication. This is viewed differently by the EU, not least because of a determination to give bite to its security and defence policy. Irrespective of EU policy, leading member states sought to establish their own satellite reconnaissance, France developing the Helios I satellite system. American satellite surveillance played a major role in the 2003 Iraq crisis, not least in target monitoring.

More generally, at the same time, intelligence was increasingly devolved to and developed at 'micro'-levels: individual units, weapons (such as pieces of artillery), and, eventually, soldiers; for each, there was more information, and it was both up to date and therefore constantly changing. This underlined the need to integrate information and activity systems effectively, and thus the extent to which command and control were under great strain at every level.

In the language of the RMA, weaponry is designed to ensure what are termed dominant manoeuvre, precision engagements, full-dimensional protection, focused logistics and information warfare. All of these are seen as the goals and methods of future military structures and particular organizational forms, and weapons are presented as intended to serve these ends rather than simply moulding structures or methods. Joint operations are seen as crucial to the manoeuvrist warfare that is advocated, and as stemming from the interest of all services in 'deep battle'.

To foster joint operations there has been a proliferation of joint organizations: inter-service or more than one service jointly conducting an operation or campaign or carrying out a strategy in pursuit of national policy objectives. These requirements and organizations have developed because alongside AirLand concepts have come greater American and British interest in sea-based strategies. In America, these organizations include the creation, in 1992, of an Expeditionary Warfare Division in the office of the chief of naval operations and, more generally, the Goldwater–Nichols Department of Defense Reorganization Act of 1986, which strengthened the position of the chairman of the Joint Chiefs of Staff and established a joint acquisition system. In Britain, the plethora of joints included the Joint Rapid Deployment Force, the Joint Headquarters, and the Joint Services Command and Staff College, while France has joint war college training. Joint institutions provide powerful advocates for new doctrines and plans, such as the American Joint Vision 2010 and Joint Vision 2020 plans. Similarly, the American defence industry is heavily committed to new weaponry designed to provide the desired RMA.

Whether or not they were willing or could afford to invest in the wider ranges of the RMA, a problem that was of particular importance for Russian ambitions, emphasis on advanced weaponry and relevant training encouraged a number of states to follow the UK and USA in moving towards a force structure that put a greater emphasis on mobility and training. This encouraged states that had continued conscription, such as France and Russia, to decide to phase it out, a process that continues today. Under President Chirac, French military planning became less concerned with nuclear defence and retaliation, and more interested in large-scale power projection, a process aided by the slimming down and professionalization of the army that followed the end of conscription in 1996. In June

2000, the Italian Parliament passed a bill phasing out conscription by 2005. It was designed to replace the army of 270,000 with a professional service of 190,000. The Turkish army has also begun to talk about abolishing conscription as part of a programme of modernization.

It is in conventional capability that advances in American power, specifically force projection, have been most important. This has reflected both American doctrine during the Cold War – particularly the determination to be able to fight a non-nuclear war with the Soviet Union, and to maintain conventional capability even if the war became nuclear – as well as the changing nature of world politics after the end of the Cold War, specifically the American practice of interventionism. Looked at differently, this interventionism has been dependent on these very advances in capability, but such an approach must not see such advances as causing interventionism. To do so ignores the role of politics in setting and sustaining goals, as was readily apparent in the Iraq War in 2003.

It is important not to exaggerate the end of the Cold War as a break, because many geopolitical issues, such as the rivalry between China and India, spanned the divide, while, as suggested above, much of the American capability deployed in the 1990s and 2000s stemmed from Cold War procurement policies, tasking and doctrine. The ability to fight a conventional war in Europe had to be translated to other spheres, which created problems in adaptation, but much of the capability was already in place. The apparent legitimacy of such interventionism is a different matter, as much stemmed from the implementation of the particular ideologies of the American administrations of the period. This indicated the central role of 'tasking', the goals set by political direction, and also the plasticity or changeability of what is referred to as strategic culture, a term that suggests a misleading degree of consistency.

The extent to which American developments in force projection have not been matched by other powers is an important aspect of world politics, as the state that benefited most in economic terms from the 1990s, China, has concentrated instead (at present) on enhancing its short-range projection capability, although that poses a major threat to Taiwan which challenges the American ability and willingness to support the latter. The contrast between on the one hand the force structures and doctrines of China and, on the other, those of Britain and France which have employed their more long-range force projection, indicates the role of politics in shaping military capability and tasks, whether those politics are reified or not as strategic cultures.

More significantly, American developments have not been countered by comparable advances elsewhere in anti-strategy/operational practice/tactics/weaponry. This, indeed, is one of the most important aspects of recent and current international relations, and is one that would benefit from careful examination. Hitherto, the general pattern in military history *on land* has been to see such a matching (at least in terms of countering) of advances in capability and responses, although there has been no systematic study of the subject. In light of the Vietnam War, it was possible to anticipate at least elements of such a matching in response to the combination of the technological pride and confidence central to the concept of the RMA and the greater intensity of American force projection that followed the end of the Cold War. In 2001, when conflict formally involving the USA began in Afghanistan, there were frequent references to past British failure there, while in 2003 it was widely argued that the conquest of Iraq would be much more challenging than its defeat in 1991. Indeed, Saddam Hussein appears to have anticipated that the problems of urban warfare would lessen American technological advantages and lead to casualties that obliged the American government to change policy, an analysis that was certainly mistaken in the short term, and that anyway could not prevent conquest by a well-organized and high-tempo American-dominated invasion force.

That American advances in capability were not matched by other powers, at least in the sense of being successfully countered in battle, does not establish a general rule that they cannot be – one of the real problems of both military history and military analysis is deciding how best to analyse and generalize from examples – but it is instructive. This is linked to an issue that divides analysts; namely, how far recent and current changes in capability constitute a military revolution, or paradigm shift in military capability and war-making, and, if so, with what results, and with what consequences in terms of analysing long-term trends in capability. The claims made for such a shift by military supporters (both in post and retired), civilian commentators and military-industrial companies are bold, but also offer instructive clues about their limitations. For example, Northrop Grumman in its 2004 advertisements under the logo 'Share information. Share victory' for its ability to define the future ISTAR battle space focused on the aerial vehicles and warships it linked in a blue world of sea and sky that left no room for the complexities of control on land.

ATTEMPTED REVOLUTIONS IN MILITARY AFFAIRS

Other attempted revolutions in military affairs require discussion, in particular those sought by terrorist groups and by so-called rogue states. In the first case, the attempt in 2001 by al-Qaeda to use terrorist methods to a strategic end by crippling, or at least symbolically dethroning, American financial and political power failed, not least because it rested on a greatly flawed assumption about the concentrated and top-down nature of American power; however, it also indicated the extent to which the terrorist repertoire was far from fixed. Although it was true that al-Qaeda did not deploy weapons of mass destruction in 2001, its ability to make use of Western technology, in this case civilian aircraft, like its determination to ignore any boundaries between military and civilian, indicated the military as well as political challenge that is posed. Similarly, in March 2004, a dependence on public transport was exploited in the terrorist attacks on commuter trains in Madrid. This terrorism is a more serious problem for international relations than those posed by particular aggressive states because the nature of a stateless entity is that it does not need to respond to the constraints that arise from claims to sovereign power, although such groups are also in a competition for legitimacy. The military equivalent is whether there is a territorial space that can be attacked or occupied.

As a result, however plausible it is to argue that there are terrorist states, nevertheless the challenge posed by terrorist movements is apparently greater, especially as they can seek to base themselves in 'failed states' where it is difficult to take action short of full-scale military intervention against them. Although most terrorism is in fact aimed at states in the 'Third World', the challenge from terrorism is particularly notable for strong powers, especially the strongest, the USA, as they have less practicable need to fear attack from other states than weaker states do: were they to attack the USA, the forces of these states would be defeated, and their territory could certainly be attacked.

This distinction, however, is challenged by the attempt by so-called rogue states to acquire weapons of mass destruction and related delivery systems. In the early 1990s it was discovered that North Korea was developing plutonium, which could be used to make nuclear warheads, and in 2002 it admitted it was trying to enrich uranium. In 1998, North Korea tested a medium-range Taepodong missile, firing it over Japan into the Pacific. Although the regular forces of states such as North Korea and Iran probably lack the capability and ability in defence to defeat the conventional forces of stronger powers, which in this case means the USA, and certainly could not stage an effective offensive war, such weapons would enable them to threaten these forces and, perhaps even eventually, home territory, while they would also challenge the aspect of international aspirations and force projection represented by alliance systems.

THE GULF WAR OF 2003–4

In 2003 and 2004 the Americans focused on Iraq – a definite and defiant target with regular armed forces – rather than on the more intangible struggle with terrorism, which challenged Western conventions of war-making. The attack was presented in terms of 'drying up the swamp' – eliminating a state allegedly supporting terrorism, as well, more specifically, as destroying Iraq's supposed capability in weapons of mass destruction, specifically chemical and bacteriological warheads, although the claims about Iraqi weapons of mass destruction were subsequently to be discredited.

Operation Iraqi Freedom, the American-led and dominated campaign in Iraq in 2003, with its rapid and successful advance up the Euphrates valley on Baghdad, was widely praised for its manoeuvrist character and for its ability to gain and seize the initiative, disorientating the Iraqi military and government, and hitting their capacity to respond. The key elements were the 125,000 US combat troops on the ground, although Britain supplied 45,000 troops and Australia 2,000. Predictions that the Iraqis would use chemical weapons and blow up bridges and dams, or that it would be hard to overrun the Iraqi cities and that they would pose problems like those faced by the Germans in Stalingrad in 1942, with the American military being chewed up in the course of their capture, were disproved.

These predictions had rested on the assumption that the Iraqis had responded to their defeat in 1991 by deciding not to contest the Americans in manoeuvrist warfare, where technology would give the Americans an advantage, and instead to abandon the desert and focus on the cities, hoping to repeat the success of Mohamed Aidid in Mogadishu in 1993 (p. 241). Indeed, both in 1991 and in 2003 Saddam Hussein appears to have counted on the Americans suffering if they could be forced to abandon the distant use of firepower for close combat.

The coherence of the Hussein regime, its ability to intimidate the population, and the possibility of exploiting American vulnerability along their long lines of advance, were all, however, hit by the tempo of American attacks. This accentuated weaknesses in the regime, including its fear of the Iraqi military and concern about the possibility of coups. The Iraqi attacks on supply lines, for example at the Euphrates bridge-town of Nasiriya, attracted considerable media attention, but the forces available for such attacks were a local irritant that could be bypassed on the drive on Baghdad, rather than operationally significant. Despite short-term problems, that were understandable given the tempo of the advance, American logistics proved able to support the offensive. The use of Fedayeen irregulars, some of whom fought vigorously, did, however, lead to somewhat naive complaints about such tactics as disguise and fake surrender.

Much of the Republican Guard ran away in the face of American firepower. Units that redeployed or stood and fought were pulverized, with particular effort being devoted to destroying Iraqi armour. This represented the tactical value of American air power, which accomplished more than the 'Shock and Awe' attacks on Baghdad from the night of 19 March at the outset of the struggle, although the latter's impact on Iraqi command and control was significant: the possible killing or wounding of Saddam Hussein in an air-strike, had it occurred, would have reflected the strategic value of air power in disrupting opposing leadership. The Americans made particular use of JDAMS (Joint Direct Attack Munitions) which used GPS to make conventional bombs act as satellite-guided weapons, and were an important addition to the improvement in American air power capability that characterized post-Vietnam developments. Although there were differences of opinion between Britain and the USA over targeting, the air assault did not face the constraints that had affected the attack on the Serbs in Operation Allied Force in 1999. Instead, with a clear target, it was possible to use air power effectively, and, in turn, to contribute to its reputation for effectiveness. About 70 per cent of the aerial munitions used were 'smart' or guided, rather than 'dumb' or unguided, in contrast to 10 per cent against Iraq in 1991.

The Americans also benefited from the use of helicopter gunships and unmanned aerial vehicles, and from improvements in the accuracy of artillery fire. The Iraqi T-55s and T-72s that were not destroyed by air attack could not prevail against the American Abrams tanks, while the American use of night-vision goggles enabled them to maintain the pace of the assault and thus to prevent the Iraqis from resupplying and regrouping. More generally, the Americans benefited from intensive realistic training from the 1980s. The Iraqis made effective use of rocket-propelled grenades, but, although there had been improvements in quality, as a honed-down force was sought, their military was far weaker than in 1991, in large part because the impact of international sanctions since then had limited the build-up of modern weaponry.

Once they had closed on Baghdad, the Americans initially, from 5 April, launched 'thunder runs', armoured thrusts into the city demonstrating that their opponents could not prevent these advances, and therefore undermining their position. Manoeuvre warfare was thus shown to work in an urban context, and tanks proved able to destroy those who fought back. Having captured Baghdad, where organized resistance collapsed on 9 April, the Americans pressed on to overrun the rest of Iraq without encountering the large-scale opposition that was feared, particularly in Hussein's homeland of Tikrit which fell on 14 April. The British meanwhile had taken Basra, Iraq's second most populous city, but were too heavily committed thereabouts to offer effective assistance further north.

A prime element of debate before the campaign, which was revived during it when American supply lines came under serious attack, had related to the number of troops required for a successful invasion. The secretary of defense, Donald Rumsfeld, and other non-military commentators, had been encouraged by the overthrow of the Taliban regime in Afghanistan in 2001 to argue that air power and special forces were the prime requirements, and that the large number of troops pressed for by the army leadership, for both the invasion and for subsequent occupation, was excessive. In the event, military pressure led to the allocation of sizeable numbers for the invasion of Iraq, but the campaign did not see the full committal of forces originally envisaged because the Turkish refusal to allow an invasion across their frontier with Iraq ensured that troops from the American Fourth Infantry Division prepared for that invasion could not be used at the outset of the war. However, American special forces, landed by air from the night of 22–23 March, helped direct Kurdish pressure (and American bombing) on Hussein's forces in northern Iraq. Kurdish and American forces captured Kirkuk on 10 April, and on 11 April Mosul surrendered. Concern that Turkey would complicate the situation by invading northern Iraq and clash with the Kurds proved unfounded, while Iran also did not intervene. The failure of Iraq to fire missiles against Israel also ensured that the internationalization of the conflict was limited.

The consequences of the rapid fall of Iraq did, however, expose one of the problems with having insufficient troops in that it proved difficult to restore order and the workings of government. Too few troops had been dispatched, in part because the difficulty of securing internal support had been underrated. The mass welcome that had been anticipated did not materialize. There was also inadequate preparation for post-war disorder and division, not least widespread looting.

Post-war disorder did not cease when the Americans handed over power to an Iraqi government in June 2004. Insurgents took over control of towns and were able to resist American and Iraqi attempts to drive them out. The insurgency drew on foreign volunteers, but also on members of Hussein's forces who regrouped during the American occupation, as well as on Shia activists, especially the Mehdi Army Militia which took over Najaf and held it against attack in August 2004.

The collapse of the Hussein regime led to American talk of pressing on to attack other states that harboured terrorism and possibly were developing weapons of mass destruction, particularly Iran and Syria. However, it is more likely that the American failure to restore order in Iraq and the costs of that commitment will foster a measure of caution and lead to a reaction against interventionism. It also encourages a focus on what was the strategic point of the operational triumph in 2003; in other words, what goals a quick victory were supposed to secure.

At the same time, the Iraq war led the Americans to devote renewed effort to their already vigorous debate about force structure and tasking. At the risk of considerable simplification, this located discussion about weaponry within consideration of the continued validity of a military centred on separate services. Donald Rumsfeld was particularly keen on breaking with what he saw as a conservative inheritance advocated strongly by the army out of keeping with what he saw as the need for rapidly delivered force. Interest in new weaponry focused on AirLand combinations, but included research into low-yield nuclear weaponry that was seen as an important way to upgrade America's nuclear capability.

Although no other power could match such developments, the impact of American weaponry in Iraq in 2003 encouraged interest elsewhere in procuring similar weapons. This was true of Britain, where the development of drones was stepped up, and also of Japan, which felt increasingly threatened by North Korea's development of rockets, leading, in response, to Japanese interest in anti-missile defences and in satellite surveillance. Japan launched its own spy satellites in 2003. Article Nine of the Japanese Constitution states that 'land, sea, and air forces, as well as other war potential, will never be maintained'; as a result, Japan has 'Self-Defence Forces', which were 258,000 strong in 2003, making them one of the most powerful militaries in the world. Nevertheless, the 1992 law authorizing the SDF to deploy abroad included strict restrictions on what they could do: they could only be sent to areas where a ceasefire was in place. SDF troops were sent to help United Nations peacekeepers in Cambodia (1992), Mozambique (1993) and East Timor (1999 and 2002), to help Rwandan refugees (1994), and to assist in peacekeeping in Iraq after the Second Gulf War.

THIRD WORLD CONFLICT

The situation was very varied across the Third World. In Afghanistan, after the fall of the Taliban and the establishment as president of the American-backed Hamid Ka'rzai, there was not chaos comparable to that in Liberia, but that was because the weakness of the central government was counter-pointed by the strength of provincial governors, such as Abdul Rashid Dostum, Atta Mohammed, Gulbuddin Hikmatyar and Ismail Khan, autonomous figures with a tradition of independence and their own armies. These, and those of local militaries, are powerful. By 2004 the militia in the city of Kunduz had a considerable force of tanks. Rivalry between these warlords – over local dominance and revenue sources such as land and drug profits – led to conflict – for example between Abdul Rashid Dostum and Atta Mohammed near Mazar-e Sharif in late 2003 and in 2004.

Government indeed involved a process of negotiation with these warlords that accepted their regional power. Peace, in turn, depended on their restraint, but it was threatened by challenges to the regional position of warlords, as well as to that of the central government. A Taliban resurgence in the summer of 2003 led, however, to the collapse of the government position in much of the south and east of the country, with the president wielding scant authority outside the capital. Support for the Taliban from within Pakistan remains important.

Angola is not a failed state, but until the killing of the UNITA leader, Jonas Savimbi, in 2002 it faced a debilitating insurrectionary war that rested on ethnic tension, especially Ovimbundu support for UNITA, and was financed by exploitation of the country's diamond wealth. Diamonds were also important in financing conflict in West Africa, especially Sierra Leone. In turn, the Angolan government benefited from control of the country's oil. Having rejected the results of the 1992 election, UNITA had resumed its conflict with the government, which was now weakened by the withdrawal of the Cuban and Soviet assistance that had greatly helped it in the 1970s and 1980s. Defeated by the scale of the country, neither side was able to win. The operational effectiveness of the government's conventional forces declined in the wet season, which favoured UNITA's guerrilla tactics. Both sides mounted attacks on the supply systems of the others, but without lasting effect other than to cause large numbers of civilian casualties and even larger numbers of refugees. However, international pressure and a failure to win led Savimbi to negotiate anew in 1994, producing a *de facto* partition of the country that lasted until 1997 when the government attacked UNITA.

UNITA now suffered from both the loss of its supply route through Congo and from divisions, with Savimbi's leadership under challenge. In 1999, Jamba, where Savimbi had established his capital in 1984, and which the government had failed to take in the 1980s, finally fell. UNITA forces were in a poor position by 2001 and the government used its oil wealth to enhance its military capability. The killing of Savimbi on 22 February 2002 was rapidly followed, on 4 April, by the signature of a peace agreement.

A different type of attempted consolidation of central control over tribal groups and peripheral areas was seen in Sudan. Its government was threatened by a serious rebellion that broke out in 2003 by the Sudan Liberation Army based in the Darfur region of the west of the country, which complained of the oppression of non-Arabs by the government. In response in 2004 the government used its regular forces, including aircraft and infantry moved in trucks, to support an Arab militia, the Janjaweed, much of which rode on horses and camels, in order to slaughter the Fur, Masalit and, in particular, Zaghawa: native tribes in Darfur. Alongside large-scale slaughter, especially of men and boys, even very young boys, and the systematic rape and mutilation of women, natives were driven away, their cattle and therefore livelihood seized, the wells poisoned with corpses, and dams, pumps and buildings destroyed. Over 30,000 people died as a result and more than a million fled. Ethnic rivalry played a role in internal conflict in many other African states, although often, for example in northern Mali in 2004, without attracting much international attention.

As a stage between Afghanistan and Angola, Congo (formerly Zaire) became both a failed state and one in which regular forces from other African countries intervened in order to influence the direction of conflict there, to dominate neighbouring areas, and to obtain control over raw materials. Mobutu Sese Soko, the dictator since 1965, fell in 1997 as a result of foreign invasion, while another invasion was launched in 1998 in an unsuccessful attempt to overthrow his replacement, Laurent Kabila. Uganda and Rwanda supported competing rebel factions, Rwanda in part in order to defeat the Hutu militias that staged the genocide of 1994 and that took refuge in Congo; Zimbabwe, Angola, Chad and Namibia backed Kabila, in part in response to the dynamics of their own internal security situation: Angola wished to stop Congolese support for UNITA, which had been important under Mobutu. The outside powers armed their own Congolese allies, particularly, for Rwanda, the Rally for Congolese Democracy and the Union of Congolese Patriots. These overlapped with tribal militia groups such as those of the Ugandan-backed Lendus, which competed with the Rwandan-allied Hemas in the north-eastern province of Ituri, a major centre of conflict.

Probably between 3.1 and 4.7 million people died in Congo from 1998 to 2003, most of disease and starvation, but many of them in ethnic conflict between tribal militias, as murderous attacks on villages proved a particularly common means of waging war. Far from being at the cutting edge of 'new-generation' warfare, this conflict saw much of the killing with machetes, and bows and arrows and shotguns were employed, alongside the frequent use of mortars and submachine guns. The conflict also led to cannibalism, and to the use of child warriors seen in West Africa. Other aspects of African conflict that were distant from Western warfare included the use of traditional charms and spirit mediums. Violence continued after the war officially ended in 2003 when the leading rebel groups joined a transitional government. In the Katanga region in 2004 insurgents reputedly cut off the genitals of victims and drank their blood.

More generally, rivalries between states interacted with insurrections and other civil conflicts elsewhere. Thus, warfare between Eritrea and Ethiopia, which involved large-scale fighting of a conventional type, spilled over into internal conflicts in Somalia. Foreign assistance was sought, and, if necessary, hired to help resist insurrection. Thus, between 1993 and 2003, Ange-Félix Patassé, the president of the Central African Republic, survived seven coup attempts, including one in 2002 by General François Bozizé, one-time head of the army, that involved serious street fighting in the capital, Bangui. Patassé turned for support to Libya, which provided backing until 2002, and then the Congolese MLC rebel group, but in March 2003 Bozizé, at the head of 1,000 men, overran Bangui. The unpaid army was unwilling to resist, and the MLC did not fight. Instability in the Central African Republic reflected the knock-on effects of war elsewhere, for conflict in Congo hit its trade links down the Congo river.

In West Africa, in 2002 and 2003, the Liberian government under Charles Taylor, whose seizure of power had originally owed much to backing from the Ivory Coast, supported rebels in the three neighbouring states, Sierra Leone, Guinea and the Ivory Coast, before being forced to step down in 2003. Guinea itself was linked to rebels against Taylor, the Liberians United for Reconciliation and Democracy – a misnamed group of thugs – as was the army of the Ivory Coast. France intervened to support the government of the Ivory Coast against the MPCI: the rebel group that failed to seize power in 2002 but that remained strong in the largely Muslim north. Britain had earlier intervened in Sierra Leone, in 2000, supporting UN stabilization, retraining the army, and, in Operation Barras, rescuing hostages from the West Side Boys, one of the gangs that intimidated much of the country.

In the Congo, Kabila was assassinated in 2001, while in 2004 his son and successor, Joseph, overcame an attempt by elements in the Presidential Special Guard to seize power by gaining control of state television and the presidential palace. This was an aspect of the continuing role of force in the seizure and retention of power across parts of the Third World, a role that puts a focus on the attitude of the armed forces and of paramilitary units. Military establishments have a disproportionate independence and impact in post-colonial systems where nothing else seems to work very well and too many countervailing institutions have lost credibility and authority. Thus, in 1999, the Pakistani army staged a successful coup, although the military lost power in other states, for example Thailand in 1992. Coups and the possibility of such action continued to play a major role in military history. An attempted military coup in Chad failed in 2003. In 2000, American and Brazilian pressure on Paraguayan military leaders led them to thwart an attempted coup, and that year the army eventually suppressed a coup on Fiji.

In turn, in some countries, groups outside the military sought to use force to seize, or at least contest, power. Thus, in 2003, organized crime linked to nationalists was responsible for the assassination of the Serbian prime minister, Zoran Djindjic, while in 2004 mercenaries were involved in an unsuccessful plot to overthrow the government of Equatorial Guinea.

Alongside the use of force to gain and hold power at the centre, force was widely used against regional separatism. Thus, southern secessionism in Yemen was crushed in 1994, the Chinese suppressed Muslim separatism in Xinjiang in 1990 and 1997, while in 1998 the Tajik army suppressed a rebellion in the Khojand region of Tajikistan where many Uzbek-speakers lived. In Nigeria, the army was used against tribal separatists in the oil-producing Niger delta, while in 1997 a separatist revolt on Anjouan, one of the islands in the Comoros in the Indian Ocean, was suppressed. The breakdown in May 2003 of a five-month ceasefire in the Aceh region of Sumatra led the Indonesian army to announce that it would destroy the Gam separatist movement, in part by moving the local population into tented camps so as to deny them cover. This conflict, which had begun in 1976, opposed a military using the means of conventional warfare, including ground-attack aircraft, amphibious landings, parachutists and tanks, against a smaller guerrilla force lacking international support but strong in determination. In some cases, separatism was not the issue. Thus, from 2002, Nepal faced a serious Maoist insurgency which posed major problems for its military.

Sales of arms continue to provide fresh munitions for Third World Forces, and their governments, encouraged by international competition as well as by concern over domestic stability, have been only too willing to spend money on the military. In 2002, African states alone spent about $14 billion on defence. Expenditure on arms by terrorist movements was restricted by measures, including attempts to restrict money laundering, but, despite the efforts of aid donors, no such restraint affected states. Instead, developments in their military capability were affected by attempts to control the trade in weaponry and its components, in particular restricting the sale of components for weapons of massive destruction. Despite the terrible poverty of much of their population, India pushed up defence spending by 14 per cent in 1999 alone, and Pakistan by 8.5 per cent, to total allocations of $9.9 billion and $3.3 billion respectively, though Pakistan's nuclear weaponry programme may have been funded by Saudi Arabia.

Rivalry over Kashmir between India and Pakistan led to the Kargil conflict in 1999, in which the attackers killed by the Indian army included Pakistani regulars as well as guerrillas, and took them close to war in 2002, with the Indians moving over 600,000 troops to the frontier. Religious hatred exacerbated a national rivalry that was made more serious by their increased nuclear capability, which led first India and then Pakistan to test nuclear weapons in 1998; that year, Pakistan test-fired its new Ghauri intermediate-range missile, while India fired its new long-range Agni 2 missile the following year: its range is 2,000–3,000 kilometres, extending to Tehran and covering most of China and South-East Asia. In March 2003 both states test-fired short-range surface-to-surface missiles that could have been used to carry nuclear warheads.

Pakistan in turn sold weapons technology to other states, including North Korea, Iraq, Iran, Libya and, probably, Egypt and Syria. Saudi Arabia probably

BOX 12.2 THE SECOND OR AL-AQSA *INTIFADA*

Negotiations between Israel and the Palestinians broke down in 2000 over the issues of Israeli settlements on the West Bank of the Jordan, Arab demands that refugees be allowed to return to Israel, and the status of Jerusalem. On 28 September, the visit of Ariel Sharon, then leader of the opposition Likud party, to the al-Aqsa compound on the Temple Mount in Jerusalem, led to Palestinian demonstrations and a forcible Israeli response in which Palestinians were killed. Violence led to growing extremism on both sides, with Arab attacks on Israeli civilians causing renewed action in what rapidly became a more violent rising than the first *intifada*. Winning election in February 2001, Sharon promised to increase the number of settlements, and the following month suicide bombers were used by the Hamas movement. Operations in the West Bank and Gaza indicated the limitations of Israeli military and political options: the killing of militant leaders did not stop attacks, while Israel failed to foster the creation of a Palestinian constituency for effective negotiations. Equally, the policies and attitudes of the Palestinian government of Yassir Arafat made negotiations difficult. In response to continued attacks by suicide bombers, the Israelis began construction of a security wall designed to block such attacks. In 2004, this appeared to reduce the rate of suicide attacks; but they continued, as did Israeli reprisals. Thus, in September, Israel launched a missile strike that killed fourteen Hamas activists in Gaza in response to a double suicide bombing in Beersheba that had killed sixteen Israelis. A cease-fire was agreed in February 2005.

funded the Pakistani nuclear-weapons programme and in the late 1980s purchased long-range Chinese missiles. These weapon programmes were designed to provide regimes with the ability to counter the military superiority or plans of other states. Thus North Korea saw atomic weaponry as a counter to American power, while Syria sought to develop chemical and biological weapons in response to Israeli conventional superiority. The Israelis in turn built up a substantial stockpile of nuclear bombs in response to the chemical weapons of its Arab neighbours. The Iraqi nuclear programme was delayed by the Israeli destruction of the reactor at Osirak in 1981 and ended by the overthrow of Saddam Hussein in 2003, while later that year Libya abandoned its own. Iran, however, proved unwilling to follow suit even after its violations of nuclear safeguards were exposed.

Weapons were not only bought by states. They were also freely available across much of the Third World. This directly contributed to disorder and civil conflict. In the spring of 2004 hand grenades could be bought in Mogadishu market for $10 and howitzers for $20,000.

CONCLUSIONS

The overwhelming majority of states in the world are neither leading military powers nor 'rogue states'. In many states, especially (but not only) in post-independence Latin America and sub-Saharan Africa, the prime purpose of the military is internal control, although its position may be rivalled by paramilitary forces. The Iranian Revolutionary Guard Corps established as a result of the Iranian Revolution of 1979 was by 2004 better equipped than the Iranian regular army, as well as more important politically. In territorial terms, the military challenge in many states comes not so much from foreign powers as from domestic regional opposition to the state, some of it separatist in character, or from resistance that has a social dimension, such as peasant risings. The resulting warfare, most of which takes a guerrilla and/or terrorist character on the part of the rebels, is asymmetrical.

It can also overlap considerably with struggles against crime, specifically wars on drugs. Thus in Mexico in the early 2000s the army was used against the powerful drugs gangs, while a paramilitary Federal Investigations Agency was established to the same end. The firepower used by both sides was considerable. In Colombia, the left-wing FARC guerrillas and the right-wing AUC (United Self-Defence Forces of Colombia) paramilitaries are both involved heavily in drugs and this ensures that their operations are often designed to ensure control over drug-producing areas. In June 2004, the two groups clashed over control of the department of Norte de Santander, an area on the Venezuelan border important for the export of drugs and the import of arms.

The porous and contested definition of war suggested by its current usage, as in war on drugs or war on terror, further complicates understandings of force and legitimacy, and makes it difficult to define the military. If the 'war on terror' is crucial, then the Saudi security forces carrying out armed raids against al-Qaeda suspects in which people are killed, or the Indian Border Security Force resisting the United Liberation Front of Asom in Assam, are as much part of the military as conventional armed forces. Similarly, troops are employed for policing duties, as in Quetta in Pakistan in March 2004 to restore order after a riot after a terrorist attack on a Shia procession. Crime also overlaps with social tension if not 'class warfare' as in kidnapping, practised for example in Mexico in order to raise money but also associated with hatred of the better off. In 2003 almost half the world's kidnapping occurred in Latin America, and with about 4,000 a year in Colombia and 3,000 a year in Mexico they represented a formidable strain on society in total terms. Colombia considered it progress when the murder rate fell in 2003, but in January and February 2004 combined there were still 3,290 officially recorded murders. In Guatemala in the first half of 2004 there were nearly 2,000 murders.

Widespread ownership of weaponry complicates these and other problems. By 2003 there were estimated to be more than three guns for every Yemeni, and the ability of the government to control the country was limited. This made the al-Qaeda presence in Yemen more serious, and, more generally, contributed to Yemeni resistance to the government. In 2004 the army launched an operation in the north of Yemen against Sheikh Hussein Badr Eddin al-Huthi, a Muslim preacher leading a rebellion.

Similarly, in Haiti, large-scale ownership of guns exacerbated problems stemming from mass unemployment and poverty and a powerful drugs and drug-smuggling culture, and this challenged its political stability, leading to a major role for street gangs or *chimeras*. The high-rate of gun ownership in Iraq proved a serious problem with the overthrow of the Hussein regime in 2003. Alongside political opposition from insurgents came large-scale property crime, as well as activity by well-armed criminal gangs, particularly smugglers trying to profit from new circumstances.

The challenge to states from domestic opposition is 'internationalized' in so far as there may be foreign support for such opposition, or international humanitarian concern about the issue. On the whole, though, the nature of conflict reflects an important aspect of international relations; namely, the extent to which the use of force within sovereign areas (i.e. states) is generally accepted. This practice is seen as a challenge to humanitarian interventionist precepts, but the latter usually lack military capability unless they conform with the goals of great-power diplomacy. The extent to which the conflation of humanitarianism with such goals sets a challenge to modern Western militaries has been apparent since the early 1990s, most obviously with the Bosnian crisis (p. 246). This challenge raises difficult issues of effectiveness, and ones in which the legitimacy of force play a major role.

In the early 2000s the key issues for concern were presented as terrorism and rogue states, and it is likely that they will continue to be issues, but it is improbable that they will continue to so dominate the agenda as they did in the early 2000s. Even then, this list of issues was in some respects misleading, as there were other conflicts and confrontations that were of great importance – not only, for humanitarian reasons, conflict in Congo, which revived in 2004, but also the serious rivalry between India and Pakistan. The dominant agenda of the early 2000s reflected American interests and commitments, an important aspect of the extent to which the Western perception of events and developments (as of military history) can crowd out other situations and changes worthy of attention.

It is unclear whether this perception will remain valid in future decades, not least as China becomes a more prominent power but also because the majority of conflicts in the world do not involve Western powers, and it is unclear how far they will feel it necessary to intervene in them. This, indeed, has always been the case, other than during the brief heyday of Western imperialism. China is often discussed by theorists in terms of a likely future confrontation with the USA, not least on the basis of a 'neo-realist' assumption that states naturally expand and compete when they can, and that China's ambitions will lead it to clash with the USA. China's pressure to bring Taiwan under control, a reflection in part of China's greater economic strength and growing nationalism, led to a major arms build-up as well as a practice landing on another island in 2004. In June 2004 there was speculation that a Chinese invasion of the island would be countered by a Taiwanese Cruise missile attack on the Three Gorges Dam in the Yangzi valley, exploiting a key point of economic and environmental vulnerability. Yet, alongside the view that clashing interests over Taiwan will lead to confrontation between China and the USA, it is possible that China's attempts to develop its strength and regional ambitions will involve India, Japan and Russia more closely than the USA.

Possibly, the USA would have a choice over how far to intervene. This serves as a reminder that the world international system involves a number of complex regional situations, with the USA taking the leading role, not because it is able to dominate the other powers (as might be implied by the word hegemony) but rather because, aside from its largely uncontested regional dominance of the Americas and the Pacific, it is the sole state able to play a part in these other regional situations.

In the 1990s and 2000s, casualties (including, crucially, refugees) were far greater in conflicts that did not directly involve Western powers than in those that did, and this was particularly true of civil wars in Angola, Burundi, Congo, Rwanda, Sudan and Uganda. In Burundi, conflict between Hutu and Tutsi has led to maybe 300,000 deaths since 1993, the last in a sequence of violence that included large-scale clashes in 1965, 1969, 1972 and 1988. The savagery of the killing was accentuated by the use of cruelty, torture, dismemberment, sexual mutilation and cannibalism to increase pain and express hatred.

Aside from deaths due to slaughter, conflicts also led to the destruction of the economy, as military units focused on plundering villages, while the infrastructure collapsed, with resulting deaths from privation as well as from disease. In part, the latter reflected disruption (for example to water supplies), but the spread of disease, by both troops and refugees fleeing conflict, was also important. In Africa, rape by troops helped transmit HIV, while refugees spread malaria.

By 2004 the brutal rebellion by the Lord's Resistance Army in northern Uganda, which broke out in 1986, had led about 95 per cent of the region's population – over one and a half million people – to flee. An extreme Christian cult, ironically backed by the Islamic government in Sudan in response to Ugandan government support for the rebels in southern Sudan, the rebels targeted children for abduction as fighters or sex-slaves.

This is an appropriate point on which to close the chapter, for the impact on civilians of war is far more intense than is suggested by the use of the concept of limited warfare, let alone the commonplace emphasis on the 'spectator' character of warfare for Western audiences. Instead, the large number of refugees in the world is a reminder not only of the use of force in waging war on peoples but also of the consequences of conflict across the globe.

Conclusions

INTRODUCTION

It is not surprising that military historians devote relatively little attention to how their subject is done. The kind of scholar who works in the field generally seeks a more 'hands on' approach, and the minority of a more theoretical disposition prefer to address the issue of the development of military thought. As a consequence, the historiography of military history, both as academic subject and as a more popular field of literature, is underwritten. This is a pity from the perspective of historiography, but also has consequences from that of military history as it encourages any one generation of writers to write with insufficient reference to the contours of the subject. If all history inevitably addresses present concerns it is important to appreciate that these concerns will change.

At the present moment these contours are apparently readily obvious, although an important caveat must be expressed at the outset: most discussion of military history focuses on the Western world in the last half-millennium; and non-Western military history is in part a branch of what might almost be discussed as area studies. The contours that can be detected for work on the Western world in the last half-millennium are a continued dominance, of both meta-narratives (overarching accounts) and work on more restricted periods, by technological interpretations, but also, on the part of some scholars, a growing interest in what are referred to as cultural interpretations.

These approaches do not exhaust the field, as much work continues to come out of the 'war and society' stable, but the latter is very varied and lacks any comparable overarching meta-narrative. Indeed, as a whole, it is descriptive, rather than displaying the implicitly, if not explicitly, prescriptive character of the technological approach. Furthermore, the 'war and society' literature cleaves more to society than to war in both its methodology and its fundamental concerns. At the same time, before proceeding further, it is important to note that analysis separates and divides what are often far from distinct. Thus, the 'cultural turn' (greater interest in cultural interpretations of war) is in some respects another version of the 'war and society' approach, while any stress, in the discussion of technology, of the impact, in the use of weaponry, of factors such as drill and discipline directs attention to the overlap with cultural and social perspectives. This approach, however, has led to accusations of ethnocentricity, in response in particular to claims that Western forces had more effective drill and discipline.

TECHNOLOGY

To approach from a different angle the same point about the extent to which scholars offer various emphases in their analyses, accepting the interrelationship of different factors, such as weaponry and drill, is not the same as giving them all equal weighting. Much writing rests on the assumption voiced by a villain in Sergio Leone's Western film *A Fistful of Dollars* (1964): 'The man with the Winchester always beats the man with the revolver', the Winchester rifle being a more effective weapon in the nineteenth century. In practice, in the film, the villain is thwarted by the ingenuity of the character played by Clint Eastwood, who produces a concealed 'low-tech' body armour; but a belief that progress stems from the improvement in the capabilities of particular weapons and weapons systems is central to much modern history. This stress on the material culture of war can also be seen in the modern discussion of earlier eras. In the case of the Iron Age replacing the Bronze Age, the emphasis is on how the superior cutting power of iron and the relative ease of making iron weapons led to a change in civilizations.

'Technology' in practice is a category of explanations rather than a single one. In particular, there are the questions of what weapons do, how they work, how easy it is to be able to manufacture large numbers of a new weapon, and at a consistent standard, and issues of their appropriateness for training, command and tactics. Royal Navy recruiters in Britain in the early 2000s produced postcards depicting modern weapons with captions such as 'Controlled by a Team of Operator Mechanics it can stop a MiG-27. Without them it couldn't stop a 27 Bus', and 'Awesomely Powerful. Deadly Accurate. But Without Highly Trained Weapons Specialists about as Lethal as a Pork Sausage'.

These factors, especially skill, quality and usability, are not fixed but vary according to circumstances. Again, depending on the emphasis, the stress on technology can be presented more or less sympathetically, but, whatever the approach, there is the widespread problem of an underrating of the role of developments in, and the application of, non-military technology. Examples include the role of railways and of barbed wire, both not originally developed for military purposes. More generally, technology has to be understood as an aspect of an entire socio-economic system.

Technology also has a major impact on morale: in particular the sense that better arms are available than those wielded by opponents. This feeling can raise morale, but can also lead to a dangerous over-confidence, in particular a misleading belief that 'better, more, faster', etc. ensures success, which has been a particular problem for societies that have a technological lead (for example, Western Europe in the nineteenth century and the USA since the 1940s). It is understandable that belief in the consequences of technological proficiency and progress is strongest in societies that enjoy such a lead, but there is a confidence that superior technology is always the answer without necessarily understanding what the question is. Indeed, faith in weaponry and technology (increasingly, for modern warfare, command, control and communications technology), rather than hard analysis of their effectiveness, frequently contributes to their designated role in military history.

The impact and role of technology, therefore, can be qualified from several perspectives. In particular, the tendency to assume that in some way 'technology' is an absolute, independent of other factors, can be questioned. The human element is often overlooked in this tendency, but, in practice, there is a complex relationship between observation, experience, perspective and perception, the last an aspect of the technological nexus that is under-explored. For example, to

Plate 13.1 *Children Playing War Games*, Barcelona 1936. The city was soon to experience the horrors of the Spanish Civil War, including bombing and the shooting of prisoners. Black and white photo © DACS 2005.

employ the same weapon does not mean that its use is understood, and this can lead to a failure to reproduce results.

Furthermore, whether something is adopted successfully may be decided by all sorts of reasons unconnected with technical merit: it is not the technology itself, but the response to it that drives change. Interpretations that suggest a near-automatic search for best practice in technology, and its subsequent diffusion, make best practice seem easier to understand and change appear far less difficult than was (and is) the case, and distract attention from the importance of understanding new opportunities. This is true for both new weaponry and for related organizational changes. An appreciation of this is linked to the reversal of the standard approach for explaining military change: instead of weapons dictating tactics, strategy, doctrine and tasking, it is the tasks assigned to the military that determine doctrine and force structure.

In addition, technological change is often considered, in both coverage and analysis, only selectively, in that it is solely the successes that are taken into account while unsuccessful or less successful ideas, inventions and developments are overlooked or neglected. Instead, failure plays an important role in the pursuit and process of change, and in the perception of what constitutes success, and this is worthy of discussion. More generally, the assumption that there is a continuity in technological improvement is simplistic. There may be no pattern other than the one subsequently imposed after the event in order to explain what has happened. Change is the product of a complex process: the interaction of intellectual achievement and practical knowledge in the context of political and social circumstances, and with respect to particular strategic cultures.

Technological change is mostly in response to problems that need, or, rather, apparently need, to be solved. This is an aspect of the extent to which broader cultural, social and organizational issues are at stake. There has to be a desire to change, and technological change is therefore affected by cultural responses to innovation. The expectation of technological change has been particularly important to developments in military capability and war-making over the last century. Political contexts, however, were important both then and earlier. Thus, during the French Revolution, there was relatively little new science in French war-making but there was a greater political will to break with tradition and apply scientific knowledge to the needs of the military.

Indeed, alongside a perception of the essential socio-cultural foundations of technological success has come a view of technology as a direct 'social construct', with social-cultural forces shaping the technology. Once adopted, societies and cultural norms are themselves shaped by that technology, not least through the consequences of economic growth and change, but the underlying initial influences remain strong. From this perspective, warfare – the form and structure that it takes, and the technology it uses – emerges as a social construct. Dethroning technology, and more specifically weaponry, from the central position in the narrative and explanation of military capability and change, does not, however, entail denying its importance. Instead, it is necessary to adopt a more nuanced approach to the different factors that play a role, considering them in a manner that allows for the multiple character of their interaction.

A stress on the role of perception in defining opportunities and best practice challenges the notion of change as equalling improvement that is so important in much of the literature. The action–reaction, and task–response models explaining change that are employed so readily by writers focus on the idea that military effectiveness is in large part a matter of responding rapidly to events and to the needs set by ably defined goals; but perception is crucial to both. Most commentators see modernization as the most sensible form of change. As a result, signs of a striving in military practice and ideas towards the present appear to be an appropriate way in which to detect merit, and thus to define relative performance, or, at least, promise, and to establish what is worthy of attention by scholars.

Such an approach, however, begs the question of what is a modern, let alone a more modern, style of military operations? Western commentators do not generally define as modern the operations currently and recently conducted by non-Western forces in 'little wars', both by regular forces and by irregulars, although in practice conflicts such as those in Congo and Sri Lanka are more typical than the Iraq War of 2003. In June 2004 Congo saw conflict in its eastern borderlands and an attempted coup in the capital by elements of the Presidential Guard. The problems posed to regional peace by such conflicts led to the deployment of international peacekeepers as a major military activity, for many militaries, and, at least in theory, for many more. In 2003 and 2004 the UN and the African Union agreed to deploy 53,000 troops as peacekeepers in Liberia, Sierra Leone, Congo, Ivory Coast and Burundi, and on the Ethiopia–Eritrea frontier, although in practice the numbers deployed were fewer and mostly all from South Africa. In the Balkans, Iraq and Afghanistan, in contrast, US and European forces played the key roles.

Considering most armies in the world, it is increasingly unclear that the central narrative (and related analysis) that has been dominant for so long – that focused on 'high tempo' symmetrical warfare – is appropriate. Instead, it is apparent that it is necessary to devote more attention not only to 'little wars' but also to issues such as counter-insurgency, let alone civil control. This suggests a multiple approach to military modernity, and an emphasis on its diversity. In this perspective, most aspects of past doctrine, organization and practice appear to prefigure aspects of the present, and there is no single pattern of modernization.

THE WEST VERSUS THE REST

As an example of the issue of bringing different narratives of military activity and change into contact, the expansion of Western power in the period encountered an opposition that combined the usual action–reaction cycle of power and warfare (for example, the Western deployment of aeroplanes was soon countered by an ability to respond to air attack) with the particular issues that arise when contrasting military cultures come into contact, as when the Italians subdued Libya from 1928 to 1932. These issues overlapped with the willingness, in *some*, but not *all* cases, to take casualties and endure burdens greater than those of the Western powers. This in turn forced decisions on the latter, decisions on how to respond to resistance and how much effort to expend, in which issues of military capability and political goals both played a role. Indeed, it is striking to contrast the British response to opposition in Egypt, Iraq and Afghanistan with that to the Arab rising in Palestine. The Third Afghan War (1919) was not used as an opportunity to try to subjugate the country, and revolts in Egypt (1919) and Iraq (1920–21) led to the British conceding authority (although a considerable amount of power was retained), but a far more forceful response was taken against the Arab rising in Palestine (1936–39).

Goals and capability as factors in the military interaction of imperial powers and non-Western peoples remained an issue after 1945. This was first seen in attempts to sustain Western European empires, which included, in the Far East, attempts to revive them after the Japanese conquests of 1941–42. The challenge to legitimacy, in the shape of colonial rule, from nationalist opposition, however, came more strongly than hitherto. Much of the colonial population was increasingly unwilling to accept the strategies of incorporation that had made empires work, and, indeed, in many, but not all, cases had been instrumental in the process of conquest.

In addition, it was more important than hitherto to note the views of international opinion, both those of other states and, albeit to a lesser extent, public opinion, which was given an edge by the role of international organizations, especially the United Nations. The hostility of the UN, the USA, and the Communist bloc, in theory, to continued colonial rule, and, in practice, to such rule by Western European states, was very important in affecting the determination of the latter (for example the Dutch in Indonesia: see p. 155), and thus in influencing the context within which force was employed. Changing attitudes within Western publics was also important, particularly in the case of France and Algeria (see pp. 159–61): the dispatch of conscripts to fight there made the war more unpopular than the earlier French struggle in Vietnam; while, in general, the ideology of national liberation was more centrally established in Western consciousness.

In contrast, enhanced military capability was of scant value to the Western colonial powers. The capability stemming from the availability of nuclear warheads and strategic bombers made no difference. The British were far more successful when they attacked Egypt in 1882 than when they did so jointly with France in the Suez Crisis in 1956 (see pp. 78, 163). In 1882 there had been an enormous capability gap at sea but a far smaller one on land. In 1956, in contrast, British forces, once landed, could draw on far superior air power; indeed, the availability of parachutists greatly expanded the range of possible 'landings' and thus enhanced the risk posed to defenders. Nevertheless, the operation was not sustained, and the contrast between 1882 and 1956 indicated a major shift in Western attitudes towards force projection. To be acceptable, such projection had to be able to conform, at least apparently, to ideological goals rather than to power politics, or the latter had to be expressed in terms of the former, as with the cause of 'national liberation' supported by the Soviet Union and the anti-Communist crusade championed by the USA.

FITNESS FOR PURPOSE

Fitness for purpose is a crucial concept when judging the applicability of weaponry, but such fitness is frequently misunderstood by putting the stress on the capacity for employing force, rather than the ends that are sought. Although the term is frequently rather overly loosely employed, these ends are 'culturally' constructed, and, in this process of construction, notions of legitimacy in the shape of appropriate goals play a major role. Furthermore, shifts in these can be seen as a motor of change in military history that deserves at least as much attention as the more habitual emphasis on weaponry. The relationship between shifts in tasking (goals) and changes in technology is, as ever, complex, and not adequately addressed by the use of organic ('dynamic relationship') or mechanistic models, imagery and vocabulary that imply or assert some sort of automatic relationship.

CULTURAL INTERPRETATIONS

A stress both on the role of perception in the understanding of best practice, and on changing notions of legitimacy, directs attention again to 'cultural' factors in military history. Here we are entering the sphere of the currently fashionable, where particular care is required as the literature is developing, and as these analyses have not hitherto received the extensive critical treatment that they merit. The application of cultural concepts to the history of war is in fact far from new. Thus, for example, Adam Smith devoted a thoughtful section of *The Wealth of Nations* (1776) to the issue, which interested Enlightenment intellectuals concerned with the anthropological character of differential social development, particularly between settled and nomadic societies.

More recently has come literature on specific aspects of culture that affect military activity and history, especially strategic culture and the organizational culture of particular militaries. Both draw heavily on work carried out by political scientists, and serve as a reminder that for military history to be intellectually acute it needs to be alive to developments in related disciplines. In many respects, the use of culture also approximates to earlier discussion of distinctive ways of war, in particular the notion of American exceptionalism. Cultural interpretations focus on perception – of norms, problems, opportunities, options, methods and success.

The detailed work that the cultural approach requires has simply not been tackled, however, for most of the world. As a result, we are overly dependent on a rather narrow range of research. Not only is much of the world only imperfectly covered, but there is scant evidence for the attitudes that are important if we are to assess cultural factors. Hopefully this will be redressed, and, in a decade or two, we will be able to look back at the current work on the 'cultural turn' and understand it as the tentative scholarship that is all that it can realistically claim to be.

An example of the problems in applying cultural interpretations is provided by the recent and current situation in Afghanistan and Iraq, in which American practice is seen as representing the apogee of a Western model of war-making, while those of its opponents are presented as examples of non-Western systems. This is a thesis that repays consideration, but there is a need to be wary of seeing in cultural or geographical terms what is in part a more widespread military practice *within* as well as *between* systems – namely, the response of the weaker power. This classically focuses on developing an anti-strategy, anti-operational method, anti-tactics and anti-weaponry, designed to counter and lessen, if not nullify, the advantages of the stronger.

Linked to the narrow range of much current research is the popularity of the concept of *Zeitgeist*, or spirit of the age, in apparently explaining situations and developments. Concepts as varied as *Zeitgeist*, national interests and strategic culture in fact underplay the diversity of circumstances and views that exist and assert a false coherence in order to provide apparently clear building blocks for analytical purposes, and, frequently, to present those who held or hold different views as failing to understand true interests and the necessary course of action. In practice, rather than there being, for example, 'Indian' or 'African' military values, India and Africa were geographical rather than cultural abstractions, with marked variations in military practice. The notion of 'Asian' or 'Oriental' military values is even more questionable. Furthermore, in South-East Asia, major, aggressive states, such as Burma and Thailand in the late eighteenth century, were able to operate not only with scant reference to Western power but are also largely ignored in subsequent Western historiography. This is a reminder of the late onset of modernity, understood in terms of Western dominance, specifically of readily-evident superior Western military capability. As a related point, Western norms in international relations also only became dominant in the nineteenth century.

Much of the conceptual problem with military analysis, as indeed with military history, stems from the extent to which it focuses on leading powers, with the corresponding assumption that other states seek to match, or at least copy aspects of, their war-making capacity and methods: the notion of paradigm powers. This approach assumes a common set of goals for militaries that does not in fact exist.

This point can be taken further by challenging the notion that paradigm/diffusion models – the spread of the methods of a paradigm power – create either a 'cultural space' (region of similar activity and norms) in war-making or, indeed, bridge such spaces as this spread takes place. Instead, the emphasis can be on how the selective character of borrowing military ideas and practices, both within and between such regions, reflected the limited validity of employing analytical terms such as 'modern', 'European' or 'Indian' warfare, as if they described an inherent reality and/or a widespread practice. This critique can be taken still further by questioning the use of particular texts and writers to describe the ideas dominant in particular conjunctures: there is the issue of the typicality of the written material that survives and also the questionable nature of the relationship between literature and practice. This is a particular problem in discussion of the Chinese, or the European, way of war as if there was only one.

The multi-culturalist approach to warfare advocated in this book underlines the extent to which pragmatism (as a factor affecting the response to problems and opportunities) can be variously understood. Therefore, it cannot be assumed that a culture's prevailing mentalities are pragmatic in a Western sense. Such points illustrate the need for, but problems of, challenging the Western-centric interpretation of military history, and of employing the cultural approach once it is understood, as it should be, in a multi-cultural context.

CONCLUSIONS

The looseness of the cultural description in military history, as well as the difficulty of employing the concept as either a precise analytical term or a methodology, does not undermine the value of the culture perspective. Instead, a synergy or interaction with the technological approach appears most attractive. Such a synergy would focus on issues such as the perception of improvement, as well as processes of learning and norm-creation. In this synergy it will be necessary to be suggestive and descriptive, not assertive and prescriptive; but that is in accord with the nature of scholarship: history as question and questioning, not history as answer.

This, however, poses a considerable 'cultural' challenge to military historians. By temperament and interest they may not be inclined to emphasize the interrogative and the tentative. In fact, there is no more reason why the subject should not encourage questioning scholarship than other branches of history. There is, however, a particular problem with the economics of military history. It is a form of scholarship especially open to 'trade' (i.e. popular market) publishing, and this helps set the contours of the subject, although it does not determine them. 'Trade' publishing is not concerned with history as questions, or with the pursuit of history as a questioning process. Instead, it has a rigid preference for history as answers, and the same is true of the visual media, as well as of the radio, and, indeed, the web-based source material employed by students.

Most book-length military history (in so far as it is not, as it will be in most cases, operational or interested in weapons and uniforms) will focus on synoptic works that offer answers, as well as an account of progressive development, and even apparently universal laws that provide guidance to such questions as how to win battles or how best to combat terrorism. However, the clarity of simple explanation in the dominant approach is unhelpful. Instead, it is useful to consider military history as a varied and changing subject, with all the consequences that entails for the contingent character of present judgements. Present-day military historians need to see themselves as operating within an intellectual discipline in which interpretations change, and their readers should be aware of the same factor.

BIBLIOGRAPHY

For two theoretical works that are especially important on the cultural turn, see John Lynn, *Battle. A History of Combat and Culture* (Boulder, Colo., 2003) and J.M. Black, *Rethinking Military History* (London, 2004). A good short introduction to the latter half of the period, albeit Eurocentric, is provided by M.S. Neiberg, *Warfare and Society in Europe. 1898 to the Present* (London, 2004). For the USA, A. Millett and P. Maslowski, *For the Common Defense: A Military History of the United States of America* (2nd edn, New York, 1994).

CHAPTER 1

For Europe, J. Black, *European Warfare, 1660–1815* (London, 1994), and P. Wilson, *German Armies. War and German Society, 1648–1806* (London, 1998). For the American War of Independence, H.M. Ward, *The War of Independence and the Transformation of American Society* (London, 1999), and for the French Revolutionary War, J.-P. Bertaud, *The Army of the French Revolution* (Princeton, 1988), J. Lynn, *The Bayonets of the Republic: Motivation and Tactics in the Army of Revolutionary France, 1791–4* (2nd edn, Boulder, 1996) and S.F. Scott, *From Yorktown to Valmy. The Transformation of the French Army in an Age of Revolution* (Niwot, Colo., 1998). For Russia, J.P. LeDonne, *The Grand Strategy of the Russian Empire, 1650–1831* (Oxford, 2003). For naval warfare, Jan Glete, *Navies and Nations: Warships, Navies and State Building in Europe and America, 1500–1860* (Stockholm, 1993) and R. Harding, *Seapower and Naval Warfare 1650–1830* (London, 1999). For European expansion, D. Peers (ed.), *Warfare and Empires: Contact and Conflict between European and Non-European Military and Maritime Forces and Cultures* (Aldershot, 1997). For North America, A. Starkey, *European and Native American Warfare in North America 1675–1795* (London, 1998). On South America, J. Hemming, *Red Gold: The Conquest of the Brazilian Indians, 1500–1760* (2nd edn, London, 1995). On Africa, J. Thornton, *Warfare in Atlantic Africa, 1500–1800* (London, 1999).

CHAPTER 2

There is no book reviewing war around the world in this period. For conflict in Europe, G. Rothenberg, *The Napoleonic Wars* (London, 1999) and Geoffrey Wawro, *Warfare and Society in Europe, 1792–1914* (London, 1999). An excellent case study is provided by Charles Esdaile, *The Peninsular War: A New History* (London, 2002). For South Asia, R.G.S. Cooper, *The Anglo-Maratha Campaigns and the Contest for India. The Struggle for*

Control of the South Asian Military Economy (Cambridge, 2004). For the Ottomans, S.J. Shaw, *Between Old and New: the Ottoman Empire under Sultan Selim III, 1789–1807* (Cambridge, Mass., 1971). For the naval dimension, J. Glete, *Navies and Nations: Warships, Navies and State Building in Europe and America, 1500–1860* (Stockholm, 1993).

CHAPTER 3

For an introduction to war in Europe and North America, J. Black, *Western Warfare 1775–1882* (London, 2001). The former is covered in greater detail in G. Wawro's *The Austro-Prussian War* (Cambridge, 1996) and *The Franco-Prussian War. The German Conquest of France in 1870–1871* (Cambridge, 2003), and in D. Showalter, *The Wars of German Unification* (London, 2004). Warfare in the 1830s and 1840s is not covered so well. For the American Civil War, R.F. Weigley, *A Great Civil War. A Military and Political History, 1861–1865* (Bloomington, Ind., 2001). For a comparative approach, S. Förster and M.A.J. Nagler (eds), *On the Road to Total War: The American Civil War and the German Wars of Unification, 1861–1871* (Cambridge, 1997). On Latin America, see C.J. Kolinsky, *Independence or Death! The Story of the Paraguayan War* (Gainesville, Fla., 1965), C. Leuchars, *To the Bitter End: Paraguay and the War of the Triple Alliance* (Westport, Conn., 2002) and T.L. Whigham, *The Paraguayan War* (Lincoln, Nebr., 2002). For naval warfare, L. Sondhaus, *Naval Warfare, 1815–1914* (London, 2000). Military ideas in the West are covered in A. Gat, *The Development of Military Thought: The Nineteenth Century* (Oxford, 1992). There is no comparable work on the Orient.

CHAPTER 4

For an overall approach, H.L. Wesseling, *The European Colonial Empires 1815–1919* (London, 2004). For European imperialism in Africa, B. Vandervort, *Wars of Imperial Conquest in Africa, 1830–1914* (London, 1998), and, for a valuable case-study, A.S. Kanya-Forstner, *The Conquest of the Western Sudan: A Study in French Military Imperialism* (Cambridge, 1969). For Russian expansion, M.B. Broxup (ed.), *The North Caucasus Barrier: The Russian Advance Towards the Muslim World* (London, 1992) and M. Gammer, *Muslim Resistance to the Tsar: Shamil and the Conquest of Chechnia and Daghestan* (1994). For the British in South Asia, T.R. Moreman, *The Army in India and the Development of Frontier Warfare, 1849–1947* (London, 1998). For the British in Australasia, N. Loos, *Invasion and Resistance: Aboriginal European Relations on the North Queensland Frontier, 1861–1897* (Canberra, 1982) and J. Belich, *The New Zealand Wars and the Victorian Interpretation of Racial Conflict* (Auckland, 1986). For North America, J.K. Mahon, *History of the Second Seminole War* (Gainesville, Fla., 1967); R.M. Utley, *Frontier Regulars: The United States Army and the Indian, 1866–1891* (New York, 1973); J.A. Greene, *Yellowstone Command: Colonel Nelson A. Miles and the Twilight of the Frontier Army* (Lincoln, Nebr., 1993). For China, P. Kuhn, *Rebellion and its Enemies in Late Imperial China: Militarization and Social Structure, 1796–1864* (Cambridge, Mass., 1970), J. Rawlinson, *China's Struggle for Naval Development, 1839–1895* (Cambridge, 1967) and B.A. Elleman, *Modern Chinese Warfare, 1795–1989* (London, 2001). For Japan, E.L. Presseisen, *Before Aggression: Europeans Prepare the Japanese Army* (Tucson, Ariz., 1965). On naval developments, L. Sondhaus, *Naval Warfare, 1815–1914* (London, 2000).

CHAPTER 5

For the conflicts on the eve of World War One, R.C. Hall, *The Balkan Wars 1912–13* (London, 2000). The best general surveys of the conflict are H. Strachan (ed.), *The Oxford Illustrated History of the First World War* (Oxford, 1998), I. Beckett, *The Great War 1914–18* (Harlow, 2001), M. Howard, *The First World War* (Oxford, 2002) and J.H. Morrow, *The Great War: An Imperial History* (London, 2003). For a far more detailed approach see H. Strachan's *The First World War* (3 vols, Oxford, 2000–). On the causes of the war, J. Joll, *The Origins of the First World War* (London, 1984) and K. Wilson (ed.), *Decisions for War, 1914* (London, 1995). On the Eastern Front, N. Stone, *The Eastern Front 1914–1917* (London, 1975), D. Showalter, *Tannenberg: Clash of Empires* (Hamden, Conn., 1991) and H.H. Herwig, *The First World War: Germany and Austria-Hungary* (London, 1997). For individual battles on the Western Front see, in particular, A. Horne, *The Price of Glory: Verdun 1916* (London, 1962), A.H. Farrar-Hockley, *The Somme* (London, 1964) and R. Prior and T. Wilson, *Passchendaele, The Untold Story* (New Haven, Conn., 1996).

For developments in fighting technique, B. Gudmundsen, *Stormtroop Tactics: Innovation in the German Army 1914–1918* (New York, 1989), P. Griffith, *Battle Tactics of the Western Front: The British Army's Art of Attack, 1916–1918* (New Haven, Conn., 1994) and J. Bailey, *The First World War and the Birth of the Modern Style of Warfare* (Camberley, 1996). On the 1918 campaign, P.R. Braim, *The Test of Battle: The American Expeditionary Force in the Meuse-Argonne Campaign* (Newark, Del., 1987), T. Travers, *How the War Was Won: Command and Technology in the British Army on the Western Front, 1917–1918* (London, 1992) and J.P. Harris, *Amiens to the Armistice* (London, 1998).

On Italy, C. Falls, *The Battle of Caporetto* (London, 1966) and J. Schindler, *Isonzo: The Forgotten Sacrifice of the Great War* (Westport, Conn., 2001). On war with the Turks, A.J. Barker, *The Neglected War: Mesopotamia, 1914–1918* (London, 1967).

For individual countries, D. Kennedy, *Over Here: the Great War and American Society* (New York, 1980), J.M. Bourne, *Britain and the Great War* (London, 1989) and C. Chickering, *Imperial Germany and the Great War, 1914–1918* (2nd edn, Cambridge, 2004); for key commanders, L. Sondhaus, *Franz Conrad von Hötzendorf: Architect of the Apocalypse* (Leiden, 2000) and M.S. Neiberg, *Foch* (Washington, 2003).

For the naval dimension, P.G. Halpern, *A Naval History of World War I* (Annapolis, Md., 1994) and *The Naval War in the Mediterranean 1914–1918* (London, 1987), A. Gordon, *The Rules of the Game: Jutland and British Naval Command* (London, 1996) and J. Terraine, *Business in Great Waters: the U-Boat Wars 1916–45* (London, 1989). For air warfare, L. Kennett, *The First Air War, 1914–1918* (New York, 1991), and for an aspect of science, K. Macksey, *The Searchers: Radio Intercept in Two World Wars* (London, 2003).

CHAPTER 6

There is no one book that pulls together the developments in this period. Instead there is a wealth of material on the Western militaries, especially those of Britain, Germany and the USA, with a particular focus on thought about tank warfare. Less has been written about conflict within Europe, and far less on wars elsewhere. For the leading militaries, see the contributions in Alan Millett and Williamson Murray (eds), *Military Effectiveness. The Interwar Period* (Cambridge, 1988) and H.R. Winton and D.R. Mets (eds), *The Challenge of Change: Military Institutions and New Realities, 1918–1941* (Lincoln, Nebr., 2000). On the Russian Civil War, E. Mawdsley, *The Russian Civil War* (London, 1987) and J.D. Smele, *Civil War in Siberia: The Anti-Bolshevik Government of Admiral Kolchak,*

1918–1920 (Cambridge, 1998). On the Russo-Polish war, N. Davies, *White Eagle, Red Star: The Polish–Soviet War, 1919–1920* (London, 1972), and on Germany, C. Fischer, *The Ruhr Crisis, 1923–1924* (Oxford, 2003). On Ireland, P. Hart, *The IRA and Its Enemies: Violence and Community in Cork, 1916–1923* (Oxford, 1998) and *The IRA at War, 1916–1923* (Oxford, 2004). On China, A. Waldron, *From War to Nationalism. China's Turning Point 1924–1925* (Cambridge, 1996).

On Imperial warfare, D.S. Woolman, *Rebels in the Rif: Abd el Krim and the Rif Rebellion* (Stanford, Calif., 1968); C.G. Segre, *Fourth Shore: the Italian Colonization of Libya* (Chicago, Ill., 1974), A. Mockler, *Haile Selassie's War: the Italian–Ethiopian Campaign, 1935–1941* (New York, 1985) and D. Omissi, *Air Power and Colonial Control: The Royal Air Force 1919–1939* (Manchester, 1990). On the USA, H. Schmidt, *The United States Occupation of Haiti, 1915–1934* (New Brunswick, N.J., 1971), B.J. Calder, *The Impact of Intervention: The Dominican Republic During the US Occupation of 1916–1924* (Austin, Tex., 1984), D. Yerxa, *Admirals and Empire: The United States Navy and the Caribbean, 1898–1945* (Columbia, S.C., 1991), D.E. Johnson, *Fast Tanks and Heavy Bombers: Innovation in the US Army, 1917–1945* (Ithaca, N.Y., 1998), L.D. Langley, *The Banana Wars. US Intervention in the Caribbean 1898–1934* (Wilmington, Del., 2002).

On the Spanish Civil War, P. Preston and A.L. Mackenzie (eds), *The Republic Besieged: Civil War in Spain 1936–1939* (Edinburgh, 1996). On war between China and Japan, F. Dorn, *The Sino-Japanese War, 1937–1941: From Marco Polo Bridge to Pearl Harbor* (New York, 1974), L. Lincoln, *The Japanese Army in North China, 1937–1941: Problems of Political and Economic Control* (Oxford, 1975), Hsi-sheng Ch'i, *Nationalist China at War: Military Defeat and Political Collapse, 1937–1945* (Ann Arbor, Mich., 1982), I. Chang, *The Rape of Nanking: The Forgotten Holocaust of World War II* (London, 1997). On Latin America, F. McCann, *Soldiers of the Pátria: A History of the Brazilian Army, 1889–1937* (Palo Alto, Calif., 2003).

On European developments in military thought and practice, J.S. Corum, *The Roots of Blitzkrieg: Hans von Seeckt and German Military Reform* (Lawrence, Kans., 1992), J.P. Harris, *Men, Ideas and Tanks: British Military Thought and Armoured Forces, 1903–1939* (Manchester, 1995), A. Danchev, *Alchemist of War: The Life of Basil Liddell Hart* (London, 1998), R.M. Citino, *The Path to Blitzkrieg: Doctrine and Training in the German Army, 1920–1939* (Boulder, Colo., 1999), A. Gat, *British Armour Theory and the Rise of the Panzer Arm: Revisiting the Revisionists* (London, 2000). On Soviet thought and practice, R. Simpkin, *Deep Battle: The Brainchild of Marshal Tukhachevskii* (London, 1987), R.R. Reese, *Stalin's Reluctant Soldiers: A Social History of the Red Army, 1925–1941* (Lawrence, Kans., 1996), D.M. Glantz, *Stumbling Colossus: The Red Army on the Eve of World War* (Lawrence, Kans., 1998). On France, R. Doughty, *The Seeds of Disaster: The Development of French Army Doctrine, 1919–1939* (Hamden, Conn., 1986) and E. Kiesling, *Arming Against Hitler: France and the Limits of Military Planning* (Lawrence, Kans., 1996).

CHAPTER 7

The best recent single volume coverage is *A War To Be Won. Fighting the Second World War* by W. Murray and A.R. Millett (Cambridge, Mass., 2000). Effective shorter studies include A.W. Purdue, *The Second World War* (Basingstoke, 1999), J.M. Black, *World War Two* (London, 2003) and S.C. Tucker, *The Second World War* (Basingstoke, 2003). An excellent earlier single-volume account is provided by G. Weinberg, *A World at Arms: A Global History of World War II* (Cambridge, 1994) and, for another look at the war in its global context, J. Ray, *The Second World War: A Narrative History* (London, 1999). The encyclopedia approach of *The Oxford Companion to the Second World War* (Oxford, 1995), edited by I.C.B. Dear and M.R.D. Foot, offers a mass of well-informed essays. The significant cartographic dimension is covered (with helpful text as well) in *The Times Atlas of the Second World War* (London, 1989), edited by J. Keegan, who has also published a single-volume *Second World War* (London, 1989).

The economic dimension is tackled in R. Overy's *Why the Allies Won* (London, 1995), while long-term perspectives are offered in P. Kennedy's *The Rise and Fall of the Great Powers* (London, 1988) and J.M. Black's *Warfare in the Western World 1882–1975* (Chesham, 2002).

The naval dimension can be approached through R.D. Spector, *At War at Sea: Sailors and Naval Warfare in the Twentieth Century* (London, 2001), C. Barnett, *Engage the Enemy More Closely: The Royal Navy in the Second World War* (London, 1991), G.W. Baer, *One Hundred Years of Sea Power: The US Navy, 1890–1990* (Stanford, Calif., 1993) and J.P. Levy, *The Royal Navy's Home Fleet in World War Two* (London, 2003). For air warfare, John Terraine, *The Right of the Line: The RAF in the European War 1939–45* (London, 1985) and John Buckley, *Air Power in the Age of Total War* (London, 1999).

For the war in Europe, the series, *Germany and the Second World War*, published under the auspices of the Militärgeschichtliches Forschungsamt, and, in English translation, by Oxford University Press, is of great importance. The most instructive of these lengthy volumes is volume six, *The Global War. Widening of the Conflict into a World War and the Shift of the Initiative 1941–1943* (Oxford, 2001), edited by H. Boog and others. On German policy, see also, I. Kershaw, *Hitler 1936–1945: Nemesis* (London, 2000) and G. Weinberg, *Germany, Hitler and World War II: Essays in Modern German and World History* (Cambridge, 1995). For the early response, T.C. Imlay, *Facing the Second World War: Strategy, Politics, and Economics in Britain and France, 1938–1940* (Oxford, 2003) and N. Smart, *British Strategy and Politics During the Phony War: Before the Balloon Went Up* (Westport, Conn., 2003).

For Germany's early successes, R.A. Doughty, *The Breaking Point: Sedan and the Fall of France, 1940* (Hamden, Conn., 1990) and B. Bond and M. Taylor (eds), *The Battle for France and Flanders. Sixty Years On* (Barnsley, 2001).

For the Eastern Front, J. Erickson, *The Road to Stalingrad* (London, 1975) and *The Road to Berlin* (London, 1987), can usefully be supplemented by D.M. Glantz and J.M. House, *When Titans Clashed: How the Red Army Stopped Hitler* (Lawrence, Kans., 1995) and *The Battle of Kursk* (Lawrence, Kans., 1999), R. Overy, *Russia's War: Blood upon the Snow* (London, 1997), D.M. Glantz, *Barbarossa. Hitler's Invasion of Russia 1941* (Stroud, 2001), R.W. Stephan, *Stalin's Secret War: Soviet Counterintelligence Against the Nazis, 1941–1945* (Lawrence, Kans., 2003).

For the war in the Pacific, R. Spector, *Eagle Against the Sun: The American War with Japan* (New York, 1985) and H.P. Willmott, *Pearl Harbor* (London, 2001).

For the war in the Mediterranean, D. Porch, *Hitler's Mediterranean Gamble. The North African and the Mediterranean Campaigns in World War II* (London, 2004). Italian weaknesses are covered in M. Knox, *Hitler's Italian Allies* (Cambridge, 2000).

For the war in Europe, A.N. Garland and H.M. Smith, *United States Army in World War II: The Mediterranean Theater of Operations: Sicily and the Surrender of Italy* (Washington, 1993) and R.F. Weigley, *Eisenhower's Lieutenants: The Campaign of France and Germany, 1944–1945* (Bloomington, Ind., 1981).

For Axis occupation and the response, M. Mazower, *Inside Hitler's Greece: The Experience of Occupation, 1941–1944* (New Haven, Conn., 1993) and B. Moore (ed.), *Resistance in Western Europe* (Oxford, 2000).

CHAPTER 8

The literature is extensive, although largely written from the perspective of the European powers. The best introduction is I.F. Beckett, *Modern Insurgencies and Counter-Insurgencies* (London, 2001), and, given the role of Africa, A. Clayton, *Frontiersmen. Warfare in Africa Since 1950* (London, 1998) is crucial. See also E.E. Rice, *Wars of the Third Kind: Conflict in Underdeveloped Countries* (Berkeley, Calif., 1988). On counter-insurgency see also T.R. Mockaitis, *British Counterinsurgency, 1919–1960* (London, 1960). On Indo-China and Algeria, A. Horne, *A Savage War of Peace: Algeria, 1954–62* (London, 1977), A.A. Heggoy, *Insurgency and Counter Insurgency in Algeria* (Bloomington, Ind., 1972), A. Clayton, *The Wars of French Decolonization* (Harlow, 1994), C.R. Shrader, *The First Helicopter War: Logistics and Mobility in Algeria, 1954–1962* (Westport, Conn., 1999), M. Connelly, *A Diplomatic Revolution: Algeria's Fight for Independence and the Origins of the Post-Cold War Era* (Oxford, 2002) and M.S. Alexander and J.F.V. Keiger (eds), *France and the Algerian War, 1954–62: Strategy, Operations, and Diplomacy* (London, 2002). On Malaya, A. Short, *The Communist Insurrection in Malaya, 1948–1960* (London, 1975), R. Stubbs, *Hearts and Minds in Guerrilla Warfare: The Malayan Emergency, 1948–1960* (Oxford, 1989), J. Coates, *Suppressing Insurgency: An Analysis of the Malayan Emergency, 1948–1954* (Boulder, Colo., 1992) and T. Jones, *Postwar Counterinsurgency and the SAS, 1945–1952* (London, 2001). On Suez, R. Fullick and G. Powell, *Suez: The Double War* (London, 1979). On the Indonesian confrontation, H. James and D. Sheil-Small, *The Undeclared War. The Story of the Indonesian Confrontation 1962–1966* (London, 1971). On Aden, S. Harper, *Last Sunset: What Happened in Aden* (London, 1978). On Portugal and decolonialization, T.H. Henriksen, *Revolution and Counter-Revolution: Mozambique's War of Independence, 1964–1974* (Westport, Conn., 1974), R.M. Fields, *The Portuguese Revolution and the Armed Forces Movement* (New York, 1976), J.P. Cann, *Counter Insurgency in Africa: The Portuguese Way of War, 1961–1974* (Westport, Conn., 1997) and L. Heywood, *Contested Power in Angola: 1840s to the Present* (Rochester, N.Y., 2000). On Rhodesia, L.H. Gann and T.H. Henriksen, *The Struggle for Zimbabwe: Battle in the Bush* (New York, 1981) and J. Cilliers, *Counter-Insurgency in Rhodesia* (London, 1985). On the Falklands, L. Freedman and V. Gamba-Stonehouse, *Signals of War: The Falklands Conflict of 1982* (London, 1990) and D. Anderson, *The Falklands War 1982* (London, 2002).

CHAPTER 9

On conflict in East Asia, S. Sandler, *The Korean War* (London, 1999) and S. Tucker, *Vietnam* (London, 1998). On American nuclear planning, B. Brodie, *Strategy in the Nuclear Age* (Princeton, N.J., 1965), H.R. Borowski, *A Hollow Threat: Strategic Air Power and Containment before Korea* (Westport, Conn., 1982), W.S. Borgiasz, *The Strategic Air Command: Evolution and Consolidation of Nuclear Forces 1945–55* (New York, 1996) and T. Greenwood, *Making the MIRV: A Study in Defence Decision Making* (Cambridge, Mass., 1975). For other powers, D. Holloway, *Stalin and the Bomb* (Oxford, 1994) and B. Heuser, *NATO, Britain, France and the FRG: Nuclear Strategies and Forces for Europe, 1949–2000* (London, 1997). On the Cuban crisis, M.J. White, *The Cuban Missile Crisis* (Basingstoke, 1995) and A. Fursenko and T. Naftali, *'One Hell of a Gamble'. Krushchev, Castro, Kennedy. The Cuban Missile Crisis 1958–1964* (London, 1997). On developments in conventional war-fighting, A.J. Bacevich, *The Pentomic Era: The US Army between Korea and Vietnam* (Washington D.C., 1986), D.M. Glantz, *Soviet Military Operational Art: In Pursuit of Deep Battle* (Totowa, N.J., 1991), L. Sorley, *Thunderbolt: General Creighton Abrams and the*

Army of His Times (New York, 1992), G. Hartcup, *The Silent Revolution: Development of Conventional Weapons 1945–85* (Oxford, 1993), J.A. English, *Marching Through Chaos: The Descent of Armies in Theory and Practice* (Westport, Conn., 1996) and W.B. Haworth, *The Bradley and How It Got That Way: Technology, Institutions, and the Problem of Mechanized Infantry in the United States Army* (Westport, Conn., 1999). On Eastern Europe, T. Snyder, *The Reconstruction of Nations: Poland, Ukraine, Lithuania, Belarus, 1569–1999* (New Haven, Conn., 2003), H.G. Skilling, *Czechoslovakia's Interrupted Revolution* (Princeton, N.J., 1976) and J. Györkei and M. Harváth (eds), *Soviet Military Intervention in Hungary, 1956* (Budapest, 1999). An accessible account of atomic power is provided by G. de Groot, *The Bomb – A Life* (London, 2004). For confrontation at sea, J.B. Hattendorf (ed.), *The Evolution of the U.S. Navy's Maritime Strategy, 1977–1986* (Newport, R.I., 2004).

CHAPTER 10

On conflict in South Asia, A. Khan, *The First Round, Indo-Pakistan War, 1965* (New Delhi, 1979) and N. Maxwell, *India's China War* (London, 1970). On South-East Asia, K.C. Chen, *China's War against Vietnam: a Military Analysis* (Baltimore, Md., 1983). On South-West Asia, D. Hiro, *The Longest War: The Iran–Iraq Military Conflict* (London, 1989), A. Bregman, *Israel's Wars, 1947–93* (London, 2000), S. Heydemann (ed.), *War, Institutions, and Social Change in the Middle East* (Berkeley, Calif., 2000), D.M. Witty, 'A Regular Army in Counterinsurgency Operations: Egypt in North Yemen, 1962–1967', *Journal of Military History*, 65 (2001) and C. Herzog, *The War of Atonement: The Inside Story of the Yom Kippur War* (London, 2003). On Southern Africa, W. Steenkamp, *South Africa's Border War, 1966–1989* (Gibraltar, 1989). On Latin America, B. Lovemann, *La Patria. Politics and the Armed Forces in Latin America* (Wilmington, Del., 1999).

CHAPTER 11

On the Gulf War, R.H. Scales, *Certain Victory: The US Army in the Gulf War* (Fort Leavenworth, Kans., 1993), R.W. Swain, *'Lucky War': Third Army in Desert Storm* (Fort Leavenworth, Kans., 1994), A.H. Cordesman and A.R. Wagner, *The Lessons of Modern War. IV. The Gulf War* (Boulder, Colo., 1996), J.A. Olsen, *Strategic Air Power in Desert Storm* (London, 2003), A.J. Bacevich and E. Imbar (eds), *The Gulf War of 1991 Reconsidered* (London, 2003). On the revolution in military affairs, R.R. Leonhard, *The Art of Maneuver: Maneuver-warfare Theory and AirLand Battle* (Novato, Calif., 1991) and L. Freedman, *The Revolution in Strategic Affairs* (Oxford, 1998). On Somalia, K. Allard, *Somalia Operations: Lessons Learned* (Washington, 1995) and M. Bowden, *Black Hawk Down: A Story of Modern War* (New York, 1999). On Haiti, B. Shacochis, *The Immaculate Invasion* (New York, 1999).

On the Balkans, M.A. Bucknam, *Responsibility of Command: How UN and NATO Commanders Influenced Airpower over Bosnia* (Montgomery, Ala., 2003).

CHAPTER 12

The analysis of the 'War on Terror', the Afghan and the Iraq conflicts, is complicated by a lack of knowledge of the perspective of America's opponents, although see S. Reeve, *The*

New Jackals: Ramzi Yousef, Osama bin Laden and the Future of Terrorism (Boston, Mass., 1999), P. Bergen, *Holy War, Inc.: Inside the Secret World of Osama bin Laden* (New York, 2001), R. Gunaratna, *Inside Al Qaeda* (New York, 2002) and J. Burke, *Al-Qaeda: Casting a Shadow of Terror* (London, 2003). However rapidly produced, analyses of American warmaking offer much, although the problem of distinguishing between battle, in which the Americans did very well, and war, in which they were less successful, is a serious problem with much analysis. A.H. Cordesman, *The Lessons of Afghanistan* (Washington, 2002) and *The Iraq War* (Westport, Conn., 2003), R.A. Clarke, *Against All Enemies: Inside America's War on Terror* (New York, 2004), B. Woodward, *Plan of Attack* (New York, 2004) and G. Fontenot, *On Point: The United States Army in Operation IRAQI FREEDOM* (2004) are useful, while the limitations of air power emerge in S. Biddle, 'Afghanistan and the Future of Warfare', *Foreign Affairs* (March/April 2003).

On the debate over how the USA will and should fight, B. Berkowitz, *The New Face of War: How War Will Be Fought in the 21st Century* (New York, 2003), W.K. Clark, *Winning Modern Wars: Iraq, Terrorism, and the American Empire* (New York, 2003), N. Friedman, *Terrorism, Afghanistan, and America's New Way of War* (Annapolis, Md., 2003), D.A. Macgregor, *Transformation under Fire: Revolutionizing How America Fights* (Westport, Conn., 2003), R.H. Scales, *Yellow Smoke: The Future of Land Warfare for America's Military* (New York, 2003) and D. Frum and R. Perle, *An End to Evil: Strategies for Victory in the War on Terror* (New York, 2004). An emphasis on energy sources is provided by S. Pelletière, *America's Oil Wars* (Westport, Conn., 2004). The second *intifada* is covered in R. Ovendale, *The Origins of the Arab–Israeli Wars* (4th edn, London, 2004). A wider perspective is offered in J. Black, *War and the New Disorder in the 21st Century* (London, 2004).

INDEX

WORLD HISTORY FROM ROUTLEDGE

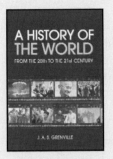

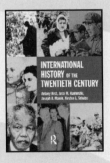

Modern History from Routledge

The Modern Middle East
Ilan Pappé

'An important survey of the vital and much-neglected cultural and social history of the region.'
John Chalcraft, *Department of Islamic and Middle Eastern Studies, University of Edinburgh*

'In his expansive survey of Middle Eastern history over the last century, Ilan Pappé questions modernization as the best framework for understanding that history and seeks to provide an alternative that devotes much-needed attention to the ways in which non-elite groups were affected by, and participated in, the dramatic political, social, economic and cultural transformations of the period.'
Zachary Lockman, *Department of Middle Eastern and Islamic Studies, New York University*

This is the first introductory textbook on the modern Middle East to foreground the urban, rural, cultural and women's histories of the region over its political and economic history. Distancing himself from more traditional modernizationist approaches, the author is concerned with the ideological question of *whom* we investigate in the past rather than *how* we investigate the past. He is keen to contribute to a more comprehensive view of the region in a post-September 11th world. Ilan Pappé begins his narrative at the end of the First World War with the Ottoman heritage and concludes at the end of the twentieth century with the political discourse of Islam. Each chapter begins with a brief introduction to the historiography of its subject, then presents case studies to illuminate the problematic issues arising from them. The geographical area covered includes the Maghrib (Morocco, Tunisia, Algeria and Libya), Egypt, the Sudan, the eastern Arab world, the Mashriq (Syria, Palestine, Lebanon, Iraq, Israel and Jordan), the Arabian Peninsula, Turkey and Iran.

Accessible and original, *The Modern Middle East* will be essential reading for students on introductory history or politics courses as well as for journalists and those working in the region.

Hb: 0–415–21408–4
Pb: 0–415–21409–2

Available at all good bookshops
For ordering and further information please visit:
www.routledge.com